A Beginner's Guide to Acting Methods

A Beginner's Guide to Acting Methods

Understanding Practitioners and their Legacies

Kim Shire

methuen | drama

METHUEN DRAMA
Bloomsbury Publishing Plc, 50 Bedford Square, London, WC1B 3DP, UK
Bloomsbury Publishing Inc, 1385 Broadway, New York, NY 10018, USA
Bloomsbury Publishing Ireland, 29 Earlsfort Terrace, Dublin 2, D02 AY28, Ireland

BLOOMSBURY, METHUEN DRAMA and the Methuen Drama logo
are trademarks of Bloomsbury Publishing Plc

First published in Great Britain 2025

Copyright © Kim Shire, 2025

Kim Shire has asserted her right under the Copyright, Designs and Patents Act, 1988, to be identified as author of this work.

For legal purposes the Acknowledgments on pp. x–xi constitute an extension of this copyright page.

Cover photograph © Mary Williams

All rights reserved. No part of this publication may be: i) reproduced or transmitted in any form, electronic or mechanical, including photocopying, recording or by means of any information storage or retrieval system without prior permission in writing from the publishers; or ii) used or reproduced in any way for the training, development or operation of artificial intelligence (AI) technologies, including generative AI technologies. The rights holders expressly reserve this publication from the text and data mining exception as per Article 4(3) of the Digital Single Market Directive (EU) 2019/790.

Bloomsbury Publishing Plc does not have any control over, or responsibility for, any third-party websites referred to or in this book. All internet addresses given in this book were correct at the time of going to press. The author and publisher regret any inconvenience caused if addresses have changed or sites have ceased to exist, but can accept no responsibility for any such changes.

A catalogue record for this book is available from the British Library.

A catalog record for this book is available from the Library of Congress.

ISBN: HB: 978-1-3504-3416-5
PB: 978-1-3504-3415-8
ePDF: 978-1-3504-3417-2
eBook: 978-1-3504-3418-9

Typeset by RefineCatch Limited, Bungay, Suffolk
Printed and bound in Great Britain

For product safety related queries contact productsafety@bloomsbury.com.

To find out more about our authors and books visit www.bloomsbury.com and sign up for our newsletters.

Contents

Preface vii
Acknowledgments x
Introduction xii

Part I Full Chapters

1 **Beginnings** 3

2 **Konstantin Stanislavski** 14

3 **Vsevolod Meyerhold** 31

4 **Jacques Copeau** 43

5 **Rudolf von Laban** 56

6 **Michael Chekhov** 72

7 **Maria Knebel** 88

8 **Bertolt Brecht** 99

9 **Stella Adler** 109

10 **Sanford Meisner** 122

11 **Viola Spolin** 135

12 **Uta Hagen** 151

13 Jacques Lecoq 168

14 Augusto Boal 183

15 Jerzy Grotowski 195

16 Tadashi Suzuki 208

17 Harold Guskin 219

18 Anne Bogart 229

19 Declan Donnellan 243

20 Patsy Rodenburg 255

21 Chelsea Pace 273

Part II Partial Chapters

22 Lee Strasberg 285

23 Frank Silvera 295

24 Barbara Ann Teer 300

25 Susan Batson 306

26 David Mamet 314

Conclusion: Missing Chapters 321

Notes 322
Bibliography 334
Index 340

Preface

I've been teaching acting since the last century. In that time, I've come across two very prevalent attitudes about the vocation of acting:

- "What actors do is magical and could not be accomplished without magical talent," and
- "Because you have so much talent, what you do is not that hard—you are basically playing all the time."

What if neither of these are true? What if many people walk away from the challenge of acting because it is not easy for them? What if there is no magic involved, but a lot of hard work?

The following pages contain a brief introduction to the methods of an assortment of acting teachers. These are not all of the methods that will be useful to you, and not all of the teachers I've chosen to highlight will help you—in fact, some of them might be counterproductive.

It is time for you to dig in. It is time for you to take seriously the craft you are endeavoring to learn. These methods will just scratch the surface for you. You must take all the steps that follow. One by one, day by day, you have everything you need to grow as an actor.

Even the legendary Stanislavski didn't think you should follow any one method. When his student, Joshua Logan, asked about his method, Stanislavski responded, "Create your own method. Don't depend slavishly on mine. Make up something that will work for you! But keep breaking traditions, I beg you."[1]

Which tools will do the trick for you? Which will push you further toward your goals? Which will trap you in your head and be counterproductive? Until you try, you won't know!

The Jesuits use a Latin term taken from Ignatian Spirituality, *tantum quantum* which means "so far as." This is the equivalent of "Consider everything. Then throw out what is useless to you." I hope you will take time to do both with each method. Consider every one. Try it on for size. Seriously engage with it. Read with an open mind. Try the activities believing they will help you. Then throw out anything that doesn't help you further your craft, and tuck the others away in your toolbox. You might be surprised by the tools that enrich your characters.

Viola Spolin, one of the acting teachers we will visit in this book said "When an actor knows 'in the bones' there are many ways to do and say one thing, techniques will come (as they must) from the total self, and beyond!"[2] It is likely the techniques that will carry you through your career come from an array of sources. Some will come from this book, but many will come from your own intuition and further study.

As for further study, I hope that you will sincerely search for the one or two methods that work best for you and delve much deeper. Being an inch deep and a mile wide in your practice will not serve you well. If all you do is grab a few tools from this book, and never dig deeper, you will be under-prepared for professional work. This is your starting point, your introduction to acting methods. You will find a muse or two here. Follow them!

The Vernacular of this Book

I have attempted to impersonate my own teaching voice in the conversationality of this book. As I envisioned the hundreds of students I have taught, I found myself writing to you, the reader, as if you were among them. I hope that comes through to you.

I have standardized my language regarding gender in a way that hopefully feels inclusive to all of you. Rather than addressing actors and actresses, I address only actors. Just as we use only the singular term "professor" regardless of gender, it is my preference to use the term actor to refer to all people of the stage. One of my other research interests is gender parity in theatre. Standardizing the way we speak about jobs in theatre is one step towards that. Can you imagine "directress? designeress? stage manageress?" Shudder.

I have discarded the antiquated use of "he/him" in reference to generic people, (although in deference to the authors I quote in my book, I have retained their pronoun use in quotes). I have likewise avoided "he/she" as equally awkward or unhelpful, using they/them pronouns when I write about you and your classmates.

Getting Started

Take a moment to choose a beautiful journal. Find a pen—or ten colorful ones—that make you feel creative. Find a spot on a hillside or under a blanket where you can turn off your phone and focus on your work.

Now read. Take notes. Mark up the pages. React to the words you see in your notebook. Bring your best, most awake self to the discussions. Bring your work to life.

A Note to the Instructor

I wrote this book because I felt you and I needed a better tool for our young actors. In practice, you will likely only use a few of these chapters in your semester. I choose fifteen chapters each Spring semester for my acting methods course and tackle one per week. I use the Beginnings chapter on day one of my semester and then organize the other fifteen chapters I have chosen in whatever order seems useful to me when I am planning. I have experimented with various orders and found that it doesn't seem to matter with the exception of needing to place Stanislavski very early in the semester since all the methods that follow are emulating or reacting against his ideas.

This book is designed so no chapter refers to a previous chapter in such a way that makes it difficult to grasp out of order—again, with the exception of Stanislavski. I hope this design is helpful to your pedagogy.

I teach this material paired with duo scenes and monologues. I find it necessary for my students to have text to work on using different methods. Throughout this text you will find activities that require your actors to have memorized material to work with in order to understand and practice various methods. May I suggest that you ask them to choose one classical and one modern monologue (perhaps even one written by a woman? I always insist on this) to experiment with each of these methods. Next assign them a Shakespeare duo scene and something contemporary with a different scene partner. This way they can use each method with a scene partner from the classical canon and something more familiar to their tongues.

In any case, it is my hope you will teach each of the methods you choose with an open mind and heart. Your experience will not exactly match theirs. I try not to inflict my opinion onto them until they have explored it fully, and even then, I try to hold my tongue. Trust them. They will discover what is healthy for their work. Near the end of his life, Stanislavski cautioned his students saying, "One must give actors various paths."[3] He wasn't the only one who felt that way. Chekhov said in his later writings,

> It is ridiculous for the artist within us to say, for example: "I love only Stanislavski. I reject Meierhold", or vice versa, or deprecate the merits of any of the theatre's other creators. Why be narrow-minded, why cut ourselves off from any of these rich heritages, when [. . .] we have the freedom to make the most of the best in all techniques? There are no prohibitions against it. All it takes is a little wisdom, imagination and courageous experimentation.[4]

I suspect you already understand this. That's why you are holding this book in your hand. Celebrate with me when you see your student's work improve using a method that has never worked for you, or that you never would have selected for them!

Acknowledgments

The seeds of this book were planted in the first few years of my vocation as an acting professor. One afternoon in class I was complaining about the absence of a good textbook for my class when one of my students said, "If you don't like the books that exist, why don't you write one?" I protested, "I can't write an acting textbook!" They assured me that I could. Without the students I worked with that fall, I would never have taken this project on. Thank you!

Once I took on the project of writing, I relied on the assistance of many:

My mother, Marie Whittaker, who upgraded my writing style. She read and copy-edited every word of this book, helping me find clarity and consistency. And then she helped me with the tedious job of verifying my sources. She's a lifesaver—and easily put in the most hours in service of my project.

Nancy Harper who scribbled on every single page of my manuscript with her brilliant skill of refining concepts to their core.

Mitchell Conway who broadened my approaches to Boal, Aristotle, Grotowski, Brecht, Bogart, and Suzuki and suggested additions to my first chapter.

Julia Harris, theatre historian extraordinaire, who offered her expertise in Stanislavski, nerding out with me and suggesting many edits to this chapter, Boal, and my history sections, as well as trying out some of my activities to make sure they work for instructors.

Lily Hoelscher who gave up many evenings to help translate Maria Knebel's work from Spanish, and edited the chapter for me.

Kellen Connelly, who loves Declan Donnellan as much as I do, and who helped me distill *The Actor and the Target* to its essential pieces.

Anna Milburn, Melissa Schmitz, Tom Trangmoe, Amber Barnes, and Joann Boswell who read and responded to some sections.

Ashtyn Reiners, Kadee Melton, and Lexi Larson who were the first students to read and reflect critically on my writing from a student perspective.

The Grandstreet Summer Conservatory class of 2023 who enthusiastically played guinea pig and helped expand many of my activities.

Andrew Hobson for critical writing/revising workshops near the end of my process.

Amber Barnes, Nancy Harper, and Julia Harris who helmed my department while I sat at my dining room table writing during my sabbatical.

Tim, Belle, and Zane Pearson who opened Casa Loca up for me as a writer's retreat.

Evie Shire who let me disrupt her homeschool schedule by playing endless hours of Sara Barellis and *SpongeBob The Musical* in the kitchen while she was trying to do math.

Samwise Shire for forcing me to take a social brain break and walk each day to reset my brain after lunch. Also for being a big data nerd like his mom.

Deaundra Shackelford, Donny Shire, Andy Shire, Jodi Fasteen, my parents and siblings who have always cheered me on as I pursue my interests.

There are so many of you who have inspired and encouraged me along the way. Thank you!

Most of all, I want to acknowledge the friendship, wisdom, mentorship, and persistent help of Dr. Jeanette Fregulia, who took me on as her project during my sabbatical, providing day to day encouragement via text and the motivation to keep plugging away on the difficult days. Homemade hummus, scones and tea in her kitchen are some of the best memories of this entire process. Cheers!

Introduction

If you are new to acting methods and the history of schools of acting, it will be helpful for you to be familiar with a few names and some major movements before you get started with this work. I remember as a young actor and director getting lost in the nuances and name-dropping of historical acting institutions, which were as meaningless to me as someone listing the Chicago Bears players from the 1960s. When I read acting texts, it felt as if I were already far behind everyone else. This introduction is intended to be a cheat sheet for you to refer to if my attempt to demystify the jargon in the following chapters fails. Please don't feel like you have to memorize all of this, but as I like to say, "If you read this first, there might be some coat-hooks in your brain for the later information to hang on." Repetition helps information stick.

- MAT—The Moscow Art Theatre was founded in 1898 by Konstantin Stanislavski and Vladimir Nemirovich-Danchenko. The list of people who are associated with the theatre are a who's who of Russian theatre: Anton Chekhov, Michael Chekhov, Yevgeny Vahktangov, Maria Ouspenskaya, Richard Boleslavsky, Vsevolod Meyerhold, Maria Knebel, and Olga Knipper.
- The American Laboratory Theatre in New York City was open from 1923–30 and run by Richard Boleslavsky and Maria Ouspenskaya. This school taught Stanislavski's System to curious Americans. It trained hundreds of people including Stella Adler and Lee Strasberg who carried this early form of Stanislavski's System to the Group Theater where the System was converted into the Method.
- The Group Theater was founded in 1931 by Cheryl Crawford, Harold Clurman, and Lee Strasberg. They invited twenty-eight actors to join them as co-founders. During the early years Strasberg's Method, or the Method, was developed and followed by the group, changing American theatre forever. The Method was based on what they knew of Stanislavski's System as it existed in the early 1930s. After an initial honeymoon phase, members began to fight for control of the direction of the company. The first outward sign of conflict came in 1934 when Stella Adler met with Stanislavski in Paris. Adler was unhappy with some of his System as it was being taught at the Group, so she challenged him. He told her he no longer taught the exercises the Group was using because they caused hysteria in his actors. Adler was relieved. She studied with Stanislavski for five weeks, then returned to the US and gave a lecture to the Group about her discoveries. Many Group members were as relieved as she was. Lee Strasberg was not. He gave his own counter-lecture the next day. One by one, members left the group to go and found their own schools or pursue careers in Hollywood. The Group Theater fizzled to an end in 1941.

- The System—Since the late twentieth century, "the System" has referred to Stanisalvski's acting method. In some early source material, his work is called "the Method," but this should not be confused with the American practitioner's creation of Method Acting developed at The Group when they were exposed to some of Stanislavski's early System techniques. In this book, and most current source materials, Stanislavski's method is called the System.
- The Method—This set of techniques came out of the work of the members of the Group Theater, but it is most closely affiliated with Lee Strasberg's later work at the Actors Studio. Scholars and journalists in the mid-1900s lumped Harold Clurman, Lee Strasberg, Stella Adler, Bobby Lewis, Sanford Meisner, and others under the label of Method teachers. However, since then, the Method has become so strongly affiliated with Strasberg's psychological approach that "the Method" really only applies to Strasberg's Method. Lee Strasberg's singular focus on emotional or affective memory work makes him unique, and Method Acting as a term is strongly correlated with these problematic techniques. The Method is an approach that come to be widely viewed as manipulative and exploitative, though it continues to be used in diluted forms into the twenty-first century especially in film acting.
- Modern Acting—This is a term that encompasses the methods of many teachers working in the mid-twentieth century, such as Stella Adler, Sanford Meisner, and Uta Hagen whose work developed out of an American understanding of Stanislavski's System. Many of these teachers were initially lumped under the Method label.

Part I

Full Chapters

1. Beginnings
2. Konstantin Stanislavski
3. Vsevolod Meyerhold
4. Jacques Copeau
5. Rudolf von Laban
6. Michael Chekhov
7. Maria Knebel
8. Bertolt Brecht
9. Stella Adler
10. Sanford Meisner
11. Viola Spolin
12. Uta Hagen
13. Jacques Lecoq
14. Augusto Boal
15. Jerzy Grotowski
16. Tadashi Suzuki
17. Harold Guskin
18. Anne Bogart
19. Declan Donnellan
20. Patsy Rodenburg
21. Chelsea Pace

1

Beginnings

Overview of the foundation of acting methods

The history of acting can basically be broken into two categories: everything before Stanislavski and the movement towards Realism in the late nineteenth century, and everything after. Methods for training actors up through this pivotal time varied widely, and it's hard to call anything prior a true acting method. They are acting conventions, or styles, rather than a codified process. The earliest creators of acting systems taught presentational, rather than emotional, performance techniques. They usually avoided evoking true emotions from the actor and instead focused on gesture and oratorical skill. There were many reasons for this:

1 Performance venues: In Ancient Greece, theatre was performed in huge amphitheatres as part of festivals and tributes to the Olympian gods. The acting style of this time had to match the size of the performance spaces and the ritualistic nature of the performance. Broad gestures and a focus on oratory skill resulted in performances that could be understood in the back of the venue without the aid of microphones.
2 The apprenticeship model: As in many other trades, the acting apprentice learned their trade by observing and imitating the work of their mentor. Originality was not valued in the way it is today. In rehearsal, actors worked to imitate their teachers or other actors they admired, copying the gestures and movements as exactly as possible. As a result, performance culture was passed down intact from generation to generation.
3 Cultural belief: For centuries, the belief that experiencing genuine feelings on stage was unhealthy for the actor was widely accepted. Plutarch disdained the idea of an actor actually feeling the emotions of the character. He wrote that an actor who feels emotions on stage shows an audience "common bare passion,"[1] whereas imitation shows skill and persuasive power. He went on to explain that emotions make the audience uncomfortable, but the skill of imitation delights them. Most people agreed with Plutarch until the late nineteenth century. Emotions were held to be dangerous, unstable, and beneath the work of a professional actor. Because of this, actors focused on skilled movements and facial expressions to portray characters in performance.

There is benefit in exploring the historical context of acting conventions created by practitioners that came before us. To that end, this chapter calls attention to a few pre-Realism practitioners.

Thespis

Thespis is called the founder of Western acting. Today, theatre people are sometimes inducted into Thespian Societies in his honor. He lived in Athens, Greece, in the sixth century BCE, during the birth of the Western theatre tradition. Aristotle reported him to be the first to step on stage and portray a character in a written play. While he most certainly wasn't actually the first person to act out a role for an audience, he was certainly the first great Athenian actor and a revolutionary theatre artist, writer, and cultural force. We don't know what Thespis would have considered good acting technique. What we do know is that he was innovative and liked to add variety to his productions.

Thespis began as a singer of dithyrambs, wild choral hymns sung by a group to the Greek god Dionysus, and then conceived of a new sort of performance in which a single actor or two would step out of the chorus to portray individual characters. He added life and spirit to these monologues and dialogues, using the chorus to add to the story, performing in conversation with the solo actor. He is also credited with adding energetic dances to the choral performances. These were very popular, and were passed down for generations. The work of this era of comic performers was punctuated by bawdy humor, phallic jokes and symbols, and partying. Tragedy and comedy were equally unrestrained and created with exaggerated motions that would read to someone sitting in the back of the amphitheatre.

He began by performing in makeup by smearing vermilion or purslain on his face. Later he exchanged that practice for masks. With this technique, he was able to exchange characters easily, by switching masks to indicate a change in character. Masks were not his invention, having been in use for many thousands of years before Thespis, but this technique for swift character switch might have been.

Thespis didn't only perform in amphitheatres. He also toured with his plays, taking his costumes, masks and props in a horse-drawn wagon from city to city performing with his troupe of actors. Thespis was the first documented winner of the acting competitions that occurred in Athens in 534 BCE.

Aristotle

About 200 years later, Aristotle was born in Greece in 384 BCE. He studied and taught with Plato, tutored Alexander the Great, and wrote copious volumes documenting the thought of the day and influencing almost every aspect of human understanding. He established rules of dramatic poetics, writing a book titled *Rhetoric* that implies that actors, poets, and orators used the same style of speaking and presentation as each other.

Aristotle focused his comments related to actor technique on clear diction. He felt that acting ability comes from nature, so it isn't teachable. Diction, however, could be taught. Because of this, he focused on oration. Aristotle's writing was influential in the foundation of later acting techniques, though he didn't specifically have an acting method. Nonetheless, his contemporaries took his rules as the gospel truth. His principles shaped drama for centuries.

Natyashastra

While the Greeks were developing their rules for theatre, their contemporaries in modern-day India were writing a book of rules for acting called *The Natyashastra*, a treatise that sets out the very specific rules for performing in Sanskrit Drama. It was likely initially written around 200 BCE, with additions by others through about 200 CE. This book focuses heavily on the appropriate gestures, musical instruments, costumes, makeup, actor positioning, and ideal set decoration for performance. The goal of these design factors was the welcoming of the gods and the transportation of the audience to a parallel reality where they could ponder the meaning of life and morality while experiencing wonder on a higher plane.

This ancient manual was created with the goal of standardizing and uplifting art. The authors of *The Natyashastra* cared deeply about the stage and the resulting transcendence for the audience. Because they wrote these things down, and because the practitioners of Sanskrit Drama had the goal of preserving and perfecting their art, we can still attend performances that are essentially the same as those being performed when time converted from BCE to CE. The careful preservation of an art form over millennia is due to ancient people documenting their methods.

Quintilian

Back in the Western world, another influential acting/orating master, Marcus Fabius Quintilian was born sometime in the range of 35–40 CE in Hispania, modern-day Spain, likely to a well-educated family who sent him to Rome to study rhetoric. He was there during the reign of Nero and several of his successors, serving as a teacher, lawyer, orator, and proponent of education.

In his professional career he was quietly influential, and knew how to distance himself far enough from the powerful to survive political upheaval while still maintaining a life of comfort. For instance, he was hired to teach Emperor Domitian's great-nephews, so he was close to power. However, he did not suffer the cruelty of that empire, possibly because of his proximity, unthreatening role, and his charming nature. As emperors rose and fell during his lifetime, he remained a respected figure with all of them. Some scholars think Quintilian died in his fifties by the year 97, others think he was still alive in 118 in his seventies.

As an orator, he was characterized to have "great strength and felicity of argument."[2] As a teacher, he is reputed to be the founder of early childhood education. As a writer, he influenced the thoughts and habits of performers, educators, politicians, and lawyers for centuries.

Quintilian's twelve-volume textbook on oratory, *Institutio Oratoria*, is where we learn the most about the influence that Quintilian has had on theatre. In one passage, Quintilian outlines his thoughts on the "eloquence of the body," claiming that the motions of the body are the same as voice—both must be engaged properly to be effective. He stresses the importance of this method, saying, "All attempts at exciting the feelings must prove ineffectual, unless they be enlivened by the voice of the speaker, by his look, and by the action of almost his whole body."[3]

Quintilian argued that a good orator must first be a good man. This "good man theory" proposes that if a man is not good, he cannot be a good orator. Quintilian considered a man good if he worked for the common good of mankind, and the prosperity of society. Quintilian spent much of his adulthood teaching boys oratory skills, considering it his duty to prepare them to be moral members of civil society. He didn't practice corporal punishment for his pupils as was common in his time, instead creating a disciplined, yet enjoyable style of instruction. In return he expected his students to be loyal to him, both obeying and loving him as their instructor.

He believed the best voices come from people who are in shape. He felt orators should be strong and flexible enough to maintain breath while speaking. He suggests certain exercises, but stated that the best sort of exercise for the voice is for the speaker to use their performative voice at all times. This practice strengths the voice and lungs while making the speaker ready to project when in court.

Quintilian also taught of the importance of pronouncing every word entirely and varying the tone of the words so that the hearer would not be not bored with monotonous speech. As he wrote about communicating emotion, he explained that while natural expression of feeling is good, it is not useful in public speaking because natural feeling is not art. Because of this, he suggested a code of gestures a speaker should use to artfully communicate feelings.

Quintilian believed gestures must be practiced using mirrors. By practicing in a mirror, the speaker could see the effect their gestures will have on the audience. He disapproved of off-the-cuff speaking with natural gestures, much preferring a practiced style of speaking with gestures choreographed to match the words and intentions of the speaker.

Quintilian's instructions regarding gestures are quite specific. Scholars of today can't quite agree on what every gesture he described looks like, but many of them are quite easy to understand. For instance, he writes rule number 83: "To shrug or contract the shoulders is very seldom becoming; for the neck is shortened by it; and it begets a mean, servile, and knavish sort of gesture."[4] He also wrote that the rules of stage acting are different from oratory—broader and cruder gestures are appropriate for actors, but not for lawyers. Even though he wrote about actors, Quintilian didn't write specifically for them. Even so, actors took his writings seriously, and for centuries followed his rules.

Zeami Motokiyo

Zeami Motokiyo was born in Japan in 1363. He discovered Noh theatre early in life and was very successful at it. He wrote many plays, acted, and documented his acting method. In his long lifetime he achieved celebrity and acclaim, though his later years were spent in exile. Zeami wrote a method for acting called *The Nine Levels* which were used to train young actors in his family. The levels described the process of development of actors from Level 9 which is completely untrained to Level 1 which is transcendent. Zeami's method is arguably the first well-developed acting method.

Zeami taught the *jo-ha-kyu* rhythmic pattern of theatre. This can be translated *beginning-middle-end*, but it can also be translated *introduction-exposition-denouement*, or *resistance-rupture-acceleration*. This practice translates to the structure of a play, but also to the movement of the actor. Every action performed on stage has a preparation, realization, and ending. For example, a person fighting with a sword performs a *jo* when they pull back slightly from their target, a *ha* when they swing the sword wide towards their opponent's sword, and a *kyu* when the swords clash. This pattern repeats many times in one sword fight, and also in calmer interactions with the serving of tea or a polite conversation.

Many acting teachers have created methods that continue or reframe this philosophy, including Anne Bogart, who wrote, "According to Zeami, every kyu (ending) contains the next jo (beginning); every ending of a gesture contains the beginning of the next gesture. Once you begin to recognize and experience jo-ha-kyu in action, you are instantly responsible to it. It can be a useful tool in organizing energy and flow of action on the stage."[5] She goes on to explain that the flow of an action is begun when there is opposition to a force, and ends when the opposition ends, thus beginning the next cycle of *jo-ha-kyu*. The tension between rhythms is riveting for the audience, and shows great control on the part of the actor.

All of Zeami's methods, including this one, were kept hidden for centuries because Noh encouraged secrecy to protect family secrets. Zeami's writings were discovered in 1883 and have informed many theatre practitioners since then.

William Shakespeare

Every actor knows his name, but the frustrating truth about Shakespeare is we really know very little about his work with actors. We do, however, have many of his plays, and one of them deals with acting technique. The instructions to actors are put in the mouth of Hamlet as he is addressing a troupe of actors. It appears in II.iii of *Hamlet*:

> HAMLET
> Speak the speech, I pray you, as I pronounced it to
> you, trippingly on the tongue: but if you mouth it,
> as many of your players do, I had as lief the
> town-crier spoke my lines. Nor do not saw the air
> too much with your hand, thus, but use all gently;
> for in the very torrent, tempest, and, as I may say,
> the whirlwind of passion, you must acquire and beget
> a temperance that may give it smoothness. O, it
> offends me to the soul to hear a robustious
> periwig-pated fellow tear a passion to tatters, to
> very rags, to split the ears of the groundlings, who
> for the most part are capable of nothing but
> inexplicable dumbshows and noise: I would have such
> a fellow whipped for o'erdoing Termagant; it
> out-herods Herod: pray you, avoid it . . .
> Be not too tame neither, but let your own discretion
> be your tutor: suit the action to the word, the
> word to the action; with this special o'erstep not
> the modesty of nature: for any thing so overdone is
> from the purpose of playing, whose end, both at the

> first and now, was and is, to hold, as 'twere, the
> mirror up to nature; to show virtue her own feature,
> scorn her own image, and the very age and body of
> the time his form and pressure.
> . . . And let those that play
> your clowns speak no more than is set down for them;
> for there be of them that will themselves laugh, to
> set on some quantity of barren spectators to laugh
> too

In this short section, Shakespeare arguably reveals some of the habits of actors in his time that he disliked. Many scholars believe Shakespeare was giving instructions to his contemporaries through this bit in the play. He could have left this out of his play without impacting the story at all. But he left it in. Why? Perhaps he was frustrated with bad acting. His instructions were:

1 Speak clearly (trippingly on the tongue)
2 Don't over-enunciate (mouth it)
3 Be grounded in movement (do not saw the air too much with your hand)
4 Control emotions (you must acquire and beget / a temperance that may give it smoothness)
5 Control volume (it / offends me to the soul to hear a . . . fellow tear a passion to tatters, . . . to split the ears of the groundlings)
6 Be appropriately bold (Be not too tame neither)
7 Be natural (suit the action to the word, the / word to the action . . . o'erstep not / the modesty of nature: for . . . the purpose of playing . . . is, to hold, as 'twere, the / mirror up to nature)
8 Don't improvise or show off (And let those that play / your clowns speak no more than is set down for them).

Shakespeare was calling for naturalness and humility in acting. Perhaps he was looking for more internal methods?

Aaron Hill

More than a thousand years after Quintilian, notable acting teachers continued to teach methods that focused on physical movements and facial expressions. Aaron Hill (1685–1750) was the son of an attorney and an Englishman. He was born fewer than seventy years after Shakespeare died. He was an actor, director, and critic. Being a man of letters, it's unfortunate he wasn't alive during Shakespeare's time, as he surely would have given us a better understanding of the mysterious man. His letters and writings give us a good picture of what the theatrical world was like in the century after the bard's passing.

Aaron Hill believed that there were exactly ten dramatic passions: joy, grief, anger, pity, scorn, hatred, jealousy, wonder, fear, and love. Like Quintilian, he wanted his actors to use a mirror while learning to communicate these ten dramatic passions. In one letter, he describes the stance an actor must take in detail. He asks actors to keep their head raised, "not rounding too lightly, as if it played with the sound of the words; and the eye fixed intently, and held, meaningly steady, on the proper object before it. This, and the nerves of the neck, arms, and feet, strongly braced in all action, whether violent or passive" the results of this action should, "warm the Player himself, into a real feeling of the passions he is acting. There is another great beauty, in a Player, who enters strongly into nature, and . . . after he has done speaking, himself, he attends to what is answered, as if it, in good earnest, concerned him."[6]

We can see that Hill felt it was important for actors to feel what they are acting. Unlike some of his predecessors, he wanted his actors to have an internal experience that matched the external, even encouraging them to react to their scene partner by appearing to listen and care about the response.

Many other acting teachers, such as Delsarte (1811–71) taught a very similar approach to acting, following in Hill's shoes. The exaggerated poses and facial expressions lent themselves well to the melodramas that were being produced in the 1800s.

Denis Diderot

Denis Diderot (1713–84) was a French philosopher and the son of a tradesman. He was educated at a Jesuit school and lived a bohemian lifestyle in Paris, earning his living as a writer. He was acquainted with David Garrick, a well-known actor who is reputed to have been able to entertain people at parties by allowing dozens of facial expressions to cross his face without feeling anything. It was a good parlor trick, and his usual method of acting. Diderot admired Garrick, and wrote an article, *Le Paradoxe sure le comedien,* which sparked a debate that continued for decades. In it he claimed that an actor with good control of their body and expressions can give the same performance show after show with great consistency. "The extravagant creature who loses his self-control has no hold on us; this is gained by the man who is self-controlled."[7] Diderot felt the audience should have emotion, while the actor should control those emotions through practiced facial expressions and gestures. He acknowledges that others in his time were arguing for more true emotion in acting: "But they say an actor is all the better for being excited, for being angry. I deny it. He is best when he imitates anger. Actors impress the public not when they are furious, but when they play fury well."[8] He believed that the most skilled actors were able to stay calm inside but imitate rage believably for the audience.

William Archer, an Australian journalist, critic, and author wrote a response to this article in 1880, almost a hundred years after Diderot's death. He agrees with Diderot. "Acting *is* imitation; when it ceases to be imitation it ceases to be acting and becomes something else—oratory perhaps . . . It is passion that interests and moves us; therefore the reproduction of passion is the actor's highest and most essential task."[9] Archer also wanted actors to imitate emotions and passion well, but he still does not ask actors to actually feel the emotions they are imitating.

Konstantin Stanislavski also reacted to Diderot's article. He wrote in *The Paradox of the Actor*, "The style of acting that most aligned with Diderot's view was called the *symbolic* style. It was presentational, not realistic. Using pure technique, actors performed highly conventionalized physical and vocal gestures that represented the emotions. Acting education involved the training of one's voice and body and the learning of the proper way to deliver specific kinds of text, usually through imitating an instructor."[10] Stanislavski, unlike those before him, presented a system of acting that taught actors to be realistic instead of symbolic in portrayal.

Stanislavski's Revolution

Diderot and the others were reacting against something they saw on stage. Many actors must have been trying internal methods even though they were cautioned not to. Clean lines can't be drawn, saying that no actor before Stanislavski used genuine emotion on stage. However, Stanislavski was the first acting teacher to proliferate a system of acting that encouraged internal work. It is impossible to overstate the impact of his work on the world of theatre.

Near the end of the 1800s, humans began to take an interest in the everyday lives of 'common' people, requiring a shift in approach. Actors, playwrights and theorists, influenced by advances in psychology, began to experiment with acting methods as the focus of the actor turned to the thoughts and feelings of their characters. These methods value experiencing true emotion on stage, delving into psychology and character development.

A new debate emerged surrounding whether it was better to have an external acting technique which focused on the movements of the body creating emotion in the actor, or to have an internal acting technique that created emotion in the actor from the inside, impacting the body movements of the actor. In other words, "Does your character's emotion come from the inside to the outside? or the outside in?" And, as per usual, others reacted against both approaches, claiming that actors don't need, or shouldn't try to use their own emotions in performance at all.

When Konstantin Stanislavski was born, the world was ready for this revolution in acting methods that shifted inward. New plays were being written about divorce, sexually transmitted infections, and other societal themes that did not work with a melodramatic style of performance. Stanislavski developed a system that was capable of teaching actors to perform in a new way. His method has dominated Western actor training in all the decades since. Stanislavski believed that in order to achieve believability on stage, the actor MUST experience the feelings of the character. Talent was directly proportional to the actor's ability to internally experience and externally portray truth on stage consistently and realistically.

In the decades since Stanislavski lived and worked, every method that has been developed is an extension of, or reaction against his work. Some methods skew towards movement based external methods, others have a strong emphasis on the internal thoughts and feelings of the actor. Today we have a legitimized choice to make. Does your work benefit more from one method than the other in a particular production? Which tools will suit your work better? It's time to find out!

Tips for taking pre-Stanislavski methods further

- Try performing in a mask, imagining that the theatre you are working in is giant, outdoors, and without amplification systems. What movements and expressions will help you communicate your story to the back of the house?

- Take a passage of an older text such as *Oedipus Rex* and deliver it as if you are delivering a speech. Now try to act it using more modern performance techniques. What do you learn from this exercise about how ancient actors might have performed?

Discussion Starters and Journal Prompts

- Summarize what early gestural acting conventions look and feel like to you as you work on them with your modern monologues. Can you find anything to apply to your own practice inspired by the ancient techniques?
- Try working on your monologue using a mirror. Use it to help you check for gestures and facial expressions that will communicate what you are trying to accomplish with the audience. Now try recreating these gestures and expressions without the mirror. Write about the experience and how it is beneficial for character building.

The Tools for your Toolbox

Activity—Quintilian Methods

- Have your students spread out on stage.
- Say: "Speak a portion of a monologue you have prepared, listening for dropped syllables and swallowed line endings."
- "Pair up and practice speaking your lines to each other while enunciating clearly from some distance using performative volume levels."
- "Have a conversation with your partner in your stage voice, practicing Quintilian's exercise for the voice: using performative style of speaking in everyday conversation."
- "Slowly walk closer to each other while conversing, but don't drop your volume."
- Have your students stand in front of mirrors.
- Say: "Stand in a neutral position and quiet your mind."
- "Cast your head down. What emotion do you think you are communicating? Quintilian felt this posture communicated humility."
- "Cast your head back. Does this communicate haughtiness?"
- "Stand at neutral again and hold your head rigid and unmoved. What is this? Quintilian says rudeness."
- "Contract your eyebrows. Do they communicate anger? Can you lower them to communicate sadness? Can you expand them to communicate cheerfulness?"
- "Shrug your shoulders. What does this gesture mean? Quintilian says shrugging the shoulders is a sign of knavishness or unkindness."
- "Turn your face a quarter turn in the direction of your hand, raise your hand above your chest, but not above your eyes. Curve your fingers and open and close your hand slowly. What

emotion do you think you are communicating now? Quintilian says admiration. Can you see it? Or is this one too far-fetched?"
- "Keep this position and look at your whole body. Make sure your stomach and chest are not sticking out, and your back is not curved inward. Quintilian said that bending backwards in any way is offensive. Try bending backwards to assess if this is offensive."
- "Touch your middle finger to your thumb, allowing the other fingers to stay open and curved. Quintilian considered this the perfect position for stating facts."
- "State facts, remembering to keep your face a quarter turn towards your gesture."
- "How does it feel to make this gesture while speaking truth? Is there any merit to this method?"
- "Now turn a quarter turn away from your gesturing hand while speaking a 'fact' that you disagree with. How does that feel? Does it work to communicate a distancing from the 'fact'?"
- "Press both palms towards the left. Does this communicate detestation?"
- "Strike your thigh with your right hand to express indignation or to excite the attention of your audience."
- "Experiment with adding Quintilian-style gestures to monologues or scenes."
- Discuss: "Does this deliberate practicing of gestures in a mirror help you develop your acting toolboxes? While we might find these methods a touch ridiculous, what can we glean that is useful from them?"

Activity—Aaron Hill, The Ten Dramatic Passions

- Have your students stand in front of mirrors. Read the following to them as they try on the ten dramatic passions.
- "Joy is expressed by bending the brow upwards, opening and raising the forehead, making eyes smile and sparkle, stretching the neck without stiffness, bracing the whole body and arms boldly, and throwing the chest gracefully back. Hill believed this would appear natural to the audience, and should be repeated every time an actor wishes to communicate joy. Do you feel the joy you are externally expressing seeping into your emotions at all? Hill believed that your body posture impacts your internal emotions."
- "Anger requires tense muscles. Add flashing eyes, set teeth, expanded nostrils, and bent eyebrows."
- "Express grief by letting your muscles loosen."
- "Speak, and the voice will sound naturally full of misery and anguish."
- "Maintain your grief-stricken stance, and add a startled look to your face to show fear. Keep the eyes wide but unfixed, the mouth still and open. Try speaking your monologue lines in this posture to see if the posture creates fearful vocal qualities."
- "Create wonder with intense muscles and alarmed eyes. Step backwards, taking a sharp breath."
- "Create love with intense muscles and respectful attachment of the eye."
- "Create jealousy with intense muscles and a thoughtful look."

- "In pairs create your own instructions or revisions to one or two of the more unnatural Hill instructions. Perhaps the descriptions written here don't work, but could we modernize them and make them useful?"
- Discuss: "What did you learn from this activity? Are Quintilian and Hill different from each other?"

Activity—Zeami's *Jo-Ha-Kyu*

- Say: "Zeami taught the *jo-ha-kyu* rhythmic pattern of theatre. Every action performed on stage has a preparation, realization, and ending. Let's play with this concept. Everyone find a partner and a space to work without being in each other's way."
- "Start by choosing who will go first. Now we are going to do a stage punch. This means no one will actually hit anyone else, but we will make it look realistic using *jo-ha-kyu*. Victims, indicate where you will take the punch."
- "Aggressors, put your fists up and perform a jo by pulling back slightly from your target. Victims perform a jo by noticing the pull back and bracing for impact."
- "Now add a ha by slowly swinging your fist wide towards your target, stopping just short of contact. Victims, perform your ha by an exaggerated reaction to the incoming motion. Your ha will sell the action."
- "Now add a kyu when the punch lands. Aggressor should not actually touch the victim, but the victim should move their body to sell the contact while the aggressor provides a recoil that also sells the impact that did not occur."
- "Practice these three steps until you can perform the action at 70 percent speed safely, then add a return punch that also has a *jo-ha-kyu*. This pattern would repeat many times in one fight."
- "Choose another action to mime that is very tame such as serving tea or having a polite conversation and use the *jo-ha-kyu* process to stage it with your partner. Remember that every kyu contains the next jo so that the end of every gesture holds the potential of the beginning of the next. You can create energy this way."
- Share work with each other and discuss: "How does beginning in an easy manner, developing dramatically, and finishing rapidly impact your acting? Do you see ways that this timeless formula could create safety, replicability, and moments that are riveting for the audience? How does control of the details help the actor?"

2

Konstantin Stanislavski

The Person

The man who looms large in all conversations about acting methods was given the name Konstantin Alexseyevs when he was born to one of the richest families in Russia in 1863. He loved the theatre, so his father built one in the family home. In his time, most actors were serfs who acted to entertain the elite, so to protect the family from embarrassment, he took the name of a retired Polish actor, Stanislavski, when he began performing.

He enrolled in The Imperial Dramatic School of Moscow, but dropped out after three weeks because he didn't want to become a copy of his teachers who were imitating their own teachers. He wanted to retain his individuality and to find a code that would help him succeed. He sought a theatre that "would ban the . . . artificial from the stage."[1]

In 1898 a man named Vladimir Nemirovich-Danchenko asked for a lunch meeting. Stanislavski accepted, and that meeting extended through the night for eighteen straight hours. Together the men formed the Moscow Art Theatre (MAT). If you haven't heard of this theatre yet, remember it now. It is one of the most important and influential developments in the history of theatre. The theatre Nemirovich-Danchenko and Stanislavski created was intended for all classes of people, and strove to use artist-actors who were willing to become a part of an ensemble, delving deep for acting and artistic values. Their fifth play, *The Seagull* by Anton Chekhov, was the play that put them on the map.

What neither the MAT or Chekhov could know before the premiere was that Chekhov's style of playwriting would be the salvation of both the theatre and the playwright. The ensemble style of the characters, the deeply real subtext behind the words, and the conflicts between classes of people were perfect for Stanislavski. On the other hand, no one knew how to produce Chekhov's unusual plays. He had almost given up playwriting after the first production of *The Seagull* had brought mocking laughter and hisses from its audience. However, he was convinced by Nemirovich-Danchenko to let Stanislavski try. That production was so successful that both the playwright's reputation and the MAT were saved. After this, the MAT produced other plays by Chekhov. They were a match for the history books. Chekhov needed Stanislavski to direct his writing, revealing the subtext embedded within his stories. And Stanislavski needed Chekhov as a vehicle for discovering his system of truthful acting.

Even though he was wildly successful at the MAT, Stanislavski felt dead as an actor. He could not connect with his characters and had reverted to muscle memory in performance. This problem, combined with the death of the playwright Anton Chekhov in 1904 which "tore out a large part of the heart of our Theatree"[2] led him to leave the MAT at the age of forty-three. He was unhappy and mixed up about what to do next. "[D]issatisfaction with myself as an actor, and the complete darkness of the distances that lay before me, gave me no rest, took away my faith in myself, and made me seem wooden and lifeless in my own eyes."[3] He wondered if he could find a system that would put him into a creative mood reliably.

He began to experiment and observed the work of actors who seemed to be able to be in a creative mood anytime they liked. These actors seemingly believed the circumstances of their character and portrayed them honestly. The next years of Stanislavski's life were spent working and writing about his discoveries. He focused on the power of relaxation, concentration, given circumstances, and action. He wrote extensively, documenting his developing system.

Something that sets Stanislavski apart from many other acting teachers is that he believed in the process of self-discovery, and each actor finding their own way. He wanted his students to keep working and developing their methods beyond his. He encouraged his students to continue innovating. This humble approach worked well for his students. They loved him, and often described his childlike charm.

While we often think of Stanislavski's System as a static standard by which all other methods are measured, the truth is that his lifelong search for truth in art was dynamic. If we focus too much on a portion of his work and writing, we miss an important part of who he was: an evolving and growing artist who continued to change and even reverse his earlier methods as he worked over his long career. Sonia Moore described this phenomenon:

> One cause of misunderstanding about the Stanislavski System is the fact that various disciples of Stanislavski were assimilating it during different stages of its formation; without realizing that the System underwent constant change in its development . . . The Stanislavski System is the science of theatre art. As a science it does not stand still, being a science, it has unlimited possibilities for experiment and discoveries.[4]

When Stanislavski died in 1938, he hadn't assembled his writings in the comprehensive way he had intended, but he left tens of thousands of notebooks and manuscripts that others have organized and translated. In 1991, when the Russian archives were opened, the extent of the censorship of his writing was discovered. Renewed scholarship has painted a more accurate version of his story.

The Method

Stanislavski studied psychology, and knew the physical body and emotions work together. For a performance to be alive on stage, BOTH must be engaged. "This means that what you experience *internally* is immediately translated into an *outer* expression, and (conversely) what your body manifests *physically* has a direct and acknowledged affect on your *psychological* landscape."[5] In other words, our inner life has a profound impact on our body, but the body also helps shape our emotions and thoughts.

In an effort to help actors find emotions through the body, he taught a system of acting that included relaxation, concentration, given circumstances, and script analysis. When all of these are in place, an actor can more frequently find a state of experiencing flow.

Experiencing

Stanislavski used the Russian word *perezhivanie* which his translator, Elizabeth Hapgood, translated into English in many ways: living the part, living a scene, sensations, emotional experience, creation, the capacity to feel, living, and experiencing. This Russian term was so important to Stanislavski that in the Russian version, he subtitled his first acting book *The Creative Process of Perezhivanie*. Modern translators might even call it *The Creative Process of Experiencing FLOW*.

Many teachers do not teach this part of Stanislavski's System because it is so intangible, and cannot be taught directly. But it was the entire goal of Stanislavski's analysis of the art of acting. He wanted to figure out how to get to this state of experiencing a role more consistently. All of his actor preparation boiled down to getting his actors into this higher state of consciousness where senses are sharpened, their inward freedom to create is enhanced, and their being is filled with a sense of awe.

Stanislavski knew that *perezhivanie* is not something an actor can force, but he taught techniques that set them up for more of it through training. The golden standard of reaching *perezhivanie* was Stanislavski's measure of success on stage.

Relaxation

Because we all carry habitual tensions that can prevent us from finding physical expression of a character, Stanislavski's training included relaxation exercises to control tension in the body. When there is unnecessary strain in the body, your five senses won't work as effectively. Twenty-first-century Stanislavski teachers tend to frame this as having an awareness of tension and the ability to release, rather than control it.

Stanislavski's relaxation exercises explore extreme tension and complete release. This task is difficult because when an actor consciously relaxes one foot, their neck picks up tension. Stanislavski offers the example of a cat. If you look at a soft surface after a cat has been lying on it, you will see a full body imprint of the animal. It was completely relaxed. On the other hand, an adult human will usually only leave the imprint of two or three contact points. The muscles and the brain can be re-trained to relax every muscle consciously, but this takes practice. His exercises are part of training and preparation so the actor can begin in a state of readiness, where they don't have to think about relaxing while performing.

Concentration

Stanislavski taught that concentration is required in order for the actor to remain mentally in the world of the play. The actor on stage must be present to the play so that the external world and audience don't pull their focus. Concentration creates what he called *public solitude*. In using concentration, a character can live on stage as if they are not being observed by the audience, creating authentic moments.

He taught that in order to avoid paying attention to the audience, the actor must be interested in something on stage. To begin learning concentration, try picking out the closest thing to you and focusing on it. Try to keep your attention there for as long as possible. You should be able to do it fairly easily. Stanislavski called this a *small circle of attention*. This area might include the actor, a small table, and a prop or two close at hand.

Your next task is to concentrate in ever-widening circles. The next is the *medium circle of attention* that might include several persons and groups of furniture. Try to expand your attention by focusing on something that is further away from you, but still on the stage. This is more difficult to accomplish than it is with closer items.

The *large circle of attention* includes everything the actor can see on stage. It is hardest of all to maintain concentration on this largest circle, but this concentration is of utmost importance. "The eye of an actor which looks at and sees an object attracts the attention of the spectator, and by the same token points out to him what he should look at. Conversely, a blank eye lets the attention of the spectator wander away from the stage."[6]

Concentration also applies to your thoughts and senses. For example, your character might smell something and their attention will shift to their senses for a moment before looking for the source of the smell. Or, your character might remember something that they have to do, or an event that happened in the past. Each of these are objects of attention for your character. These circles of concentration are elastic and can contract to focus on a tiny detail on a prop or expand to include a fellow actor or some part of the set as needed. Concentration and practiced control allow the actor to control what the audience notices. You can create truth on stage by allowing your concentration to jump from one object to another just as you do in real life.

If you are having trouble with concentration, you might be trying too hard. "An inexperienced actor always feels that he does not give enough. 'Cut ninety-five percent,' said Stanislavski. 'An actor need not try to amuse the audience. If with the help of his imagination he sees the object . . . the audience will also be interested.'"[7] He recommends only giving as much attention to the object as you would in a real life situation.

There are other benefits of good concentration. Concentration is part of grounding your character. If your concentration is genuine and complete, your feet and hands will stop causing you trouble.

Voice

Stanislavski taught that an actor should work to speak so the audience can understand them without effort. He said, "every actor must be in possession of excellent diction and pronunciation, that he must feel not only phrases and words, but also each syllable, each letter . . . We do not feel our own language, the phrases, syllables, letters, and that is why it is so easy for us to distort it."[8] We mumble and blend sounds in our everyday life, so it is difficult to learn the skill of communication from the stage. We tend to slur words into an incomprehensible mess.

The work of learning to have clear diction, good pronunciation, and skillful singing are imperative for an actor. This work has to begin with a qualified teacher, and continue as a discipline of the actor to practice every day. The control of the voice is a tricky skill to gain, and it can be frustrating and time consuming. Stanislavski did not teach a particular method for speaking or singing well, but he did spend time working with his students on their voices in order to convince them to work with experts in singing and diction.

The work you do on Relaxation, Concentration, and Voice are the tools that prepare you to work as an actor. All the concepts from this point forward are what Stanislavski considered artistry.

Meeting Your Script

Stanislavski recommends carefully choosing where and when you read the script the first time. It is like a first date, and first impressions are important. Make sure that place is comfortable and free of distraction, where you can freely feel and express emotions. Take your first impression of your script very seriously. Lock those first instinctive impressions into your memory.

Given Circumstances

Your next step is the analysis of the script, starting with the given circumstances. This is simply a list of facts that can be found in the script. The playwright may give you many details about the history of the character, the present situation, and the future aspirations of the character, or they may not.

The use of given circumstances helps the actor integrate themselves with the character. Your job as a Stanislavski-based actor is to put yourself into the circumstances that are given to you and respond to them with belief. You can't actually become the character, but you can put yourself in that character's shoes and circumstances and respond in a reasonable way. Because the character's inner feelings are brought about by their given circumstances, you must delve deeply into what those circumstances are.

Imagine that you are playing Romeo in the famous balcony scene. What are the circumstances given by the text?

- You have climbed a wall into a garden by Juliet's bedroom window.
- It is night time after the masquerade ball.
- Juliet is on a balcony at a higher level than you are.
- You have a massive crush on her.
- Your families are bitter rivals and being found here could mean death for you.

There are many other things you could pick from the text, but this is a good start. Now think about what circumstances you might have been given by the set designer, costumer, and director?

- You have a dark cape that covers your light colored party outfit.
- There is ivy growing on the walls and a trellis covered with lilies.

- There is light coming from a source behind Juliet so she is a silhouette.
- Your director has told you to deliver the first line you say to someone in the front row of the audience.

Now you add your own circumstances. Your imagination is an important part of Stanislavski's circumstances. Perhaps:

- You are pretty sure your armpits stink.
- You have always hated Juliet's family, so this new love is surprising to you.

This list will get longer and longer as you analyze the text and circumstances.

The Magic If

Now it is your job to put yourself into these circumstances and ask the question, "How would I respond if I were in this situation?" Stanislavski called this the *Magic If*. You, as the actor, imagine yourself in this situation. What would you do as Romeo? No two actors would handle the situation in quite the same way. Maria Knebel, one of Stanislavski's assistants, said he often told his students that living in the *Magic If* was a wonderful state that does not impose anything on the actor. The *If* frees the actor to imagine.[9] Since you aren't coerced to certain emotions, you are freed to approach your work as if it had happened to you. In other words, ask the question, "what if this were me?" and let the work answer the question. You create the answers based on your own personal experiences. You do not have to believe you are Romeo, but you can believe in the way you are responding to Romeo's circumstances.

The unique *Magic If* you create for this scene will transport the character's aims to be your own, creating inner and physical actions for you. You won't have to worry about over-acting or mechanical performance since your actions will be truthful. Let your artistic imagination run wild, giving life to the list of circumstances you have compiled. Stanislavski calls this process a waking dream. You can live the "I am" state of the character in your imagination, living in the character's world, feeling their soul.

Table Work: A history

At the beginning of his career, Stanislavski worked in a very director-centric model in which the actors did not do any analysis, but followed the director's orders without question. In 1904 this changed. For the next thirty years, his actors spent an enormous amount of time around a table discussing the script and marking it up. (The final four years of his life were devoted to Active Analysis, which you will read about at the end of this chapter and more extensively in Maria Knebel's chapter.) This table-work process was extremely collaborative, and required the actors to contribute all of their ideas. He wanted his actors to take responsibility for the creation of their roles. By the first rehearsal, everyone had done a lot of work on the script.

Contemporary theatres do not spend weeks at the table, but much of the language that was developed around the tables at the MAT are still in use today. It is useful to understand what they mean in your own work.

Table Work: Super-Objective and Throughline of Actions

One of the first expectations of table work is for each actor to identify their character's overarching goal for the course of the play. This is the character's super-objective. Knowing that goal sets the foundation for further script analysis. Every action a character performs should add to the throughline of action towards the character's super-objective. What is Romeo's super-objective? Is it finding love? To find someone to give himself to? Stanislavski felt that any actions that did not match with the super-objective would stand out to the audience as superfluous—even as wrong. Actions that aren't connected to each other will appear as chaos instead of inspired art. Each actor is free to choose their own super-objective for the character as long as it can be justified within the playwright's text.

Table Work: Bits (or Beats)

Next, a script must be dissected into bits that each have their objectives and counter-objectives. There is much confusion about the term, some scholars preferring the more rhythmic *Beats*, others insisting that *Bits* is simpler and more closely translates from the Russian term. Either way, a Bit or Beat is a small segment of the script, chosen for its bite-sized ability to be analyzed as one unit of a play.

There are different methods to break a script down into bits. For example, a new bit might begin when a character exits or enters (called the French Scene), or when the subject of conversation switches. The bit shouldn't be more than about a page, but also shouldn't be so short that it isn't useful as a rehearsal unit. A helpful tip is to understand that each bit should contain an action that meets some resistance.

Table Work: Objectives

Next, each actor participates in the analysis by choosing one verb to serve as the bit's objective for their character. For example: *to entice* or *to trap*. The objective is sometimes called an action. The action, simply put, is what the actor does—even if it doesn't include movement. Stanislavski wrote, "You may sit without a motion and at the same time be in full action."[10] Action is everything.

Sharon Carnicke wrote about the Russian word *zadacha* and how it is translated into English, "One of the most misunderstood of Stanislavsky's terms continues to be 'objective' . . . When reading Stanislavsky's discussion in Russian, I understood perfectly that in every scene the character faces a set of given circumstances that pose a *zadacha*, which the actor (as the character) must attempt to solve by taking action . . . the most apt translation is 'problem.'"[11] Once you understand the problem in your bit, you can choose an objective that motivates you to solve it. If you dread going on stage, it might be time to adjust your objective, creating compelling internal motivation.

Table Work: Obstacles and Counter-Actions

In the process of striving to meet your objectives, you will find that there are obstacles in the way of reaching them, and counter-actions you perform in order to reach your goals. These counter-actions are sometimes called adaptations or tactics. If an actor uses the same counter-action to get something from another actor for a whole scene, it will become boring. Therefore, tactics must shift. Obstacles met by a variety of counter-actions create fun.

Table Work: Subtext

If your audience only wanted to know the words of the script, they could read it at home. They come to the theatre to see you enact the subtext, or meaning beneath the text. Underneath the words "I have a headache" written on the page of script could be many different realities to act. Perhaps the character wants guests to leave a party so they can go to bed, or they are worried about their overall physical health, or they want their partner to offer a backrub. Your imagination will fill out the meaning behind the request even if the playwright doesn't offer one. Remember, sometimes the characters lie. How will the audience know it is a lie if the actor doesn't communicate the subtext?

One of the reasons that Stanislavski's System pairs so well with Anton Chekhov's plays is that those scripts are full of subtext where the characters rarely speak what they are thinking. Stanislavski claimed we only speak about 10 percent of what's happening in our heads. The remaining 90 percent is the unspoken subtext. This subtext is seen by the audience in the way we handle our action followed by counter-action and then resolution.[12]

Table Work: An Example

Put into practical terms, if you are working on a scene in which your character is working with their mother and sister setting up for a party, the super-objective of the play might be "to find a suitable spouse." You would write this super-objective at the top of your script. Next, you would break the script into bits and write objectives for each bit that serve the super-objective of the play. Sometimes you would find objectives shift quickly; other times they cover longer sections. Perhaps in one moment of this fictitious play, the objective might be marked as "to impress my mother with my flower arranging skills," and in another, "to be a better helper than my sister." While they are smaller objectives, they both serve the greater overarching super-objective by impressing the mother to assist the character in their hunt for a mate.

Within these objectives are actions such as "to bend the red rose in a pleasing shape" or "to induce my mother to look at my bouquet." What a character wants and does are often intertwined.

As you analyze each bit, you will find the obstacles in the way. Perhaps your sister has an objective "to distract mother from looking at my sister's bouquet." This obstacle will push your character to try other tactics or counter-actions to win mother's attention. Your imagination can fill in the subtext with the collaboration of your scene partners.

Living Truthfully Under Imaginary Circumstances

Now that your table work is done, it's time to embody your role. Hopefully the work you have done makes you excited to get up and work on your feet. Stanislavski taught his students the goal on stage should be *living truthfully under imaginary circumstances*. He taught his actors to train their bodies and study the text, but then to allow themselves to be present on stage and allow each performance to have a truthful life of its own. He believed that if an actor were to try to recreate exactly the performance of the night before, their performance would become dead. He wrote,

> The great actor . . . must feel an emotion not only once or twice while he is studying his part, but to a greater or lesser degree every time he plays it, no matter whether it is the first or the thousandth time. Unfortunately, this is not within our control. Our subconscious is inaccessible to our consciousness . . . The result is a predicament; we are supposed to create under inspiration; only our subconscious gives us inspiration; yet we apparently can use this subconscious only through our consciousness, which kills it.[13]

This predicament means that we have to work very hard to train our bodies and minds. We must prepare many creative moments in our work, and then be ready not to interfere when flow takes over. The work done to prepare the body and voice for the work of the stage is what frees the subconscious to do the work of living through the character.

Tempo-Rhythm

All of life runs on rhythms. The seasons, hours, days, heartbeats, breath . . . Acting has rhythm too. Stanislavski taught his students to think about the tempo-rhythms of their characters and use them to create truth on stage. You have a particular tempo-rhythm as a human being, and an important part of you finding your character, is finding your character's unique tempo-rhythms both internally and externally. Inner tempo-rhythm and outer tempo-rhythm are two different things. For example, if you are teaching a teen to drive, your inner rhythm will be fast and furious. Externally, however, your methods will necessarily be slow and controlled. The calmness on the outer facade contradicts the internal tempo creating tremendous tension.

Communion

We are always in communion with someone or something. When we have a blank stare, we are in communion with something far away from where we are. We are thinking about a past moment, or a person who is elsewhere, and we aren't really in the room. Actors sometimes bring their lives and thoughts with them onto stage. In that case, they are in communion with something outside the four walls of the set. Stanislavski observed that this makes them uninteresting to the audience. Actors must stay present to the stage reality.

Stanislavski believed any direct communication with the audience "disrupts the truth of the performance and distracts the audience from the play itself. An honest, unbroken communion between actors, on the other hand, holds the spectators' attention and makes them part of what takes place on stage."[14] This means that the fourth wall must be in place and respected.

How then, would Stanislavski coach an actor to perform a monologue which is often supposed to be spoken directly to the audience? Stanislavski taught actors to be in communion with themselves. You can create two versions of yourself that are speaking to each other. Your audience will be riveted by the internal communion between you and you. The idea is simple: communicate honestly with your scene partner who is another piece of your character.

A Note on Emotion Memory

Stanislavski experimented with emotional memory exercises early in his work. These exercises have also been called affective memory and emotion recall exercises. They were the starting point for the affective memory work Method actors use which can be found in the Strasberg and Batson chapters. Since memory of the senses can have a powerful effect on stage, bringing back powerful emotions can be effective in authentic performance.

When he developed these exercises, Stanislavski was trying to help his actors experience emotional moments repeatedly on stage with genuine emotion. His exercises were designed to remind an actor of a moment when a real life trauma or joy occurred so that the real emotion could be triggered on command. It is important to note that when Stanislavski did emotion recall work with his actors, he asked them to do the work at home alone. "His concern for actors' privacy and their 'mental hygiene' as well as his own modesty prohibited him from asking actors to perform affective recall in front of others."[15]

By the early 1930s, Stanislavski had abandoned the practice of emotional memory because he found that it produced hysteria in his actors and damaged their mental and emotional health. Our bodies don't know the difference between living the trauma the first time and reliving it in our minds over and over on stage. He replaced this work with his system of physical actions described in this chapter: objective, action, counter-action.

When Stanislavski worked with American actor, Stella Adler, he recognized that she was being taught the main tenets of his method, but that the emotion memory piece was way out of proportion. Stanislavski taught his actors this tactic as a small piece of their work, staying mindful of mental health. It is a finicky tool that will work for some performances, and fail in others. He stopped using it completely by the end of his career.

Active Analysis

In the last four years of his life, Stanislavski did almost no table work with his actors, preferring instead to use the natural tendency of the actor to enact their analysis, skipping directly to the stage for a method called Active Analysis. This was not a change in how much analysis an actor did, but a giant change in how the analysis was done. Instead of using pencil and paper, they used their bodies. Stanislavski realized that dividing mental work from physical behavior in long sessions around the table led to actor disengagement and wasted time.

Boris Zon, a prominent Russian theatre teacher who had built his career on Stanislavski's System, attended an Active Analysis rehearsal under Stanislavski's supervision. He was moved to tears over the complete transformation of the System that he had been taught and finally understood at a deeper level. After the rehearsal, Stanislavski pulled Zon aside and asked for his impressions. Zon told him that his ideas about the Stanislavski System had been strongly shaken. Stanislavski, understanding the transformative moment replied, "we have had to rethink a lot of things, and give up much that seemed indisputable to us earlier." Zon replied to Stanislavski, "So now I have this feeling . . . that until today I have been blind and suddenly I can see clearly. Everything I knew so well actually looks so differently now that it needs to be learned all over again."[16]

What Zon had observed was a new paradigm. Stanislavski now believed the only logical way to approach the text was through action. "The fact is that over-reliance on table work led us to 'indigestion.' Like a capon [chicken] fed on so many nuts that its stomach no longer digests any food, so too the actor is preconditioned with so much 'food' at the table that he cannot reproduce it immediately, cannot use one-hundredth of what was accumulated."[17] The way the company now approached the work of analyzing bits and finding objectives was to act it out and notice when one beat/bit is complete. In this method, the objective appears spontaneously, so everyone simply notices, then reaches for the next action to play.

What does Active Analysis look like? It begins with the actors reading a script together for the first time, but on their feet making movement decisions on their own as they read. In this way, they are actively and physically analyzing the script as they have their first impression of it. Next, the director has a moment to speak broadly of their vision of the theme and characters in the play. Immediately afterwards the actors and director break the script down into fragments, or rehearsal units. Each fragment is analyzed and then performed in what Stanislavski called an etude.

The actors are given some time to quickly analyze the etude for storyline and shifting actions/objectives in the selected fragment. Then, the director instructs the actors to put the script aside and improvise it by creating an etude. Afterwards, the actors and director discuss what was discovered, then the director sends them back to their scripts to study and see if they managed to remember and represent the actions of the piece. In this way, they are starting with a method of analyzing through physical actions, before the words are in place. Acting starts with action.

James Thomas describes this post-etude analysis this way: the actor

> returns to the table excited and energized by the experience of analysis in action that had just taken place, and consequently he carefully identifies his omissions, mistakes, and the shallowness or superficial understanding of this or that circumstance of the play. Right there he reads the text again. Right there he grasps the author's wording, and he recognizes it happily. (How much better, more precise, and more significant the text is than he, the actor, could express with his own words!) The omissions lead to disappointment, and a desire arises in the actor to go on stage and rehearse again.[18]

This process is repeated over and over. The director subtly helps the actors unify their individual work by asking good questions, prompting them to explore and discover the answers on their feet. The end result of this process leaves the actors in control of their own blocking and mental work.

This process fit well within Stanislavski's later focus on communion, both communion with the audience and the other actors. "Collective creativeness, on which our art is based, necessarily demands ensemble . . . Those who violate it commit a crime . . . against the art which they serve."[19]

Using Active Analysis, communion can be achieved and all the participants can stay present with each other in the service of their art.

It is inspirational to know that the most influential acting teacher in the history of humankind was a person who humbly understood he hadn't solved all the problems of acting even after a lifetime of work. Late in life he completely shifted his approach to his work in order to find a better way to reach truth.

Professionalism

How can an actor achieve all of Stanislavski's objectives? As a starting point, his System emphasizes professionalism. Gifted actors work persistently on their craft, always searching for a technique that will unlock their performances. Stanislavski said,

> Let someone explain to me why the violinist must daily perform hour-long exercises or lose his power to play? Why does the dancer work daily over every muscle in his body? Why do the painter, the sculptor, the writer practice their art each day and count that day lost when they do not work? And why may the dramatic artist do nothing, spend his day in coffee houses and hope for the gift of [inspiration] in the evening? Enough. There is no art that does not demand virtuosity.[20]

He believed that success relies on dedication to the practice of art.

Stanislavski believed an actor needs four types of discipline:

- Psychological—in order to separate your own emotional baggage from the character's
- Physical—to rigorously prepare your body for acting.
- Imaginative—to color your performance.
- Collective—to understand your responsibility to your fellow actors.

Konstantin Stanislavski's Legacy

In his seventy-five years of life, Stanislavski managed to completely change the way actors thought about their profession. He had created a System by obsessively observing and perfecting a method that seemed to enliven the best actors in performance. A true mold breaker, Konstantin Stanislavski focused on the internal emotions and meaning that an actor can bring to the stage. He wanted his students to behave truthfully on stage in imaginary circumstances blending the internal with the external. And he never stopped searching for the key to truthful acting. Every method of acting since he developed his has to contend with this man's work and legacy.

Tips for taking this method further

- First and foremost, get a copy of Bella Merlin's *The Complete Stanislavsky Toolkit*. It is the most readable and complete text on the System, and it should be required reading for all serious acting students.

- Read the three English language books that cover the evolution of his system: *An Actor Prepares, Building a Character,* and *Creating a Role.*
- Read good translations of Stanislavski's journals. I recommend *My Life in Art* translated by J. J. Robbins.

Discussion Starters and Journal Prompts

- Write one paragraph about observations from your reading. Write one paragraph defining internal and external acting, then explain which style you find most appealing and why. On a scale of 1 to 10, 1 being fully internal and 10 being fully external, where do you fall? Where does Stanislavski fall?
- Write a reflection on this reading and some Google research that you completed about Stanislavski. What did you learn? What did you already know? What do you agree with? What do you want to try? What bothers you?

The Tools for your Toolbox

Activity—Relaxation and Concentration

- Have your actors stand and tense all the muscles of their bodies.
- Say: "Relax your muscles. Now try to tense only one side of your body while leaving the other side relaxed. This is very difficult to do! When you are on stage and part of you is tense, it is easy for other parts of your body to unconsciously pick up that tension. You have to work to learn to control this phenomenon."
- "Stand using only enough tension to hold yourself upright."
- "Bend over slowly, one vertebrae at a time until your upper body is hanging limp at the waist."
- "Reverse that motion until you are standing at neutral again."
- "Lie on the floor and imagine yourself somewhere you can be completely at peace: perhaps in bed, or in a hammock, or on a beach."
- "Relax every muscle of your body, imagining its imprint forming underneath you."
- "Concentrate on your breath. Don't try to control it. Simply allow your attention to notice the air going in and out of your body while you remain relaxed."
- Note: It would be appropriate at this point to do a yoga relaxation and visualization exercise focusing on the various chakras, keeping in mind that relaxation in the context of theatre should be energizing rather than sleepy.
- Say: "Develop a sense of self, connecting to your creative imagination."
- "Return your thoughts to a visualized place of peace resting in the imprint of your body."
- "Open your eyes and return to the room slowly."
- Discuss: "Were you able to find an energetic relaxed state? What was that like?"

- Say: "Close your eyes. Imagine your favorite mug is sitting on the floor in front of you. Get a picture of its shape and color in your mind, then reach out and pick it up. Remember its weight. Hold it as if it is empty and examine it in your imagination."
- "Now set it down again and imagine I have filled it with hot cider. Pick it up. Bring it slowly to your lips, taking in the sight, scent, and feel of it. As you carefully take a taste, react to the heat and taste. Did you like it? Now set it back down carefully."
- Discuss: "Tell a partner what it was like to imagine a familiar item and engage all the senses in exploring your imagination."
- Say: "Close your eyes again. Take something that has meaning to you out of an imaginary bag. Feel its weight. Explore its shape. Use it as you usually would. Think about the history of this object. What are your emotional ties to it? Examine all the details of it using all five senses."
- "Concentration is not about staring at something or someone intently. It is about studying everything about it, exploring emotions, histories, judging and reacting. The attention you paid to this item is the same as the attention you should pay to all the items in your circle on stage. Don't just glance at things. See them. Expand your ability to concentrate by practicing this skill on your own time."
- "Remember waking up today. Use all five senses. What did you hear, smell, taste, feel, see? And how did you react to each of these things?"
- "Get up and walk around the room. Remember coming home after a day at school when you were nine. Imagine it is a rainy day. What are you wearing? How do you respond to the rain? Is anyone walking with you? What will you do when you get home? Is there someone waiting for you? Are you hungry? Happy?"
- Discuss: "How can concentration on details, emotions, and memories help you as you progress as an actor?"

Activity—Subtext and Analysis

- Have your actors pair up to play with open scenes. You can use the following originally from *The "Open Scene" as a Directing Exercise* in *The Educational Theatre Journal*:

ONE: Oh.
TWO: Yes.
ONE: Why are you doing this?
TWO: It's the best thing.
ONE: You can't mean it?
TWO: No, I'm serious.
ONE: Please . . .
TWO: What?
ONE: What does this mean?
TWO: Nothing.
ONE: Listen . . .
TWO: No.

ONE:	So different.
TWO:	Not really.
ONE:	Oh.
TWO:	You're good.
ONE:	Forget it.
TWO:	What?
ONE:	Go on.
TWO:	I will.

- Give the class a scenario or two such as:
  - A Military General is looking at a battle plan. A subordinate comes in and disagrees with the plan.
  - A dance instructor and a shy uncoordinated person.
  - A worker is packing up their desk to walk out on a job when a co-worker walks in and tries to dissuade them.
  - "A couple lost their only child before the baby reached three. The tragic death occurred about six months ago. The wife has often been found lately, sobbing hysterically over the box of toys belonging to the child. The day has come when the husband is determined to get rid of the toys, because of the way they continue to haunt his wife and himself."[21]
- Say: "Work with your partner to create a scenario that would work with this scene and act it."
- "Write your own open scene and create three very different scenarios for it."
- "Break the scene into bits/beats then write objectives, actions, and counter-actions for your scene, both for the lines and for the actions between lines."
- "Practice acting your scenes, adjusting and performing again."
- Discuss: "What is the value of scene analysis and understanding the subtext?"

Activity—The Magic If

- Have your students pair up.
- Say: "Improvise a scene in which Person A is a Bible-thumping, snake-handling preacher in the Appalachians. Person B is a devotee. OR a hillbilly and a member of royalty."
- They will likely give stereotypical portrayals.
- Say: "Step deeper into the given circumstances of your roles. In order to play the parts with truth, walk through the process of understanding the mindset of each character until you believe that if you were in the same circumstances, you could do nothing other than believe and act as these characters."
- "Run the scenes again without the stereotypes."
- Discuss: "What is the difference between truth and stereotypes? How did you make your characters believable while acting stereotypes?"

Activity—Tempo-Rhythm

- Have your actors do a walking exercise, running a metronome while they walk. Change the speed at random intervals.
- Say: "Justify your tempo-rhythms internally so your physical state matches your psychological state."
- Turn off the metronome and ask them to improvise the following scenarios:
  - Fixing and eating breakfast while late for work
  - Fixing and eating breakfast when there is plenty of time
  - Writing a text to a person you are in love with
  - Writing a text to someone you must reply to, but are annoyed with
  - Defuse a bomb using different inner and outer tempo-rhythms.
- Discuss: "What did you learn about internal and external rhythms?"

Activity—Sitting with Purpose

- Choose a student to start this activity and ask them to perform a scene on their own from *An Actor Prepares*.
- Say: "The curtain goes up, and you are sitting on the stage. You are alone. You sit and sit and sit . . . At last the curtain goes down again. That is the whole play."[22]
- Allow the student to sit there in discomfort for longer than seems good. They will likely either feel helpless, or try to please and entertain the audience. Ask them to come to you and whisper an instruction to them such as: "This time go on stage and sit in the chair in order to count how many students have brown eyes (or how many seats are in the auditorium)."
- Give other students a chance to try this activity.
- Discuss: "Stanislavski said whatever happens on stage must be for a purpose. What changed for the audience when the actor had a purpose for sitting on stage? Does the purpose for your movement and stillness have to be related to the script?"

Activity—Moving with Purpose

- Start by placing an assortment of furniture pieces on the stage. Choose a volunteer.
- Say: "Go up and arrange the furniture until I say to stop."
- Let the scene go on until it is clear to everyone that the actor is bored.
- Discuss: "Why was the actor arranging the furniture? Was it because I told them to? Is it enough for an actor to move because the director tells them to?"
- Say: "You are arranging the furniture because you have invited people over to listen to you read some of your original poetry. Your favorite professor is coming."
- Discuss: "What difference does purpose for action give to a scene?"

- Have two students go onstage and sit on something. Give them each a blocking instruction like "Cross to the door!" without giving them a purpose for the activity. After they have done this, ask what their purpose was. If they did not have one, ask them to find a purpose and repeat the activity.
- Say: "Directors will often give actors blocking without a purpose. It is the actor's job to create the action or the purpose of that movement."
- "Get into groups of three or four and designate a director. Each director should give blocking while the actors use their imaginations to motivate their movement."
- Discuss as a group.

Activity—Psycho-Physical Involvement

- Have your students stand in a circle.
- Say: "Let's count together to thirty. Clap if a number is divisible by three."
- "Count again with the same rule, but this time also clap twice if a number is divisible by five, if a number is divisible by three or five, clap three times."
- "Stand in lines an arm's reach apart."
- "Move your right arm forward. Move it up. Move it out to the side. Move it down."
- "Create an image in your mind of what you are doing. Make your body match the image."
- "Move both arms forward. Now up. Now out to the side. Now down."
- "Create an image in your mind of what you are doing. Adjust your body to match."
- "Move both arms forward, but keep the motion of the left arm slightly behind the motion of the right. Now up. Now out to the side. Now down."
- "Create an image in your mind of what you are doing. Adjust your body."
- "Continue your motions while walking in circles."
- "Create an image in your mind of what you are doing. Adjust your body."
- Discuss: "The purpose of this activity was to help your body express mental images, attaining psycho-physical involvement. What effects might these activities that combine concentration and motion have on performance?"

Activity—Text Analysis

- Bring in copies of a scene and break it down into etudes, bits, objectives, counter-objectives, super-objectives, given circumstances, etc. . . .
- Act the etude as broken down by table work.
- Use Active Analysis to perform the next etude.
- Discuss: "What do these two styles of analysis have in common? What are the merits and detractions of each style? Which helps you most with your character?"

3

Vsevolod Meyerhold

The Person

Born in 1874, Vsevolod Meyerhold was an original member of the MAT alongside Stanislavski. He was born in rural Russia, the son of a successful vodka distiller. Being the eighth child, he would never inherit the business, but the family money provided Meyerhold the opportunity to attend Moscow University. After one year of law school he switched to studying drama. Vladimir Nemirovich-Danchenko, who was one of his teachers, invited Meyerhold to be one of the first members of the MAT. He agreed.

Four years later there was tension between the headstrong Meyerhold and the leaders of the MAT, and his name was not included on the 1902 shareholder's list. He left, taking more than a dozen MAT actors with him. He assembled a company in Ukraine experimenting with performance methods and structure. Three years later, Stanislavski invited him back to Moscow and helped him open a studio to continue his experimental work. This studio was ultimately unsuccessful, and lost a lot of Stanislavski's money, but this failure didn't deter him from pursuing his style of theatre.

Meyerhold began to train his actors since Stanislavski's students were not as physically expressive and balanced as he envisioned, too trapped by realism. Towards this purpose, he created a system he called Biomechanics, referring to the mechanical operation of the body. He recruited a group of actors who split their days between working on tumbling mats with Meyerhold and studying the System at the MAT.

The physicality that Meyerhold was reaching for had a purpose. He felt that audiences of Russian theatre were lulled into a spell in the theatre of the real, protected by the fourth wall. He wanted to awaken them. His theatre tried to make the audience and the actors mutually aware of each other during performance, shocking them into social action by opening their eyes to the struggles of the working class.

Meyerhold's career spanned three revolutions, one in 1905 and two in 1917, which required him to be nimble and play political games for Tsar Nicolas II, Lenin, and Stalin. Experimental work like his was encouraged in the 1920s, but in the 1930s it was dangerous. Unlike Stanislavski, who appeared apolitical, Meyerhold was outspoken, but politically savvy, keenly aware of the danger of what he was doing.

In 1922, during a time of government endorsement of his experimental ideas, he conscripted designer L. Popova to create a constructivist set for him that was different than anything his audiences had ever seen. It consisted of a wooden scaffolding that resembled a jungle gym for adults. It had slides, ladders, and ramps which his actors used like a play structure depicting the essence of modern man and the new Soviet life.

When Meyerhold gave his first public demonstration of Biomechanics it was clear that he was moving in the opposite direction of realism, creating a purely physical style of acting. He engaged intentionally with the theatrical worlds of pantomime, commedia, Noh, gymnastics, and clowning. He celebrated the presentational and theatrical, rejecting realism in acting.

Unfortunately for him, the political environment at this time dealt harshly with artists who fought against realism, the accepted style of the current government. In 1938 his theatre was closed and his methods were declared anti-Soviet because they were avant-garde. He didn't stay quiet, criticizing the Communist policy of socialist realism and "was arrested on charges of espionage, of plotting to assassinate Stalin and of being part of a counter-revolutionary Trotskyist organization."[1] He was put in prison in Moscow, and then, in 1942 at the age of sixty-six, he was tortured, forced to confess to being a spy, and fatally shot. Meyerhold had devoted much of his career to furthering the cause of the Soviet regime, but his experimentation was a perceived threat to Stalin. When he died, all mention of his name was erased from publications. It was fifteen years later before his work could be safely mentioned in Russia. We only know of his work today because of his students who remembered and reconstructed his system after Stalin died.

The Method

Meyerhold believed the physical and psychological are inextricably connected. While Stanislavski emphasized psychological truth, Meyerhold focused on physical truth, teaching his actors to comfortably feel the positions and movements of their bodies. Meyerhold used choreographed movement to achieve emotion in the audience, not necessarily in the actors. If an actor felt comfortable in a position, but the audience would see the position as discomfort, he insisted the actor adjust to create the appropriate audience response.

He strove to create productions that only half of the audience would love. In this way, a lively discussion would happen on the way out of the theatre. "He filled his productions with self-conscious theatricalities, arranging the order of the scenes in such a way that they might collide against one another rather than seamlessly fuse together."[2] Meyerhold's audiences could see their own complicated lives reflected on stage in theatrical ways, prompting thought and conversation.

Art and Music

Meyerhold used art as inspiration for the stage pictures and compositions that he created with his actors. He said that great art has, "interesting compositions, original rhythmical solutions."[3] He told his actors to look at paintings and examine the hand and foot positions of the subjects in order to imitate them. His actors were taught to perform an uninterrupted flow of movements creating a moving painting. The term Meyerhold used to explain this style of movement was a French word *raccourci*, meaning shortcut, indicting an efficiency of movement. The actors performed a prescribed series of continuous motions that ended in a static poses. Meyerhold used mirrors to help his actors experience the raccourci in their body, while observing themselves from the outside, allowing them to create beautiful and elegant lines and shapes. If they thought of themselves as a work of art, they could enjoy every body position even if it was demeaning in some way.

Meyerhold also inspired his actors with music. The musical rhythms helped actors find the tempo-rhythm of their acting. This was not meant to create an actual rhythm with the music, instead, the music inspired feelings and an internal rhythm that matched or contradicted the music. They worked *over* rather than *under* the music. He said, "The actor in the music drama must absorb the essence of the score and translate every subtlety of the musical picture into plastic terms. For this reason he must strive for complete control over his body . . . *Man*, performing in harmony with the *mise en scéne* and the musical score, becomes a *work of art* in his own right."[4] The *mise en scéne*, or design elements of the production, in conjunction with music and the artful movements of the actors created living, moving art.

Athletics

Meyerhold's actors trained not only in fine arts, but also in sports. They were trained in boxing to create an alert stance, ready to give and take. They worked on acrobatics learning to be ready for action at all times. Some exercises required actors to effortlessly leap onto the backs of their classmates at a signal. Athletic training helped Meyerhold's actors be present in action without extraneous movements, with rhythm, stability, and correctly placed center of gravity. Meyerhold claimed people who move in this way are riveting to watch.

Biomechanics

Meyerhold's system of actor training was called Biomechanics. Unlike many modern systems of acting, Biomechanics trained actors to be precise and replicate their movements exactly each time they were on stage. This technique requires actors to have:

- Control—a healthy, coordinated, trained body.
- Education—an attentive, imaginative mind complemented by knowledge of the artistic culture of the past, major trends of the past and present, evolution of acting methods including Western and Eastern traditions, history, science, literature, and play analysis.
- Precision—the ability to exactly repeat every action.
- Balance—the ability to perform movements in a balanced way without a wobble.
- Coordination—the coordination of their own body first, then coordination with the movements of others so everyone is working together, operating in shared space with musicality.
- Efficiency—wasting energy on stage is uncomfortable for the audience and unnecessarily tiring for actors. A factory worker has to boil down each movement to the essential elements. If an actor can do the same thing, their work will be compelling.

- Rhythm—the ability to perform each gesture in three parts: a prologue, the realization, and an epilogue. This rhythm is precise and replicable.
- Expressiveness—the ability to create expressive stage pictures to communicate the central idea of a scene.
- Responsiveness—the ability to give an immediate response to any stimuli.
- Playfulness with Discipline—the ability to balance play and discipline in performance and rehearsal. Too much playfulness leads to self-indulgence; too much discipline leads to a lack of creativity and spark.

In his training program, actors studied all sorts of physical movement styles "without dwelling on any of them too long, in order not to develop heavy muscles which hinder ease and freedom in movement."[5] They also studied Biomechanical gymnastics, a prescribed series of physical actions that helped the actor have control of physical movements so they could create both *legato* (smooth, flowing) and *staccato* (sharp, quick, distinct) movements in a large range of motion.

The effect of these movement sessions was to focus the actor's attention to their waist and the springiness of their legs. These exercises have the following stated objectives:

1. To enable the actor to feel the balance and center of gravity within himself, that is, to develop complete control over one's own body.
2. To enable the actor to position and coordinate himself three-dimensionally in relation to the stage space, one's partner, and the stage properties. In other words, to facilitate the development of a "good eye" so that the actor becomes a moving part of a harmonious whole.
3. "To develop in the actor physical or reflexive arousal for instantaneous and non-conscious reaction."[6]
4. "To develop in the trainee a director (a control over one's material) in coordination with the playing area, one's partner, one's costume and the stage properties."[7]

The training of the body in Meyerhold's school created a sense that the body is an instrument for the actor to play. The torso is mass that can be balanced in various ways. Extremities can be positioned in efficient and rhythmic ways. The head and voice can be controlled as well.

Meyerhold was fascinated by industrial society and he thought of the body as a machine. However the quality of movement in Biomechanics was never robotic or rigid. The use of muscles and movements was both musical and exact. The actor had to learn to move as if on springs in a quality of "dancingness" which has a quality of acceptance: "Strike me! I will gladly receive your attack, and then we will trade places."[8] In this way, movements are natural even if the situation is aggressive, with wrists and hands moving freely unless a specific posture such as a fist is requested. Beginners usually find this looseness of Biomechanical motions to be a challenge.

The efficiency of movement takes training also. Every movement must engage every muscle. Can your foot muscles help as you twitch your nose? Can you involve the pelvis in squaring your shoulders? When you involve every part of your body, no motion can be wasted. For instance, if your movement is to shift your weight from left to right, Meyerhold would not allow you to also adjust your hair. This level of focus takes discipline and practice.

Since his training was so complete and drilled into his actor's bodies, Biomechanics exercises today are essentially unchanged from a century ago. The students who studied in his laboratory learned the routines, or etudes, so thoroughly that when the period of suppression of Meyerhold's legacy was over decades later, his students could still remember and teach them exactly as they had been taught.

Training Sessions with Meyerhold

If you were to study with Meyerhold, you would start with learning the *dactyl*. The dactyl is performed both at the beginning and the end of each biomechanical exercise to signal the exact beginning of the activity and the exact conclusion. The dactyl is a quick contraction, expansion, and re-contraction of the body punctuated with claps. Many videos are available online to help you visualize and embody the form.

Once you learned the dactyl, you would learn a series of other precise etudes bookended with the dactyl. As you learned the movements, the instructor would call "Hup!" after each freeze moment to instigate the next stage of the etude.

Each movement of each etude has a rhythm:

- The first part is the *Otkaz*, meaning recoil. It is the preparation for any movement or "gestural prologue."[9] In this initiation, an actor pulls back, indicating their intention to move. This has both a functional purpose: pulling back to provide more force to the movement, and an expressive purpose: pulling back to signal their intention to the audience by contrast. It also creates stability for the movement.
- The second stage is the *Posil*, meaning settling or sending. This is the realization of the movement.
- The third part is the *Tochka,* meaning period. It is the moment where the motion is completed, a sort of "frozen epilogue."[10]

For example, in the etude called *Shooting the Arrow*, the actor indicates their intention to shoot an arrow at a target by pulling back. Next, they realize the action by actually releasing the arrow at the target. Finally, the actor poses in completion of the action. These motions are not fully realistic, but carefully choreographed to communicate the spirit of the action. Every etude is built around this *Otkaz-Posil-Tochka* rhythm.

This careful choreography helps you as the actor by:

- giving you form and structure for everything you do on stage
- making your rhythmic choices very clear
- giving you freedom within a clearly defined set of boundaries
- establishing a language that can be used to communicate with collaborators
- putting you in a musical mindset from the very beginning of the process.

Biomechanics work created physically fit and responsive actors who could perform any action. After completing training, an actor had balance, physical control, and the skill of readiness.

Biomechanics in Performance

Meyerhold's Biomechanical etudes were not performed on stage. Instead, the actor trained in Meyerhold's school was ready to create stylized movements on the stage under the direction of their director. This actor's motion was not realistic. For example, a worker hammering a nail must learn to use only the forearm and wrist. An actor, however, needs to use their entire arm and shoulder in an exaggerated way to efficiently communicate the hammering of a nail to the back of the house. The actor's goal is not actually to place a nail, but to show placing a nail. These two have different goals, so the motion is different.

Stylized movements simplify ideas down to their core essence, paying attention to rhythm. For example, in Ibsen's *A Doll House*, there is a scene in which the husband is supposed to teach his wife a dance. In a naturalistic or realistic portrayal, this would be done quite literally. In Meyerhold's stylized performance, the husband instead treated his wife like a marionette while she created a series of poses that illustrated the controlling relationship of the couple by moving her like a mindless puppet, submitting to her puppeteer's instructions.

Meyerhold liked stylized performances because they put the emphasis on the actor instead of realistic sets and props. This forced the audience to be more active, using their imaginations. His plays were like living art museum with controlled rhythm in performance that didn't conform to realism. As the director, Meyerhold served as a conductor of the production, creating a carefully planned score of movement that the actors brought musicality to. For example, in one staged moment, Meyerhold's actor slid down a slide to his lover expressing his delight to see her. Meyerhold believed this was far more emotionally effective in conveying emotion than realistic blocking.

Masks

Meyerhold liked to use masks as tools in performance and rehearsal. Masks have a certain duality about them. In one sense, they are comforting to hide behind. But, on the other hand, they are also really good at revealing when an actor is relying too much on their face to communicate at the expense of their body. The mask forces the actor to externalize communication to their appendages and core.

Masks also require a certain level of theatricality. Masks only work when facing forward. Actors using masks must face the audience in a fully open stance. This means that actors in masks cannot be realistic.

The mask has another advantage to the actor: objectivity. An actor in mask can stay emotionally detached from their role, and comment on the behavior of the character.

Unpredictability: the Grotesque and Montage

Meyerhold despised predictable theatre. "For this reason Meyerhold turned to the grotesque, the genre of surprise, about which he said: 'The grotesque isn't something mysterious. It's simply a theatrical style which plays with sharp contradictions and produces a constant shift in the panes of perception.'"[11] The grotesque keeps the audience on its toes, holding their breath, unable to know what is coming next. It mixes opposites together, as *Romeo and Juliet* mixes comedy and tragedy, so does the theatre of the grotesque. It celebrates the unpredictability and incongruous life we live. It is tinged with the demonic, borrows from unexpected traditions, and "stretches the natural to the extent that it becomes *un*natural or stylised."[12] The audience can't catch its breath and doesn't know whether to laugh or cry.

Since Meyerhold encouraged and relished moments that did not mix well in a production, he also liked the concept of montage, where one event would collide with another in an unexpected way. This forced the audience to think, to make connections, and to stay alert. The moments any two factors joined together in points of transition were the highlights of Meyerhold's productions. The audience was meant to see these happening. They pulled the audience's attention to stylization, to rhythm, to the mixing of opposites.

Vsevolod Meyerhold's Legacy

Meyerhold's approach to acting left a permanent mark on the study of acting. His way of enlivening the bodies of his actors and confronting the audience have persisted in many other acting methods. Something that particularly stands out about Meyerhold is his connection of social causes to his art. His belief that art has the power to change culture and his willingness to risk his life for what he believed about art and humanity makes him one of our heroes.

Tips for taking this method further

- Study the biology of your body and muscles.
- Start by looking up online tutorials for performing the Biomechanical Exercises students were taught in their first two years at the Meyerhold Workshops: I suggest video archives of Aleksei Levinski and Gennadi Bogdanov.
- Apply to study at GITIS Russian Academy of Theatrical Arts.

Discussion Starters and Journal Prompts

- Watch an online demonstration of one of the Biomechanics etudes. Try to follow along and copy the movements keeping your movements rhythmic and controlled, with no extra motions. How did it feel? Was it easier or harder than you expected?
- What do you think might be the benefits to your acting if you performed these activities every day for several hours? Will a week-long workshop on this method have any lasting impact on your practice?
- Look at the list of traits of Meyerhold's actors and think about which of these tenets you most embody already as a performer, and which of them would be the most important for you to work on. Why? What could you do to accomplish this?

The Tools for your Toolbox

Activity—The Dactyl

- Look up a video of an actor such as Austin Jones performing a dactyl.
- Say: "The dactyl is performed at the beginning and end of each of Meyerhold's etudes."
- "Stand alert and firm with your feet about one foot apart in a neutral position."
- "Your hands should be open and relaxed at your sides and your head should be up and facing forward."
- "Swing both arms back as far as you can while bending your legs and bending forward as if you were about to leap forward."
- "Swing your arms up in an arc while breathing in, keeping your feet on the ground and your fingers relaxed as they shoot up as high as you can comfortably reach in one smooth action."
- "Bend your knees and body and clap your hands loudly near your knees, sending quick and strong energy into the ground."
- "Begin to straighten."
- "Repeat the motion of the clap again—it should seem as if the two claps are one action that includes the release of the body between claps in a very quick rhythm."
- "Return to neutral."
- "Practice this motion until you can do it smoothly as one fluid motion."

Activity—Shooting the Bow

- Look up a video of "Shooting the Bow." Seth Thomas has posted a good one. Have your students watch the sequence a couple of times.
- Now have them spread out.
- Say: "Keep your feet attached to the floor and move smoothly, but strongly through these motions."
- "Stand upright on your toes."
- "Clap twice quickly."
- "Pose bent over like a runner getting ready to run with left foot in front of right, both knees bent, left arm bent with fist near your face, right arm extended behind and above your back."
- "Fall to the floor onto your left arm (don't fall over)."
- "Extend the right arm higher above yourself while both legs are bent at the knee, your head still facing down as a racer in the blocks."
- "Move backwards to sit next to your right foot while pulling your right arm in to rest against your side."
- "Twist smoothly and rise to your feet with your weight on your right foot and lean to your left shifting the weight to your left foot."

- "Make your right leg fairly straight while bending your left."
- "Straighten your right arm as though holding a bow."
- "Bend your left arm as it begins to draw up the bow."
- "Shift your weight to balance between feet and raise your left arm straight out."
- "See and point at a target, shifting your weight from right leg to the left."
- "Crouch down, placing your right hand on your right kidney as if reaching behind yourself and take out an imaginary arrow."
- "Straighten your legs suddenly, keeping your torso bent so that it is at a 90 degree angle to your left leg."
- "Put both arms straight with the left arm reaching to the ankle of the left leg, and the right arm stretched out with a fist 180 degrees from the left one."
- "Lift your torso up to a standing position, retaining your arms in position so that your left fist is straight back and your right one is straight forward."
- "Stretch your right arm backwards and down while your left hand and arm move to the right by about a foot."
- "Move your right arm forward to meet the left, placing an arrow in the imaginary string of the bow while your knees bend slightly and weight is shifted to your front leg."
- "Pull the arrow back with your right hand coming just below your chin and your body leaning back, shifting weight to your back leg."
- "Release the arrow, let your right arm come forward to join your left quickly at the same time as your shift your weight forward and bend your knees."
- "Thrust your right arm straight down and raise your left elbow up above your head quickly, straightening both legs."
- "Bend your knees forward, right knee almost to the floor and left knee bent, bringing both arms up together with hands grasping each other as if in prayer to heaven, head facing the sky."
- "Curve your upper body over to the right, thrusting the right arm straight down in 180 degree opposition to your left arm, weight shifting to your right foot with right leg slightly bent."
- "Stand strongly with face turned toward your left shoulder looking out at eye level, arms straight down from shoulders."
- "Clap twice quickly."
- "Pose bent over like a runner getting ready to run with left foot in front of right, both knees bent, left arm bent with fist near your face, right arm extended behind and above your back."
- "Clap twice quickly."
- You can assign your students the job of looking up different etudes online to learn and recreate for the next class.

Activity—Twentieth Century Non-Realism

- Put on a song such as Pink Martini's *Pure Imagination* or Post Modern Jukebox's *Creep* or *We Can't Stop*—the goal is to have a soundtrack that is a bit quirky and where the style doesn't quite match the lyrics.

- Get your students moving using some sort of gymnastic, ballet, or circus movement. Perhaps pile up some acting blocks and ramps and create an environment of play similar to what Meyerhold would have done with his constructivist sets.
- Say: "Imagine you are a marionette, with strings attached to your body. You should move as if you are being controlled from above."
- "Now move like a light organic force of nature such as the wind or a snowflake or a feather."
- "Now move like you are a specific modern machine. Perhaps a typewriter or washing machine."
- "Now move like an animal, bird, or insect."
- "Create a movement style to implement while performing monologues or scenes in pairs."
- Discuss: "How does it feel to separate from realism by freeing up the movements the body is performing from the context of the dialog?"

Activity—Stylization

- Group your actors in threes and hand them copies of The Tarantella scene from Ibsen's *A Doll House*:

    Nora: Oh, do sit down and play for me Torvald dear. Correct me, lead the way, the way you always do.
    Helmer: Very well, my dear, if you wish it. [He sits down at the piano. Nora seizes the tambourine and a long multi-coloured shawl from the cardboard box, wraps the shawl hastily around her, then takes a quick leap into the centre of the room and cries.]
    Nora: Play for me! I want to dance! [Helmer plays and Nora dances. Dr. Rank stands behind Helmer at the piano and watches her]
    Helmer: Slower, slower!
    Nora: I can't.
    Helmer: Not so violently, Nora.
    Nora: I must!
    Dr. Rank: Let me play for her. . . . [Rank sits down at the piano and plays. Nora dances more and more wildly. Helmer has stationed himself by the stove and tries repeatedly to correct her, but she seems not to hear him. Her hair works loose and falls over her shoulders; she ignores it and continues to dance.]

- Have your students work to create a stylized performance to show the class. Say: "You have a free rein with the text, but you need to communicate the essence of the scene with a conscious eye for *form, line* and *color*. Above all, you need to draw on the *physical expressivity* of your performers, concentrating at all times on *rhythm*: the rhythm of the dialogue, the rhythm of the actors' movements, the rhythm of the shapes created when the actors come together in a tableau."[13]

Activity—Rhythm or Otkaz, Posil, Tochka

- Have students spread out in the space.
- Say: "Create a motion: something simple that you perform every day: perhaps picking up a water bottle or checking you cell phone."
- "Divide the motion up into the Otkaz, Posil, and Tochka, making sure that the finish of the activity anticipates more action after."
- "Perform the action repeatedly saying *And* for the Otkaz, *One* for the Posil, and *Two* for the Tochka."
- "Now continue with exaggerated physicalization."
- "Now perform it in an understated style."
- "Pair up and work together creating one action per person. Suggest new rhythms to each other and perform as a duet, one action leading to the other or performed simultaneously."
- "Find another pair and add your motions together, focusing on rhythm."
- Continue combining groups until the entire class is working together to create stylized motion and rhythm.
- Discuss: "How does the recoil at the beginning and the freeze at the end of the motion effect the entire sequence? What emotions are created? How is it to work with a partner on motions with this specific set of boundaries?"
- Assign volunteers to play: Ilinski, the father, the maid, the Chopin player (who pulls up Chopin music on their phone ready for their cue.)
- Say: "I am going to read you a description of an actual Meyerhold production using the Otkaz, Posil, Tochka technique. Volunteers, act it out as I read."
- "In [Chekhov's] *The Proposal* . . . the simple direction, 'He drinks a glass of water,' becomes a small scene. Ilinski breaks off his speech, clutches his heart with one hand, his coat lapel with the other. The father rises, steps back a pace and holds out both his arms, as though Ilinski were about to swim to him. The maid in the background raises her broom and holds it poised in mid-air over her head. There is a pause. The Chopin music begins to play. Ilinski, still holding his lapel, reaches out with the other hand for the glass on the table. He holds it at arm's length from his mouth; his eyes grow bigger; the music plays louder. The father and maid stand motionless. With a quick jerk Ilinski draws the glass to him and downs the water. The music stops, the maid returns to her sweeping, Ilinski carefully smooths his lapel and returns the glass to the table. The father continues with the next line."[14]
- Perhaps have everyone try a simultaneous re-enactment while you narrate.
- Discuss: "What does this technique communicate? Can such non-realistic acting and direction be effective? How?"

Activity—Throwing a Stick

- You will need a sturdy meter/yard stick or dowel for each participant.
- Say: "Spread out in the room and hold your sticks vertically about halfway up the stick."

- "Practice tossing it to your left hand and back so that it lands perfectly and exactly each time. You should shift your weight from foot to foot as you perform the toss."
- "We are going to perform this toss simultaneously. Toss when I call out *Hup!*"
- "Go back to tossing on your own, then gradually develop you own group rhythm."
- "Switch which foot is forward. Keep them parallel so you are a bit unstable. Spread your feet so if you touched your back knee to the floor, it would be even with your front foot."
- "Hold the stick near the bottom, about a quarter of the way up."
- "Toss the stick up so that it spins and catch it at the other end."
- "Try to make it feel soft."
- "Don't move your hand up to catch it. It should arrive softly in your hand."
- "Practice this, making sure the energy for the action comes from your legs."
- "Swap leg positions and repeat."
- "Pair up and divide the action into the Otkaz, Posil, and Tochka."
- Try adding music to this activity (Jonathan Pitches recommends trying some early Louis Armstrong Dixieland music, and then contrast that with Charlie Mingus.)
- Say: "Work with the rhythm and then try working against the rhythm."
- "I'm turning off the music now. Work with the music internalized."
- Variations you could try: make the Posil a full 360 degree rotation, try balancing the stick on a different part of the body, walk in a circle balancing the stick and switch directions on *Hup!*, work in pairs tossing and catching the stick at various distances, or trading sticks each time with a rhythm. Or, create an etude performance with the sticks or balls to music. In performance, switch the music to something contrasting to what they were rehearsing to.
- Discuss: "In which ways were you working with the music and in which ways against? Both are encouraged! What is the underlying rhythm of all Biomechanics work? How did this play out in your stick activity? What was your body/center of gravity doing while you were focusing on the stick?"

4

Jacques Copeau

The Person

Jacques Copeau was born in Paris in 1879. His parents owned a small iron factory and were comfortably upper middle class reaping the benefits of a country that had recently found peace at the end of the Franco-Prussian War. This environment allowed Copeau to develop his artistic dreams. As a child his parents introduced him to theatre. He was hooked and spent his money on seeing everything produced in Paris.

When his father died in 1901, Copeau quit college and traveled for a while. In his time abroad he met and married Agnes Thomsen, a Danish woman, and they had their first daughter. He brought his young family to Paris, and had to give up his pursuit of theatre to run the family iron factory for two years until the business failed. Freed from that burden, he took a job in an art gallery.

He couldn't shake his love of the theatre, however, and Copeau began to write about theatre, quickly becoming an important critic in Paris. He took this responsibility seriously, attending plays more than once before he wrote a review, giving each his full attention. This effort turned him into an expert in acting and directorial choices. Becoming frustrated with his ability to change theatre from the outside, he decided to become a participant. He wanted to recreate theatre from the base up.

He planned to create a simple and inventive form that would engage the imagination and sense of play in both actors and audiences. In his theatre there would be no stars, they would produce both new and classic plays, and his plays would be performed in repertory with many productions in each season. In 1913 he founded his theatre with one cattle-call audition where he selected ten actors to be his company. He took them to the countryside for training and re-normalization. Re-normalization was an important part of actor training for him as he felt the actors of his time were insincere, obsessed with fame, and superficial. By taking his actors to the country, they could develop a team spirit and the ensemble sense of play he required for his art. That summer in the country, his actors rehearsed five hours a day, studied classical theatre, fenced, swam, and played team building games.

He planned a season of fifteen plays, choosing his season so his actors would be forced to be versatile rather than stuck in one type. He believed specialization is the enemy of the artist.

At the end of training, they returned to Paris to perform. Audiences were surprised to see non-realistic sets. They had no painted scenery and very few pieces of furniture. He didn't want the set to obscure his actors or their acting. This first season did not go well until the final of fifteen opening nights. The show was *Twelfth Night*. That play worked beautifully with playful actors who clearly loved to perform with flamboyant, colorful costumes, and no fourth-wall separation between audience and actor. It truly embodied Shakespeare in the way his work was meant to be performed, and it worked. Audiences and critics alike loved it.

Unfortunately, the onset of the First World War disbanded most of the company. Copeau could not serve in the military because of tuberculosis, so he spent the war time codifying his methods. He borrowed heavily from the Greek chorus model with its open performance spaces and powerful ensembles, as well as Commedia Dell'arte with its physicality and improvisation. Both forms used masks. Copeau found this fascinating and began to incorporate their use in his training method.

Before the end of the war, the French government sent Copeau to New York to serve as an artistic ambassador for France. He was allowed to recall some of his actors from the army and brought them with him to America to perform in Manhattan. Copeau's troupe was only in the United States for seventeen months from November 1917 to March 1919, but in this time, they had a significant impact on the development of the American Little Theater movement which we call community theatre today. Copeau's vision of simple sets, ensemble casts, and the encouragement of new work development inspired a middle-class theatre for every community in the United States.

Their return to Paris was a welcome change for everyone involved. Copeau returned to his theatre and renovated it, reducing its seating capacity and removing the footlights and proscenium arch. He added a platform on the center of the stage with stairs on all sides the actors could sit on, run over, climb, etc. The stage created a setting that worked for all his plays and practically begged his actors to play. This new staging was well received.

In 1920, Copeau, together with his former student Suzanne Bing, opened a school of theatre, providing training for those seeking a professional career in theatre. At first he had a school for teens and one for older actors. He found his attention focused on his younger actors who didn't have bad habits from previous training. Eventually he closed the school for older actors, focusing on fourteen to twenty year olds.

His school and theatre were critically acclaimed, but Copeau closed the theatre at the height of its success and moved his school to the countryside of Burgundy. Some people said he did this because he couldn't stand success. Others said his theatre was losing money because he refused to produce commercially appealing work. Others believe he was exhausted because of his non-stop work coupled with tuberculosis.

In the countryside with his students, he worked to create the style of theatre that he was craving: a new Commedia. In this form, the actors created new stock characters to suit themselves. The students accomplished this, and though he was initially pleased, the next day he condemned their work as "dust." They were crushed. They parted ways soon after and his students went to Paris to perform in their home theatre. His dreams of a re-imagined theatre were realized, but without him. His students continued to develop his work for decades after they left him.

Meanwhile, Copeau remained in Burgundy where he wrote and produced religious plays, did some freelance directing and lecturing, and returned to writing theatrical critiques. He died in 1949 after a long struggle with tuberculosis.

The Method

Jacques Copeau was a teacher who believed firmly that the actor must both "have an internal knowledge of the passions he expresses" and "the anatomical knowledge, the muscular mastery of his instrument"[1] when acting. Because he was so determined to get his method right, he worked hard to train the whole person. Physical training, rhythm, imagination, diction, and movement were important in the course of study. But he also included art, music, philosophy and literature because these would cultivate a well-educated whole person who could understand and react to the material they were given. With this training, his actors were ready for all genres of theatre. They could pivot to work in abstract theatre, broad comedy, slapstick, or naturalism. And because the sets were minimal, they could perform a different play each night in a different style on the same set.

Play

Copeau had a fascination with children and their natural, unspoiled ability to play. In all of his acting techniques, he sought to learn from children and to return his actors to a state of play. He said,

> The trainee actor returns to the games of childhood not only in order to develop further their skills in improvisation and imagination, but also to rediscover a form of playing/acting which is more 'authentic', more connected to the organic sources of the actor's creativity, more 'natural'. The child/actor nurtures their innate capacity for imaginative play whilst giving it focus.[2]

It is important to give credit to Copeau's teaching partner who worked with him for most of his effective years. Suzanne Bing was one of the young actors he hired in 1913. She quickly became invaluable to him, serving as his associate, as a teacher to his new students, and a co-writer and adapter of staged work. She eventually gave up acting in favor of helping to develop Copeau's method, to do research with children, and to hold the company together when Copeau's moods or travel prevented him from being actively involved.

As a woman, she was often not credited for the significant contribution she made to Copeau's work. In truth, she was responsible for testing Copeau's ideas, developing corporeal mime techniques, and mask improvisation. We will never know how much of the method we attribute to Copeau is actually Bing's. It is likely his method would have failed to thrive without her holding things together and pushing his ideas further than he did. I find it interesting that so many of the men whose methods have been codified have a woman to thank for a substantial portion of their success. Stanislavski had Knebel. Copeau had Bing. Without her we might have lost not only Copeau's method, but also the methods of those who were inspired by this work.

Animal Work

Copeau's curriculum in his school included the first record of animal work done by Western actors. This is a natural result of his interest in children's games. He and Bing observed children impersonating animals, and created activities inspired by those games. Animals move without self-consciousness. They have a primal and simple way of embodying their needs and desires. Copeau found value in teaching actors to respond physically to their intentions as animals. His students were taken to observe animals at the Paris zoo and later embodied and gave voice to the animals in class.

Natural Gymnastics

Copeau wanted his actors to learn to use their bodies before using their voices. He would often read stories to his actors and have them act them out as he read. By doing this, he avoided the trap of many young actors who often start with the text and totally forget the body. By starting with the body, the actors could not shortcut their skills by starting with words. Since action was the only vehicle left to them, they learned to move.

Copeau had his actors train in sporting activities to strengthen and add flexibility to their bodies. They did push-ups, jogging, high jumps, balance bars, obstacle courses, swimming, and trapeze work. He didn't want them to be stuck in any one form, so he created a method making his actors capable of flexibly switching from one mode of movement to another. He phrased it this way, "We are going to try to give our pupils *awareness and experience of the human body*. But this does not mean that, by appropriate methods, we are going to train athletes. Anyway, that would be impossible for us . . . What is needed is to make normally developed bodies capable of adjusting themselves, giving themselves over to any action they may undertake."[3]

Breath

Copeau trained his actors to reserve breath so there is always something left to give. He said "Breathing makes lightness possible, which is one of the supreme virtues of the artist."[4] One of the techniques he used in helping his actors with this was two hours of cold reading each day. Actors paired up and took turns listening to the other read.

Mask Work

Copeau used neutral masks in an attempt to free up actors from timidity, but also to push them to simplify and extend their gestures. Further, these expressionless masks forced his trainees to use their bodies to express emotions. With their faces obscured, they had no choice but to communicate with their bodies.

The masks were so revered that they were put on with a ritual the company developed called *shoeing the masks*. This process was an important part of the training that Copeau created. As actors advanced, they could change this ritual, but never ignore it. The placing of the mask was significant.

While in mask, the actor's primal and even demonic instincts were free to express themselves. Masks also de-individualize an actor. All of the qualities that make an actor unique are stripped away, giving them the ability to start over without cultural expectation. It was important to Copeau that the masks be neutral so the movement of the actor would be the expression of the mask. He believed our living impulses want to express themselves, but that we stifle them. By being inhabited by a mask, we are able to let these impulses control our bodies.

Motionlessness

Copeau once diagnosed an actor problem of incoherent pantomime, "What he is not succeeding in doing, I think, is *to establish silence and calm within himself.*"[5] Copeau taught that an actor needs to learn to start pantomime from a place of silence, calm and motionlessness. "An actor always makes too many gestures, and many too many unintentional ones, on the pretext of being natural . . . He does not know that motionlessness, like silence, is expressive."[6] Grounded motionlessness prepares the way for the gesture or sound that follows since stillness contains the seed of the action to follow.

Character Development

Copeau believed in sincere external acting. Because of this, his actors did not try to become the character. Instead, they trained to create calm and control inside themselves, creating the ability to express emotion and not be possessed by it. This was achieved by being outside the character, almost like a puppeteer. The actor imagined themself as an observer of their own work. Copeau taught that this distance between actor and character is essential.

Copeau, unlike Stanislavski, did not think actors should spend a tremendous amount of time in textual analysis. "It isn't necessary to do analysis to get into a character or a play. It is an instinct or a talent which one either has or not, and this instinct alone gives the sense, the rhythm, the pulse of the character or of the play to the actor, just like a director."[7] Copeau didn't mean actors shouldn't be intellectual, but he saw instinct as the most important tool in creating a character. Perhaps you have felt this too. Some actors find that if they do too much analysis, the character becomes dead, or they get too stuck in their heads.

In the rehearsal room with Copeau, actors were often asked to improvise their scenes as they developed their sense of what the characters required of them. The playfulness and enjoyment of the process were paramount because Copeau felt that emotionality often displayed itself through the feeling of movement. The plays Copeau directed had a quality of a dance with a sense of exuberance and play that audiences loved and critics knew came from careful thought and planning.

In Copeau's mind, even one wrong gesture in an insignificant part of a production could ruin the overall effect. As a result, he worked to create carefully scripted movements with his actors. He also worked to differentiate the movement rhythms, gestures, and postures of different characters. Different characters made different sounds as they made contact with the floor. The auditory and visual differences between the characters set them apart and helped establish character.

These character features were supposed to slowly fill an actor as they worked, but Copeau "simultaneously held that there be a limit to the character's takeover. The actor's intelligence, sense of proportion, and taste must always guide and shape the character and the performance. The actor should stand *outside* the character, hopefully unseen and exercise control over it."[8] Copeau desired the character to come to the actor rather than vice versa.

Jacques Copeau's Legacy

Jacques Copeau had a massive impact on international theatre because of his emphasis on the training of the body in the development of a school of physical theatre that is based on ensemble work and versatile actors. His teachings encouraging play to take center stage at rehearsal, and encouraging actors to let characters take over their bodies created a new way of energized, selfless acting that more closely resembles the work we most appreciate today.

Tips for taking this method further

- Study some of the disciples of Copeau: Leon Chancerel, Étienne Decroux, Jean-Louis Barrault, Michal Saint-Denis, Jacques Lecoq, Jean Vilar, and Ariane Mnouchkine.

Discussion Starters and Journal Prompts

- Write about Copeau's use of expressionless masks in his acting schools. Why do you think that the masks worked to force the actors to focus on their bodies? Would this technique work for you?
- What role did childhood play take in Copeau's method? Do you think this feature is particularly useful for all actors?

The Tools for your Toolbox

Activity—Warming Up

- Tell your students to spread out in the space with room to stretch.
- Say: "Begin your work with Copeau with the appropriate attitude: one of lightness, playfulness, and focus. This is a place where your creativity is inspired to work. This state of mind allows you to be alert to the work of your peers, responsive to shared rhythm, space, and emotion."
- As a group, lead some basic body rolls, stretches and physical limbering activities as you would in any basic acting course. The spirit of Copeau's classes has been continued on into today, and the basics of physical warming remain the same.

- Do some isolations where the actors become aware of the physical movements of each body part as individual pieces. Have them move just ribcage, just pelvis, hips, etc . . . .
- Optional: ask the actors to perform some basic tumbling and acrobatics. I recommend you lead them in activities that you are familiar with and can instruct comfortably. Perhaps forward and backwards rolls, cartwheels, juggling, etc . . . .
- Pair students up.
- Say: "Perform the following scenario silently: You are hiding outside a store at closing time in preparation to steal something from inside. One of you is scared to death of being caught and the other is confident of success. Work together to break in and get away with law enforcement in pursuit."
- Say: "Sit still and find calmness in your stillness. Begin your work in pantomime with that stillness as the base. Allow your movements to begin from stillness. Perform your scene again starting with this calm grounded energy."
- Discuss: "What did you need to do in order to communicate with your partner since you couldn't use words? Did rooting your work in stillness change anything for you?"

Activity—Emotional Communication

- Have students pair off and face each other sitting in chairs.
- Say: "Choose who will go first."
- "Think of an emotion and communicate it to your partner when I signal. You have one second. Go!"
- "Partners guess what emotion was communicated."
- "Swap who is communicating. Again you have one second. Go!"
- "Now guess what emotion was communicated."
- "Partner one, turn your back on your partner. It is much more difficult to communicate an emotion without the face. Your back is functioning the way a mask does. It must help your audience understand."
- "Keep working on this game, taking turns until you succeed."
- Now have your students stand shoulder to shoulder facing the audience in lines of five to ten people per line.
- Say: "The person in each line closest to stage left, choose an emotion."
- "Tap the person on your left and perform it with restraint."
- "Second person add a little to the emotion and pass it to your left."
- "Continue this to the end of the line until the emotion is in full force."
- "Reverse the action back down the line, bringing it slowly back down to neutral."
- "As the emotion reaches the top or bottom of its expression, it may transform for instance from peals of laughter to a wail of sadness."
- Play this game a few times, perhaps switching the low level of emotion to stage right.
- After a while, give them a task to pantomime: for instance setting up a campsite.
- Say: "Continue the waxing and waning of emotions as you work, in the same order."

- "Do the same task, but respond emotionally in any order, no longer linked to the intensity of emotion you had in the past."
- Discuss: "Emotions wax and wane as they come and go in everyday life. Do you see how this might be true in a scene you are familiar with? (Quarreling scene of lovers in Midsummer Night's Dream III.ii or the growing panic of townspeople waiting for the inspector in Gogol's *The Government Inspector*.) Copeau teaches that the flow of emotions belongs to the ensemble, not the individual."

Activity—Improvised Play

- Say: "A very common activity in Copeau's first year of training involved the teacher reading a text to their students and asking the students to improvise movements and soundscape along with the story. I am going to tell you a story now. Add non-verbal sounds and actions to illustrate. If my story includes a storm, create a soundscape for that. If my story includes animals, embody the animals. Be bold and playful."
- Read or improvise a story and encourage them to be fully engaged in embodying the text.
- Discuss: "What are the advantages of embodying and vocalizing a story. Do you think that being active from the beginning of a process is useful? Or is it better to sit and read and listen first?"

Activity—Mask Work

- Prepare the space by covering or removing mirrors. Place a table in the space with adhesives and small pieces of foam.
- Give each student a neutral mask and elastic band. Have them adhere some foam into the mask so that the mask itself does not touch their face, and they can wear it comfortably. Say: "Tie on the strap when you are finished with the foam, and make sure it fits comfortably. But do not leave the mask on yet."
- Say: "We are going to experience the ritual of placing the mask. Copeau called it 'shoeing the mask'" (I suggest you participate in this activity to help them understand your instructions.)
- "Sit firmly in the center of a chair without leaning back and with feet planted hip-width apart and flat on the ground. Think of balancing your spine on your pelvis.
- "Stretch your left hand out forward and shoulder height, holding the center of the elastic strap of the mask."
- "Reach your right hand out and grasp the mask so that the thumb grabs the chin of the mask and the index and middle finger hold the mouth opening."
- "Pull the elastic around the back of your head with your left hand, and onto your forehead with your right hand."
- "Lower your mask over your face while simultaneously breathing in and closing your eyes."

- "With eyes closed, adjust your mask and arrange your hair. Only your arms and hands should be moving. Once the mask is in place, you are not allowed to touch it, so make sure it is seated comfortably."
- "Simultaneously place your hands on your thighs not quite to your knees while your elbows contact your torso and your arms rest on your thighs."
- "Open your eyes and inhale."
- "Close your eyes, bend your head forward, and exhale. Bend your back slightly, creating a curved posture."
- "Relax completely and think to yourself, 'I am not thinking of anything.' Repeat until you are fully relaxed, ready to be inhabited by characters. If you are struggling to relax, focus on the colors behind your eyelids as they shift color and shape."
- "Inhale, sit upright, and exhale while opening your eyes."
- "You are now ready to begin work in mask."
- "Walk around calmly."
- "Hold onto imaginary items and explore their weight and shape. (baking sheet, rubber band, snow boot, cast iron skillet, paring knife, etc. . . .)"
- "Explore physical sensations (heat, cold, fatigue, sun worship, hunger, etc. . . .) Avoid cliché and clownish pantomime."
- "Explore physical motions like throwing, lifting, pulling, etc."
- "Find a comfortable posture and settle into a comfortable breathing rhythm. Now pantomime shooing away a fly that is disturbing your relaxation."
- "Notice each other. Act out an improvised story called *The Farewell* by improvising goodbyes, embodying various feelings about the departure of others."
- "Try to avoid cliches, and respond naturally to what happens."
- "Play the same scene, but with abstract responses."
- "As you play *The Farewell*, play it with a feeling of: liberty, democracy, knowledge, Broadway, rainbow, summer, etc." Try a few of them.
- "This time add non-verbal sounds and/or gibberish to your scenes."
- Remove the masks and reflect on the effects of Mask on performer and performance.

Activity—Pantomime

- Gather your students in groups of six to eight and read them the following prompt slowly twice:

    The Sailor: "A group of pupils come to the front of the stage. They must produce, despite their masked faces, a vision of a strand and of fisher-folk peering out upon a stormy sea. Their bodies create not alone their own emotion, but by a subtle fugue the heave of the water. A rowboat comes up. It is created by two actors in a rhythmic unison of propulsion. They leave their boat and mount the stairs to the apron. They have news of the drowning of a comrade: the news transfigures the group. The scene shifts to what is an interior of a fisher cottage. The wife and children await the master. The friends come in with the tragic tidings."[9]

- Say: "Prepare your scene to perform in five minutes. The rules are that every actor must be involved either as a character or inanimate object in each scene and you may not speak. Each person should morph from character to character seamlessly. You can talk and decide positions, how to mime the rowing of the boat, which actors will play which role before you shoe the masks, but get the work on its feet as soon as possible. The talking should be brief."
- Have the groups perform simultaneously after five minutes.
- Do not provide specific feedback. Instead, say: "Go back to working on your scene. This time, notice the points in the story where the mood shifts. Also, think about good and bad feelings. Where do you feel those in your body? How can you communicate the story using your body? How can you insert a sense of play in a sad tale? How can you communicate social status and groupings? What is the rhythm of the scene?"
- "You have ten more minutes to work."
- Have each group perform for the rest and comment on the ways they succeeded in embodying the masks.
- This activity works well repeated several times, or as a warm-up to subsequent sessions. Try mixing or combining the groups and having them improvise together with the same story, varying the number of participants.
- For variety here is another prompt from Copeau's school:
- *The Tree:* "The scene is bare let us say, save for a table. A boy jumps on this, masked. He is portraying a tree in a sunny field. He is not acting a pantomime: he is improvising a drama; and the first factors to convince are his associates. His arms and body marvelously swaying, convey the shady scope of bole and branch moving in a breeze. A wayfarer enters (like all the others, masked). He espies the shade and goes to it, escaping the heat of the sun. He sleeps. Enter a flock of sheep ... They see the trees, nibble at its leaves, seek its shade. They come in collision with the man. Man and beasts are frightened off."[10]

Activity—Animal Work

- This activity requires advance homework. Have each student select an animal that they identify with in connection with a character they are working on. Tell them to observe their animal in real life outside of class time, or at a zoo. If a live observation is not possible, they should observe their animal online.
- They should be able to answer the following questions:
    - What is their natural environment like? Arid? Humid? Cold? etc . . . .
    - Where is your animal most comfortable? High in a tree? A cave? etc . . . .
    - What are the movements of the animal like?
    - Where does it's center of balance sit?
    - How does it make contact with the ground? Decisively? Heavily? Gracefully?
    - What is it's walk, run, stand, sit, etc. posture?
    - What are the rhythms of that movement?

- What leads the animal? The head? stomach?
  - How flexible is it's spine?
  - What is the creature's breath like?
  - What do it's vocalizations sound like?
  - What is the focus of the animal like? Is it fixed? Wide open? Flighty?
  - How does the animal eat? Mate? Interact with its own species and others?
- In class, give the class time to experiment physically with the movements and rhythms of the animal.
- Say: "Remember to play the animal as it is, not as you imagined it to be."
- "Start by working alone, without interacting with others."
- "Act out sleeping, feeling the heartbeat and breath of the animal."
- "Wake and stretch, relating to your environment, then begin to forage for food."
- "Begin interacting with each other, remaining in your animal personas. Don't forget to vocalize as the animals would."
- "Begin to introduce human characteristics to your animal—morphing towards the character you are working on. Maintain as much of the animal as possible while becoming fully human."
- "Slide further into human."
- "Slide back to fully animal."
- Discuss: "Did you learn anything about your character? What was it like to embody an animal based on observation?"
- "Run your scene or monologue, incorporating as much of your animal into your character as you can without losing the humanity of the character."
- Discuss: "Talk to your scene partner about what you learned."

Activity—Slow and Fast Motion

- Say: "Walk around the space."
- "Vary your speed from full run to stillness."
- "Think about what qualities give each speed a dramatic effect."
- Have them perform a pantomime activity again (the sailors on the strand, the farewell, setting up a tent)
- Say: "This time, find ways to work in slow motion or stillness to dramatic effect."
- "Do it again, adding fast motion."
- Discuss: "How long can the stillness be maintained without ruining the effect of the story? Where does fast motion work well?"
- Have the groups pair up and show each other their work, responding specifically to the successes and failures of the speed experiments. Encourage them to go ridiculously hard digging in on both extremes, trying in and out of mask.
- Discuss: "Does it make a difference if you are masked or unmasked? What have you discovered about the connection of storytelling to tempo?"

Activity—Choral Acting

- Break into groups of five or six students standing in a formation in which every person is lightly, incidentally touching at least one other person with all eyes closed.
- Say: "Begin swaying together, never losing contact with the others. The swaying can begin with a pattern, but must then develop into a swaying that moves in random speeds and directions as the group learns to move together. No obvious leader should be discernible."
- "Add vocalization to your motions. Again, the sounds should be choral so the group is working together without an evident leader."
- "You may open your eyes and begin to move forward and back in the space."
- "Allow groups to begin to merge until the entire room is one group."
- "Bring the activity to a close with no foreplanning or signal by rushing forward as a group and stopping at the front of the stage with a shout. This should come at the impulse of the group."
- Now suggest a group activity to act as a chorus. Remind them that this activity is to create the appearance of a group mind. Ideas for group work: Riding a boat across choppy water. Perhaps there are two or three boats, and as they pass each other the wakes affect the others. Another idea: The group watches a train pass, a tennis game, or an airshow together.
- Discuss the work of choral acting. "How does it work? What is hard about it? What do you gain by working on this?"

Activity—New Commedia

- For this activity, your actors will need half-masks that cover eyes and nose. You can give them masks in advance to decorate or they can work in blank ones. It might also be useful if they were somewhat familiar with commedia as a form. Perhaps prepare them by having them watch some video footage of commedia, along with a handout to read.
- Say: "Begin with the animal characters you have been working on. Shoe your half-mask and breathe in your animal character, playing with their movements and morning rituals."
- Now create a scenario, and interesting place for two of the animal characters to meet and interact. Have the two of them meet while the rest of the class observes. Words are allowed, but not jabbering. You could also start with gibberish.
- Once you have seen a story develop, set the class loose to play in the space, interacting and focusing on creating human/animal characters.
- Now suggest some more contemporary character types: goth kid, stoner, Karen, f@#boy, soccer mom, etc.
- Say: "Take on a new character incorporating your animal, creating new postures and attributes. Create characters that are not like you. Crossing gender, class, etc. are encouraged."
- "Find the physical signatures of your new character type."
- Have them remove the masks and sketch the costumes and props that might help their new character to live for the audience and for their portrayal. They should name their character. Perhaps bring out a chest of stock costume and prop pieces for them to experiment with.

- As they play with the choices, have them begin to find the voice of their new character that suits the mask. Tone, pitch, where the voice is centered in the body, are all important in developing the voice of the new commedia character.
- Have the new characters find short scenarios to enact, uncovering the dramatic potential of their new stock characters.

5
Rudolf von Laban

The Person

Rudolf von Laban was born in 1879 in Austria. He did not receive formal training in theatre or dance. However, he studied with a painter in childhood and learned to observe and perceive in those studies. He also spent a lot of time in nature, receiving the answers to questions which only the earth could answer.

He traveled extensively because his father was a prominent military governor. While traveling in his teen years, Laban was introduced to Sufi Dervish dancing inspiring him to believe in the magical quality of movement. He also watched military parades, battle maneuvers, and other military movement. All of these helped in his emerging choreographic instincts. While in military boarding school, he organized a festival performance of different folk dances that originated in the other cadets' home regions. This fascination with movement led him away from the military career that was planned for him and towards a career as an artist.

In 1923 he moved to Hamburg and converted some old zoo buildings into a theatre, forming a theatre troupe that began touring internationally almost immediately. In 1930 he was appointed as the Director of Movement at the State Theater in Berlin, and the ballet-master at the Berlin State Opera. He felt movement was something that all humans have a natural instinct for and developed movement choirs bringing large groups of people together to experience the joy of movement together. He even created a one-time mass movement choir for the Pageant of Craftsmanship and Trade involving 20,000 participants from movement choirs and the working class in Vienna.

In 1936 Laban was tasked with organizing an international dance competition for the Berlin Olympics. He was cooperating with the Nazis for a time, but when his dress rehearsal for the opening ceremonies was observed by a government official, it was banned. He was interrogated and placed in house arrest. Hitler banned his work. He left Germany in 1937. After devoting his life to the arts in Germany, he was left with nothing at the age of fifty-eight.

He settled in the UK where he remained for the rest of his life, slowly rebuilding his career from scratch, studying movement in industry and education. When he was sixty years old, he began to study industrial workers and their movement to help them be more productive, and also healthier. He and a woman named Lisa Ullmann opened The Art of Movement Studio in Manchester in 1946. It later moved to a country estate where he spent the last five years of his life studying the movement and needs of both industrial workers and psychiatric patients. This work laid the foundation of what would become movement and dance therapy. He struggled to make a living all his life, but he wrote, lectured, and taught all the way up to his death in 1958.

The Method

Laban's method, called Laban Movement Analysis (LMA), is a theoretical framework for analyzing movement. Laban appreciated precision in terminology. He created a language that described the qualities of movement and sound, helping actors and dancers by giving them terminology to describe their work. Where Stanislavski-based systems of acting focus on the who, what, where, why questions, Laban's method focuses on the how. As you read about LMA, you may find it to be very technical. This is ironic, because the work of learning these concepts is visceral and deeply embodied. The following descriptions of Laban's LMA must be experienced to be understood. There are activities at the end of the chapter to help you explore the themes and movement qualities of Laban's system.

Before learning about the technical elements of LMA, it might be helpful to understand the four major themes of LMA that Laban taught:

- Mobility/Stability—This theme is seen throughout Laban's work. He teaches actors and dancers that the body is always in a state of flux on the continuum between stability and mobility. This is true even while the body is still. A still body may be stable, or it may be crouched and ready for mobility.
- Function/Expression—Functional movements have expressive results, and expressive movements have functional form. The two together create meaning in movement. In other words, as you reach for your toothbrush (functional movement), your body expresses your inner mood and state. Are you tired, stressed, relaxed? Your movement expresses that. On the other hand, if you expressively communicate your emotions in a dance, the movement has the function of moving you from one place to another and providing exercise. Function has expression, and expression has function.
- Exertion/Recuperation—Laban taught that the body needs to rest to recover from movement. The body seeks rest after exertion. It also has a natural desire to complete one action, and then it's opposite. The moment of recuperation provides meaningful pause to punctuate the movement as well.
- Inner/Outer—Laban taught that the motivation for movement comes from both inner and outer places. The outer influences the inner and vice versa.

These themes are present in Laban's BESS which stands for Body Effort Shape Space. All of your movement can be analyzed by thinking about your Body as a Shape in Space using Effort.

Space Harmony

Laban's theory of Space Harmony claims the environment around us is interacting with us. In fact, Laban believed the space around us has life in it. As our bodies move, they are responding to *spatial pulls* around them. In other words, every movement you make is connected with the space around you. He believed empty space doesn't exist, and, in fact, when you extend your arms, "that movement produces 'trace lines' that continue to travel beyond the corporeal self, a phenomenon that we will call 'body resonance.' This possibility can be likened to an echo or perhaps the tone that lingers when a musician has stopped singing or playing an instrument."[1] Laban developed exercises for his actors to explore Space Harmony by connecting the "dots" in space as they attempted to harmoniously connect with the universe.

BESS—Space

As you think about Laban's theory of Space Harmony, can you begin to form a relationship with the air around you? Barbara Adrian, LMA teacher, writes, "Space is perhaps the most elusive concept for the actor to absorb . . . **Space** and its relationship to the **Body** is what dancers, gymnasts, and . . . athletes of all types understand, capitalize on intuitively, and develop further with each practice. Actors, however, can be prone to remain focused internally or only on their scene partner, forgetting that in the theatre, there is a larger environment to be filled with dynamic energy."[2] Can Laban help you buck this generalization by helping you develop a kinship with Space?

Laban's concept of Space describes how the body moves in relationship to the three-dimensional space that surrounds it. There are three one-dimensional planes we work in:

- The Door Plane which is a Vertical surface in the Height dimension.
- The Table Plane which is a Horizontal surface in the Width dimension.
- The Wheel Plane which is a Sagittal (forward-backward) surface in the Depth dimension.

These three planes are all in what Laban called your "kinesphere." He defined your kinesphere as the spherical space that your limbs can reach at fullest extension when you are stationary. As you work in movement, try to discover your kinesphere in all three dimensions. What space is yours? Can you expand your kinesphere to encompass your entire reach?

Laban taught his students to work with Spatial Intention. In other words, to intentionally use the Space around them to communicate meaning. Even standing still, you can change what a wave goodbye to another character means by changing the distance your wave is from your center. Try waving with your hand reaching to the far edge of your kinesphere, then as close to your body as possible. Now try intermediate distances. How does this change the meaning of the wave? Do you see how the way you choose to wave changes the intention quality of your movement?

It is possible to create a character, beginning with dimensional thinking. Your character might stretch forward and left or downward and back. Finding center and dimensional qualities for your characters gives them nuance and grounds them.

BESS—Shape

Another element of BESS is Shape. It describes how our body continually changes its shape in relation to ourselves, others, and the room or Space. Laban broke down shapes of the body into five still shapes: Pin, Ball, Wall, Screw, and Pyramid. Try to create these shapes, and you will see that they encompass the extremes of shapes you can create with your body. For instance, the Pin shape is open, tall, thin, straight, and extended; while the Ball shape is closed, round, and compressed.

Transitions are essential in the work of a Laban actor. Laban started with the five shapes and then had his actors practice various modes of shape change or Shape Flow from one shape to the other. These transitions could have three different styles:

- Arc-like—a movement outward in a curved shape that collects the environment, claiming it.
- Spoke-like—a movement outward that is directional and targeted that stretches straight for the goal in a bridge-like movement.
- Carving—a process-oriented movement that interacts with the environment, creating a relationship between actor and Space.

The Shape Flow modes apply to all sorts of movement. Imagine you are playing Hamlet in the scene where Ophelia tries to return his letters. Take on a Screw shape with your body as you ponder your mortality, then use Spoke-like shape flow to transition to a Pin shape as you confront Ophelia. Many actors find that using vocabulary like this to describe their movement frees them up to move with intention and confidence. Try it! Just reading that description won't help you understand it until you feel it in your body.

BESS—Body

Your body is your physical instrument that creates movement and voice. Work on the body increases awareness and articulation of your physical instrument. Part of your body awareness is recognizing dimensional thinking. Laban taught his students to think of their body as the center of their three-dimensional kinesphere, feeling the experience of existing on one plane at a time.

Your breath is the foundation of body work and awareness. Laban taught that breath is where inspiration for creative work begins. As a performer, you must start your work on your body by consciously becoming aware of your breath and learning to breathe in a way that supports your artistic expression. Barbara Adrian reminds us that, "The sound of your voice radiates beyond your body's corporeal boundaries. You cannot propel your body, without serious consequences, through walls, off rooftops, or instantaneously up six flights of stairs. But the voice can and does make such leaps."[3] Your voice can do more than your body can, but it is your breath in your body that gives it this power. As you control your breath, you can use your Body and voice to interact with the Space, giving Shape to your performance.

BESS—Effort

Effort can be seen in all human movement, but also in the movement of nature and objects. Hold on, because there is a lot to Laban's Effort category of terminology. Laban broke down every Effort, or way of moving, on a continuum of Elements: Time, Weight, Space, and Flow. These Elements are the four components of movement that can be seen in all movement combining in various ways. Every move can be characterized somewhere between the opposite ends of each scale:

- Time = sudden to sustained—Time explores impulses and rhythms. In sudden movements, time is interrupted like an explosion or the falling of a tree. In sustained movement, time continues like the waves of the ocean.
- Weight = heavy to light—Weight explores the effect of gravity. A feeling of heavy weight means that the body is pulled down by gravity. Light weight movement quality means that the body is released from gravity.
- Space = direct to indirect—Space explores the destination of movement. In direct movements the body finds the most direct path from A to B, moving in straight lines. In indirect movement, the movements are circling, spiraling, and meandering.
- Flow = bound to free—Flow explores the freedom of your energy. In bound states, the body is constricted. In free movement, the body moves without restriction.

The Elements can be combined to create other hues of movement, just as different colors can be combined by an artist to create shades. Laban created a shorthand for describing combinations of the Elements into eight Effort styles:

- Floating—light weight, sustained time, indirect space, free flow
- Dabbing—light weight, sudden time, direct space, bound flow
- Wringing—heavy weight, sustained time, indirect space, bound flow
- Punching—heavy weight, sudden time, direct space, bound flow
- Pressing—heavy weight, sustained time, direct space, bound flow
- Flicking—light weight, sudden time, indirect space, free flow
- Slashing—heavy weight, sudden time, indirect space, free flow
- Gliding—light weight, sustained time, direct space, free flow.

Each of these Effort styles is a combination of the Elements at an extreme end of the Element continuum. For example, a Floating Effort is light and gravity doesn't impact it much. That is combined with time that is sustained, meaning no sudden movements. Floating also has the feature of indirect space and free flow; the actor using Floating Effort will lightly move in a sustained way without a clear destination or restriction of movement.

Imagine you are playing Gertrude in the scene where Hamlet confronts you in your bedroom. If you choose a Floating Effort quality, you would play Gertrude as if gravity didn't pull her down (light weight), as if time was experienced as steady waves, and in a spiraling movement quality (indirect space) that is free (free flow). Your Gertrude would be evasive and not grounded in reality. A different actor could play the same lines with a Punching Effort that was heavy, sudden, and direct. She would be more calculated and grounded. Both portrayals have value.

Each of the Effort styles deserve exploration through exercises. As you are working, remind yourself that your goal isn't to learn to do the Efforts, it is to *become* the Effort. As you develop characters, think about the movement qualities you naturally have versus your character's. Do they handle weight differently than you? Is their quality of flow more Slashing, while you are a Pressing person? Try out a few possibilities and see what you discover. Active experimentation can lead to compelling characters.

As you work through each of these styles of movement, you will build a vocabulary to describe different ways of moving that your body will remember. After you practice a Dabbing movement quality, your body will store this way of moving and you will have the Dabbing movement at your disposal when your character calls for it. You will be able to experiment as you are creating a character by cycling through the different effort factors until you land on the combination that works.

Effort Archetypes

Sometimes your character shifts from one Effort style to another during a production. Other times, you might prefer to use just one. In this case, you are employing an Effort Archetype. For example, an actor might play the role of Ophelia in *Hamlet* with a Wringing Effort Archetype. In the scene where she speaks with Hamlet, trying to return his love letters, both her movements and her thoughts would be heavy in Weight as she understands the importance of the moment and is resolute in completing her mission though she dislikes it. Time would also be sustained in her thoughts as the important moment stretches out, each small movement and effort painfully lengthened. She would communicate her dislike of her task through indirect Space as she doesn't aim clearly for any end goal. This Effort has a bound Flow, so Ophelia would express movement that is constricted and trapped. An actor could choose any of the Effort Archetype for Ophelia. None of them are correct or incorrect, but they profoundly impact the scene.

One Laban teacher advises, "Invest fully in the simplicity of the one choice you have; by remaining true to themselves and their overriding Effort, each Archetype has an inherent openness and integrity. If the actor can commit wholeheartedly to the work, each Archetype also has the power to express something fundamental about the human condition, which is, ultimately, both recognizable and very moving."[4] This teacher goes on to recommend that you name the Archetype you are using with names like "Ms. Press," "Mx. Glide," or "Mr. Dab." By giving your character a nickname, you remind yourself that they are defined by a single Effort.

Archetypes can also lead to some fun relationships. You could work with a scene partner as "the Dab Siblings" or "Mr. and Mrs. Wring." Or you could find a relationship between two Archetypes by accentuating the differences and similarities. "Ms. Float and Ms. Wring, for example, may appear to be very different types of people who would have little in common. However, they share the same Elements of both Sustained Time and Indirect Space, and differ only in Weight. This helps explain how people understand and empathize with each other, even though they might appear to have no obvious connection at first glance. Often, relationships occur between people because of the partially overlapping Effort Affinities."[5]

Effort Weaves

Laban taught students to explore how one Effort moved to another. He didn't use the term Effort Weave, but his students coined the term because it helped them think about how one Effort interacts with another as it transitions both externally and internally. Laban likened this to the gradient in a rainbow as one color gives way to another. Instead of being in Dabbing Effort and then abruptly switching to Gliding Effort, the actor creates a weave where the two are forced to cohabitate for a while.

As you play in this middle ground, it might be helpful to think of it as a journey. You can play with the thoughts and movements of both Efforts in various ways as you transition. Also, remember to keep the two distinct from each other. Just as a woven rug has different colored threads woven together, your Efforts will remain distinct, but in close proximity to each other.

One author describes the process of an Effort Weave:

- Stage One: You express one Effort only.
- Stage Two: A neighbouring Effort appears in the body very briefly, and then disappears.
- Stage Three: The same neighbouring Effort reappears. It stays for longer this time and the two Efforts coexist in the body.
- Stage Four: The invading Effort 'wins.' It becomes the new sole Effort as the initial Effort disappears.[6]

The Effort Weave can also be internal. While your external Effort remains constant, your internal Effort might shift through Weaves. As you are developing your Internal Weave, it might be helpful to verbalize your internal transition by thinking out loud and using external gestures.

Incidentally, an Internal Weave is a great option for a solo warm-up activity when a group warm-up isn't possible, your space is limited, or you must remain silent. Sit or stand still and internally transition from Gliding thoughts to Slashing thoughts to Dabbing, etc.

Effort Duos

As with Effort Weaves, the term Effort Duos comes from the work of Laban's students. This Effort style occurs when two different Efforts coexist in a body, creating conflict. Laban described this effect as one *disguising effort* and one *revealing effort*. Perhaps a character has a Slashing inner effort and a Gliding outer effort that is trying to hide the inner effort. The conflict is between the inner attitude of the character and their outer demeanor.

Other times the Effort Duo might be a conflict between a character's inner thoughts and their inner feelings. Perhaps as Ophelia is confronting Hamlet with the letters he wrote her, she uses an inner Effort Duo. Her inner thoughts are logical and know that Hamlet is not a good match for her. The actor might choose an inner Effort of Punching for thought as the character logically tries to return the letters with directness and strength, while her inner feelings are still in love with and connected to Hamlet. The actor might choose an inner Effort of Floating to express the feelings that are warring with her thoughts internally. These two will take turns being the *major* Effort in control while the other is the *minor* Effort that is repressed. The actor playing Ophelia will carefully map out the scene and decide which Effort is dominant in each moment. This will play up the anxious quality of the character in the scene as she vacillates from Punching to Floating.

Sounding

Laban actors learn that part of their movement work includes the movement of air in the body. If you allow unstructured sound to happen as you explore your breath, you are performing what LMA teachers call Sounding. As you work, you see the movement of your breath in your torso changing the shape of your body as you grow and shrink. These movements are on the three dimensions or planes of the body. Your body

- lengthens and shortens on the table plane
- widens and narrows on the door plane
- hollows and bulges on the wheel plane.

Your breath radiates in all three dimensions when it is being most efficient. This three-dimensional breath occurs when you breathe on the wheel, door, AND table planes simultaneously.

Laban teachers encourage their students to explore their breath in conjunction with body shapes. For example, they might coach you to lie on the floor in a Screw shape and transition to Ball shape, while doing that, they coach you to use Sounding by allowing unstructured sounds to ride on your breath as it leaves and enters your body. These sounds allow you to analyze whether or not your breath is matching your intended shape or effort style. You can also explore Sounding by allowing a character to express itself through unstructured sound as you use various Effort styles.

Just as your body has a kinesphere, so does your voice. Its reach is further than your spatial kinesphere, but it has the same divisions. Your near vocal kinesphere is where your voice reaches in intimate conversation, and your far vocal kinesphere is the furthest reach of your voice. Your voice can have spoke-like, arc-like, and carving qualities to it. What does calling attention to this fact change in the way you breathe and vocalize?

Your body can lead your voice, and your voice can lead your body. And, just as you can break down your movements into individual parts, you can break down your speech into its components and work on them individually. If this concept is interesting to you, Barbara Adrian has written a book with an integrated approach to voice, speech and movement called *Actor Training the Laban Way*. She teaches how to break down each word into its components and learn to strengthen each piece of your voice. For example, she breaks down each vowel sound and encourages her readers to play with the effort quality of the sound. If the sound you are working on is an "OO" sound, you can play with creating the sound with light weight and direct space, then slowly transition to a strong weight and indirect space.

Efforts with Text Work

After you practice using BESS through movement, breath, and inner attitudes, you will be prepared to add them to your text. Laban drew lots of pictures and graphs as he was working, and you could easily start working on your text by doing the same. You could map your Efforts on the page as they weave from one to the other in a section of text. Then, try it out. At this point, don't try to communicate the meaning of the words. Simply perform and see if the Effort style you chose unlocks anything for you. As you work, allow body gestures to happen even though you are focused on your text. Try different combinations of Efforts the next time. Take note and add that to your map. Notice that when you pinpoint your Effort transitions, it won't ever be at the end of a sentence. The feeling will originate on a word in an exact way that doesn't exactly line up with the words.

Character Development

Working on development of characters using Laban's BESS brings up questions such as: "How does your imagination respond to creating a character that exists on a Table plane, and who has a heavy Weight and dislikes Directness?" See which qualities of movement inspire you in performance. These questions will lead you to a place of experimentation and away from cliché and generalization.

Barbara Adrian, who is a Professor and a graduate of Laban/Bartenieff Institute of Movement Studies encourages you to individualize your work with LMA as you develop your craft,

> The order in which you explore text through LMA is not sacrosanct in any way. You must assess each character and the text to determine which explorations are going to be the most beneficial to you and your work. Beneficial doesn't necessarily mean the easiest. Some of the most beneficial explorations may also be the most challenging . . . be patient and allow the text to unpack its mysteries as you explore . . . let curiosity be your guide. LMA and its many component parts make up a kaleidoscope of possibilities. Eventually, your explorations will become the scaffolding that supports an integrated physical and vocal wholeness . . . To arrive at that point takes time, discipline, dedication, and a huge amount of curiosity. You can't be in a hurry. Trust. Let go. And don't forget to bring your joy![7]

Recuperation

A good reminder at the end of an exploration of Laban's method is that he valued both exertion and recuperation. Every movement exercise has moments of recuperation built into it. Every movement or gesture on stage must be punctuated by rest. The body and mind are focused as they work through an Effort, and they need time to recuperate. It is part of the natural cycle of movement, breath, speech, and nature. Each has a beginning, middle, and end which need to be punctuated by pause.

Rudolf von Laban's Legacy

Laban struggled with mental health and poverty throughout his career, but he lived a long life and contributed an astounding amount to the fields of dance, acting, movement therapy, and industry. His persistence, energy, creative boldness and vision are inspiring. One element of his work was the creation of Labanotation, a method of writing down movements through notation so that other practitioners can duplicate a movement piece simply by decoding a written code. Professionals have used this system to restage dances using Labanotation scores.

His work has inspired generations of acting and dance teachers who have taken his concepts and used them in their own work and to inspire other acting methods. Many practitioners give him credit for being the basis of their methodologies.

Tips for taking this method further

- Look into LMA training programs. Experts recommend: Laban/Bartenieff Institute of Movement Studies in Belgium, China, Israel, Scotland, and the USA; Integrated Movement Studies in the USA; Laban-Eurolab in Germany; Laban Guild in London; Giles Foreman Center for Acting in Europe and the USA; Trinity Laban Conservatoire of Music and Dance in the UK.
- Try mapping your movement through a script you are performing. Draw, make graphs, sketch the shifts in Efforts and Elements as they progress using the LMA vocabulary.
- Spend time observing and imitating people like Laban did. Notice someone in public and sense their movement in your own body. Try their effort styles, imagine what their inner monologue is like. Take notes on what you observed using Laban vocabulary.
- Look up Effort States and Effort Drives and add them to your exploration.

Discussion Starters and Journal Prompts

- Formulate your own description of the Elements of movement that Laban taught: Weight, Time, Space, and Flow. Explain how these Elements work together to create the Efforts.
- Discuss how you respond to the written description of LMA before you experimented with it. How did putting it into practice change the way you experienced the method? What is the value of codifying a method into terminology and notation?

The Tools for your Toolbox

Activity—Dimensional Awareness

- Have your actors spread out in the space.
- Say: "Imagine you are standing on a one-dimensional rectangular Height plane as if you are bisected by a door. Let your body widen, stretching side to side. Let your body narrow itself and then widen again."
- "Reach to each of the four corners of your plane with your fingertips. Define the edges of your door."
- "Take a walk around the stage maintaining the idea of being a one-dimensional being on a door plane."
- "Wave at others, while staying completely in your door plane."
- "Find a wall and place your door plane on it. Peel your plane from the wall and feel what it is like to be a parallel plane to the wall of the space. Lean back into the wall. What does it feel like to be a part of the space? What does it feel like to be free-standing?"

- "Imagine you are standing on a circular one-dimensional plane as if you were a wheel that stretches out in front and in back of you. It is your forward-backward dimension in a wheel shape. Allow your body to stretch forward and back, filling onto your wheel. It wants to grow outwards, forward and back, then retreat, then grow out again. Surge forward, then push backward."
- "Reach to each of the edges of your wheel plane with your fingertips. Define the edges of your wheel."
- "Take a walk around the stage maintaining the idea of being a one-dimensional being on a wheel plane."
- "Shoo others away, while staying completely in your wheel plane."
- "Imagine you are standing in the center of a rectangular one-dimensional plane as if you are bisected by a table top. It is your table plane."
- "Reach to each of the edges of your table plane with your fingertips. Define the edges of your table."
- "Take a walk around the stage maintaining the idea of being a one-dimensional being on a table plane, extending your lower arms and hands from your elbows, smoothing the table top."
- "Reach out to others, but stay in your table plane."
- "Experiment with spreading into different planes unevenly, perhaps spreading to back and left. What character choices could this visual create for you?"
- "Begin to play with existing on all three dimensions at once. This is your kinesphere."
- "Play with your kinesphere. How much space does your bubble expand to? Can you enlarge it and shrink it, assigning a color to each size of kinesphere?"
- Discuss: "What can three dimensionality teach you about your body and shape? Can your voice also be three-dimensional? How?"

Activity—Shape

- Say: "Lie on the floor in Wall shape with your back to the ground and arms reaching out and up from your core, while your legs are extended out and down."
- "Notice the bony parts of your body in contact with the floor."
- "Notice that the inner architecture of your body changes with your breathing, subtly growing and shrinking from your center. This is your Shape Flow."
- "Imagine you're a single cell floating on water."
- "Now inhale into your Wall shape, and then as you exhale, shrink into a Ball shape, which is curled into yourself as tightly as possible."
- "Repeat the shrinking and growing on breath from Wall to Ball."
- "Now shift to Pin shape by stretching your feet straight down. Inhale."
- "On your exhale, compress your shape into Screw by reshaping your arms so that one extends upwards in a curve and the other down into a curve. Keep one leg straight, while the other curves."

- "Inhale to Pin shape, and out to Screw shape."
- "Try breathing in and out into all four shapes for a minute."
- "Change your position so you're standing, and repeat the exercise, breathing into all four positions."
- "Remember that you are inhaling and exhaling towards these shapes, not pushing or pulling the body to achieve them. The movements must happen within a single breath, so they will not be perfect or complete each time."
- Discuss: "How difficult was it for you to move on your breath? What did you learn?"

Activity—Exploring Motion Elements

- Have your actors lie on the floor.
- Say: "Release all your muscles, including your face muscles, and allow your body to relax. Pay attention to your breathing."
- "Explore the Element of WEIGHT by feeling the lightness of the air as it fills you and let the air gradually lift one part of your body from the ground. Take your time. Let that body part feel weightless."
- "Allow the air that brings a feeling of lightness to travel to a different body part. Shift the portion of your body that is weight bearing as needed to continue to explore weightlessness in one body part after another. Enjoy the feeling of weightlessness."
- "Stand up and continue to explore WEIGHT through the lack of gravitation on one body part after another. Find lightness in your core. Now shift it to your shoulders. Now to your knees. Now to your arms, etc. . . ."
- "Walk in a way that would look normal in public, but with a sense of lightness."
- "Lie back down. Explore the Element of WEIGHT through heaviness. Allow your body to sink into the floor, enjoy a feeling of being partially submerged."
- "Imagine you are lying in sand and slowly sinking into it. Allow the sand to start to fill your body. Every time you exhale, sink further into the sand."
- "Imagine that gravity is weighing you down further, as if you are under a weighted blanket, so that you could not get up if you wanted to."
- "Imagine the sand filling your body shifts slightly allowing you to move one shoulder slightly up. As the sand moves about the body, feel your ability to move shift from body part to body part."
- "Keep this sensation of heaviness as you stand and begin to walk around the room. Explore the sensation of heaviness as you move."
- "Walk in a way that would look normal in public, but with a sense of heaviness."
- "Explore the Element of SPACE by taking large steps."
- "Even larger steps."
- "Now take less SPACE with each step."
- "Even smaller steps."

- "Try to walk in a way that would seem normal in public, but with varying ideas of SPACE. Try a sense of taking space, of wandering aimlessly, of trying to compress your footprint. Contain your body in the space you are claiming with each step."
- "Stand still and raise one hand. Point it as you scan the space, focusing on details, to find a destination. Stay present to SPACE."
- "Move towards the place you have selected using different qualities of movement. When you get there, pause and point out to a new point in space to move to."
- "Shift to focusing on the Element of TIME. Walk quickly to a specific place as if on an urgent errand."
- "Speed up!"
- "Begin to walk with leisure. You have all the time in the world, and no specific place to go."
- "Work with a SUDDEN TIME quality. Create sudden movements of sitting, standing, folding arms, stopping and starting."
- "Walk with SUSTAINED TIME quality. Everything you do contributes to continuity."
- "Play with variations on purpose and pace. How does your character exist in TIME?"
- "As you move, focus on the Element of FLOW. How does your character express emotion through movement? Move with a FREE FLOW in a way that is carefree and generous."
- "Move with a BOUND FLOW in a way that is cautious, precise, or sneaky."
- Discuss: "How did this activity help you understand the continuum of Laban's Elements?"

Activity—Exploring Effort Styles

- Say: "We are going to explore the eight Effort styles. Begin by embodying the Effort of Floating—light weight, sustained time, indirect space, free flow. Allow your eyes to float from thing to thing in the room without landing on anything. Begin to float the head on the neck. Allow your shoulders and arms to join the eyes and the head. Your body is off-center, asymmetrical, continuously moving without a plan or direction, working against gravity."
- "Imagine you are a silk scarf floating on a calm lake."
- "You are smoke billowing gently up from a campfire. You are a cloud floating through the air, breaking up and reforming in new patterns and shapes."
- "Add Sounding to your work. Focus on your breath and allow sound to ride on it. Sounding happens both on the inhale and the exhale; it should sonically represent the movement of the body."
- "Embody the effort of Dabbing—light weight, sudden time, direct space, bound flow. Notice that your eyes are constantly blinking without your notice. Imagine dabbing red wine spilled on a white carpet."
- "Now travel in the room, dabbing things that catch your attention. Keep the moves light, sudden, and direct."
- "Imagine you are a light rain landing on a still lake. Dab the molecules in the Space around you with different parts of your body. Your body is centered, symmetrical, continuously moving with clear purpose, working tirelessly."

- "Add Sounding to your work. Start by saying 'dab, dab, dab,' but let the sound morph. Remember to keep your sound light; it should sonically represent the dabbing movement of the body."
- "Make sure you know where you are going . . . that you are using a variety of wide and narrow movements . . . that you are avoiding repetitive rhythm . . . that you are avoiding circular movements."
- "Embody the Effort of Wringing—strong weight, sustained time, indirect space, bound flow." Remember the feeling of a really big yawn. This is the Effort of Wringing."
- "Begin by wringing out a cloth to get it as dry as possible, allowing all of your body to wring it out."
- "Imagine you were swallowed by a snake and you are struggling to get out of it. Wring your body out. Your body is off-center, asymmetrical, gravity pulls you down to the ground. Your movement is continuous with no particular end-goal."
- "Add Sounding to your work. The sound of Wringing is continuous and deep. 'It can seem quite extreme at first. you may feel you want to scale down or diminish the sound but instead ask: how can you stay Strong/Heavy?'[8] Remember to keep your sound moving and morphing; it should sonically represent the wringing movement of the body."
- "Make sure you keep momentum, this is not slow-m0tion . . . that you are shifting your center of gravity . . . that you are contracting as well as expanding."
- "Embody the Effort of Punching—strong weight, sudden time, direct space, bound flow."
- "Remember the effort of throwing something really heavy as far as you can. This is the Effort of Punching."
- "You are the pistons of an engine. Your body is centered, symmetrical, stable. Your movement has sudden bursts towards a specific end-goal. It is explosive. It doesn't st0p to listen, and changes its mind with force."
- "Add Sounding to your work. Start with saying monosyllabic words. Support your strong voice. It should sonically represent the punching movement of the body."
- "Make sure you are not tense . . . that you avoid stamping . . . that you are avoiding circularity."
- "Embody the Effort of Pressing—strong weight, sustained time, direct space, bound flow."
- "The effort of pressing is a downward, sustained push. Straining and squeezing are other terms that describe this single-minded effort."
- "Imagine pressing clay into a mold. Use other parts of your body to press."
- "The room is closing in on you and you need to use your body to press the walls and ceiling away from you. Your movement has sudden bursts towards a specific end-goal. It is centered, stable, and symmetrical."
- "Add Sounding to your work. The sound of pressing is one note; it should sonically represent the pressing movement of the body."
- "Make sure you are not using diagonals . . . that you never reach an end-point . . . that you are avoiding circularity."
- "Embody the Effort of Flicking—light weight, sudden time, direct space, free flow."

- "Remember a moment when a large bug landed on your arm. The sudden startle you felt is the Effort of Flicking. It is a reflex."
- "Imagine a fly landing on your sleeve. Flick it away being careful only to flick the garment, not the skin. Move around the room flicking things you imagine. Now use other body parts to flick. Imagine you are wearing a grass skirt and flick it with your hips. It is off-centered, sharp, and asymmetrical."
- "Add Sounding to your work. Begin with a sudden, sharp inhale and then let the breath carry a sound; it should sonically represent the flicking movement of the body."
- "Make sure you are not making decisions, be spontaneous . . . that you don't hold shapes in your body . . . that you are adjusting your center of gravity."
- "Embody the Effort of Slashing—heavy weight, sudden time, direct space, free flow. Slashing is like Flicking with more weight, and can cause damage if you are holding tension. Stay aware of your body and the bodies of others, and don't become out of control. Anything that appears out of control should be an illusion. If you are truly out of control, you are a danger to yourself and to others."
- "Remember a surprising sneeze. This is the effort of Slashing. It is a reflex."
- "Explore Slashing by imagining your clothes are on fire. Without moving your feet from the floor, imagine you are throwing furniture around the room."
- "Sit on a chair and slash with your legs like you are trying to shake off spider webs. While still sitting, slash the air with your arms like they are knives cutting through underbrush."
- "Pause and locate where the control is in your movements. Develop a habit of always knowing where the control is. Just as you would always know who is in control when you are in a flying harness, you should always be fully aware of who is in control in any movement work. Safety is grounded in control."
- "Add Sounding to your work. Begin with adding a monosyllabic word to your breath by saying 'Slash.' Let the sound change, committing to fully pronouncing the ending consonants; it should sonically represent the slashing movement of the body."
- "Make sure you move past gestures . . . that you maintain strength and weight . . . that you are adjusting your center of gravity."
- "Embody the effort of Gliding—light weight, sustained time, direct space, free flow."
- "Recall a deep sigh of satisfaction. This is the effort of Gliding."
- "Allow your eyes to scan the horizon where the ocean meets the sunset."
- "Imagine you are smoothing a tablecloth on a table."
- "Move through the room as if you were smoothing your body out across the space. Your body is centered, symmetrical, and stable. You move with purpose but not force."
- "Add Sounding to your work. Gliding rides in the space between breath and audible sound; it should sonically represent the gliding movement of the body."
- "Make sure you don't zone out . . . that you maintain a feeling of being free from gravity . . . that you never reach a destination."
- Discuss: "Which Effort Qualities were most natural for you? How are you connecting best with the movement efforts? What does Sounding do for your work?"

Activity—Single-celled Amoeba Improvisation (with Effort Weave)

- Say: "You are transformed into an amoeba. An amoeba has to keep moving to survive. Accept yourself as a single-celled organism. You are an incredibly skilled survivor. Allow your movement to be what it is. You are your effort. You don't react to your experience. You are your experience. You have no thought or feeling. you simply move to survive."
- "Move with the effort quality of Floating—light weight, sustained time, indirect space, free flow."
- "Transition to Dabbing—light weight, sudden time, direct space, bound flow."
- "Transition to Wringing—strong weight, sustained time, indirect space, bound flow."
- "Transition to Punching—strong weight, sudden time, direct space, found flow."
- "Transition to Pressing—strong weight, sustained time, direct space, free flow."
- "Transition to Flicking—light weight, sudden time, indirect space, free flow."
- "Transition to Slashing—strong weight, sudden time, indirect space, free flow."
- "Transition to Gliding—light weight, sustained time, direct space, free flow."
- "Now create an Effort Weave between Gliding and Floating. You are already doing Stage One because you are expressing only Gliding."
- "Begin Stage Two by allowing Floating Effort to appear in your body very briefly, and then disappear."
- "Begin Stage Three by allowing Floating to reappear and stay for longer so the two Efforts co-exist."
- "Complete your Effort Weave with Stage Four by allowing Floating to 'win.'"
- Discuss: "How does improvisation help you? Which Effort styles were the most natural for you? What was the Effort Weave like for you? Did it feel successful?"

Activity—Leaving or Staying[9]

- Have your students partner up.
- Say: "You are a couple at a party. One of you wants to stay, the other wants to leave. Improvise a scene between the two of you using archetypal efforts using both body and voice. When one tactic, or effort type, doesn't work on your partner, try another one. For instance, you might start with Dabbing to convince them to leave while they use Floating to convince you to stay. Then you switch to Gliding and they switch to Pressing."
- Discuss: "How did it feel to do tactics work using efforts instead of motivations? Do you like this way of working? How does it feel to work with another human who is also using efforts?"

6

Michael Chekhov

The Person

Michael Chekhov, a man who laughed easily and acted from childhood, was born in St. Petersburg in August of 1891, the nephew of Anton, the playwright most of us think of when the name Chekhov is mentioned. This family relation may have helped him to begin in the theatre industry, but he resented the idea that nepotism led to his success. He studied theatre formally at the Alexei Suvorin Dramatic School where he was known as a comic actor, and was admitted to the MAT in 1912. Chekhov worked closely with Stanislavski who was proud of Chekhov, but was also worried for him during times in Chekhov's life when he was struggling with his mental health.

Chekhov was not easy to direct since he felt he must use methods that worked for him, not bowing to the micro-management and line readings which were common at the MAT. During Chekhov's time there, Stanislavski believed in using past personal experiences to create real emotion on stage. Chekhov instead focused on imagination. Once, in Stanislavski's class when he was supposed to be using a past moment of grief, he created an emotional scene at his father's funeral. Stanislavski was pleased until he found out that Chekhov's father was still alive. Chekhov used the anticipation of what that funeral might be like to create emotion rather than a real memory. Stanislavski was angry and expelled him from the course because of his "overheated imagination."

Chekhov's alcoholism and depression created many problems for him. His wife took their newborn daughter and left him during one bad episode. He had psychotic breaks that were not under control even on stage and Stanislavski had psychiatrists and hypnotists treat him. These methods did seem to help, and he had a spiritual awakening, diving deeply into spiritualistic practices taught by Rudloph Steiner such as Eurythmy, a form of movement or dance said to make music and speech visible. He also explored Anthroposophy, a belief in a tangible spiritual world. Using Steiner's teachings, Chekhov gained perspective on his addiction and found freedom from his self-indulgence. This spirituality spilled over into his career. He taught Steiner's methods as well as telepathy and yoga. At one point he pushed his students to spend days in meditation, attempting to become reincarnated as their characters.

In his late twenties Chekhov alienated Stanislavski by publishing an analysis of Stanislavski's method. This caused a huge stir because Stanislavski did not want his methods published, partly because of the political danger of drawing attention to his work. Chekhov added insult to injury by including some of his own methods in the analysis, attributing them to Stanislavski. It took the teacher two years to forgive his student.

Once they patched things up, Stanislavski gave Chekhov the directorship of his own theatre, the Second Moscow Art Theatre. Here Chekhov experimented with his methods, delving into rhythmic exercises and telepathic communication between actors. His work continued there for five years, at which point seventeen of his actors quit in protest of his techniques. The Russian government was also in opposition to many of his ideals, and sent him a letter, asking him to refrain from teaching Anthroposophy.

He realized he was in danger and moved to Berlin in 1928, barely escaping arrest. During his time in Berlin, while acting in one production, Chekhov's character taught him how to perform. He became a spectator of his performance and developed the concept of divided consciousness, in which he could be both aware of performing, and attentive to the direction of his character. He called this experience "Obeying the Higher Ego," a technique in which the actor allows the character to use the actor's body and voice.

Chekhov spent time traveling and teaching in England, Paris, and New York where he encountered and taught at the Group Theater under Stella Adler's leadership. In 1943, he settled in California where he spent the remainder of his life acting in films such as Hitchcock's film, *Spellbound,* and teaching his method. He died in Hollywood of heart failure in 1955 at the age of sixty-four.

The Method

Imagination is the most important piece of Chekhov's method, because he believed that imagination has the ability to create inspired acting when it is activated. Chekhov used the example of several painters all painting the same vista. If they agreed to paint exactly what they saw, their results would still be wildly different because artists don't "paint the landscape, but their own individual conception of it, one made possible by each painter's Creative Individuality."[1] Your imagination brings your unique artistry to your work.

Chekhov taught actors to develop flexible imaginations. You, as the actor, can create an image in your mind, and then collaborate with it deeply through your "fiery gaze."[2] As you develop an image-rich focus in your practice, your images will flex and change before you. Chekhov recommends allowing the images to lead you, merging with each other, following a logic that is not your own.

Character Development: Imaginary Body and Center

Chekhov's method of character development begins with your imagination. When you are handed a script for the first time, let your imagination, or gaze, imagine the setting, see the characters, live in the atmospheres of the moments, anticipate the reactions of the audience, and create the play in your mind.

With the play living in your imagination, your next job is to transform into the character you have imagined, rather than playing a version of yourself. Chekhov recommends you create a mental image of your character and make friends with them. Begin by imagining a body for them, and then ask them questions. For example, ask it to show you its face, arms and hands. Then, instead of guessing what they would do in the given circumstances, ask them. "What would you do in this situation?" Chekhov even recommends you develop a divided consciousness so you can watch your character perform their actions in your mind's eye. Your character can create multiple approaches for you to choose from.

Now, imagine that you need to play the role of Don Quixote, a tall and lean character, but your body does not have those qualities. This is not a problem. Your developed imagination can see the tall, lean character before you, and step into it. When you imagine the long, graceful arms of your character's imaginary body rising to meet the horizon, your arm will move with it.

Chekhov called this process of living your imagined body *Incorporation*. "The actor imagines with his body. He cannot avoid gesturing or moving without responding to his own internal images."[15] As you visualize a character, it gradually clarifies in your mind. You will naturally want to physicalize it. Chekhov advises you to start with just one part of the body, for instance, your hands. As that part of the image manifests naturally, then you can add another part of their body to the incorporation. He teaches you to stand before your imaginary character, then step towards them, incorporating the character bit by bit until you have absorbed it all.

Once in the character's body, your first goal is finding the center of the character's body from which all impulses come. Think about every movement of your arm coming not from the shoulder, but from the character's center. Each type of character has a different center in their body. If you are playing a curious character, for instance, your center might be on the surface of your nose. Chekhov recommends asking the image of your character where their center is. They might show you something you hadn't thought of. Respectfully allow the character to show you what you need to know.

Movement Qualities

When you are on stage, new actors often focus on the "what" of their movements. It is important to know what you are supposed to do in your blocking, but it is more important to know the "how" of your movement. This is the work of your imagination. Chekhov identified four qualities of movement: Molding, Flowing, Flying, and Radiating. They aren't the only ways of moving, but they work very well to get you started. As you read, try moving your hand in each of the qualities to get your imagination engaged.

Molding is a quality of movement that seeks to shape the space around you. Your task is to create movements "with inner power and awakened activity, so that you will feel as if you mold the air, or even a thicker, heavier substance, around your body. Each movement must leave an outline in your surroundings."[3] Molding movements must be free of muscular tension.

The next style of movement is **Flowing**, in which each successive movement is "slurred into another in an unbroken line."[4] Each shape you make is clearly defined, but does not have a clear beginning or end. The movements are continuous and powerful like a wave, with a dynamic growth of power and then a subsiding. When done properly, you will feel the surrounding air support you "as if it were the supporting surface of a wave."[5]

Flying is a quality of movement where your imagination helps you create infinite lightness. "While making these movements you must imagine that each of them continues in space indefinitely, flies away from you, departing from your physical body."[6] While you are moving with flying motions, you will desire to sustain your movements so they have time to fly on beyond you into space.

Radiating requires you to imagine invisible rays streaming out of you through your movements. You send these rays from every part of your body with the goal of sending your inner activity outward. As you work on radiating movement, imagine filling the air around you with light. "The practice of radiating creates sensations of confidence, power, freedom, happiness and inner warmth, and in its most fundamental application strengthens the actor's presence. Regular practice of it counteracts self-consciousness, doubt, fear and anxiety."[7]

There are other useful movement qualities that can be added to the four primary ones, or used separately. **Staccato** and **Legato** are two examples. A staccato movement is rhythmically sharp, quick, and exciting. A legato movement is rhythmically slow, connected, and liquid.

When you think about and try these movement qualities, you can take it further, deciding if your character thinks in staccato or legato rhythms. Does their outer movement quality match their thoughts? Are they a flowing movement character with a staccato thought rhythm? Of course, every character can break their normal patterns to create drama or suspense. Try acting a moment with a staccato movement pattern, switching a critical moment to legato, noticing how this impacts your storytelling. This could be a powerful tool in your repertoire.

Images

Another way to add a Quality to your work is to incorporate an image. Three images Chekhov used to spur his imagination are a stick, a ball, and a veil. If you are working on a character that has a stiff quality about them, you can try to incorporate stick qualities into your movement. Starting from the outer, move stiffly about as if you are a stick. Next, allow the outer body to soften, but retain the image of the stick on your inner, energetic body. That stick can now transform into an arrow, a toothpick, an iron pipe, a sword, etc. Perhaps through the course of a performance, your energetic inner self embodies many rigid images to help you.

The ball work begins the same way. Roll around and move with the physical qualities of a ball. After a time, shift that movement into your energetic self, and stop physically moving as a sphere. That image can help you contain the qualities of a planet, a marble, a cannonball, etc.

You can easily see how this work translates to a transparent, airy veil or any other sort of simple image that you might take on as a performer.

This skill of incorporating an image can also be used to sharpen your center. Imagine that the ball image is a sun, and that it is radiating from your center which you have identified as your pelvis. Now move that radiating sun up to your chest and see what that changes in your being. How does it feel if your center is in the intellect of your head? Take notice of the changes and give yourself over to the image.

Emotions

Chekhov used Qualities of movement to solve other problems. For example, he used Qualities to help his actors move past thinking about how to create feeling. He noticed actors trying to force themselves to express emotions. "It seems that such forcing is rarely successful. In most cases, the actor's Feelings, the most valuable element in his profession, remain dormant in spite of all his efforts."[8] Instead of asking for an actor to be more angry, he would ask for the actor to add a quality of anger. His actors found the desired feeling often emerged from the movement.

As an actor, you can move with the *Quality* of suspicion even though you don't actually feel suspicious. After a while, you may experience the *Sensation* of suspicion, and eventually even the *Emotion*. Try it! Say to yourself: "I want to experience the sensation of defeat." Without forcing, sit in the sensation, noticing the heightening of your emotions.

Chekhov taught that it is dangerous to use a specific personal moment in your life to get to an emotion. For example, using the memory of your dying grandfather is not ideal. However, as an actor with a vivid imagination, you can easily use all of the dying grandfathers. A general group is safer for your emotions to work on. Your imagination can use an atmosphere of dying grandfathers to get to the place you need to be emotionally, without exploiting the memory of your grandfather on his deathbed.

Psychological Gesture

Another approach Chekhov used to create the emotions of a character was the *Psychological Gesture*. He taught actors to develop a motion to physically communicate the desire of the character. This technique can be used for a problem moment, or to communicate the super-objective of a character. For example, an actor playing a character who wants "to push my friend to make a decision" might create a pushing gesture and use it in rehearsal. Physicalizing your imagination is a powerful tool.

Chekhov wrote of the time he discovered the power of psychological gesture.

> While working upon the part of Erik XIV . . . I asked my director, Vakhtangov, many questions, trying to penetrate the very heart of the character and to grasp it all at once. Vakhtangov struggled . . . endeavoring to find a satisfactory answer to my questions. One night at rehearsal he suddenly jumped up, exclaiming, 'That is your Erik. Look! I am now within a magic circle and cannot break through it!' With his whole body he made one strong, painfully passionate movement as though trying to break an invisible wall before him or to pierce a magic circle. The destiny, the endless suffering, the obstinacy, and the weakness of Erik XIV's character became clear to me.[9]

The character that had eluded him for weeks was clear to him in an instant as he used an image paired with a gesture to communicate the heart of his character.

Although psychological gesture can be used on stage as an outward action, Chekhov intended it to mostly be reserved for internal work. For example, if you are working on a scene in which you are trying "to trap" your partner, act out a trapping motion while performing the scene a few times.

Next, return to your usual blocking and internalize the action, retaining the intensity in your words. If you ever lose the intensity of the action, you can repeat the action off stage to regain the power of the internal gesture.

You can take this objective further by creating a picture in your mind of your character reaching their goal. Chekhov gives the example of a mother who wishes to hold her child. In her vision, she has already gathered them to her chest. If your character's objective is "to get revenge," you can physicalize a psychological gesture, then internally fix an image in your mind of your character stabbing the object of their hate. When you foresee the thing happening in your imagination, you reach inspired acting.

Atmospheres

Some practitioners call the theatre an empty space. Chekhov disagreed. "The stage is always filled with Atmospheres, the source of ineffable moods and waves of feeling that emanate from one's surroundings."[14] Atmospheres are not just in the theatre. They are in your home, in the park, at the mall, and on cruise ships. They can be either physical, as in the temperature, or psychological, as in a feeling. You experience them by listening as you go about your day. Become aware of them and their influence on you. Think about a time when you went down to a basement and had goosebumps because the atmosphere was creepy, or a time when you walked into a room and felt foreboding. You can become attuned to atmospheres by paying attention.

Chekhov said it is the atmosphere of the theatre that draws people to it, not the people who are performing there. The atmospheres are not created by you, but you must open yourself up to experience them. These atmospheres fill the theatre, with both the performers and audience experiencing the same permeation of a mood. The actors amplify an atmosphere by radiating it out to the audience, while they receive the support and empathy the audience is radiating back to them. The radiating and receiving of all participants create a symbiotic theatre experience.

You can develop your use of atmospheres as a team with your director and your fellow actors investigating and trying out different atmospheres, eventually deciding which atmospheres to amplify. You can then score your script with a succession of atmospheres to assimilate into your performance.

The atmosphere will create different feelings for your character than it will for others. Imagine that you are on a crowded beach. Some people will feel delighted and relaxed in that situation, others will be afraid, others will be frustrated. The same is true of your character. If the atmosphere of a scene is one of foreboding, your character may feel fear or determination. Your scene partner might feel power or weakness. Chekhov asked his actors to imagine the feelings of an atmosphere coming from outside, become aware of the reaction within themselves to the atmosphere, move in harmony with the atmosphere, and radiate it back out to the room.

Atmosphere can also take the form of a personal bubble so that different characters are working with different atmospheres. Your personal bubble can be filled with anything you like. Your bubble might be filled with laughter, causing you to easily find the humor in the room. Your partner might fill their bubble with the smell of rotten eggs. This bubble acts like a filter between the character and the outer atmosphere. Everything that is radiated or received goes through this haze of laughter or odor.

Radiating and Receiving

When you radiate, you send out invisible energy to the audience and other actors on stage. But where did you get the energy in the first place? When you receive, you accept what is radiated from the audience and other actors. You welcome the impressions that come to you, drawing others in. "Embracing the notion of acting as receiving can revolutionize our relationship with performing and teach us how to play into the elusive 'present moment.' The most liberating aspect of it . . . is that it means that everything doesn't have to start with us . . . Acting is *a result of* receiving."[12] If you make yourself open to what is happening in the room, and respond to that, your style of acting will be contagious. As you generously receive from your partner, they will open up as well. Your other techniques will flourish if all the actors on stage are radiating and receiving each other's feelings and atmospheres. Chekhov even teaches that the only true moment of Pause on stage is a "moment of absolute radiation."[13] Try this at the end of a scene, extending the moment of radiation as long as possible, holding the moment.

Chekhov suggested asking your character if they are primarily a radiating or receiving character, being aware that this can change from scene to scene. This flow from receiving to radiating can be easily overlooked. Sometimes remembering to breathe is as simple as re-focusing on radiating and receiving.

The Four Brothers

Chekhov used another image to teach an important concept of his acting method. He claimed all great works of art have four "brothers" in common: Ease, Form, Beauty, and Entirety.

- **Ease**—Where Stanislavski talked to his actors about relaxation, Chekhov focused on a feeling of ease, achieving the same result with less effort. Chekhov told his actors to remember times in their lives where they felt light and festive as well as times when they felt heavy and sad. Remembering these times, they could remember the feeling of physical lightness versus the feeling of weight. Even while playing a dark, down-trodden character, a feeling of ease is important for acting. Audiences worry about actors when they aren't at ease.
- **Form**—Chekhov taught that you must expressively sculpt your own body in service of the play. As you concentrate in your imagination on the form of your own body, you will create a feeling for yourself and your audience. By continuing to work on developing your imagination and conception of the form you inhabit, your body will be stronger and more willing to work. The form of your body will influence your inner life, which will, in turn, influence your body, creating a positive feedback loop.
- **Beauty**—Chekhov taught that within every actor or artist is a "wellspring of living beauty and harmony of creation."[10] Be aware of this and allow it to flesh out your work even while playing "ugly" characters. A feeling of beauty has to come from inside yourself, and cannot be

inspired by trying to impress the audience or director. As you practice the feeling of beauty, don't add to its natural vibrations, but let them radiate. This beauty is tied to unselfconscious authenticity.
- **Entirety or Wholeness**—You can frame an entire play from beginning to end as an actor and help the audience find that wholeness as well. It is your job to communicate the wholeness of a character in context of the whole piece of art. "The feeling of the whole requires an awareness that every action, every piece of stage business, every speech, has a beginning, middle and end which needs to be clearly defined."[11] For example, since characters are rarely fully evil or fully good, your job is to find the vice in the heroine and the heart of gold in the villain. This will help you portray truth in entirety. You must also think of yourself as a part of the whole of your company as well as all of theatre. You are tied to something much bigger than yourself.

The Three Sisters

Chekhov, later in his career, spoke about the three sisters, or three sensations that express a dynamic state of movement in a character. They are Rising, Falling, and Balancing.

- **Rising** refers to a quality of movement on the vertical axis. In this state, you are moving upwards, but with an understanding that falling will likely follow.
- **Falling** implies downward momentum or a state of collapsing. This is an active state where there is a sensation of descending that has not ended yet.
- **Balancing** is in between rising and falling. It is a place of trying to find equilibrium. On stage we are never truly balanced. We are forever vacillating between rising and falling.

The three sisters reinforce another concept that Chekhov taught his professional actors: Sustaining. Actors were taught to remember that inner momentum and movement are essential to keep energetic acting alive. When you focus on sustaining, you are internally continuing an action even after it is completed. For example, when you rise from a chair, you continue to rise internally even after you are standing at full height. When you trip and fall in a stage combat sequence, you sustain falling even after you have completed your fall until you reverse your momentum and begin rising to continue the fight.

Spy Back

Chekhov taught that actors should be fully in that moment, not analyzing their work while they are acting. However, after completion, he taught them to "spy back" to the work they just completed and ask themselves some questions. Intellect is an enemy during performance, but it is vitally important afterwards. One Chekhov Method teacher suggests that asking a series of questions after performing:

- What was I concentrating on?
- What does this movement mean to me?
- What is my experience of this?

- Where is my connection to this?
- Do I recognize this?
- Can I do it again?
- Where can I use it?[16]

Michael Chekhov's Legacy

Chekhov's legacy is alive and well today because many actors have chosen his methods as their own, and find freedom and joy working on stage through enlivening their imaginations and incorporating images.

Tips for taking this method further

- Read Sinéad Rushe's book *Michael Chekhov's Acting Technique: a Practitioner's Guide*. It is thorough and inviting to read, and goes into great detail with practical tips and explanations from a career of using the methods.
- Read Lenard Petit's *The Michael Chekhov Handbook: For the Actor*.
- Read Michael Chekhov's book *On the Technique of Acting*. This book has eighty-seven exercises created by Chekhov that you can use alone or in a group.

Discussion Starters and Journal Prompts

- Summarize Chekhov's acting method in two sentences for an actor who has never heard of him.
- What portions of Chekhov's Techniques are you most excited to apply to your own practice? What do you think you might gain from them?
- After practicing radiating atmospheres, what have you learned about the nuance this adds to your practice of scene work?
- When you work with the external acting method of Chekhov's Qualities, how does that impact your internal emotions? Do you find this easier or harder than starting with generating internal emotion? What about the psychological gesture?

The Tools for your Toolbox

Activity—Staccato Legato[17]

- Have your students spread out.
- Say: "We are going to start this class the same way Chekhov started many of his classes moving in the six directions of right, left, up, down, forwards and backwards one at a time."

- "Stand in present time."
- "Begin by turning to the right and lunging onto your right foot, shifting all your weight there. Do not travel far, but make a strong commitment to the right, completely facing right from your feet to your forehead."
- "Do the motion again in one smooth motion, while imagining you are holding two tennis balls, one in each hand, flinging them as far as you can. Your final position should include your arms stretched out in front of you with palms downwards."
- "Do the motion again, sending your inner energy out to the right, radiating out your fingertips, face, chest, and knees."
- "Do the motion again smoothly, this time imagining flinging your energy through the wall across from you in staccato tempo. Let it continue briefly, then return in staccato to your neutral starting position, standing in present time, as if you never left."
- "Now that you have the first gesture learned, repeat it to the left, committing to the direction of left. Radiate then return to your starting neutral."
- "Now do the gesture upwards, committing to the up direction, radiating, and return to neutral."
- "Throw down into the earth, bending knees, radiating down through the floor, and return to neutral."
- "Lunge forward onto your right foot and radiate in the forward direction, return."
- "Lunge backward onto your left foot , turning your body, and radiating in the backward direction, return."
- "You have completed one cycle of six directions in the tempo of staccato. Repeat the cycle in staccato one more time."
- "Repeat the cycle in legato two times."
- "Repeat one time in staccato, then one more time in legato to complete the thirty-six gestures."

Activity—Imagination

- Have your students sit or lie on the floor and close their eyes.
- Say: "Imagine a scene of transformation. A frog is turning into a prince or a tundra is transforming from season to season."
- "Imagine the whole process of transformation without skipping anything."
- "Now repeat the exercise, but make it more complicated and detailed. Heighten the previous transformation without skipping any steps."
- Discuss: "Chekhov asked his students to repeat this activity using the same imagery day after day until the image would take over under their creative gaze. What do you think the benefit could be of this activity?"
- Say: "Imagine you are in your character's home. What do you see surrounding you?"
- "Imagine you are looking in the mirror. What do you notice about your character? How are you dressed?"
- "Ask your character to run for you. Observe them. Ask them to sit down. What do you notice as they move around the space?"

- Discuss: "What value do you see in giving your character private space and questioning them in your imagination?"

Activity—Atmospheres

- Have your students space themselves out on stage.
- Say: "Imagine the air around you is filled with the Atmosphere of fear. Allow the atmosphere to envelope you. Use concentration to sustain the atmosphere without adding any justification for the fear."
- "Try to relate your internal reaction to the atmosphere outside yourself. Don't force anything. Just realize the feelings coming from the atmosphere around you."
- Repeat with other atmosphere words such as joy, festivity, gloom, horror.
- Say: "Choose a line from your monologue to say while fully engaging an atmosphere, allowing it to play on your feelings. Chekhov said, 'Frequently, we are able to maintain a strong Atmosphere if we are silent and motionless but as soon as we speak or make a movement we are inclined to destroy it. The Atmosphere must remain around you and your movements and words must be born out of it.'[18] Can you keep an Atmosphere while speaking lines?"
- "Pair up with scene partners and talk about what the temperature is in your scene. Choose a specific temperature like zero degrees, not something general like *very cold*. Run your scene with this new physical atmosphere information."
- "Adjust the temperature and try again."
- "Act your scene again, adjusting to the temperatures I shout out to you."
- Discuss: "What new things do you discover when you heat up or freeze out the characters?"
- Say: "Spread out in the space and imagine your own bubble physically around you. Stretch your arms out and explore the space inside your bubble, defining the thin membrane on the edges."
- "Fill your bubble with a scent—perhaps something foul like urine or skunk, perhaps something wonderful like fresh cookies or a favorite cologne."
- "Now wander the space, bumping into each other's bubbles, imagining bouncing off of the others around you."
- "Approach others and laugh through the atmosphere in your bubble, and take in the laughter of others through the scent they have."
- "Now fill your bubble with smoke. Interact to see how that impacts your acting."
- "Fill your bubble with the taste of sweet, sour, bitter, or savory. Interact with others through your bubble."
- "Pop your bubble and *Spy Back*. Chat with each other about what happened to you psychologically as you worked?"
- "Work with your scene partner to score your scene with shifting atmospheres of mood, temperature, senses, etc. and practice them in a heightened way, then bring it back to realism. Remember to let the atmospheres create feelings in you, not the reverse!"

Activity—Psychological Gesture

- Have your students spread out in the space.
- Say: "We are beginning with the psychological gesture of expansion and contraction. Stand at neutral. Now, slowly open your bodies into a star shape."
- "Say to yourself: I am expanding, growing, waking up to life."
- "Hold this position for fifteen seconds, breathing easily, radiating energy out through your fingertips and the rest of your body. Imagine you are growing larger energetically, far beyond your physical limitations."
- "Gradually pull back your energy and shrink to a position of contraction crouched near the floor. Say to yourself: 'I am contracting, getting smaller, shrinking, withering away, becoming invisible.'[19]"
- "Hold this position for fifteen seconds."
- "Repeat the expansion and contraction mantras and gestures a few times."
- "Change your expansion mantra to 'Yes' and contraction to 'No.' Repeat the gestures a few times."
- "Move around the space while playing with the internal gesture of expansion and then contraction, repeating the words yes and no while using reduced external motions."
- "Now attempt an outer expansion, while experiencing an internal contraction and vice versa."
- Divide your students into two groups and spread them out to work individually.
- Say: "Group One work on gestures that communicate pulling, while Group Two works on gestures of holding back. Remember not to complicate your gestures with acting, you are simply performing a motion that communicates the action."
- "Use your whole body to complete the action, spreading out to use more space and committing your full essence to the gesture."
- "Make the gesture smaller, but allow your whole body to feel the effects of the gesture."
- "Everyone find a partner from the other group so pulling people have holding back partners."
- "One of you is a parent trying to talk their teenager into staying home from a Black Lives Matter protest. Improvise the scene using their psychological gestures only without words."
- "Add words in while continuing to use your gestures."
- "Intensify the gestures on a round, and then perform the scene without using the gesture at all."
- "Find the sweet spot of the gesture, and use your energetic body to engage that psychological gesture while you act the scene."
- Discuss: "Talk to your partner. What were the effects of the gesture when performed in small, big, and invisible/energetic ways. What do you find useful about this method of improving acting?"
- Say: "Perform your scene again, attaching a quality to the gesture such as stubbornly, pleadingly, decisively, hopelessly . . . Then try again with a different quality."
- "Perform the scene again trying out two different qualities each in one improvisation."
- Discuss: "How did the combination of qualities with a psychological gesture increase the range of your performance? You each have one psychological gesture to use now. What other gestures could you create?"

Activity—Movement Styles

- Have your students spread out in the room to create space to work.
- Say: "Close your eyes and imagine a center in your chest that is the seat of all impulses to move."
- "With your eyes still closed, begin moving your arms gently, imagining that the movement starts with impulses from your center."
- "Open your eyes, and take a few steps forward and backward, still imagining the impulse to move radiating from your center."
- "Now pick up an item or move a chair using this same focus on the impulse coming from the center."
- "Imagine that the air is thick. Make molding movements with your arms from your center in a way that sculpts the air around you. Make your molding movements slow and deliberate."
- "Speed up your molding movements to be faster, deft and purposeful. Continue your molding movements, using your legs moving around in a small area, changing your speed and intensity. Experiment with your molding movements."
- "Move a chair again, but now with the quality of molding."
- "Imagine that the air is supporting your movements as if it were the surface of a tropical ocean. Instead of molding, perform flowing movements by moving your arms using the impulse from your center in a way that flows organically from one movement to the next without settling on a beginning, middle, or end of each movement. Make your flowing movements wavelike, speeding up and then slowing."
- "Continue your flowing movements, using your legs moving around in a small area, changing your speed and intensity. Feel the support and thickness of the air around you as it ebbs and flows. Experiment with your flowing movements."
- "Move a chair with the quality of flowing."
- "In a flying movement quality, imagine your body tends to lift off the ground as if gravity doesn't hold you down. Move your arms from your center in a way that lifts your movements and sustains you as you fly out to outer space. Try different speeds and tempos with your flying motions. Think of your movements as if they have a life after they have left your body."
- "Continue your flying movements, using your legs and move around in a small area, changing your speed and intensity, experimenting with your flying movements."
- "Move a chair with the quality of flying."
- "Move with the quality of flying, imagining that your movement radiates out from you in the direction of the movement. Keep your feet in place, but move your body from the impulse at your center in a way that sends rays out from your chest, arms and hands. Make your radiating movements legato, then staccato."
- "Continue your radiating movements using your legs and move around in a small area, experimenting with your radiating movements."
- "Move a chair with the quality of radiating."

- "Pair up and improvise a scene in which you are packing up a kitchen. Decide which movement quality you will focus on for the improvisation and complete the full scene with one quality. After the first run, do it again, experimenting with spontaneously changing your movement quality as you progress through the scene. Also experiment with each partner making a different choice."
- Discuss: "*Spy Back!* What discoveries or thoughts did you have while completing this exercise?"
- Have your students spread out.
- Say: "Do a stage movement a few times until you can do it repeatedly in nearly the same way. Perhaps move a book from one side of the room to another, stand up and sit down again, etc."
- "Do the movement again, but with the quality of Molding."
- "Now Flowing."
- "Now Flying."
- "Now Radiating."
- "Now combine qualities, doing the same action with the quality of *Slyly Molding*."
- "Now try *Angrily Flying*."
- "Play with combining the four qualities with others such as: calmly, fiercely, thoughtfully, angrily, hastily, painfully, decidedly, slyly, wilfully, rigidly, softly, soothingly. Try several things to see what you discover."
- "Try switching from legato to staccato while playing with the movement qualities."
- Discuss: "Did legato and staccato create additional drama or suspense?"
- Say: "This half of the room is *the house of curved* and that side is *the house of straight*. Move freely and broadly around the space, switching from curved to straight as you cross the line of demarcation in the center."
- "Now speak lines of your monologue while moving and notice the way your acting changes as you cross the line."
- "Try qualities to your Curved and Straight side performance. Remember not to act emotions, but simply add a quality to your movements."
- "Find groups of two or three."
- "Improvise a scene of moving into a new house, changing qualities as I suggest them. Begin with just movement. Start with shyly."
- "Angrily! Condescendingly! Sweetly! etc."
- "Add dialog! Complimentary! Gently Flying! Awkwardly Molding! etc."
- Discuss: "How did the qualities work for you?" This is an external acting technique that is designed to impact the internal acting. Did it work that way for you? In what ways?

Activity—Tossing Balls

- Begin in a circle. Start with one ball. Hand it to one person.
- Say: "Toss the ball across the circle to another person, saying the name of your target as the ball leaves your fingers. Play this game for a while."

- "Now say your own name as you toss the ball."
- "What are we doing?"
- Guide them to the two action statements "to toss" and "to catch."
- Say: "These are the actions we are doing to get what we want. This is a metaphor for actions. As you toss and catch you are communicating with your castmates, and acting with them."
- "Now say your own name as you catch the ball, and say the name of the person you are throwing to as the ball leaves your hands. Maintain the shape of tossing until the ball is caught."
- If someone throws the ball overhand during the exercise, say: "We are tossing, not throwing. Our actions need to be clear."
- "If someone were to walk into the classroom, they would immediately know that we are tossing and catching. In acting, our actions should be this clear as well."
- "Now toss and catch with a feeling of ease."
- "Now replace your names with 'I toss' and 'I catch.'"
- "Play with the feeling of form by holding the position of catch longer than feels comfortable before transitioning to the position of toss."
- Add more balls if you like, reminding them to continue to play with a feeling of ease.
- "Now imagine that the ball is hot. Each person who gets it wants to send it away quickly."
- "Play hot potato with the ball, passing the balls to the right around the circle."
- "Stop and notice your tension. Relax. Whoever has the balls should accept and allow the warmth of the ball. Respond to the warmth."
- "Continue the game, passing the balls quickly, staying present."
- "Start tossing the balls again. Play with tossing as a form of radiating and receiving."
- "Pair up with your scene partners."
- "Find another scene group to work with."
- "Read aloud the lines of the other group's scene while the actors silently throw the ball back and forth. Think about the connection movement has with your role and emotions as you toss the ball with intention."
- "When you have finished, trade places."
- Discuss: "*Spy back* on this activity. How did replacing intentions and words with tossing and catching feel? Could you do it with a feeling of ease?"

Activity—Timeline[20]

- Have your students stand and close their eyes
- Say: "Lift one arm to point at something on the imaginary horizon."
- "Feel all the way to the ends of your fingers, then imagine you can reach beyond your fingertips to the space just beyond your hands. This is Chekhov's energetic reaching. Believe it is possible and it will become fact."
- "Remember to release tension in your body."
- "Now as you reach beyond the body, feel you are *radiating* into tomorrow."

- "Continue reaching further into next week, then even further into next year."
- "Feel energetic rays leaving you and radiating out beyond the wall."
- "Reach with your other hand behind you. Continue looking straight into next year, but also now find yesterday behind yourself. This moment is not about visualizing actual events that have happened or will happen, but to reach into the past and future on an energetic timeline, sending rays to both at once."
- "Focus on the timeline of energy you have created, from behind you in the past, into the present where you are, and beyond you into next year. Say 'yes' to your timeline."
- "Lower your physical arms, but continue to send rays to both ends of your timeline through your energetic body. You are part of this line. Allow it to exist. Be comfortable."
- "Take steps forward into the future, then step backwards into the past."
- "Find the present moment again, raise your physical arms back to match your energetic arms on the timeline."
- "This time, as you lower your arms, take back the rays from the past and future and stay in the present."
- Discuss: "Take a moment to *spy back* on what was occurring in the creation and maintaining of the energetic body and connections with the past and future. What were you concentrating on? Can you recreate this moment? When could the timeline be useful to you as an actor? Does it create a feeling of ease? Can you project this timeline in your everyday life to take back control of your ease in stressful situations?"

Activity—The Train Station[21]

- Have the class choose a location such as a train station to improvise with.
- Say: "Evenly space yourselves out in the space with your backs to the wall so there is an imaginary threshold in front of you in the center of the room."
- Have one volunteer cross into the playing space and behave as if they are in the location.
- Ask a second student t0 join them and say: "Have an interaction that includes speaking, then the first participant should leave."
- "All students take turns entering and leaving the location, one or two at a time until everyone has had a turn."
- "You have created a *form*. Repeat the form, but with one element of Chekhov's Techniques at a time. First we will try Molding."
- Repeat with other elements alone or in pairs: Floating, Flying, Radiating, Stick, Ball, Veil, Staccato, Legato, Center in the heart/nose/knees, Inner Gesture of Push, pull, lift, expand, throw.
- Discuss: "What impacts do the different elements of Chekhov's Techniques have on your work?"

7

Maria Knebel

The Person

Born in pre-Soviet Russia in 1898, Maria Osipovna Knebel had a happy childhood. Her father was a preeminent publisher of art and children's books. She developed a love of art and literature and she wanted to be an actor, but her father discouraged her because she was painfully shy, short, and not very attractive. At first, she did what he wanted. Because she had an analytical mind and was very good at chess, she went to university to study mathematics.

One night when she was nineteen, a friend took her to the home of Michael Chekhov who was giving acting lessons from his home while he was recovering from a mental breakdown, and she was given the task of acting as if she were made of glass. She was seized by the fear of breaking, and became engulfed in the role. Chekhov was watching. After class ended, he convinced her she would be good at character roles and invited her to study with him. After working with him for a few years, Knebel enrolled in the MAT and studied acting with Stanislavski. Her work there was very successful and she became a member of the professional company in 1922. Knebel's father was proud of her career once he realized she was employable as an actor. She acted at the MAT until 1950 playing many memorable character roles.

In 1936, Knebel was called to the home of Stanislavski who was under house arrest. She described this meeting by writing that he invited her to teach Artistic Recitation at his Studio. She answered "I have never studied it myself or given any concert recitals." He was pleased with this answer, "'Even better,' he said, 'then you haven't had time to develop any bad habits. There hasn't been much practical exploration in the field so far. It needs to be considered at length. We need to find a new approach to it. How about: teach and learn?'"[1] This conversation began a season of her life where she was allowed by the government to work closely with him, though he was considered dangerous by Stalin, and only a few actors were allowed close to him. They worked on Artistic Recitation, and Stanislavski taught her Active Analysis, which she immediately took to and began using in her directorial work. Stanislavski monitored her work from afar, pushing her to take the method to its limit. She loved it, and delved deeply into it, even writing her doctoral dissertation on the method. In Russia she is now considered to be "the most clear-sighted witness to Stanislavsky's last experimental work."[2]

The political landscape of Stalin's Russia in the 1940s and 1950s made the work she was doing illegal. Nevertheless, she continued to teach Stanislavski's System after his death, and to teach about

Michael Chekhov even when she could not use his name safely. She was eventually fired from the MAT by the new artistic director, probably because she told a different story about what Stanislavski's last work was about, but also because she was a Jewish woman.

After leaving the MAT, she directed at Moscow's Central Children's Theatre, eventually becoming its artistic director in 1955. She worked with brilliant adult actors, playwrights, and directors to create a world of theatre for children that did not condescend to them. Working for children gave her the escape from the notice of the government she needed. She expected excellence in everything, and she believed children deserved honest theatre. Parents flocked to her productions with their children, the superior quality of her work making it one of the most popular theatres in Moscow.

She is not well-known in the West for several reasons. For one, her work was illegal during the most prominent time as a teacher and director. She had to keep a low profile. When her work was once again encouraged by the government, she left directing in order to teach full time. She summed up this complex problem quite simply: "Being a woman director is not easy."[3] In the last years of her life, with Gorbachev's reforms in place, she was able to realize a lifelong dream of collecting Michael Chekhov's writings together to publish in Russia. She did not live to see them in print, but she did manage to get all of his writings prepared for the first ever Russian language volumes of his work.

She died in 1985 at the age of eighty-seven. She taught and wrote right up until her death. When she was too feeble to walk up the stairs to her classroom, she enlisted students to carry her up so she could work with them. She loved teaching, because it filled her with "incomparable minutes of joy."[4]

The Method

Knebel created a new method of acting, collaging the work of her favorite teachers. She was a trusted person at the center of a revolutionary time in Russian theatre, and as such, she had a front row seat to the best work of Michael Chekhov, Nemirovich-Danchenko, Meyerhold, and Stanislavski. She was able to reconcile the best of each of their methods into one method called the Knebel Technique of Acting. But, since she was a Soviet citizen, she was required to teach the officially sanctioned curriculum. Therefore, her work is still enmeshed with Stanislavski's. It is likely that many things she attributed to him were really her own invention. She has been so overlooked in the West that most of her writing hasn't been translated into English.

Observation and Concentration

Knebel taught that an actor has both inner and outer objects of attention. These can be paid attention to simultaneously. The outer objects of attention are physical and material. The inner objects are spiritual, mental, and psychological. Knebel emphasized working on your acting as you move through your everyday life. She taught that you can strengthen your ability to concentrate by paying attention to both your inner and outer focus, committing the objects of your attention to your memory because

"Everything you hold in your memory is a treasure."[5] Knebel taught a three-step process to strengthen your concentration:

1. Perceive the object
2. Memorize your perception of the object
3. Know how to recreate the perception.

As you observe things, your job is to see the detail that actually exists, not to invent any embellishment on the truth. Take time to see the details in life that others find ordinary. Knebel taught that there is an important connection between memory and attention, and between memory and concentration. It's the actor's job to fortify this connection.

Knebel worked with her students to sharpen all of their senses. She even asked them to recall the tastes of foods from their past, telling them the events and the emotions of the past are tied closely to memories of tastes and scents. She told the story of the wife of Anton Chekhov, Olga Knipper-Chekhov, who always wore the same perfume when playing a role until the war, when resources were scarce. Knipper-Chekhov was distressed because she could not play the role without the perfume since her sense of smell was too closely tied to the role for her.

Knebel also worked on her student's vision. She taught that visualization is essential because actors can't influence the audience with empty words. Actors can learn to visualize the life of the character with clarity and precision. For example, when Juliet gives her monologue before taking the poison, she has to visualize with clarity and precision making it seem difficult for her to drink the vial. Visualization creates enlightened subtext, and brings life to the performance for the actor and audience. Nothing can be general. Visualization should be so specific that it becomes a memory for the actor.

Knebel recommended that her actors spend two months paying attention to others in public spaces as if they were preparing to paint a masterpiece or sculpt a sculpture. She felt they would soon realize they haven't been paying good attention to people their entire lives, but the habit of preparing to make a piece of art would help build attentive habits.

Sense of Space

Knebel played a game with her students that required them to create a labyrinth with chairs and tables. Next they were given time to study the space. Then, one at a time, they would try to cross the space blindfolded. Anyone who touched a piece of furniture was out.

She had them study paintings, public spaces, and literature, learning to be artful in their arrangement of humans and items in space. Composition of the stage picture is important for an actor to understand because it helps them find their place in the design of the stage. When she sent her students out to people-watch, she sent them to study what physical relationships and arrangements and positions seemed interesting to them. This work attuned her actors to staging and awakened their imaginations.

After this observational work with paintings and humans, the actors then worked to create stage pictures matching and heightening the atmosphere. If you try this, it could potentially lead you back to art, compelled to find art that reinforces your inner and outer work.

Speaking the Text

Knebel wrote that "the art of 'the word sung by the heart' is much more complicated and difficult than the art of false emphasis."[6] Because of its difficulty, text work was saved for later in the progress of her students. Knebel started her work with her students on improvised and devised scenes. Once they were established in their own identity as artists, she introduced the text. "Our problem is to maintain our creative activity and not lose our 'I' when encountering the playwright."[7] The individuality of the actor had to remain intact, creating a collaboration between the playwright and the actor.

The playwright gives the actor a lot of material to work with, but Knebel taught that the actor must supply the goals of the character. The director can help them find it, but it is the actor's job to graft the character's motivations, or objectives onto the text.

Super-objectives

Knebel considered Stanislavski's super-objective to be foundational to the actor. In Spanish she called it the *tarea suprema*, or the "supreme homework." Knebel believed our main assignment as actors is to find the super-objective of our characters. Without a clear goal, our characters will fail. Knebel taught that all actors need to know the specific goals of their actions. She knew that finding the super-objective requires a lifetime of work in strengthening your imagination, relating the circumstances of the play to modern ideas.

The questions that Knebel asked in all her classes led back to the super-objective:

- What is the reason to present this play?
- What is its central idea?
- What do you wish to say with your behavior?
- How is this work viewed in our time?[8]

Communication

Knebel taught that people exchange invisible, but tangible rays of energy when they communicate with each other. To clarify your communicative energy while working with your partners on stage, ask yourself "What do I want from them? What action will achieve my desires? What do I sense about my partner's actions?" Then, color your actions with the answers to those questions. Your attention will lead to good, living communication with your scene partner that includes both your actions and active listening.

The First Time

Knebel wrote that "Stage acting is always built in the present tense."[9] Building each stage moment as if it were "the first time" is difficult. The actor knows the story and lines backwards and forwards, but they must not appear to. Knebel said, "that is precisely the nature of the art of acting: the actor must . . . respond so spontaneously to what is happening at any given moment that it is as if they are unaware of where it is all going."[10]

The work of the first time begins with deeply understanding the character's story. You build memories of their backstory with your imagination, then tell the story in a first person narrative, making it your own. These stories lead directly to the text and make it ring true as if it were the first time you spoke them because they spring from the logic of the character and story. And then, when you perform your scene, don't try to do it the way you did it the last time or the time before. See it all today with fresh eyes as if it was the first time.

Inner Thoughts and Images

If you pay attention to your own thoughts for a while, you will see they are wide-ranging and distracted. They go from thinking about what people might be thinking about you, to a trip you took as a child, to a friend that is struggling, to the meal you will eat next. Your character thinks all the time too. Knebel taught her students that they must think like their character on stage, in a torrent of ever-changing thoughts boiling in the mind of the character. A character's inner monologue can't be pretended. To act thinking is a skill that you have to learn and practice. The unspoken thoughts of the character will spur you to action.

You can practice this skill by working with your scene partner, speaking what you are thinking instead of your lines. Or, you can write down the thoughts you have based on what the other character is saying and then practice thinking them when your partner is speaking. When you work on your internal monologue in a role, you are forced to become intimately acquainted with your character. This is another way the actor collaborates with the playwright.

Knebel taught her actors that thinking as the character extends beyond inner monologue to inner mental images. In real life, our minds are full of vivid images, but actors often forget that when they are on stage. If an actor can work on imagining the vivid mental images of the character, the result can be unparalleled truthfulness onstage. This work can bring about stronger images for the audience as well. Knebel wrote, "The more actively the actor exercises their capacity to see vivid images of reality behind the writer's words, the more they can call to mind pictures of the things being talked about, the greater the effect on the audience."[11] Knebel believed actors must train themselves to visualize the life events of their character's life as clearly and concretely as their own.

This process begins when the actor creates a library of mental images for the character. "This enormous job is mostly undertaken outside of rehearsals. The actor gathers up and stores material that helps them to create the living past of their character . . . those inherently unique ideas and beliefs that firmly bind the actor to the unfamiliar author's text, and help them to breathe life into it."[12]

The second phase of this process happens when the actor speaks to their scene partner's eye rather than their ear. The actor can speak life into the images by engaging the sight of their scene partner in shared imagining.

Active Analysis

Active Analysis is a rehearsal technique that Knebel learned from her time with Stanislavski. He had become aware of several disadvantages of doing table work before putting his actors on stage. The actors were passive and it created an artificial separation between the actor's mind and body, "instead of actively searching for a way to get closer to their roles from the very start, relied on the director to show them the way."[13] Thinking on their feet seemed to remove this divide.

It was a huge shift in his method to get actors on their feet quickly, and without a fully fleshed out plan. During the time he was developing Active Analysis, Stanislavski was under house arrest. He didn't document it because of the danger to himself and his actors. Active Analysis might have been lost to history except for the fact that Knebel chose to document it, even expanded upon it, using it extensively in her own directing work for the rest of her life, even when it was forbidden. Her writing tells the story of Active Analysis, a method which should be credited as a collaboration of Stanislavski and Knebel, because she refined and developed it for almost fifty years after he died.

In a nutshell, Active Analysis asks the actors to do the work of analyzing the text mostly on their feet. Before the first rehearsal, a prepared director does all the usual analysis and research. They know the playwright, relevant historical and cultural facts, the throughline of the play, and have broken the play down into events. The prepared actor will have done less than the director, but still have completed some preparatory work with historical research and reading of the play. The real analysis happens together in the rehearsal room.

It starts with a three-part activity:

1. The first step is dividing the text into etudes: Director and actors agree on which portion of the script is the event or etude to be worked on. They find that every action in a play meets resistance. This resistance is called counter-action, which could be a conflict, but it could also be a part of a negotiation or collaboration. To isolate one event, actors find an action, and its counter-action, which comprise an etude. Once an etude has been isolated and named, work can begin.
2. The second step is called *razbor* in Russian, or the "reading of the facts."
   a. The actors read their selected etude out loud, closely looking for dramatic structure, style of speech, and given circumstances. They also pay attention to their personal responses to the material.
   b. The actors find the gaps in the text, providing an opportunity to collaborate with the author. What subtext is missing from the words that the actors need to fill in? Are there jumps in logic? Are there contradictory words and actions? This is the place where active discussion between actors and director gets to the bottom of what's really going on in a scene.
   c. Each actor makes a decision by choosing the verb that describes their action or counter-action in the etude.
   d. Finally, each actor takes a quick look at the etude again and creates a map including the facts of the scene, the order of things that must occur for the event to unfold according to the text, and the playable verb that describe the action or counter-action. Some actors might

want to write these down; others collect them in their heads. Either way, no notes are allowed on the stage. As soon as they have finished gathering their thoughts, they move to the stage.

3   The third step is to perform the first paraphrased etude, an improvisation based on the scene maps. Knebel never used the word improvisation to describe this portion of the work. Instead, she always called it *a search*. This search was done to find "the interactive possibilities within a play's text, thus emphasizing its purpose as analysis."[14] The actors improvise paraphrased language, pantomime, and fragments of remembered script, searching to discover why the characters speak, and what they might be unable to say for some reason. (Note: Actors are often timid about this step when they are learning. They are used to having a script to rely on, and this process asks them to be experimenters who know how to enjoy making mistakes, because mistakes turn into discoveries.)

Now that the first etude has been enacted once, the rest of the process involves three steps that repeat over and over until the play is ready for performance. These steps are very similar to steps two and three.

4   The actors discuss the scene with their director, deciding if their chosen verbs helped or hindered them. Do they want to try a different verb? What discoveries were made on their feet? In some acting methods, the motivational verb actors choose is hidden from scene partners, but since Active Analysis is about collaborating, discussing them together is useful and in the spirit of the practice.
5   The actors return to their scripts briefly, looking for missing moments and connecting dots. They ask themselves: What did I remember? What did I forget? What do I want to change about my map? What is my character's problem that drives them to take action?
6   These discoveries will compel them to want to get back up on stage and re-perform the etude, experimenting with their new map and making new discoveries with their bodies. After the paraphrased etude is complete, the actors go back to step four.

As they repeat these steps, the actors get closer and closer to the written text, but memorization is not the goal. In fact, sometimes the director might call for a silent etude because the actors are too into the words and not their bodies. Or, they might ask the actors to choose only one line from the text and do a one-line etude that asks them to perform the entire etude with only the words from one line.

Steps four through six repeat many times until the director is ready to move on to another etude. By working this way, the rehearsal is not a place for preparing a performance, but rather a way of analyzing the script actively. Sharon Carnicke describes the benefits of rehearsing this way from her own experiences in the rehearsal room:

> Active Analysis turns the usual way of rehearsing inside out. Traditionally we learn the lines, get the blocking from the director, and then use rehearsals to justify both lines and blocking. Yet, when you memorize by rote, you risk, at worst, a recitation of the play instead of a dynamic performance, and, at best, a performance that skims the surface of the text. In contrast, Active Analysis confronts you with the dynamics that prompt characters to speak and move before you memorize anything ... words and movement [are] 'tools' ... to help you push and pull at one another, as you explore the scene's human interaction.[15]

After repeated work in this mode, the playwright's words emerge from the work on their own. "Only when they understand the dynamics of a scene intellectually, physically, and emotionally do they memorize the text. At this point however, act0rs often find that the text is already inside them."[16]

Knebel strongly advises against memorizing alone. All of the work of the play should be done in communion with other actors and the director. Because exploring random inspirations can lead to a beautiful shift in thought for the whole team, blocking is not locked in until Active Analysis is done. Setting things too quickly leads to a loss of possible outcomes.

Some people say that Active Analysis takes too much time, but Knebel was convinced it took the shortest possible amount of time. Try it next time you are doing scene work. Maybe you will agree with Knebel.

Maria Knebel's Legacy

Maria Knebel's legacy is still being created. In her lifetime, newspapers attributed her success to the work of her collaborators. Scholars also missed her impact and didn't recognize that her method was distinct from her colleague's methods. More recently, scholars such as Alison Hodge and Marie Carnicke have tried to right this wrong. Hodge writes: "Knebel taught actors to use every aspect of their artistic beings, from soul to finger tips, as they embodied the playwright's words. Not only did this approach defy atheistic Marxist philosophy by embracing spiritual dimensions in art, but Knebel's term for the rehearsal process stressed the actor's holistic usage of body through 'action' and mind through 'analysis.'"[17] Carnicke wrote books giving Knebel credit for her work and collaboration with Stanislavski. Knebel was someone without vanity, and didn't speak of her own accomplishments as her own. While we will never know definitively how much of Active Analysis was actually her own invention, she deserves a place of honor in the annals of acting methods history, both for her own work, and for the selfless way she devoted her career to the documentation of her colleague's work.

Tips for taking this method further

- Study Active Analysis and use it in your scene study work.
- Take time to develop your skills of observation, purposefully studying art and nature.
- Build inner monologues and inner images for your characters.

Discussion Starters and Journal Prompts

- Summarize what makes Knebel's method distinct from Stanislavski, Meyerhold, and Chekhov.
- Reflect on the process of Active Analysis. Describe it for someone who doesn't know anything about it. Theorize about the benefits of this method over other rehearsal methods you have experienced.

The Tools for your Toolbox

Activity—Tossing Balls

- Ask students to stand in a circle and toss a ball to random people.
- Say: "The person who throws the ball should say a noun, the person who catches says a verb." For instance: "Bird" (toss) "Flies" (catch) "Milk" (toss) "spills."
- Have them play for a while, say: "Think and act at the same time!"
- Say: "Pass the ball around the circle saying words that relate to each other in free association. For example "Cow" "Horse" "Barn" "Smell" "Food truck"
- "Stand with your scene partners. Each pair should have one ball."
- "Give the ball to the person who speaks first in the scene."
- "Each person should say their line and then pass the ball to the person who speaks next."
- "The way you toss the ball should match the intent behind the line."
- Discuss: "How does throwing a ball serve as a useful tool in communication while rehearsing a scene?"

Activity—Inner Monologue

- Prepare for this activity by either bringing in some hand sewing projects, table settings, or personal hygiene items like combs.
- Say: "Everyone come get a prop."
- "Pair up. One of your pair should complete a simple task with your prop while masking an attitude towards your partner such as anger, avoidance, manipulation, or disgust."
- "The observer must watch and listen intently."
- "Switch roles and do the activity again."
- Now set up an improvisation where an actor must make a choice.
- Say: "Get into groups of three and decide who is A, B, an C."
- "Actor A and Actor B have decided to skip school in order to attend a concert. They want Actor C to come with them."
- "Improvise your scene once."
- "Actor C speak a monologue while you are acting the same scenario again. In it, first talk yourself into saying yes, then into saying no or vice versa. The important part is to verbalize your struggle to decide."
- "This activity can help you if you feel stuck in a moment of a script where there are internal struggles going on. By improvising an inner monologue during rehearsal, you can find the train of thought that leads you to the next moment.""
- Play this game three times with three different scenarios so each person gets to try being Actor C.
- Discuss: "What did this activity do for your understanding of Knebel's inner monologue technique? Can you think of a time when this would have been useful for you?"

Activity—Tempo-Rhythm

- Bring in a stack of coats or large shirts with buttons.
- Say: "Everyone take a garment and button and unbutton them as fast as you can."
- "Button and unbutton them as slowly as you can."
- "Create a new rhythm as you button and unbutton your garment."
- "Create a new rhythm as you button and unbutton your garment. This time build a scenario in which a character is doing the task, and match the rhythm to the inner monologue of the character."
- Discuss: "Find a partner and tell them what your inner monologue was, and how the exercise helped you develop your character."

Activity—Observation Games

- Needed for this activity: chairs and one painting of a person for each student.
- Ask one student to leave the room.
- While they are gone, say: "Switch a few items of clothing with each other."
- Invite the missing student back into the room and say: "Your classmates have traded clothing items. How many of the switches can you identify?"
- Now ask students to pair up.
- Say: "One student from your pair should move a chair from one position to another, then move it back."
- "Partners, exactly recreate the movements of the first person."
- "Add on more and more complexity, taking turns creating, observing, and recreating."
- "Everyone come pick up one of these paintings and study it silently for thirty seconds."
- "Describe with as much detail as possible what you observed to a partner while they are looking at your painting, but you are not. This observation should be physical details as well as emotional impressions."
- "Look at your portrait again and think about the ideas of the painter about this subject. What would this character like to say?"
- "Create an inner monologue for the character in the portrait."
- "Perform your internal monologues for your partner."
- Discuss: "Ask your partner what their impressions were of your painting and if they would have gone a different direction if their assignments were switched."
- Discuss: "Tell the class what you think the value is of studying art for actors."

Activity—Devising a Story through Gestures

- Have your students sit on the floor in a semicircle with a chair or stool in the center.
- Tell the group: "Close your eyes and take three deep breaths, clearing your minds."

- Begin by asking one of the people at the edge of the semicircle to begin a story.
- Say: "Step forward to the stool and complete one gesture. For example, perhaps look at your watch to check the time. Then return to your seat."
- Say to the person next to them: "Go to the stool and copy the gesture of the first player and add another gesture to the story: For example, check your watch and then turn your head towards the exit, leaning to look for someone who should have arrived already. Continue the game with each person adding one gesture to the story."
- Discuss: "What difficulties did you encounter while repeating gestures? Did you find that you could remember exactly which arm the watch was on? What skills do you need to play this game effectively? Knebel felt that an actor can learn the good habits of 'relaxed attention, careful observation, efficient memory, the will to collaborate with others, and the ability to connect thought to gesture and tell stories through your body.' Do you think this is true?"
- Repeat the game, asking the actors to focus on building these skills.

Activity—Acting with Figures

- Required material: two scripts and two cardboard characters for each actor, also art supplies for decorating the figures. (You can use chess pieces or other objects if you like, but Knebel used cardboard.)
- Give your students two scenes each in this way:
  - Print two copies each of duo scenes in which there is a character who drives the action, and one who does not. Label the top of one copy as Driver, and the other as Not Driver. You need one unique scene for each student you have in the class: If you have ten students, you need ten scenes, two copies of each.
  - Prepare two stacks of scripts labeled: Driver and Not Driver.
  - Say: "Take one script from each pile and two cardboard figures. If you happen to draw the same scene from the second pile, trade with someone else."
- Select half of your actors and say: "Find your scene partners for your Driver script."
- "Read your scene with your partner and identify the super-task of your characters."
- Optional: "Decorate your figures making decisions about your character's appearance."
- "Enact the scenes with your figures so it is clear from the movements what the super-task of each character is, and how that shows itself in movement."
- Repeat activity with the other set of scenes.
- Discuss: "What is the usefulness of doing this activity with figures instead of your own bodies? What did you learn about finding the tasks and actions of the scenes you worked on?"

8

Bertolt Brecht

The Person

Bertolt Brecht was born in 1898 in Augsburg, Germany. His teenage years were spent in a war-torn country, leaving him angry and skeptical. This outlook was put to good use, as it compelled him to create revolutionary theatre with a social purpose. He began writing plays at sixteen, and at nineteen founded The Berliner Ensemble, a theatrical company that outlasted him. With the help of his company, he created what has come to be known as Epic Theatre.

When he was a child, the dominant theatre of his country was Stanislavski-based. He did not enjoy realism, preferring theatre to be more radical, sarcastic, and full of humor. He felt realism was designed to put the audience in a trance. He wanted to create a theatrical experience that caused the audience to become socially awakened.

Brecht used a style of design which reminded the audience they were in a theatre. Instead of trying to get them to suspend disbelief, he wanted them to use their natural skepticism and disbelief to stay aware of where they were. He did things like place signs and random projections on the set to remind the audience the play was not real. The house lights were often on, the actors wore their own clothes, props were obviously fake, and set changes were done un-artistically in full view of the audience. Even music used in productions was intended to reduce emotions rather than heighten them.

One of the really interesting things that Brecht (in conjunction with Erwin Piscator) is credited with is bringing historical context and modern problems together. Sometimes, a Brecht play would project slides or film of an seemingly unrelated event from history as a background projection. This was intended to help the audience make intelligent connections between current socio-political issues and events of the past. In this technique called historification, the audience was faced with the cyclical nature of history.

Brecht was also a man who understood entertainment. He wrote frequently that theatre needed to be fun for everyone. If the playwright doesn't enjoy their work, then the actors won't have any fun and the audience won't either. His secretary and lifelong collaborator, Elisabeth Hauptmann wrote in her diary, "If Brecht gets no fun out of what he has created . . . he immediately goes and changes it . . . He says that Shakespeare was undoubtedly the best member of his own audience, and wrote things primarily that he and his friends got fun out of."[1] In fact, when he was interviewed, Brecht said that he wrote his plays not for the audience members who wanted their hearts warmed, but "For the sort of people who just come for fun and don't hesitate to keep their hats on in the theatre."[2]

The onset of the First World War changed everything for Brecht. He had a traumatic experience as a medical orderly that turned him into a fervent pacifist, dead set against capitalism and what he believed it does to governments, turning them into power brokers who send innocent people to slaughter. He left Germany in 1933 as the Nazis rose to power and settled in Scandinavia for a while before moving to Santa Monica, California until the war was over. While in self-imposed exile, Brecht wrote *Mother Courage And Her Children* and *The Caucasian Chalk Circle*, two of his most famous plays. During the fifteen years he spent away from home, he gained name-recognition and acceptance in Europe and the United States.

He returned to Germany in 1948 after being blacklisted in Hollywood for being a Communist. If you are a Brecht fan, you might enjoy watching his testimony before the House Committee on Un-American Activities. He eloquently dodges their insinuations, and speaks with intelligence and humor. However, he returned to Germany soon after the hearings. He spent the remaining eight years of his life in Berlin where he died of a heart attack in 1956 at the age of fifty-eight.

The Method

You have heard the term "Brechtian" thrown around plenty if you have been around theatre much, but it's likely you don't fully know what that means. In most cases, "Brechtian" is a blanket term used to describe a design that intends to remind the audience they are in a theatre. The Brechtian style also extends to acting. A Brechtian actor is a completely external actor because Brecht didn't want actors to "hypnotize" themselves into believing they were the characters, or to put the audience in another world, disconnected from reality. Brecht wrote of audiences in realistic theatre, "They look at the stage as if in a trance . . . This detached state, . . . grows deeper the better the work of the actors, and so we, as we do not approve of this situation, should like them to be as bad as possible."[3] He didn't really want his actors to be bad, but he taught them techniques that would seem bad to anyone who wants realism on stage. The sort of acting he was asking for would keep the audience active in thought rather than contentedly observing.

Alienation

Brecht often used the term *Verfremdung* which means *to make the familiar seem strange*. In English, we refer to this as the A-effect, or alienation effect. The A-effect means actors cannot pretend they are actually the character. They must separate their own experience from that of the character.

Brecht admired ancient Chinese forms of theatre such as Jīngjù that have the A-effect built into them. In these forms, actors wear symbols on their clothing. For example, a poor character might wear a silk costume that has expensive silk patches on it to represent a garment that has been mended rather than actually wearing rags. Another character might use makeup as a mask rather than changing their facial expression.

The A-effect is intended to create an inquisitive and critical spirit in the audience. Brecht tried to prevent the actor from creating empathy in themselves or the audience. Real emotions on stage were repulsive to Brecht. When an actor feels an emotion, and also shares it, Brecht asks, "has one the right to offer others a dish that one has already eaten oneself?"[4] Brechtian actors were required to represent emotions instead of feel them. He asked them to work against realism, looking for contradictions in a character and portraying them without explaining why the contradiction exists.

One way for the actor to achieve the A-effect is to memorize their first impression of the script. Usually, as an actor becomes familiar with a play, they take on the role as their own. Brecht coached his actors to remember the skeptical spirit they had when they encountered it the first time. The actor should be "astonished and resistant" to the events and characters of the play. Since the audience is seeing the play and characters for the first time, the actor can help them to remain critical. He believed it is difficult for actors to "conjure up particular inner moods or emotions night after night."[5] Instead, they can simply do the external movements that help the audience understand what the character is feeling. This also helps because it avoids making the audience feel empathy with the character.

This sort of acting can appear unskilled. In other styles of acting, "showing" or "indicating" is considered bad acting. But in Brecht's theatre form, this intentional practice of showing is the goal. Robert Lewis, who had seen a famous Brecht play said, "It amused me that, after the performance of *Mother Courage*, in a discussion with some theatre people, a theatrical journalist who was present said of the one performer some of us felt was the least adequate because she was 'indicating' her feelings instead of experiencing them, 'Ah, but she was the one who was doing the alienation business.'"[6]

An actor who remains outside their role can appear to be detached. Brecht thought this was the best possible way to perform because it is healthier for the actor, who is allowed to use their knowledge of humanity and social situations creatively. The actor is allowed to stay distant from the trauma in the story, intellectualizing it instead.

Brecht felt this sort of acting was natural. He writes, "The alienation effect does not in any way demand an unnatural way of acting . . . On the contrary, the achievement of an A-effect absolutely depends on lightness and naturalness of performance."[7]

Brecht's actor doesn't transform into the character. Brecht claims this is perfectly natural. After all, the actor is not really Lear, Lady M, or Mother Courage. The actor instead reproduces the character's words as authentically as possible and completes actions for the character, but they never try to persuade themself or the audience that they are transformed. The actor is free to represent with naturalness the actions of a character or type, but not to pursue inspiration as Stanislavski encouraged.

Brecht encouraged his actors to over-rehearse and round off gestures so they look rehearsed to the audience. He wanted them to watch Eastern acting styles like Noh and Kyogen in which the actors openly observe their own gestures. This self-aware and polished performance is the pinnacle of achievement in many forms. The actor who performs this way is neither a servant who must present emotions to the audience, nor are they "high priests of art."[8] Instead, they are political human beings who use art to further their social causes. They get to be critics of their characters and society. Brecht wrote that a critical attitude is positive because it is active, creating revolution and change.

If you try Brecht's style of acting, but are having a difficult time creating the A-effect, here are some techniques that might help. Try reading the script:

1 in the third person
2 in the past tense
3 while also speaking the stage directions.

For example, when reading a role during rehearsal, you might comment on your character between the written lines. "He got up and slammed his hand on the desk because he was angry at his wife." This will help you separate yourself from the gesture and the emotion. You will be able to communicate that you, the actor, do not approve of the belligerent character you are playing.

Truthfully, while using the A-effect, actors cannot simply demonstrate the role as they want to without also experiencing the role, empathizing with the character. Brecht taught his actors not to feel like a failure for having both empathy and criticism while acting. Instead, he encouraged them to let the struggle between the two create interest for the audience. Struggling to stay alienated from a character is the point of Brechtian *Verfremdung*.

Historical Knowledge

Brecht required his actors to be students of history, including current events. As scholars of the past and present, Brecht felt actors must maintain a healthy level of skepticism, destabilizing "facts" on stage. Peter Brook, after observing Brecht's company said,

> What Brecht introduced was the idea of the intelligent actor, capable of judging the value of his contribution. There were and still are many actors who pride themselves on knowing nothing about politics and who treat the theatre as an ivory tower. For Brecht, such an actor is not worthy of his place in adult company: an actor in a community that supports a theatre must be as much involved in the outside world as in his own craft.[9]

His actors were taught to question everything they observed, and to understand that the answer to any question is another question. Because of this, their powers of conscious observation equaled success on stage.

Gestus

The gestus, or social gesture, is something a Brechtian actor might be asked to perform. The gestus clearly communicates the social status and personality of a character without delving into the emotions of the character. For example, a Nazi soldier saluting as they march across a stage crowded with dead bodies communicates the ideology of the character without saying a word. It was important to Brecht that every scene used gestus for clear communication.

The most famous example of a gestus is the silent scream of Mother Courage in *Mother Courage and her Children*, when her son is shot by the military. In Brecht's production, her expression was one of abject grief, but no sound emerged from her mouth. The strangeness of that gesture caused the audience to think about why she must hide her emotions.

The gestus can also be a design element, such as Napoleon's face being replaced with a skull as a political statement. Makeup and costumes can be suggestive of a feeling, such as white faces for soldiers to represent fear. Sometimes the gestus is a seemingly random element inserted into a show such as a protest song performed at an inappropriate time in the script, pulling focus from the storyline and forcing the audience to rationalize the message of the song at that particular moment.

Using gestus, a Brechtian actor tells the story with a series of contradictory stage movements and sounds, odd design elements and non-linear text. Brecht compared the gestus to a knot tying the cords of a story together. The knot has to be accentuated so the audience notices the odd transitions in the flow of the story.[10] This is designed to spark thought that carries beyond the walls of the venue.

Voice

Even though Brecht wanted his actors to communicate their scenes through gesture, without the need for words, he also insisted on clear speech. Clear vowels and consonants are essential, but clarity of meaning is much more essential than a beautifully spoken line.

Brechtian actors need the body control of Asian acting techniques and a voice that is trained in both realistic and non-realistic style of speech so they can communicate the nuance necessary in their work. Brecht liked to include juxtaposition through dissonant singing, chanting, and expressionistic vocalizations in his plays. Because of this, Brechtian actors were trained in non-Western vocal techniques.

Social Function

One of the skills of a Brechtian actor is the ability to represent a stereotype rather than an individual. An actor trying to make a social comment on workers or the elite has to be able to create a generalized portrayal free of nuance so the audience understands they represent a group rather than an individual. If an actor is playing the part of a street demonstrator, they are not playing a fully fleshed out person, but rather the entire movement. This demonstrator's actions in each moment are carefully planned. They must pay "exact attention . . . to his movements, executing them carefully, probably in slow motion; in this way he alienates the little sub-incident, emphasizes its importance."[11]

Because Brecht's work is about social change rather than storytelling, the stories and characters are meant to encourage everyone to change the oppressive social constraints in their society. Portraying a whole class of people at once helps the audience see the problems that need addressing.

Spass

The literal translation of *spass* is "fun." Brecht was a playful artist who used fun to get his audience to think. Laughter is a great tool to get people to think, so he used it liberally. Even if a play had a very serious message, Brecht inserted comedy to break tension. Since he didn't want the audience to follow the character on their emotional journey, he created moments where the experience of the character was quite different from the audience. A comic song about horrible trauma or a slapstick fight in the middle of a war can make social commentary through silliness.

One article gives an example: a serious play addressing the topic of suicide could use spass by projecting a parody of an American advertisement on the wall behind an actor in a moment of poor mental health: "'Are you feeling low? Depressed? Think there's no way out? Then you need new 'End it All' … The poor taste of this would be shocking for an audience. But it actually highlights the pain of depression through contrast and black comedy. The audience will laugh and then question why they laughed."[12] Spass is a tool used liberally in Brechtian productions.

Brecht wrote that theatre should be pleasurable. Art can entertain as well as provoke thought. "They must be entertained with the wisdom that comes from the solution of problems, with the anger that is a practical expression of sympathy with the underdog, with the respect due to those who respect humanity … with whatever delights."[13]

Character Development

Brecht didn't want his actors to become numb to the strangeness of the actions and feelings of their characters. He wanted the audience to notice when a character could make a different choice. In these moments, or "nodes," the Brechtian actor wants the audience to understand they have the power of choice as well.

If you want to try this, don't worry about creating contradictions in behavior from scene to scene. Instead, ask yourself:

- "What am I?"
- "What action am I doing?"
- "What are the social and economic consequences of this action?" (Don't do internal work to differentiate the character from others. Instead, develop a representative of a certain class and culture.)
- "What is my social function?"
- "What is the political intent of the play?"
- "What choices can I make to illustrate my social function in the scene?"
- "Is there a physical gestus I can perform that will call attention to the socio-economic function of my character?"
- "Can I create a character gestus to use throughout the play in relation to costume or props that will emphasize my social or economical function?"
- "Can I show emotions as something that can change?"
- "What is my character doing wrong?"
- "How can I continue to be surprised by my character's behavior?"
- "What does my character do in one scene that contradicts another scene? And how can I accentuate the difference?"
- "How can I help the audience stay in the moment, not entranced by the story?"
- "How can I help the audience think critically about the play and my character?"

In an interview, Brecht addressed the common misconception that he wanted actors to be purely technical and inhuman in their portrayals since they aren't allowed to transform into the characters.

Of course, the stage of a realistic theatre must be peopled by live, three-dimensional, self-contradictory people, with all their passions, unconsidered utterances and actions . . . The actor has to be able to create such people (and if you could attend our productions you would see them; and they succeed in being people because of our principles, not in spite of them!) . . . There is however a complete fusion of the actor with his role which leads to his making the character seem so natural, so impossible to conceive any other way, that the audience has simply to accept it as it stands.[14]

Brecht wanted his audiences to believe that the character could have made a different choice. Can you play your characters in a way that sheds light on the plight of human beings, motivating your audience to action?

He also realized the limits of his acting theories and techniques. He told Lotte Lenya near the end of his life that she shouldn't worry so much about following his method in her performance. "Once aware of and rehearsed in the Epic techniques, follow your instincts and play the role without worrying about the theory."[15]

Bertolt Brecht's Legacy

Bertolt Brecht was probably the most influential theatre theorist since Stanislavski. His Epic Theatre movement was based in an optimistic view that people can and will change if presented with intelligent calls to action. He has inspired generations of artists to make their productions both entertaining and thought-provoking. And he gave us all permission to remind the audience that they are in a theatre through design choices and dissonant gestures, text, and voice.

Tips for taking this method further

- Take some time with each role you play to set yourself outside the character and criticize them. Figure out what you disagree with, and try to bring attention to it in a rehearsal. Ask for feedback from the director about what social problems they think the play is highlighting, and how you can help.

Discussion Starters and Journal Prompts

- Reflect on your own past experience with theatre and write some Brechtian concepts you have witnessed or performed, perhaps not understanding where the techniques came from. What was your impression? What did you like and dislike about these methods?
- What do you think about Brecht's claim that actors should not share genuine emotions with the audience?

- Think about productions that have smooth and artistic transitions. What do you think the effect of purposefully breaking this tradition would have on the audience and the actors?

The Tools for your Toolbox

Activity—Character and Emotion in Brecht's Epic Theatre

- Pass out copies of a Brecht scene to your class and divide them into groups, giving them a portion of the stage to work in.
- Say: "Quickly assign the roles."
- "Practice a few of Brecht's acting techniques for character and emotion as I call them out":
    - "Perform while paying attention to the feeling of being watched."
    - "Look at the floor, showing the audience that you are making decisions about your movement."
    - "Make your vocal timing disconnected from your movements."
    - "Stay physically and emotionally distant from the other actors."
    - "Let your groupings be loose so you can make your own decisions about movement."
    - "Acknowledge the diversity of your audience by speaking to them both as parts of social structures as well as individuals. For example, focus on a group, and then focus individually on each person."
    - "Stand center stage and directly address the audience in open stance."
    - "Say your lines as if you are delivering a third person speech."
    - "Sometimes speak your stage directions."
    - "Think of your character's actions as if they occurred in the past. Be critical."
    - "Trade roles with other actors to simplify ideas and to stay unattached to your role."
    - "Study your gestures in front of a mirror."
    - "Try robotic, mechanical, dream-like, and stylized movements."
    - "Use a fresh acting style completely opposite of your usual approach."
- Choose a few of these fourteen elements. Tell your students to perform using these techniques.
- Say: "Now perform again, using strictly realistic manner."
- Discuss: "What is the impact of Brechtian style? What could be useful to take into your acting toolboxes?"

Activity—Poem in the Round

- Give your actors the following poem[16] on sheets of paper:
    A dog went into the kitchen
    And stole an egg from the cook,

>   The cook took out his cleaver
>   And cut the dog in two.
>   The other dogs came in
>   And dug him in a grave,
>   And put on it a headstone
>   With the following epitaph: (repeat)

- Assign your students the roles indicated in the poem: the dog, the cook, the other gravedigging dogs.
- Say: "Each character should recite the poem in their own attitude, adding in some context—for example, the dog that has puppies to feed, the dog who likes to steal things, the cook who is afraid of dogs, the cook who is afraid of seeming weak."
- "When I point at each of you, begin saying the poem until it is a round, with many different voices and attitudes."
- Discuss: "What effects does this activity have? How does it relate to what we have learned about Brecht?"

Activity—Social Mirrors

- Have students spread out in the space.
- Say: "Pair up and establish eye contact with each other."
- "Perform mirrored actions. The goal is to hide who is leading and who is following any given movement. Work as a team."
- "You are performing a role in the mirror. Start by performing machinist."
- "Now perform homemaker."
- "Now chef."
- "Postal worker."
- "Wall Street executive."
- "Unhoused person."
- "Now mirror socio-economic situations starting with global warming."
- "Immigration."
- "Feminism."
- "Civil rights protest."
- "Start walking around the room, no longer mirroring, instead working alone."
- Give them scenarios to act out. Say: "You are wearing shoes that are much too big for you, one of your body parts has swollen to triple its natural size, the air is too thick to move through easily," etc. . . .
- "Now play archetypes as you walk around developing movement rhythms and gestus. For instance: lawyers, soldiers, teachers, mothers, fathers, police, musicians, doctors, patients."
- Now spend some time playing with these archetypes and gestus. Give pairs a scenario to play within using only the archetypes you have rehearsed. For example, a lawyer suing a teacher for teaching a banned topic or soldiers conscripting fathers into military service.

- Say: "Remember that the focus should not be on the emotions, but on the representation of the socio-economic role of each player. You should make specific choices to illustrate the plight of the entire class of people you represent."

Activity—Folding Linens

- Choose two actors to fold cloth napkins or washcloths, or some other sort of menial and regimented task.
- Say: "Begin folding the linens calmly. And then, give each other a knowing look and begin to have a fake jealous fight for the benefit of your spouses who are in the next room. All the while, you must continue folding calmly."
- Discuss: "What are the challenges of performing an activity that contradicts the scene? Did this game highlight an activity that would normally go unnoticed by the audience?"
- Now have another set of actors perform the same scene, but this time play the argument genuinely and not for the benefit of an audience in the other room.
- Discuss: "What changed? Do we still notice the strangeness of the folding?"

Activity—Said the Man

- Prepare copies of a scene, perhaps something from *Mother Courage*. Assign students to read each role.
- Say: "As we read, each actor should add 'said the man' or 'said the woman' at the end of each of their lines."
- Discuss: "This activity is designed to show the actors that their personal emotions do not need to be the same as the character's. Did this technique allow you to critique your character better?"
- Say: "Repeat the scene speaking the stage directions instead of saying 'Said the man/woman.'"
- Discuss: "Did this technique have the same effect as the other?"

Activity—Not . . . But

- Create a setting on the stage where there are three exits.
- Ask one actor to come on stage.
- Say: "Choose a door and exit."
- "Repeat the action, but communicate to the audience that there are three choices before making a choice."
- Discuss: "How does giving the audience an understanding of the options help them try to choose differently than the character? Does it help the actor to remember that the character rejected other options?"

9

Stella Adler

The Person

Born in 1901 to a famous Yiddish-American theatre family, Stella Adler had her first acting role on Broadway at the age of four. She acted in London and New York and on the vaudeville circuit, often at the expense of her schooling. Adler grew up at an exciting time for acting. She was twenty-one when Stanislavski brought his troupe to the US for a tour in 1922, profoundly changing American theatre. She joined the American Laboratory Theatre in 1925 where she learned Stanislavski's System from Maria Ouspenskaya and Richard Boleslavsky.

She was a stunning talent. Harold Clurman, who would become her husband, describes meeting her: "At this juncture I had, to my surprise and almost against my will, fallen in love. The lady in question was Stella Adler, poetically theatrical, reminiscent of some past beauty in a culture I had perhaps never seen . . . she was somehow fragile, vulnerable, gay with mother wit and stage fragrance, eager to add knowledge to instinct, spiritually vibrant."[1]

She joined the Group Theater in 1931. She had great respect for the Group, though they were much less experienced than she was. Over time, she found that what the Group called Stanislavski's System was destructive to her. She once said that drawing on personal trauma to produce feeling on stage was sick. If that is what acting took, she didn't want any part of it.

In 1934 she traveled to Europe. While in France, she learned that Stanislavski was also in Paris, and decided to call on him. She told him about her struggles with his system. He wondered if the Group Theater was doing it wrong and asked her to share their techniques with him. He was appalled at what was being taught in his name, explaining that he had discarded his affective memory exercises long ago because they tended to cause hysteria in his actors. He explained his newer approach to acting, and offered to help her with her current role. She agreed, and they worked together for several hours a day for five weeks.

When Adler returned to America, she gave a series of talks about Stanislavski's System to the Group, making Group member Lee Strasberg furious. He believed strongly in the methods he had been teaching, and he perhaps felt betrayed or threatened by this new information. On the other hand, some of the members of the Group were quite excited about the things she had to say and began to assert their will over Strasberg, producing plays they wanted rather than allowing him to choose and direct all the plays. Adler, rejuvenated by the work in Paris, approached her craft with new joy and purpose. "While continuing to act, I started to teach and direct, trying to correct the mess that was made of Stanislavski's technique."[2]

Later, in 1949, she founded her acting studio called the Stella Adler Studio of Acting in New York City where she taught for many years. At the same time she taught at The New School, Yale School of Drama, and led the undergraduate drama department at New York University. She made a name for herself as an effective acting teacher and became sought out by both stage and film actors. Adler died in 1992. Her school is still in operation today.

The Method

Stella Adler's method of acting fits squarely in a category of acting strategies and philosophies called Modern Acting that emerged in the mid-1900s. Her method was based on Stanislavski's. One of her students wrote that Adler wanted her students to find artistic independence, "If the actor truly understood and absorbed the System, he would contact his own creative powers and rise above any explicitness of the System. Adler had herself absorbed Stanislavsky's concepts and imaginatively reworked them; she was no longer able to say precisely which aspects of her method were his and which were exclusively hers."[3]

Adler told her students when they enrolled in her classes that they must stop relying on the opinions of others. Growth comes from self-awareness, and self-awareness leads to success. She recommended making an honest assessment of your assets and flaws, writing them in two columns. Once you understand the work you need to do, you can begin working on your body, speech, mind, and emotions. She wrote, "Know what you want and have the courage to pursue it. **It is important to say aloud:** 'I am myself and have my own standards.'"[4] Adler worked with her students to become independent, recognizing the freedom that comes from being responsible for their own development. She expected her students to create the standards by which they would judge themselves.

Disciplined Body and Voice

Adler started with the voice. She emphasized that while your volume may go up and down, the energy in the voice must remain high. She emphasized the actor's responsibility to have a resonant voice. This responsibility begins with daily practice of reading something aloud to someone who is a good distance away. She insisted that her actors be powerfully articulate. "Your professional obligation from the stage is to make your partner and the audience understand . . . Get over using your everyday voice. This voice doesn't communicate."[5]

Adler also required her students to be disciplined with their bodies. She was upset by the casual trends in physical conditioning and posture that she observed in youth culture. She required her actors to straighten their spines and hold their heads up so they could move in a normal and functional way. She emphasized posture and movement that create a solid base to work from in movement studies. She objected to what she called Puritanized bodies. "You find yourself either ashamed of your body or defensive . . . there is a lot of contraction, shame, pulling in, and making everything less than it is. It is a tradition of restriction, from which you need to free yourself . . . There is room for everybody on this earth. No one is taking up anybody else's place."[6]

This statement exemplifies Adler's mission to end cultural obsession with smallness. She pushed for fully formed actions, unconstrained presentations of self on and off stage, and using of maximum capacity in gesture and movement. Following her training allows energy to thrive in the performer's body.

Ways of Seeing

Adler taught three ways of seeing that she believed would help an actor to live a full life on stage. These ways of seeing are practiced outside the theatre in everyday life.

- **Banking**: This way of seeing requires you to describe what you see in simplest terms, "I went to the grocery store and there were apples, bananas, and oranges." This is seeing like an accountant. It is not good for the actor because when you describe facts, you kill the thing you describe.
- **Seeing the Life**: This way of seeing requires you to see things in relation to the world around you, "I went to the corner store and I saw some expensive looking raspberries, red and delicious. I also saw some pears that were past their prime, but beautiful. And I saw some green grapes that looked sweet and crisp, the kind you can eat by the pound without breaking the bank." This is seeing more like an actor. Each item has some extra detail.
- **Traveling**: This way of seeing requires you to let the observed thing lead your thoughts, "I went to the store and I saw some big, red strawberries, the sort of thing you might purchase for a picnic date with someone you want to impress. They would go well with a baguette like the ones at Park Avenue Bakery, some brie like what my mother used to serve at fancy dinner parties (that I would sneak into, pretending to be a grown-up until I was discovered), and all of that would look so pretty in a picnic basket like the one I foolishly sold in my last garage sale. Oh, I wonder if my neighbor still has it!" The observation of one thing leads the viewer to remember and travel from one thought to the next, enriching each moment with a string of associations.

Traveling is the optimal way for the actor to see. "With the object as catalyst for a chain of references, the viewer goes and keeps on going, traveling as if he could go on forever, discovering, uncovering, recovering what he holds within . . . every object contains one's whole life."[7] This way of seeing trains the actor to recognize that they contain everything they need for every role.

Given Circumstances and the Imagination

As humans, we always know our own circumstances. We usually know where we are, what is happening, what our goals are, etc. But as actors, we often step onto stage with the disconcerting feeling of not knowing the circumstances. We are lost until we figure out where we are and what is going on. Adler believed that living in the circumstances is more foundational to acting than the script. You cannot ignore circumstances and be a successful actor. They must become real in your imagination. Adler taught that imagination is the secret to successful acting. She, "in fact credited imagination with nine-tenths of the acting. Imagination makes the actor's work honest. Without the use of imagination, words are just words, the place is no place, the objects are nothing, the characters are nobodies, and the actor is empty, his acting a fabrication . . . Everything on stage is a lie until you make it truthful."[8]

Actors can see specifically and rapidly, differentiating between different shades of colors. They put those details into the imagined circumstances of a play. Adler recommends actors document the specific things they see in a journal at the end of each day. This practice cultivates the imagination, and helps the actor see the stories behind things most people don't even notice. "From now on your work will lead you to live imaginatively. You will see and act in imaginative circumstances. This is not hard if you accept that everything you imagine is truthful . . . Anything that goes through the imagination has a right to live and has its own truth."[9] For example, the playwright will give you a description, perhaps telling you that "the day is gloomy and oppressive." However, it is up to you to discover what is "gloomy and oppressive" since the playwright can't give you a cloudy day that belongs to you. You have to create that yourself.

The filling in of details must be specific and include everything on stage. Adler says,

> if you pick up your tumbler in a Shakespeare play and say, "Health to the King," and if you don't know what you are drinking, then you are drinking the words. The actor manages the circumstances by assimilating the logic of where he is. He figures out what kind of drink that place has to offer, as well as the nature of everything else coming his way.[10]

Adler claims that all of human knowledge and history is in each of us, ready to be accessed. We don't usually use this trove of information except on stage. Part of training your mind to use these things is taking advantage of the resources around you. Your study of history and the world can be expanded by attending museums and imagining yourself in the worlds of emperors, native islanders, and czars. You can also read books of art and architecture at the library.

Acting is Doing

Adler wrote, "Acting and doing are the same. When you're acting you're *doing* something, but you have to learn not to *do* it differently when you *act* it."[11] In other words, every action is truthful in life, you have to make actions just as truthful on stage. For example, imagine your action on stage is to perform surgery. You can't perform actions that are too general, so you have to break down your actions into single item steps. So, you compose a list of activities such as putting on gloves, focusing the light, and preparing the incision site by shaving, taping, and sterilizing it. This is the same principle that Stanislavski teaches: be specific in everything you do.

This physicalization of actions also gets you onto stage. For instance, as you are entering, give yourself an activity that carries you into the action. Perhaps you are taking off your coat, or smoothing your hair, or carrying a flower to a vase already on stage. In your real life, you are always doing activities as you enter a room. The stage is no different. Pay attention to your entrances into rooms. You will be surprised! Can you find a single instance of an entrance you make that does not include activities?

The great thing about Adler's method is that these simple actions are what helps actors find emotion. For example, the director might tell you to slam a drawer shut angrily. You can't just act the emotion "angrily," you need to find a justification for slamming it angrily. Your justification isn't the emotion. You don't justify slamming the drawer by thinking "I'm slamming the drawer closed because I'm angry." Instead, think "I'm slamming the drawer closed because my winning lottery ticket wasn't in it." If you try it and the needed emotion doesn't come, then find something that works.

In building a character, an actor justifies every action, and they also create a ruling action. Like Stanislavski's through-action, this is the motivation behind all of the character's actions. So, if you are a surgeon, perhaps your ruling action is to win a promotion at your hospital. Your individual activities of picking up scissors and stitching up an incision are done with the goal of appearing skilled enough for that promotion. In this way, your motivated series of physical actions lead to your ruling action.

Adler taught that physicalizing actions takes emotional pressure off the actor. "When I ask an actor to physicalize his actions, and use his circumstances, the purpose is to take the burden off the actor . . . In life, as on stage, not 'who I am' but 'what I do' is the measure of my worth and the secret of success. All the rest is showiness."[12] The physicalization of circumstances causes emotions to emerge. Rather than squeezing emotions out of actions, Adler taught her students to physicalize and allow the emotions to come. For example, if your character must feel miserable because of the cold, rather than grimacing and shivering, close a window or button your coat all the way up to your chin. This action should create belief in the circumstance and cause misery to emerge.

Adler strongly advised against using your past experience to create emotion on stage. She wrote,

> To stay with your personal past, which made you cry or gave you a past emotion, is false, because you are not now in those circumstances. You are in the play, and it is the circumstances of the play that have to be done truthfully by borrowing what was physical in the action you had in the past, not the emotion.[13]

In other words, if you are having a hard time finding an emotion in the play, for instance, pleading with a lover to stay with you, you should not bring a past experience of desperation into that moment. Instead, remember that desperation is "reaching" and physicalize reaching on stage so that you can experience the appropriate emotion in the circumstances of the play rather than in your past.

Creating Characters

Instead of delving into emotions and the past, Adler required her actors to do the internal work of dramaturgy (historical and cultural research). Her students study the text extensively and make choices based on what they learn from it. She taught that the actor who doesn't do their homework goes onto the stage "naked" and fakes it. If a character talks about recipes, the actor needs to learn about cooking or they will fake it on stage.

When building the character, an actor's job is to do research about the time period, for example, the politics, leading artists, music, science, daily routines, clothing, and religion of the time period. The actor must also create a full backstory for the character and figure out what the social status of the character is, what that status means for the day to day life of the character in their time, what their specific political and religious beliefs are, and what those beliefs would mean day to day for the character. These details are not simple to figure out; the process of birthing a character is difficult. Adler didn't believe in shortcuts to creating a character.

In this first stage of research the work is general; in the second, the actor gets to be imaginative and specific. For example, if most people in the setting of the play are Muslim, the first stage of your work is learning about the Muslim faith in the setting of the play. The second stage allows you to ask questions like: does your character believe in this faith? or does the character merely go through the motions of the faith because they must in order to avoid the disapproval of a parent?

In this second stage, the actor also personalizes the immediate circumstances of the play. You do this by walking around the set and personalizing the environment. If the setting is the character's home, the character has a history with the items there, the decor on the walls, and the furniture. Just as you have a favorite place to sit in your home, your character does too. Take time to make the set of the play a real space for your character.

Your character also has character traits. Take the time to list them and then think about the actions you have built. For instance, if the character you are playing is a meticulous person, you will sew on a button in a different way than if your character is a distracted person. You might write in the margin of the script: "He sews on the button deliberately because he is meticulous." or "She loses her needle because she is distracted."

Those character traits lead to attitudes. Your character has an attitude about smoking, God, their mother, spiders, and the other characters. You have the ability as an actor to portray things that are not in your personality. Adler taught, "In some area of your life you are a killer, a crook, a liar, and a whore. You are a genius, a god, and pure. You are everything."[14] The process of turning yourself into something that isn't you involves first identifying a time in your life when you were that thing, even briefly. Perhaps you were so angry at a co-worker that you hoped they would die and stabbed the air with an imaginary knife in their back. You can amplify and activate the essence of that anger and action, expanding your murderous tendencies until your character can be Ms. Murderer. Your characters are "manifestations of our shared human potential."[15]

Adler stressed that actors cannot feel superior to their characters. Her instruction was to, "Understand your character and, even if you disapprove of him, find him in you. The great actors always did that . . . A good exercise is to ask, 'Where am I, in my own circumstances, like that too?' Let your imagination take you to the experience of whatever you don't like."[16]

Characters are sometimes types that you can embody. For instance, the character might be an Ivy League type. In these cases, you can learn what characteristics they all share: superiority of education and opportunity, lack of understanding of the plight of the underprivileged. The posture of this type might include a wide, confident stance and carefree head tilt. As an actor you can embody and physicalize this type. The outer mannerisms of physicalizing this type will change the way you portray the character and the internal way it feels to be on stage.

Adler also taught her students how to heighten a character. She instructed them to think of their character in the way their opposite would imagine them. For instance, if playing a Nazi soldier, you can heighten your character by imagining how a gay person or Jewish mother would see him. If you choose to heighten those characteristics the oppressed see in your character, your character will be heightened. This isn't appropriate in all plays or for all characters, but is a helpful tool for many roles.

Approaching the Text

The play itself is completed when the playwright publishes the play. It exists as a frozen thing that has no life, but exists in the past. Your job as the actor is to honor the words that you have from the playwright and make them live on stage. "Adler sees establishing a version of truth in performance as embracing the past-ness of the play text and the present-ness of performed actions."[17]

Your first task when approaching the text is to interact with and understand it. Adler recommends starting by paraphrasing the text in your own words. The text is full of empty words that actors need to fill by creating a series of doable actions. Doable actions have an end goal. For example, not simply "to think." Instead, "to think about what I will make for lunch." If the action you create for yourself is doable, then you will get to experience the doing. Adler told her students not to consider a task done until they had done every step of it. For example, an actor can't sew on a button without threading the needle, placing the button, stitching every stitch, knotting the thread, and cutting it. This is easier if you actually perform the action on stage. However, if you are tasked with pretending to sew on a button, you cannot skim over any of the steps simply because it isn't real. To your character, every step is real.

Objects in real life are complicated. They might have dog hair on them that needs to be removed. They might get knotted up. Can your character also have real objects with real complications? Of course! Adler taught her students to first learn the action step by step, then to add complications to them. The complications will help you invest in the action more deeply.

Once you have established the circumstances of the play, it is time to personalize the role. Instead of speaking in the third person about your character, start to use the first person. For example, instead of saying: "Juliet stands on the balcony looking at the moon and daydreaming about a boy," say, "I feel the moon on my face and wonder what it would be like to kiss Romeo." The feelings will be stronger when you take on the character in the first person.

The last step of approaching the text is memorization. Adler says that it is deadly to start with memorization. As you do the work of understanding the circumstances, actions, and world of the play, the words of your character will become yours and memorization will happen automatically.

Approaching Stage Design Elements

Adler learned from childhood that an actor is responsible for learning to own their costumes. If your character is a modern one, then the job of learning to own the costume is relatively easy. If, however, your character is historical, you need to learn to own the cape or corset that your character wears. Learn how the style of the clothing indicates social status. Learn how to move in it as if it were yours. It is also your job to endow it with the qualities that its historical counterpart would have. If your costumer gives you a dress that is light and cotton, but the historical equivalent would have been heavy, scratchy wool, you must know that, and treat it as if it were heavy and scratchy.

Similar work must be done with props. You must befriend your props by paying attention to them. Each prop deserves to have a history. What did it look like when it was first made? How did you get it? How has it changed since then? If the prop is an item you aren't used to using, for instance, a newspaper, then you need to become familiar with using it and give yourself a task. With the newspaper, you might decide that you are looking for stock prices. Quickly find the index and turn back to the correct page and begin studying them. Never just open the paper and pretend to read. Use it as if it were something in the world of the character for which your character has a purpose. It is time consuming, but "When the actor gives a prop a history and a current condition, it ceases to be a prop and becomes a living object . . . there is no costume—there are clothes—there are no props—there are personal belongings."[18]

Knowing Your Playwright

One of my favorite things to teach actors is Stella Adler's approach to roles and her insistence on knowing not just the play, but also the playwright. She said, "It's a big stretch for an actor to live up to the playwright. But you can't do less."[19] Since the actor is the interpreter of the work of the playwright, they must understand the playwright deeply. "More than anything, it is an actor's job to penetrate the playwright's creation—the subtleties and mysteries that the playwright's ideas contain."[20] She believed this firmly, and even published a book teaching actors how to work with the texts of different playwrights.

She taught actors that they have a different job when performing a Brecht play, than a Gunderson. If you are doing a Brecht play, such as *Mother Courage and Her Children*, you have to know about Brecht. If you don't understand that he was ideologically a Communist and working to expose capitalism as the destroyer of society, you won't play the part well. If you don't understand that Gunderson writes to create positive change for women in community, you will miss the point of her work.

In the interest of grasping the value of Adler's insistence that you understand the playwright, let's explore what she taught about Tennessee Williams. If you are not familiar with his work, go watch some of his plays online, or stream *A Streetcar Named Desire* with Marlon Brando, one of Adler's most well-known students.

Tennessee Williams' plays, like many of the most influential plays in history, are about people dealing with change. Adler starts her chapter on Tennessee Williams by bringing up another playwright, Arthur Miller, who wrote *Death of a Salesman*. The characters in this play are trying to find out who they are in a changing world. "Tennessee Williams doesn't do that. He's very different. His characters don't really want to find out who they are. They cannot face the reality. They run away from it. That is why he so captivates us—because of the romantic way in which he escapes the filth, the dirt, the frustration. His characters don't blame society."[21] Adler explains the genre of his plays is *poetic realism*. In other words, the world that the characters live in is a real place. The reality of the situation is very much rooted in the South at the time it was written, but the characters exist as if the world were not decaying around them. They speak with more flowery language than they deserve, and they refuse to see the truth.

Tennessee Williams, the man, was wealthy, but lived in run-down shacks. He drank, did drugs, and spent time in mental hospitals. Adler met him and recognized that he was escaping the middle-class life that was available to him. "He couldn't get to his truth . . . there is nobody that smells the poetry of life the way he does and yet lives the life of a Bowery bum. No money can help Tennessee, no success. In this escape business, he writes really about himself."[22] She said that he spoke the way his characters do, with unrealistically poetic language. His words and scripts drip with poetry. He sees the downfall of a formerly proud Southern lifestyle, but he does not blame this on the government or society. And he doesn't hide from the ugliness of the soul of the fascist. "But Tennessee isn't political. He has no real social or political concern . . . He is a bohemian, and his interest is in the individual."[23] The world that Williams creates is full of unadorned failure. "He doesn't like a beach that doesn't have bums on it . . . Everybody is raw to the bone."[24]

Here is a quick list of the claims that Adler makes about Williams' characters:

- They are the best of Southern society, but they are in the process of being defeated.
- They have the capacity and options to save themselves through their own action, but they don't.
- They create their own reality and stay in it with determination.
- They have a right to run away from the changes in society because the changes are commercialism and competition that are destroying the beauty of life.
- They all fail, but each fails on their own terms.
- They fail in order to live. Tennessee Williams sees their failure as a virtue. They have escaped!
- They are humans at the end of their ability to cope with life.
- There are often foils in his plays: the person who can survive in the new reality is contrasted with the person who cannot. (Watch for other sorts of opposites pitted against each other.)
- The male character he creates most often is the fascist brute who would slit a throat without thinking about it. He is crude and violent. He is a powerful, mesmerizing bully. He resists being pushed around.
- The women in his plays are often vulnerable and self-deluded. They create a fairyland, and bring other characters into their worlds. They speak with artificiality.
- The character who is an artist is never weak. That character sees the truth. This character is "humble, he's pushed down, he's defrocked, because there's no need for a poet in society. But when Tennessee writes about him, . . . he is a fighter against middle class values, against his mother's values."[25]

If you have the opportunity to play a character in one of Williams' plays, you will serve the production, your own role, and society by learning as much as you can about the poetic realism of the place they come from. You must know that you can't trust the words of your character or the other characters. As you depict these people, can you show us a character that doesn't know they are failing? Can you fully grasp this world in which the playwright much prefers failure to success? Can you help the audience to identify with your character's inability to cope with the hand they have been dealt? Your work exploring the playwright's world will enrich your performance just as much as your other dramaturgical research.

Stella Adler's Legacy

Even though Adler developed her own method based on Stanislavski's work, in direct opposition to Strasberg, she is still often classified as a Method teacher. This is not right. She created a method of her own that stands alongside the work of other American acting teachers now recognized as Modern Acting teachers. In her time, she could not fully pull herself out of the grip of Strasberg. We are correcting that error in the twenty-first century. One scholar wrote,

> In Adler's case, she had questioned, but had been unable to challenge, Strasberg's training and direction for three years—until 1934, when she effectively contested his authority by showing that his interpretation of Stanislavsky was at odds with Stanislavsky's actual views. One might note that Adler was able to overturn Strasberg's interpretation only after she could reference notes from her period of study with Stanislavsky. That Adler needed to cite Stanislavsky directly is significant, for it reveals that her credentials as a respected actor . . . were not enough to debunk Strasberg's self-appointed role as the authority on Stanislavsky within the Group Theater.[26]

She was a respected teacher, whose students made a name for her. Her students include: Robert DeNiro, Warren Beatty, Martin Sheen, Benicio del Toro, Mark Ruffalo, and Marlon Brando. Brando never worked with Strasberg. Nevertheless, Brando's training was credited to Strasberg in Strasberg's obituary in the *Los Angeles Times*. Brando refuted this, writing,

> Stella Adler is much more than a teacher of acting. Through her work she imparts the most valuable kind of information—how to discover the nature of our own emotional mechanics and therefore those of others. It is troubling to me that because she has not lent herself to vulgar exploitations, as some other well-known so-called 'methods' of acting have done, her contributions to the theatrical culture have remained largely unknown, unrecognized, and unappreciated.[27]

Brando's statement does not call out Strasberg by name, but everyone understood who he was referring to. Ellen Adler, daughter to Stella Adler, in a letter to the editor *New York Times,* May 30, 1997 wrote,

> In 1943 Marlon Brando studied with Stella Adler. It is certain that what Ms. Adler taught in her class was the technique she had evolved. Marlon Brando never took acting classes again and so the interesting question is why Stella Adler's student [has] been put forth . . . as the very embodiment of Lee Strasberg's "Method" . . . Even more puzzling is why this myth persists decade after decade despite anything Brando or anybody else has said.[28]

Today the longevity of her method speaks for itself. While Strasberg's Method is obsolete, actors still attend conservatories that teach Adler's method. Rooted in deep research, physicalized actions, respect for mental health, and imaginative characterization, her method has stood the test of time.

Tips for taking this method further

- Start building your imagination by paying attention to everything and writing in a journal each night what you have seen during the day.
- Find a conservatory or workshop that teaches the Adler method of acting.

Discussion Starters and Journal Prompts

- Summarize Adler's struggles with acting before her visit with Stanislavski, her discoveries when she met him, and her lecture on returning to the United States. What impact do you think her work as an actor and student of the System and the Method have had on your acting training through today?
- How is Adler's method different from Stanislavski's? What methods does she help to clarify and expand for you in a way that is more useful than Stanislavski?

The Tools for your Toolbox

Activity—Finding a New Norm

- Ask your students to get out their journals.
- Say: "In your journal create a chart that has two columns: Assets and Faults. Take some time to fill in this chart with some very specific things about your bodies, speech skills, mind, and emotions. Write down things such as: Assets—Desire to get better, Good health, flexibility; and under Faults—Insecurity, poor diction, untrained body."
- "Stella Adler firmly believed that an actor must begin by being honest with themselves about what must be fixed, and then to be disciplined about working on their body, speech, mind, and emotions. She claimed that the actor's new norm should be to have a will to survive. She said, 'One's core must be made of steel. An actor has a right to survive, to grow as an artist. This entails a special strength, a new discipline, and self-awareness. Know what you want and have the courage to pursue it.'[29]"
- Discuss: "Talk to a partner. If you were Adler's student, what goals and activities would you create for yourself to improve as an actor? Do you think this approach is healthy?"

Activity—Reaching the Audience

- Have your students stand on the stage and simultaneously rehearse a monologue as if their audience is ten feet away.
- Repeat this activity with an audience fifty feet away, then one hundred feet away in the back of the balcony.
- Say: "Find the deep resonance in your voice, and use this every time you perform on stage."
- Discuss: "What is required of you to reach the audience? How does this change with distance?"

Activity—Physical Controls

- Have your students spread out in the space.
- Say: "Choose an ailment that would impact your ability to move well. Maybe a stiff knee or a broken finger in a splint."

- "Walk upstairs with your ailment."
- "Put on and take off a piece of clothing."
- "Dance to some music."
- "Pack up a suitcase or backpack."
- "Stella Adler asked her students to put on an ailment for several hours a day, for weeks at a time. This would provide them with the truth of the movement work. They would be able to reproduce this physicality at any time when they needed to, and the movement would be truthful and unconscious."
- "Work on a series of activities using muscular memory to complete imaginary tasks:
    - clean imaginary glasses, or your glasses that are already clean—focus on the detail of the task and imagined grime
    - open a jar that is too tightly closed
    - thread a real needle with imaginary thread and 'sew'
    - thread an imaginary needle with real thread and 'sew'
    - use an imaginary needle and thread to sew a hem on a real garment
    - clean mud off shoes
    - pour water from an imaginary pitcher into a glass
    - take imaginary feather or fuzzball off of your real clothing."
- Discuss: "How does using muscle memory help you as an actor? Do you think that practicing an ailment could be beneficial?"

Activity—Physicalizing to Cause Emotion to Emerge

- Ask your students to get into scene work groups and pull out their scripts.
- Say: "Find an emotion you think should come from a moment in the play."
- "Create physical actions you could do that might bring the emotion out of you."
- "Try the new physicalized actions to see if the emotions come without forcing or squeezing them out. If the emotions don't come, try a different physical action. The problem isn't with your ability to emote, but in the choice of actions."
- Discuss: "What worked for you in your rehearsal?"

Activity—Stop Faking!

- Provide each student with a needle, thread, button, scissors, and a garment. (Or substitute for a detailed project you know how to teach.)
- Teach them to unspool the correct amount of thread, cut it, thread the needle, tie a knot, stitch on the button, tie a knot and inspect their work.
- Say: "Now say your monologue while stitching on a button. No faking! It must be real thread, needle, etc."

- "Try again, but this time do the actions without the needle, thread, and button. Use the scissors, spool, and garment, but make the audience believe you are actually sewing."
- "This time add a complication to the process: perhaps the thread gets a knot, or you lose the needle."
- "Decide how your character feels about this task. Remember that you are not your character, but you can find your character inside you."
- "Think about your character's backstory. Are they familiar with this task? Or is it foreign to them? Why are they doing it? How are they doing it?"
- "What is the story with the garment? How is your character connected to the items and furniture on the set?"
- "Say your action to yourself. For example, 'I stitch on a button badly because I am distracted by my father's disapproval.'"
- "Try the task again, but with the motivation and backstory firmly in your mind."
- Discuss: "How does the work of personalizing an action, and learning not to fake it impact your performance? your emotions? How does this apply to other things you might do on stage?"

10

Sanford Meisner

The Person

Born in 1905 in Brooklyn, and the child of Hungarian Jewish immigrant parents, Sanford Meisner was called Sandy by his friends and colleagues. When he was only five, while his family was on a trip to the Catskills with the intention of helping Sanford's health, his three-year-old brother died after being given unpasteurized milk which caused bovine tuberculosis. Meisner's parents blamed him, since they wouldn't have gone to the country if he hadn't been ill. He was haunted by this death for his whole life. He said it was "the dominant emotional influence in my life, from which I have never, after all these years, escaped."[1]

As a first grader, Meisner told his teacher he wanted to be an actor, but rather than study acting, he played the piano. He trained in music at the Damrosch Institute of Music (which later became Julliard) for a year. After this, he worked briefly in New York's garment district for his father's fur business. His father wanted him to have a career there; instead, he pursued acting.

His first acting job was as an extra with the Theater Guild where he met the founders of the Group Theater: Harold Clurman, Cheryl Crawford, and Lee Strasberg. He was among the twenty-eight actors invited to be founding members. You have, most likely, been impacted by the theories and methods of this group of actors, directors, and teachers. Meisner claimed that if it weren't for the Group, he would have returned to the fur business. Meisner attended Stella Adler's famous lecture about what she had learned from Stanislavski and his methods. She explained that Stanislavski no longer worked in affective memory, but in given circumstances. At this revelation, a fog lifted from him. He had been oppressed by affective memory, and was pleased to break free from it. He helped to refocus the Group Theater into a stronger ensemble approach.

It was soon after this that Sanford Meisner began to teach at the Neighborhood Playhouse School of the Theatre. He took over leadership about a year later and remained with the school the rest of his life. At the Neighborhood Playhouse, Meisner created a two-year process for training actors. In his classroom, each student was gradually developed under his careful eye.

Meisner had much success as an actor with the Group Theater, but the only thing that fulfilled him was teaching. He loved analyzing the technique of his students. He continued teaching at the Neighborhood Playhouse until his death even though he suffered a series of health difficulties and a bad accident. He had to wear heavy glasses because of cataract surgeries, then had cancer of the larynx which took his voice. He learned to speak again with great difficulty by "inhaling air into his esophagus and releasing it in controlled burps."[2] This technique was a bit disturbing for people who were not used to it. He had to wear a microphone on his glasses to magnify and transmit his voice through a speaker on his desk, which gave it a disembodied quality. You can find documentary footage of him speaking in this way online. Just as he had settled into his routine with these tools in place, he was struck by a delivery truck. The injuries caused him to have to walk stiffly with a cane for the rest of his life. "Now, with all my limitations—I can't talk, my eyes are bad—I came back to this freezing city to teach again! Some people think they've talked me into it. That's not so. No one can talk me into anything that I don't want to do. I want to do it. I'm happiest when I'm teaching."[3] Meisner taught until his death in 1997 at the age of ninety-one.

The Method

Meisner claimed it takes twenty years to really become an actor. His students thought he was exaggerating, but he wasn't. Meisner had observed that while it only took two years to learn his method in his school, it took two decades to make that technique automatic for them.

Meisner took a great deal of inspiration from Stanislavski's System, but he created unique methods to give actors the tools to do the work quickly and with truthfulness. One of his students, Bill Esper, who worked with him for seventeen years, said that "Teaching Stanislavsky doesn't work for contemporary actors. The realities faced by twenty-first-century actors are completely different than those faced by Russian actors of the nineteenth century. In Stanislavsky's world, if actors wanted to rehearse a play for three years, they could."[4] Obviously, modern actors have to work quickly with some professional productions getting less than a month to rehearse. Actors who study Meisner acting develop the skills that make them available for truthful acting without the time it takes to do the depth of analysis the Stanislavski System requires.

Living Truthfully Under Imaginary Circumstances

Meisner's definition of acting is "living truthfully under imaginary circumstances."[5] In many ways, it is simpler to be present on stage. For instance, instead of pretending to read a letter, actually read it. This way, the audience gets to experience your eyes moving over the page in the appropriate way without you putting in a tremendous effort to fake reading. This is the essence of Meisner's method. This was also the first thing he taught his students. He taught them that if they were supposed to be listening to a scene partner, the easiest way to act is to actually listen rather than faking. Since the other actors on stage are the fuel an actor needs to perform, they must pay close attention to what is happening, staying receptive and open. In Meisner work, every part of the actor is welcome and seen by their scene partners. The greatest gift an actor can give to their scene partner is attention. Instead of perpetuating "partial attention culture" on stage, Meisner teaches us to attend fully. Actors sabotage themselves by focusing on being good actors instead of keeping their attention on the scene.

Another aspect of living truthfully under imaginary circumstances is learning to create "the first time" every time. The character doesn't know there will be a knock on the door in minute three of the second act, but the actor knows because that moment has been carefully rehearsed over and over. Meisner's method to solve this problem is to bring actors into the now. Rather than simply repeating the same actions over and over because they worked before, Meisner worked to help the actor find the *right now* each time in performance.

Emotions

In Meisner's method, emotions come from doing something, not from emoting. When our mind isn't occupied by trying to manufacture emotions, the emotions come easier. Many actors in his time used a technique of Strasberg's Method called affective memory that required actors to relive their past emotional experiences to bring out emotions on stage. Meisner was troubled by affective memory because it detracted from what Stanislavski called *communion*. Meisner believed the connection between actors on stage was the most important part of being in the moment. When actors used their past memories to recall emotions, they temporarily vacated the communion of the stage. He told Strasberg, "You introvert the already introverted."[6] He reasoned that reaching back to dredge up old experiences is not natural. Humans don't do that purposefully. Additionally, he reasoned, human memory isn't effective and reinterprets moments, reframing them until they are much different from reality.

Meisner firmly believed actors should stay present to themselves and their scene partners, allowing emotions to come from actions rather than the past. Because you are in the present with your partner, you don't have to try to repeat the same feeling each time. Different moments will hit you differently on different days. Your scene partner will find a new take on something that will hit you differently too. This is the beauty of trusting your partner and the moment to create truth and emotion on stage.

Get out of your head

Not only do Meisner actors get to be free from emoting, they are also encouraged to stay out of their heads. For example, Meisner did not like the extensive paraphrasing of the text done by the Group Theater. He felt this exercise put the actor in their heads and took them out of the moment. On Meisner's stage, the actor's impulses come from the heart, not the head. Their job on stage is to act on impulse, before thought. Instinctual responses to the stage environment and actors create honest moments in a way no well-thought-out response can.

Repetition

Meisner's most well-known, and very first actor training activity is repetition. Because it is first, and unique, it is often the only thing people remember about this method. It is a necessary entryway, but only a small portion of Meisner work. Meisner's repetition activities teach actors to really connect with each other. They learn to feed off the responses of their scene partners, creating an energetic dance between actors on stage.

Examples of these activities are given at the end of this chapter for you to try, but for now, imagine that your job in Meisner's class is to notice something about your scene partner and say it without censoring yourself. And your partner's job is to repeat what you said back to you without any pause for thought. For example:

"You have red hair."
"I have red hair."
"You have red hair."
"I have red hair."

Imagine your instructor asks you to do this for twenty minutes without a break. You will likely feel like you are wasting your time. What is this teaching you? This activity, according to Meisner, is teaching you to work outside yourself so you don't have time to watch yourself act. You only have time to be yourself, not a character. You don't need to be Hamlet to notice the red hair. *You* notice the red hair. This work is training you to play with your impulses which are the source of all creativity.

The next step in repetition is to make assumptions about your scene partner in repetition. For example:

"You have red hair."
"(sigh) I have red hair."
"You don't like your red hair."
"I *don't* like my red hair."

The repetition turns into real speech, allowing one actor to make assumptions. Perhaps they are wrong. Without censoring yourself, your job is to respond. Let's try that again:

"You have red hair."
"(sigh) I have red hair."
"You don't like your red hair."
"I *do too* like my red hair."
"You REALLY like your red hair."
"I REALLY like my red hair."
"You really like your red hair."
"You wish you had my red hair."
"I do wish I had your red hair."

All of this is done in the moment, on instinct, without taking time to think about responses. You are doing these exercises correctly when you no longer plan your answers, speaking instinctually. "'You try to be logical, as in life. You try to be polite, as in life. May I say, as the world's oldest living teacher, *Fuck* polite!' Meisner says passionately. 'You have one thing to do, and that is to pick up the repetition from your partner.'"7

Larry Silverberg, who has written some of the best books on the Meisner Technique, compares this repetition work to practicing scales when you are an instrumentalist. The skills built by the repetition of the scales lead to virtuosity in musicianship, and eventually they aren't needed anymore. You don't start your first piano lesson by playing Mozart for an audience any more than you should start acting by performing on the stage. The same is true of Meisner's repetition exercises. "Ultimately, the rules will fall away, the original structure will no longer be needed because the skills encouraged by the repetition have been absorbed into the actor's instrument and the actor is unleashed into the zone of total freedom."[8]

Repetition isn't an excuse for being mean, but it does require honesty. In real life, you edit yourself and try not to hurt the feelings of others. You aren't honest when you leave a boring party by telling the host that it was a terrible party. You want them to still like you. In acting you must stop yourself from trying to appear nice. Say what you mean. This is a skill polite society doesn't teach, so you have to practice.

After working on unchanging repetitions for a while, your Meisner instructor will begin to allow you to change the dialog under four circumstances:

1. You give an honest answer to a question instead of repeating.
2. You get exhausted by the pileup of repetitions and force a change.
3. You have a point of view about something, and you say it.
4. You respond to your partner's behavior.

The scenes you work on will now change. Obstacles and challenges are added gradually to allow you to apply your skills of reacting to your partner with honesty.

When Meisner reflected on the reasoning he had for creating these repetition activities, he says they sprang from observing and participating in improvisations based on the text in Stanislavski's System, which he felt was "all intellectual nonsense." He created an activity that removed intellectuality to get away from "mental manipulation and get to where the impulses come from. And I began with the premise that if I repeat what I hear you saying, my head is not working. I'm listening, and there is an absolute elimination of the brain."[9] He went on to say that actors don't need to know how to make conversation. Instead, they need to react to something in the other actor.

The Pinch and the Ouch

Two key rules of Meisner's acting technique are "Don't do anything unless something happens to make you do it." and "What you do doesn't depend on you; it depends on the other fellow."[10] So, wait for your partner to say or do something and then react. That's what repetition teaches you. Don't pre-plan. Let your partner provide the *pinch* that justifies the *ouch*. If you wait for the pinch to provide the ouch, then you will be acting truthfully. This does not mean the responsibility for your good acting depends on your scene partner to cause your response. It does mean that your reaction should come from the relationship between you in the moment.

Improvisations

As a Meisner actor continues to work, they transition to improvisations that begin with repetition. Acting students begin with "taking the first thing" and then allow the repetition to grow into a scene. This challenge is not to make a scene out of the repetition, but to let one happen. William Esper, a prominent Meisner teacher, suggests surfing as a metaphor for this moment by moment improvisation:

The only thing you can control is paddling out to a place where you know a wave might rise. Then you work moment to moment in order to see what the wave has to offer. Sometimes it turns out to be a dud . . . If you're lucky, you pop up onto your board and start to ride. The wave has its own life, a life that you can't control. You'd come to ruin if you attempt to impose your will too profoundly over the flow of ten thousand gallons of raging water. Your job isn't to command . . . Your job is to *surf* . . . You never know what'll happen next. Who cares? That's never the point. The point is to surf—no more, no less. Improvise. Follow the truth as it develops. Enjoy each ride because it only happens once.[11]

The creation of scenes using improvisation creates actors focused on each other and living in the impulse of the moment. Esper says actors have to learn to stop stifling their impulses. "Stop judging them. Get out of their way and follow wherever they lead. When people are spontaneous, they're always charming. They're interesting to watch because they're really and truly alive; we never know what they'll do next because *they* never know what they're going to do next."[12]

Fast and Flat

After improvisations, actors in Meisner's classes are given their first scripts to work on before coming to class. Their first assignment is to read it silently. They will immediately have thoughts about how to play it, and Meisner encouraged them to allow the thoughts to happen, but let them go. The next step is to copy the scene into a journal without any punctuation or stage directions because Meisner felt punctuation is not useful to an actor. Humans don't punctuate actual speech, so getting rid of it frees actors to speak naturally.

Next it is time to get off book. At this point, the memorization must be by rote without any emotion, meaning, or inflection. Meisner describes this type of memorization as "fast and flat," like a machine. This way of working eliminates the emotional cadences we tend to memorize. When you memorize fast and flat, you don't store any preconceived ideas of what the text means, this way on stage emotion can come from responding to your partner in the moment, and every performance can be different.

At Rehearsal

A Meisner actor comes to class memorized, emotionally alive, but without pre-planning for the scene. Meisner recommends warming up before rehearsals or performances by tossing something back and forth with your partners on each line while saying the lines with no emotion or pauses. If anyone messes up or pauses, go back to the beginning of the scene.

After warming up, actors sit in chairs facing each other and speak their lines as if they are having a private conversation with each other, focusing on the other just as in repetition activities, without trying to control the scene.

> The urge to control a scene is an actor's biggest enemy. It takes a big dose of actor's faith to get you into free fall, but it's always worth the trip. And it's the trip that only ever really matters. Give yourself up to every moment with a sense of reckless abandonment. There's no greater gift you can give to an audience, and no greater gift you can give to yourself.[13]

It's important to do the exercise exactly the way you've always done it. Focus on impulses rather than thoughts. The script will tempt you to return to your old ways of acting. Don't do it. Stay with your partner and out of your head.

After class Meisner recommends getting together with your scene partner in public somewhere and running your scene in several locations, focusing on reacting to your partner and your environment. Don't worry about character development. Really speak and really listen without forcing anything to happen. See where the scene takes you.

Character Development

Character development is not really a part of the Meisner Method. As you work on your character, you begin and end with developing the emotional life of the character because the emotional life *is* the character. You develop this emotional life by using your imagination. Meisner compared this process to daydreaming: your inner life is transformed and humming with imagination.

Remember Stanislavski's *Magic If*? This part of Meisner's work is similar. Meisner called it particularization. He talked about using the circumstances of the play, but also relying on outside thoughts when the circumstances don't work for you. For example, imagine you must play a part where you are scandalized because you discover another character fathered a child out of wedlock and you must say "Shame!" to him. You personally probably don't really care about the marital status of the parent, but if your character can find a substitute particularization to work with, you will be able to achieve the necessary emotion. For example, perhaps you imagine that the child is the result of incest. Now can you find the scandal? This tool could be quite useful for you any time you must react in a way you don't naturally feel within a story.

Put another way, "actors are wonderful liars ... but the difference is this: Their lies are always grounded in truth, and always—*always!*—their lies serve the purpose of the art."[14] If you take the time to figure out how you would respond if you were in the character's place, your resulting emotions are imaginary, and not necessarily ones you have had in real life. "If you allow it freedom—with no inhibitions, no proprieties—to *imagine* what would happen ... your imagination is, in all likelihood deeper and more persuasive than the real experience ... we can recall from our past."[15] Meisner never asks his actors to use their own past experiences to create emotions. Imagination is more powerful than memory.

It is tricky. It takes time to learn how to prepare your character to live emotionally. Meisner knows that this work isn't easy because from childhood we have been taught to restrain our emotions to follow social norms. In acting it is better to let go of boundaries and freely express emotions.

Meisner teaches using the text can help create your character as well, "The text is like a canoe ... and the river on which it sits is the emotion. The text floats on the river. If the water of the river is turbulent, the words will come out like a canoe on a rough river. It all depends on the flow of the river which is your emotion."[16]

All of your preparation is with the goal of being alive and available to your impulses and emotions on stage. If you have the emotional fullness in the moment you are acting, the emotion will impact both you and your audience. But, Meisner teaches, if the emotion doesn't come, "don't bother; just say the lines as truthfully as you are capable of doing. You can't fake emotion. It immediately exposes the fact you ain't got it."[17] Your emotional preparation has to get you through the door and onto the stage emotionally alive, but then your interactions with your scene partner take over.

Relationships on Stage

As you work with others on stage, simply saying "we are married" won't do the trick. You have to make the relationship very specific. William Esper writes the example of Nora and Torvald Helmer in *A Doll's House*. Just knowing they are husband and wife doesn't tell you nearly enough. To bring that relationship to life, you have to realize their relationship is like an indulgent father with his beautiful little daughter. He infantilizes her just as her actual father did. She grows up during the course of the play, and has to leave home. The specifics of what their courtship and early married life were like are essential to understanding the play. And if the actors don't add that specificity, the audience won't understand the relationship either.

But what if your scene partner gives you nothing? Then you still do your job. You can work off the meaning of their words. Or you can act as if your partner is giving you the emotionally full performance you need.

A Word of Warning

William Esper warns us:

> One pitfall of the Meisner Technique is that the beginning exercises are easy to learn and easy to teach. This attracts a lot of under qualified practitioners. They teach versions of Repetition and claim that they're teaching Meisner's work without progressing to the next steps, all of which are necessary to build genuinely accomplished actors capable of creating characters with deep and compelling inner lives.[18]

The work you will do on Meisner in this chapter only scratches the surface of the tools you could obtain with two years of study. The progression of the work is successful for most who take it on, but it does require a lot of time up front to learn and embody the work. This chapter does not detail much of the latter half of the method. That you will have to find in your future work.

Sanford Meisner's Legacy

Sandy Meisner was a beloved and long-lived teacher who believed that actors must remain present on stage, responding to their impulses and their partners in order to create authentic moments on stage. His methods are practical and accessible to anyone who is willing to leave other ideas about acting and give themselves to the process. Many actor training programs teach only his method, and many of his students are well-known actors of film and stage. His method has stood the test of time.

Tips for taking this method further

- Begin working on your skills of taking the first thing in your daily life. Notice what you notice first about the coffee shop you go to, your roommate, your waiter, etc. As you encounter your life, practice bringing awareness to your responses to the world around you. This might just make your life richer in the process of attempting to become a more present and available acting partner.
- Buy and read Larry Silverberg's *Meisner Complete* and Meisner's *Sanford Meisner on Acting*.
- Research acting programs and workshops in Meisner Technique and enroll in one of them. Some colleges and universities specialize in Meisner Technique, but there are also a plethora of non-credit-bearing classes in most urban centers.

Discussion Starters and Journal Prompts

- Summarize Meisner's method for someone who doesn't know it. Be sure to both explain repetition and why that is not the crux of his method. What is the purpose of starting that way?
- How do you think studying Meisner's method for two years would help you? Do you believe his claim that it takes twenty years to become an actor?

The Tools for your Toolbox

Activity—Warm-up

- Have your students sit in a circle and choose a person to start the activity.
- Say: "Your mission is to tell a story as one person so there are no gaps and no planning ahead. You must all work as one to tell this story so that the story takes you somewhere, not vice versa. The story must have two main characters."
- "As a group, get in as tight as you can and close your eyes."
- "Tell a story as a group. One word at a time, moving clockwise. The first person says one word, and the second says the next, etc. If someone says two words, start over. Continue until you can't stand it anymore, and then continue anyway."
- Afterwards discuss: "Can you control the story? How did you know what to say in the moment? Did you have to listen harder than you usually do on stage? What implications could this have for your work?"

Activity—Repetition: Taking the first thing

- Have students pair up and face each other sitting in chairs with a foot or two between their knees. Set the pairs up in lines so there are two lines facing each other.

- Say: "Everyone on my left look away from the other then turn back to your partner and say something about the first physical trait you notice about your partner. For example: 'glasses.' This is called *taking the first thing*."
- "Everyone on my right, do the same thing."
- "Did you actually say the first thing you noticed? It is important to notice when you censor yourself and bring it to your own awareness."
- "Everyone on my left, rotate so that each partner has a new person facing them. Take the first thing. Then let your partner take the first thing."
- Repeat this activity until each person is again facing their first partner. Leave them with this partner for the remainder of the class time. This gets some of the giggles out and they get practice with taking the first thing multiple times.
- Say: "This time, after the first partner says the first thing they notice, have the second partner repeat it. So, if the first partner says 'gray hoodie' the response would be 'gray hoodie' continually."
- Allow this to go on for a minute or two, giving them a chance to feel the monotony and stay focused on their partner anyway.
- Say: "Did you notice the words changing or the way they were said changing? Did your partner add a word or a sound to the statement? As that happens, simply accept and repeat what you heard. Be available to whatever happens, not attempting to circle back to the 'correct' phrase. It is in the past, so continue to work with what is in the present."
- "Be careful not to copy the intonation or style of your partner's voice. Just let the words come out of your mouth. Don't suppress your emotions as they repeat. Let the emotions come and express themselves. Those emotions are coming from the connection you have with your partner. This is the goal!"
- "Get rid of the desire to entertain your partner. No one should try to be interesting. This is manipulation, and a bad habit that must be broken."
- After a few minutes, say: "Did you have pauses between your words? Take those out. Stop thinking and just react!"
- Tell them Silverberg's rules: "1. Don't do the repetition, let the repetition do you. 2. Trying to do the exercise right is not doing the exercise right, 'trying' is always a step removed from simply 'doing'. 3. There is no need to keep the repetition on track because there is no track. 4. There is nowhere to get to so you might as well be there."[19]
- Continue the repetitions for about twenty minutes.

Activity—Repetition: Real Talk

- Continue the repetition work with partners.
- Say: "Use simple sentences when you notice something about your partner. Instead of repeating 'glasses,' say 'You are wearing blue glasses.' or 'You have glasses.' or even 'On you there are glasses blue.'"
- "First partner, look away and take the first thing by making a statement. Second partner, repeat it."

- "Who was speaking the truth in the repetition activity? Only the first partner was speaking the truth in most cases, right? It is unlikely that both partners are wearing blue glasses. Speaking the truth is important in repetition activities. It's time to modify your repetition. If the first person says, 'You have blue glasses on.' The response should now be, 'I have blue glasses on.' Now both partners are speaking from a truthful point of view."
- "Work this way for a couple of minutes, changing the repetition when needed to keep speaking from a truthful point of view, or to reflect changes your partner introduced into the repetition."
- "Do not pause to think. If your partner says something you disagree with, disagree without pause. If they say, 'You look like a frog.' Respond, 'Hey! I don't look like a frog.' Then, 'You don't look like a frog?' and so on. What we know takes no thought, so don't take time to censor your thoughts in repetition. Just respond with your instinct. Allow the repetition to go where it goes."

Activity—Repetition: Three Moment Game

- Set the students up for repetitions. Start with a sample pair for the others to watch before doing the activity independently.
- Say: "Think of a provocative question to ask your partner that will create an emotional response. For example, If I asked you 'Why do you hate men?' I would get an emotional response."
- "Partner A, ask the question, Partner B repeat the question back, permitting yourself to have whatever reaction to the question you have."
- "Partner A, observe the reaction of your partner and deal with it out loud by stating your observations of the response directly to your partner. For example 'You squirmed when I asked the question and seemed annoyed with me. That made you mad.'"
- "This is the end of the game. It is simply reflecting emotions back to your partner."
- "Play this game with your partners, asking a few questions each. Remember we are not actually interested in the answers to the questions, but the behavior that the question evoked."
- "Stop and reflect on if you have been using qualifiers in your answers (it seems like you are mad, or it looks like you are embarrassed)? If so, stop. It takes courage to be direct. In real life, we use these qualifiers to be direct and give the other person a way out. In acting, we don't give our partner a way out.'"
- "Continue the three moment game, but let the three moments lead into repetition: 'That made you mad.' 'That made me mad.' 'That made you mad.' and so on."
- "Pause your repetition. You now have permission to change the repetition as the behavior of your partner changes. Don't think! Respond to what your partner gives you. Don't give the ouch without a pinch. This is 'working off' your partner. Let it happen. Be aware of when you censor yourself, and try to stop. Usually when a repetition goes on for a long time without change it is because you had thoughts you didn't share, or because you weren't really listening."

- Discuss: "What was that experience like? Do you enjoy making your partner stay in the moment with you and experience their feelings? Does it feel interactive even if you don't talk about what caused the reaction?"

Activity—Knock on the Door

- Start this activity with two volunteers to demonstrate, then repeat the steps with everyone working at once.
- Divide the group into pairs, and each pair into an A and B.
- Say: "Person A is outside the room. Person B is in the room."
- "Stay in the moment. You don't know what will happen. You both simply exist. When you hear a knock, you don't know who it is. Your job is to simply respond to the knock. When you knock, you don't know who will respond. You just knock."
- "Do the same repetition activity you did before with the exception that you are standing at a door instead of in chairs. One person knocks, the other answers, someone takes the first thing, and the repetition begins."
- Discuss: "Did Person B invite Person A in or block their entrance? How did that feel? Did the dialog match the feeling of dis-ease that was created by standing at a door instead of sitting?"
- Say: "We are now going to take it to the next level. Person A find a task to do that is specific, and real, without mime. For example, you could try to balance a pen on its tip or make a pyramid out of white board markers. Person A, imagine a mob boss is watching you over security camera and will shoot your dog if you can't complete the task." (Note: Whatever task you give must come from a recent piece of information, for example, they just got off the phone with the mob boss and immediately started working on it just before the knock.)
- "Person B, wait for a minute and then knock on the door. Your job is to convince Person A to stop working on their task and leave the building because it is going to explode in four minutes. You are Person A's sibling who lives ten miles away. You just found out about a bomb in the building and need to get them to leave. You are not allowed to discuss your given circumstances directly, but instead use repetition."
- Discuss: "Did this activity force you to focus on the behaviors and attitudes of your scene partner rather than the storyline or scenario? Did repetition heighten the conflict? What discoveries did you make? How could training like this benefit an actor in a scripted situation?"

Activity—Repetition: Doing Something

- Have one partner sit in a chair, and hand the other partner a stick or broom handle.
- Say: "Balance the end of the stick on the tip of your non-dominant thumb so your thumb is pointing to the ceiling, and do it as if your life depends on not dropping it."
- "The sitting partner give the balancer some time to get into the activity, then begin repetition by taking the first thing just like when you were sitting together."

- "The balancer should focus both on balancing the stick AND the repetition."
- "Switch places and try again: balance for a while, then begin repetition."
- "Come get a deck of cards. This time try the activity while one person is trying to create a five story house of cards. You should each create your own high stakes motivation such as your dog will die if you don't complete the task in three minutes."
- Discuss: "Was the sitting partner the one that did most of the subject changes? Were you fully doing what you were doing on stage? How can this apply to your work in scenes?"

Activity—Fast and Flat

- Give your students a short scene to take home prior to this activity.
- Say: "Please memorize these lines 'fast and flat'—which means you should not attempt to figure out what they mean, or analyze them in any way. By the next class you should be able to rapidly repeat your lines with no inflection or emotion. Work alone on learning the lines, no assistance allowed."
- When the students arrive in class, say: "Run your scenes with each other, focusing on listening, and allowing the circumstances of the play and your scene partner's words to create emotion in the moment on stage."
- Discuss: "Is there wisdom in not spending time working on inflection separate from your scene partner? Does it help you be alive on stage and in the moment with your partner?"

11

Viola Spolin

The Person

Viola Spolin was born in 1906 to Russian Jewish immigrants. She grew up surrounded by her extended family that loved to gather, play games, and perform for each other. She and her cousins free-ranged around dangerous areas of downtown Chicago, creating their own games and fond memories. Her love of theatre came both from her family performances and from attending the opera with her father who was a police officer on duty at the performances. As a high school student, she was athletic and non-conforming. She sometimes wore men's clothing and cut her hair short. She also wore bright red lipstick and drove around in an old Model T Ford truck. She was nicknamed "Spark" by her friends, and it was an appropriate name for her, since she had a talent for creating fun for everyone wherever she went.

After high school Spolin worked with Neva Boyd at Hull House in Chicago using games to work with children living in poverty. Boyd's philosophy was instrumental in the development of Spolin's. Boyd believed that non-competitive games helped immigrant children to learn language, socialization, and cooperation because games aren't fun if the rules aren't agreed upon and followed. Spolin discovered these games brought life to the children, and increased their creativity. Over time, Viola Spolin took Neva Boyd's ideas and further developed them into a system of theatre games, first just for children, and then also including adults.

During this same period of time, Spolin married her high school sweetheart and gave birth to two boys: Paul and William. She divorced when the boys were small, but continued to host improvisation nights at her home while she was stuck at home raising her children. She told one historian that she liked to prop her baby up so he could watch their games.

After her work with Boyd, Spolin acted in Chicago area productions and studied dramatics in night school at DePaul University. She also worked as a stage manager and acted in a Heinz show five times a day during the 1934 World's Fair. In 1935 she left her children in the care of her family and went to study with the Group Theater. She worked with these prominent theatre people for a while, but missed her children, so she returned to Chicago.

Back in Chicago, Spolin rented a lakeshore mansion with a group of other divorced, working mothers so they could communally raise their children. They called their home The Educational Playroom. These mothers figured out a system that kept the children fed, cared for, and allowed the women to pursue their careers. One of Spolin's children, Paul, said they received visits from a who's who of theatre leaders in that home.

Spolin worked at the WPA Recreational Project in those years, training teachers how to use dance and creative drama as teaching tools. They were amazed at the effectiveness of her methods. She was promoted to drama supervisor and worked with children and immigrants in low-income neighborhoods, incorporating the benefits of play. She knew children didn't need acting techniques. She found that play reached across cultural differences and language barriers. She said: "The games emerged out of necessity. I didn't sit at home and dream them up. When I had a problem (directing) I made up a game. Then another problem came up, I just made up a new game."[1] Likewise, when she was short on students, she rounded them up from the streets, inviting them to transfer their games from the street to the stage. These games became public productions. In one *Chicago Daily News* article, the author, Howard Vincent O'Brien wrote:

> Few will ever see this play, and I doubt if any professional critic will ever hear of it. Yet for importance I think it is worth about a dozen Broadway successes rolled into one . . . There were about 150 people in the cast—Italians, Greeks, Mexicans, Negroes . . . They were all ages and both sexes. What they were doing is not exactly a play. It was perhaps what is called a revue. But its form doesn't matter. The important thing about it was that it was conceived, written and played by the people themselves.[2]

Spolin remarried in 1940, and together, the couple and her teenage boys moved to California. During the Second World War, Spolin worked as a riveter in a San Francisco shipyard and conducted theatre workshops on the side.

She further developed her methods after the war, establishing the Young Actors Company in Hollywood which trained young actors while also functioning as a professional repertory theatre. It was here that she replaced the word "actor" with the word "player," and the word "feeling" with "physicalizing." Spolin was troubled by the way Stanislavski's methods were being taught, causing all sorts of blocks, over-seriousness, and angst. She believed adults had stopped playing, and this was a serious mistake which robbed them of their joy. Her technique is full of anti-authoritarian philosophy and emphasizes collaborative interpersonal work.

Spolin's oldest son, Paul Sills, gathered a group of actors at the University of Chicago and taught them using his mother's methods. They invited Spolin to come direct a play and to teach workshops. This group of actors eventually founded the Compass Theater which later founded The Second City, a premier theatre company that now has locations in three major cities. In 1959, Sills invited his mother to teach workshops for The Second City. She later joked that a two-week visit turned into a seven-year stay. She became the director of workshops at Second City as well as teaching improv to local children with her son. Audience members were invited to join the games, reflecting her belief in the democratization of theatre.

Spolin continued to teach, collaborate with her son, and write about her methods after she returned to Los Angeles. Spolin lived a long and playful life until her death in 1994 at the age of eighty-eight.

The Method

Viola Spolin's method of acting encourages play and experimentation. She teaches that anyone who wants to, can become stageworthy. Spolin teaches that you get better and more talented at acting by opening yourself up to more experience. These experiences are intellectual, physical, and intuitive. She joins the ranks of theatre professionals who found that all humans are capable of learning to act effectively. She also realized her methods could democratize teaching ability. For some naturally gifted individuals, teaching and acting come easily. But these individuals are rare. With a process like Spolin's, anyone who is open can become an actor or acting teacher. It requires bravery to step out into the unknown together, but "Though many may pull away fearful of leaving the familiar cage, some of us will find each other and together preserve the vital spirit of the theater."[3]

Improvisation

At the core of Spolin's method is improvisation, because improvisation is freeing. It forces you to fully engage the present moment with your community of players. She writes, "Acting requires presence. Being there. Playing produces this state. Just as ballplayers in any sport are present in the playing, so must all theater members be present in the moment of playing, in present time."[4] When an actor practices improvising, it teaches them to stay alert to the present moment, ready to pivot based on what their fellow players do. While many acting methods ask you to carefully plan each moment on stage, Spolin's method asks you to instead act intuitively on stage. She called this "direct experience," the ultimate goal of acting.

As an actor, your greatest chance at finding the present moment is to open up to and follow your intuition. The spontaneity of acting on intuition is dependent on being in an environment where you can freely experience and express yourself. Improv is the perfect avenue for finding this freedom. In order to be successful in improv, you must be free of your inhibitions, your attitudes, your opinions, and the same must be true of your scene partners.

This work in improvisation will eventually help you in scripted and blocked work, but at first, you will focus on being in the moment on stage, playing with your fellow players. This is the realm where you explore the all-important WWW, or Where, Who, and What. By improvising, you learn to communicate through your behavior who your character is, where they are, and what they are doing.

Spolin taught her players that communicating the Who includes portraying age not by stereotyping the character, but by portraying an attitude towards life. An old woman can play a young girl by skipping up to a "bus stop" and chewing gum, looking around at her environment, playing with her hair, etc. An eleven-year-old girl can be a business man by focusing on taking notes on a notepad while impatiently looking at his watch and looking for the missing bus with frustration.

Spolin warns against delving into conflict in improvisation too soon. Actors must first learn how to focus well in the WWW of the scene without delving into their own psychology. The addition of conflict early on might feel like acting, but if the inner motion of the actor is not on physicalization of the character, they won't really be acting, but working out their own conflicts in the moment. Once an actor is adept at focus, they can then move on into conflict work.

Games

Spolin taught improv skills through games. She said that improv provided the perfect tool for developing acting skills because games open actors up in a way that allows them to learn skills. In a game, your ingenuity and inventiveness are available to you as long as you follow the rules of the game. It seems a bit counterintuitive to think that rules free you up as a performer, however, structure, through rules of a game, actually creates expressive freedom. Within the structure, agreed upon by the group, a problem can be solved collaboratively with everyone paying keen attention to the impulses of the members of the game.

In order for you to grow personally as an actor, you must progress as a team with your fellow players. Every person in the group must give full participation. If any member of your team dominates, it destroys the growth and pleasure of the others in the group. Competition is actually good for a group if the competition is for the group to find a solution to a problem together. If the individual is trying to "win," they have to tear down or show up other actors. If, instead, the whole group is working for a "win" in a scene together, the excitement and collaboration will fuel growth for everyone.

This is why Spolin believed that authoritarian situations stifle growth. She believed the teacher must be on a level playing field with their players. They might have 1,000 solutions for a problem, but if the players feel free to find the 1,001st solution because of the nature of their environment, they will be able to grow. This doesn't mean Spolin felt the teacher is unnecessary. Rather, she taught teachers to see themselves as the guide in the room with deeper experience in the technical and artistic aspects of theatre.

Using Space Awareness to Achieve Direct Experience

Spolin taught actors to work together, but emphasized that we are each responsible for ourselves and finding our way into the present tense. One tool she taught to help players was taking responsibility for their relationship with the space. She taught them to build a relationship with their playing space by actively choosing to notice and feel the space and how it impacts them. Spolin wrote, "Each player becomes a receiver/sending instrument capable of reaching out beyond the physical self and the immediate environment. As water supports and surrounds marine life, space substance surrounds and support us."[5] She recommends starting this work by imagining you are exploring the space as a fish would explore the sea, feeling the support of the water around and through them.

She used slow-motion movement to get her actors to feel the space because that made space more tangible. As an actor, if you are struggling to understand how to feel the space, she suggests you work on your own in slow motion. It will bring the space into focus for you as you exaggerate the resistance of the air around you, even breathing and blinking in slow motion.

Curing Acting Obstacles

Spolin said that direct experience is the cure for acting obstacles. Do you ever find yourself focused on how you are being perceived? If so, you are probably failing to truly be present. You are trapped in someone else's mind. Or perhaps you get stuck with a thought that you won't be ready by opening night. In that moment, you are living in the future, not the now. You are not directly experiencing the present. This can be changed, bringing you freedom to explore without your self-critic causing you trouble.

Spolin teaches actors to find this freedom by truly exploring themselves and their environment in the moment. "It is necessary to become part of the world around us and make it real by touching it, seeing it, feeling it, tasting it, and smelling it—direct contact with the environment . . . The personal freedom to do so leads us to experiencing and thus to self-awareness (self-identity) and self-expression . . . Very few of us are able to make this direct contact with ourselves."[6]

Spolin said there are five obstacles that prevent you from having direct experiences:

1 Approval/Disapproval—This is the need to be validated by the approval of others. In our effort to avoid being "bad," we lose the ability to explore possible solutions to our problem. When this obstacle is in your way, you hear your inner critic say things like "The director hates me" or "My scene partner thinks I'm the best" or "I need to memorize these lines so my director will like me."
2 Self-Pity—This obstacle comes in the form of a debilitating feeling that you can't accomplish something, stubbornness, or excuses. In this obstacle, you hear your inner critic say things like "I don't have the time" or "They want too much from me" or "I won't compromise" or "She's the director's favorite."
3 Success/Failure—We have a cultural obsession with being successful and eliminating failure. Our inner voices that are crippling us tell us "You're a failure" or "You can't succeed." It is your job in dealing with this obstacle to transcend a black and white outlook. Instead of focusing on success or failure, focus on the problem you are trying to solve. You can accept any outcome of your effort, because your intuition helps you overcome any obstacle.
4 Attitudes—Attitudes make it difficult to directly experience and work on a problem. If you catch yourself approaching a problem with a chip on your shoulder, you are creating an obstacle for yourself. You can choose a calm attitude to work through obstacles rather than freaking out.
5 Fear—Fear gets in the way of being in the moment. It stirs up anxiety and creates confusion and self-doubt. Fear sounds like "I don't know what to do" or "I'm helpless!" or "I can't move."

Spolin identified two main ways to overcome the negativity of these five obstacles. The first is direct experience itself. When you catch yourself saying one of the statements in the list above, side coach yourself.

1 Tell yourself to pause.
2 Choose a new focus, for example: slow motion. In a state of focus on slow motion, you will directly experience connection with the space and the moment you are in.
3 The obstacles have no power over you when you are focused and connected to right now.

Her second strategy is a game she called Scoring. Scoring helps you identify and dissolve these obstacles by scoring yourself for a set period of time. Your job is not to fix yourself, but simply to observe. This is how the game is played:

1. Get a notebook and keep it close while you are playing.
2. Observe your inner voice creating an obstacle for you.
3. Name what the obstacle is and write it in your notebook. The second time and beyond when this obstacle comes to mind, make hash marks after the word. This moment of scoring is the "pause." (If you notice a thought when you don't have your notebook handy, you can create your pause by coughing or making some other noise.) In the moment of pause you are indicating you know what is happening, resulting in self-awareness and direct experience.
4. If the feeling or thoughts increase after you score them, make more marks.
5. If a different feeling or thought replaces it, score that.
6. Keep observing yourself without judgment. Spolin says, "Don't take responsibility, take note!"[7] In fact, don't justify, interpret, or analyze the obstacle, just notice what is happening in the right now moment. Directly experience the moment, and the obstacle will dissolve.

In this game, you accomplish a few things. (1) You detach from the obstacle when you score it, letting it dissolve. (2) The hold of the past negative emotions is interrupted. (3) You take personal responsibility for your emotions and behaviors. (4) You find yourself in the present, focused on scoring the game. She suggests you can play Scoring for all sorts of other things: boredom, overexplaining, mannerisms you dislike, being too helpful, thinking "I wish." You can choose to focus on one behavior to score on a "theme day." This scoring work is between you and you, and it is "not designed to force you to change ... matters will take care of themselves without your interference. Don't change. Don't not change. Just keep score."[8]

Gibberish and the Voice

Language has a physiological structure you can play with. Spolin taught the use of gibberish words for teaching actors many skills, forcing them to communicate through actions and tone rather than through words. She suggests that if you struggle with gibberish at first, it is likely you rely mostly on words instead of experiencing directly.

She taught her players to experiment with sending their sounds through space, forming first gibberish, then words, then spelling the words, then emphasizing vowels and consonants. By visualizing the sounds being supported in space and landing in specific locations, you can gain control of your voice and articulation. Rather than focusing on the formation of the words as most acting teachers do, she placed the emphasis on imagining the sounds in action.

Script Work

Spolin had a few unorthodox rules for work on scripts. For instance, she felt it was a bad idea to take a script home to work on lines. The Spolin actor's only homework outside of the rehearsal room or stage is to experience life, to open themself up to observation and action in the world.

Spolin recommends actors turn their scripts into sides. A side is a script which only has one character's lines and the last few words of each of their cues from other actors without stage directions. This way, when on stage in rehearsal, actors won't be tempted to silently read their partner's lines on the script, pulling them out of connection with their scene partners. With sides prepared, actors are forced to actively listen and react while waiting for a cue to speak.

Emotion

As an actor in the Spolin universe, your own past emotional experiences cannot be used to create emotion on stage. Spolin explains that using the stage as a place to work out old emotions is psychodrama, or drama therapy, a therapeutic and legitimate use of theatre, but not appropriate for audience's entertainment. When an actor is using theatre to work on a personal emotion or trauma, they are not in the room directly experiencing with the rest of the ensemble.

Instead, she says, "The emotion we need for the theater can only come out of a fresh experience ... This prevents the use of old emotion from past experiences being used in a fresh moment of experience."[9] As you work on stage, you can create fresh emotions each time by playing in the joy of the WWW collectively with your fellow players.

In fact, Spolin used the term "inner action" instead of emotions. Inner actions are physicalized, creating outer action. For example, an actor should not first say "I'm angry!" then stomp a foot and grimace. The inner action happens first. Spolin gives the example of hunger. The first thing that happens when you become hungry is an inner action that is a physical response in your body. Your salivary glands activate and your stomach growls. Then, you go to the refrigerator. The last thing that happens is the inner dialog of "What do I want to eat?" The inner action comes first, motivating the action, which motivates the text. Coach yourself to first physicalize your inner actions for more genuine moments of acting.

Character Development

Character work is approached last in Spolin's classroom. This is because she emphasized actors' need to relate to other actors, not the character. Just as in team sports we play with other people, not their uniforms, on stage both actors know the other is also playing. The actors working off of each other do not react to the character, but the other actor.

In rehearsal, Spolin led activities in learning to create characters in which actors would choose six or more character qualities that represent their character. For example:

Character: Mailman

1. animal: golden retriever
2. image: tennis ball
3. rhythm: staccato
4. prop: mail scanner
5. costume pieces: messenger bag, hat
6. color: blue.

Then Spolin had her actors play the character in improvised scenes, allowing the qualities they chose to color their characterization. She explained that extensive intellectual character work is useless because a student can do all the painful work of analysis but still be unable to communicate the role physically. Intuition is the source of inspiration, not intellect. Play is the focus of character work, and leads to actors who stay in the moment with each other, ready to react and play intuitively.

Side Coaching

In teaching directors and teachers, Spolin uses the analogy of a first base coach whose job is to be outside eyes and support for the batter. In this situation, the actor is the batter. The actor's body is in motion, trying to meet the objectives of the game. The side coach is there as a teammate and "a guide, a directive, a support, a catalyst, a higher view, an inner voice, an extended hand . . . to help you stay on focus. Side coaching is a necessary message to alert your total organism, your whole self, to keep you in process and in present time, while releasing spontaneity, hidden wisdom, and intuition."[10]

If you can think of your director in this way and begin to respond quickly and freely to the instructions you are given as you work, the creativity you have inside yourself will come out. And, as you play improvisational games with your cast and side coach, you will develop the skill to hear and respond to incoming information in the moment. If your director is a Spolin-based director, they might even coach you while you act, expecting you to keep rehearsing without stopping while they call out instructions from the sidelines.

You can also internalize this process by becoming your own side coach. By internalizing the voice of your coach reminding you to directly experience, you will learn to let the space support you. You will learn to diagnose your problems while you are working and your internal voices will learn to give you helpful feedback. If those internal voices are opening up the space for you, then you have correctly identified your internal side coach. Side coaching can be carried into character development. Your internal coach can tell you things about your character such as, "she's excited to see Romeo again" or "he's afraid he looks like a fool." Spolin called this "shadowing your character," a technique that helps you artistically detach from your character so you can put on the attitude of your character.

Audience

Spolin claims that the audience has to be a major part of theatre training. She is dead set against the fourth wall and any attempt to ignore the audience. They are there.

> The audience is the most revered member of the theatre. Without an audience there is not theatre. Every technique learned by the actor, every curtain and flat on the stage, every careful analysis by the director, every coordinated scene, is for the enjoyment of the audience. They are our guests, our evaluators, and the last spoke in the wheel which can then begin to roll. They make the performance meaningful.[11]

The audience should be invited into the scene to participate and give your work meaning.

Viola Spolin's Legacy

Today's improvisational theatre movement comes directly from Spolin's approach and writings. She also informed an entire movement of theatre teachers and directors. If you have worked with a director who encouraged you to follow your impulses and stay in the moment with your fellow actors, they were probably influenced by the work of "Spark." She encouraged others to follow their natural tendencies and get out of their own way through play. Her legacy can be seen through television shows using sketch comedy, in classrooms, and in non-hierarchical theatre.

Tips for taking this method further

- Do some research into Second City and see if applying for a class or residency is right for you.
- Read *Theater Games for the Lone Actor* by Viola Spolin and do the activities in it. Begin working on side coaching yourself, learning to find the useful self-talk that pushes you in positive directions.
- Try playing the Scoring Game from this chapter. Come up with a theme for a day and observe yourself, scoring each time you catch yourself doing something or thinking something. See if observing and scoring the behavior creates change.

Discussion Starters and Journal Prompts

- Write about a time in theatre when you were too interested in competing with another actor for approval, or when you have observed others doing this. How can Spolin's techniques help the theatre world as a whole grow into something stronger and more engaging?
- What do you think of Spolin's ideas about side coaching yourself and the Scoring Game? Do you think that keeping track of your negative thoughts could have a positive impact on your mental health and your acting?
- Reread Spolin's ideas of emotions. Summarize what she means when she forbids psychodrama in the rehearsal space. Explain why you do or don't agree with her.

The Tools for your Toolbox

Activity—Feeling the Space

- Have your actors spread out in the space and sit cross-legged.
- Have them sit and breathe without thought.

- Say: "Allow your bodies to align themselves and release tension."
- "Exhale with a hissing sound."
- "Roll your heads, letting the weight of your heads do the moving."
- "Relax your shoulders and keep them out of it."
- "Send your sight to the four sides of the room one at a time while your head is rolling far to the left, right, front and back."
- "Extend your peripheral vision to see behind and underneath you. Allow your vision to be active! Send it out to look into the things you see! Bring your vision back! Send it on another adventure!"
- "Now close your eyes. When you open your eyes, see objects in the room without labeling them. Now close your eyes again and look in a different direction. Open your eyes and see without labeling what you see."
- "Do the same thing with people. You are allowing yourself to see with new insight when you don't allow words to cloud your vision."
- "Feel yourself with yourself! Feel your feet with your feet! Feel your feet inside your stockings and your stockings on your feet!"[12]
- Expand this coaching to other items of clothing, and awareness of body parts such as feeling tongue in mouth.
- Say: "Touch the floor with one finger. Now, allow the floor to touch your finger. Does that feel differently?"
- "Now feel yourselves in the space, and the space around you as you stand up."
- "Move around the space experiencing the substance of the air around you. Can you feel it against your backs? Feel it with your whole body."
- "Explore the space, feeling it on different parts of your body."
- Say: "Allow the space to flow through your body. Feel inside your spinal cord! Up and down your spine! Feel your inside with your inside! Observe, note, take note! Feel your skeleton moving in space with your skeleton! … Allow your body to align itself! Feel your pelvic bones! … Feel where the space substance ends and you begin! Feel your own form! Allow the space substance to flow through you and you flow through the space! Allow your sight to flow through your eyes! Take a ride on your own body and view the scenery around you!"[13]
- Say: "Begin supporting yourselves. You are the only support, holding yourself together. How does it feel to be solely responsible for holding yourself together?"
- "Allow the space to support you fully. What does that feel like? Can you feel the expansiveness and fullness of the environment? Did you already knew the environment wanted to support you?"
- "Pair up and play with the space substance between the palms of your hands. Can you feel it and believe it is there to support and energize them?"
- "Allow an object to appear between you and keep it between you by playing with it."
- "Let the object go, and begin to play with space together. Swing on it, wind it around each other, let it pull you …"
- "Everyone get an object out of your backpack or purse and let the space give it life. Move it around the space. Avoid manipulating it yourselves. The space is animating it, not you."

- "Now stand facing a partner, and send a sound to land on your partner. Take turns. Move around the space at various distances and angles, landing sound on each other."
- "Stand together and take turns sending sounds to land on items around the room, extending your ability to direct your voices. Coach each other where to send the next sound, to keep it in space, and to land it on the object, holding it there until instructed to stop."
- "Coach each other to send sounds in slow motion and as fast as you can."
- "Send words, and let them land, taking the word or phrase given by your partner and sending it as coached."
- "See your words visually extending and landing. What color are the words? What do they smell like?"
- "Try placing the emphasis on the vowels, then the consonants, sending them through space."
- Discuss: "What new understanding of the space have you gained? How could it serve you? Which other acting teachers also use this animation of space in their methods? Is there a difference in how they approach it?"

Activity—Give and Take

- Divide the class into two groups. Put one group stage left and the other stage right.
- Say: "We are going to play with Give and Take. To Give is to fade into the background and to allow the other to Take focus."
- "Group one is operating room 1, the other is operating room 2. Assign yourselves roles of inanimate objects and characters and arrange yourselves in a good stage picture in less than twenty seconds. Go!"
- "Begin your scenes until I side coach you to give and take the attention of the audience."
- "Operating room 1 TAKE!" and then trade off which room is the focus from time to time. Side coach as needed.
- Say: "Discuss with your group what giving and taking techniques worked and failed."
- "Each group split into Group A and Group B. Each Group A should sit at a table facing each other and near their Group B which is also sitting at a table. Be near enough to each other to be able to hear the other."
- "Begin to have a conversation with your table."
- "Table A Take! Table B Give! Do not freeze. Stop talking but continue in relaxed motion, ready to take again when it is your turn."
- Trade back and forth alternatively for a while.
- Say: "Now continue your conversations when you give, but still give the focus to the other group."
- "Try to give and take without side coaching. Can you give and take without talking about it just by being responsive to the table next door?"
- Discuss: "How well were you able to read when your teammates wanted to give and take. How does this exercise relate to stage work?"

Activity—Exits and Entrances/What's Beyond?

- Create teams of 4-6 players and put the first one on stage.
- Agree on a scenario (WWW).
- Say: "This game is played by the actors finding as many excuses as possible to exit and enter the stage. Each entrance and exit must include the full involvement of the other players. If you fail to fully involve the others, the audience will side coach by yelling 'Go back! Try again!' Some players may try to make a big scene with noise or tricks to get involvement with the group. This is not legitimate. Exits must come from the involvement with the WWW. Entrances and exits should be organic and spring from paying attention to the scene."
- After one group has the idea, allow other groups to play simultaneously or one at a time. Always have a watcher to side coach as needed.
- Discuss: "In theatre our job is involvement, not attention. How often were people satisfied with simply gaining the attention of the others rather than getting involved in the story?"
- Say: "All players go to one side of the stage. Think about what room you are in before you go on stage, and what room you are going to after."
- Now, have one player at a time come onto stage and exit, communicating non-verbally what room they just came from, and where they are going after they exit. Coach them to explore, heighten, establish WWW, reflect where they were, stop mid-stage, reflect where they are going.
- You can continue this game adding words, gibberish, or allow them to work in pairs.
- Now add time to the game. Either ask them to select a time, or have them draw times out of a hat. Ask them to cross the stage communicating where from and where to while also communicating the time of day it is.
- Give them a weather condition or place to communicate (cold jail cell, rainy day in a tree house, coffee shop, dentist office, drug store, dorm room, forest).
- Discuss: "What is the impact of always reflecting the where from and where to when acting? Do you remember actors who do this well? Does adding weather and time make an impact?"

Activity—Bus Stop (The WWW)

- Set up three chairs or a bench on stage.
- Have the players sit in the audience and create a character in their mind.
  - Who are they? What age, gender, vocation, etc.?
  - Where are they? What is the weather, scenery, place? This portion should be done as a group, or you, as the side coach, can establish this for them since they all will be interacting in this Where.
  - What are they doing? Where are they going? What is the reason for taking the bus today? What is their goal?

- Now that they are settled, ask for a volunteer to get the game going.
- Say: "Approach the bench and establish the WWW before anything else happens."
- Select another player. Say: "Approach, also establishing the WWW before interacting with the person on the bench."
- "Once you have established the WWW, while accepting and continuing the work your partner has done, start an interaction with the other." (If you would like to avoid playing with words at first, you can start with gibberish.)
- If someone begins a conversation before carefully establishing the WWW, coach them to back up and try again to establish the missing W.
- Once the new relationship is fully established, call out "The Bus is Coming!" and cross the stage playing the bus driver who will pick up the first actor, leaving room for another actor to enter the space and continue the game.
- Don't allow anyone to repeat their visit to the stage until all have played once. And, when they return, they should play a significantly different character with different WWW. Actors usually love this game and will play unendingly, but if you don't focus on the purpose of the game, it will devolve into showing off. Remind them the goal isn't to be funny, but to communicate the three Ws to the audience.

Activity—Slow/Fast/Normal

- Ask for three volunteers to play.
- When they come up, give them the WWW and have them improvise a scene in which the three Ws are clearly communicated, everyone is saying Yes, with a clear beginning, middle, and end.
- Now, ask them to replay the scene in slow motion.
- Now, ask them to replay as fast as possible without losing the scene.
- Now have everyone divide into small groups of 3–4 and spread out. Suggest a new WWW, and give them time to improvise at normal speed.
- At your signal switch speeds.
- You can now play the scenes and change speeds throughout at random intervals.
- Discuss: "What does slow motion require of you? What does it teach you? What happens in fast motion? What do you learn in each mode?"

Activity—Exposure

- Divide your players into two equal groups. Have one group sit in the audience and the other stand on stage in a line.
- Say: "The goal of the game is for both groups to look at each other and observe."
- When the group on the stage becomes uncomfortable and giggles or shifts positions, coach them to stop and just look at each other. "You look at us. We'll look at you."[14]

- Once they all have shown some discomfort, give them a job to do like counting the floorboards or the seats in the audience. This task should relax them so that you can see the difference.
- Now switch positions of the groups of players and do the exact same set of steps.
- Discuss: "Describe the experience of this game. What discoveries did you make? How did you feel standing on stage? How did the players look when they stood on stage? What changed when I gave you a job? Did anything change about how you felt?"

Activity—Mirroring

- Have the players sit in the audience and call up two volunteers.
- Say: "Play mirrors, facing each other and mirroring each other's activity with the goal of not revealing who is leading the activity."
- After they have played for a moment, ask the audience to vote for the player they think is the leader while the players keep playing. This small demonstration will set the expectations for everyone else. If you skip this step, you will often find that some partners will attempt to trick their mirror into making mistakes which is counter to the goals of the game: intense heightened concentration and involvement.
- Say: "Everyone come to the stage and pair up. Decide who will lead first. I will side coach you to switch from time to time."
- Call out "Change!" or "Switch!" at random moments, coaching them: "Make the transitions look seamless between leaders. Work together!"
- "There is no longer a leader! Work together, initiating and following each other's moves. Follow the follower!"
- "Add mirroring of sound to your movements."
- "Keep the sound going! Keep paying attention to body movements."
- "Pause mirroring. Quickly decide on a subject to discuss, like the best flavor of ice cream, and who will start the discussion."
- "Initiator, start talking about the topic. Reflection say the same thing as your partner at the same time out loud."
- "When I call Switch, do not interrupt the flow or pace of the conversation."
- Call changes and then set them free to follow the follower.
- "Break into groups of four or six."
- "Decide on a team activity to do and mirror. For example, a stylist cutting the other's hair or a parent pitching to a child."
- "Groups mirror each other."
- "Change!" and later "Follow the follower!"
- Other ideas for taking mirroring further:
  - Send one player from the room and have one leader in the room lead a series of movements that the whole group must reflect. Bring the player back to join the group and give them three guesses to figure out who is initiating the motions.

- Groups of four or more play three-way mirror. The group sets up a WWW for the scene in which one person does an activity like trying on clothes and the others mirror them. This can be complicated further by having two people do an activity like fixing a car together while being reflected by a three-way mirror.
- Play the mirror WWW activity above with amusement park style distorted funhouse mirrors.
- Group them up into groups of three and have one of the people be the side coach. They will call the changes for their pairs until you call "Change coach!"

Activity—Gibberish

- Note: You will need to demonstrate gibberish to your students in this lesson, so practice in advance if you aren't already fluent in the use of representational words. Do NOT tell your students that gibberish teaches them to show instead of tell. Let them learn this experientially. In fact, don't tell them you will be speaking in gibberish. Show them!
- Ask your students to sit in a circle and ask one player to stand up using a gibberish word. (Gallorusheo!), accompanying your made-up word with a gesture that can be understood.
- Now tell someone else to stand up using a different gibberish word, but the same gestural language (Rallavo!).
- Then tell them both to sit down using another word (Moolasay!).
- Now ask the whole group to sing for you (Plagee?).[15]
- You can demonstrate a few more gestural/representational commands by telling one student to get up and complete a series of activities while you speak to them in gibberish. If they say something in English, pretend you don't understand until they use gibberish.
- Now, using gibberish, ask them to converse with each other in gibberish, commanding each other to do things. You will know they are on the right track if they are all speaking another language and completely understanding each other.
- Spolin recommends some English side coaching comments for you at this point in the game: "Use as many different sounds as possible! Exaggerate mouth movements! Vary the tone! Try gum-chewing movements! Keep your usual speech rhythm! Let the gibberish flow!"[16]
- Say: "Switch partners!" Note: make sure those who get it quickly are paired with players who are struggling when possible, by rearranging them using forceful gibberish.
- Say: "Switch partners and sell a product to each other in gibberish. Have a clear object to sell in your mind."
- Now have them split into larger groups and take turns teaching the others a task or subject. For example: playing an instrument, photography, anatomy and physiology.
- Say: "Create groups of four where two of you speak one language, and the other two speak a different language. Come up with the WWW, for example, exchange students trying to get directions from police officers. Then play the scene!"
- "Divide into teams of three. Each team should pick a conversation topic and begin talking in English. The third person in the group is the side coach that switches them from English to gibberish and back. Switching can be made mid-word, or mid-sentence."

- "In your group of three elect a teacher who speaks gibberish, and another who is the translator who speaks English. The third is the student. Ask the teacher to pause for interpretation from time to time. The interpreter is to reflect the sound and meaning of the teacher spontaneously in translation for the two students."
- "Switch roles so everyone gets a turn as teacher and interpreter."
- "Play a game where you have one English translator that helps the other two understand each other as they speak gibberish. Each team gets to create their own WWW, for example: diplomats negotiating a peace treaty."
- Discuss: "What do you learn from speaking gibberish? Which tools do you have to communicate with when you can't understand the words being spoken?"

Activity—Shifting Inner Action

- Choose one actor to set a WWW for a disaster or emergency of some sort (car accident, fire, etc.).
- Say: "Start the scene with an enactment of the disaster, and each player should then enter the scene one by one filling in the scene—for example: a police officer, an ambulance driver and team of EMTs."
- "Enter with physicalized inner actions. What would your character's inner action be, and how would they physicalize it?"
- "Repeat the exercise. This time, play the same character, but physicalize a different inner action. Perhaps the first time you checked your phone because you were physicalizing disinterest, and this time you touch the patient's shoulder because you are physicalizing empathy."
- "Try a new WWW: Where: the greenroom of a college theatre. Who: a college theatre troupe. What: they have heard a rumor that their favorite professor took a job with a different school for the next school year."
- "Remember you need to physicalize your feelings rather than emote. Start with the inner action of self-pity. Begin to improvise the scene."
- Side coach them to physicalize self-pity. Once you are satisfied that they are doing the activity correctly, introduce new feelings for them to physicalize one at a time. Spolin recommends: anger, hostility, guilt, grief, sadness, affection, love, self-responsibility, understanding, self-respect, admiration for each other.[17]
- Discuss: "What is the difference between emoting and physicalizing? Did you feel the exercise was a success or did it devolve into meaningless chattering?"

12

Uta Hagen

The Person

Uta Hagen was born in 1919 in Germany. Her mother was an opera singer and her father was an art historian and musician. They immigrated to Wisconsin in the Midwest of the United States when she was six. As you might expect, because of her parents, her childhood was full of travel, culturally enriching experiences, intellectual discussions, and the training she needed to be a successful artist. In childhood she traveled to Europe, studied modern dance and piano, attended plays and museums, practiced stage makeup in her room, and read biographies of actors as well as all the classical dramatic literature she had access to. What she lacked in friendships, she made up for by using her imagination and the fine arts.

Hagen graduated high school at sixteen and traveled to London to study theatre at the Royal Academy of Dramatic Art. She didn't like their methods of actor training which focused on imitation of inflections and gestures. She only stayed a year before she returned home and began auditioning. She was unusually successful, and was performing on the New York stage quickly. She, unlike most important acting teachers of her era, did not train with Stanislavski or any of his acolytes. She developed her methods in parallel with the Group Theater, but not connected in any way to them. She learned her methods through performing.

Hagen was successful but deeply unhappy with the canned way she had found success as an actor. She was able to use the tricks she had learned from watching others, but she was confused. "I got great reviews, I was 'starred' on the marquee, and still I was left with an empty, hollow feeling . . . The approval, applause, and good reviews were not enough. I actually began to dislike going to work."[1] At twenty-eight, she was cast in a play directed by Harold Clurman, who insisted she stop using acting tricks and become the character. In this production she played opposite of Herbert Berghof who she would eventually marry. Berghof, a European actor, helped her develop new techniques to replace her old tricks. The two of them were romantic and professional partners until he died in 1990.

In 1947, Hagen was among the actors placed on the Hollywood Blacklist which meant the movie studios denied her employment along with many others believed to be Communist sympathizers. Hagen became falsely connected to the movement which meant she could not act in film or television. She took this opportunity to focus her efforts on stage acting and the teaching of acting. The loss to her film career was not a huge problem for her, but "it was the only time in my life when

I was made fearful or felt that I had lost control over my own destiny. And for that, I have the right to remain outraged."²

Her students loved her. One student, Pauline O'Driscoll described her:

> She . . . had a wickedly acerbic sense of humour, a raucous laugh, a deep raspy voice, a mischievous nature, and an uncanny ability to hone in on the element of your scene or exercise that wasn't working. As a teacher was consistently supportive, respectful, encouraging and generous. She possessed an extraordinary insight which she used with laser sharp accuracy to guide her students lovingly and respectfully to better awareness and more truthful performances . . . but neither did she suffer fools, or tolerate lateness or ill preparedness. She smoked like a train and took her dog GB, named after her favourite playwright George Bernard Shaw and her cigarettes everywhere with her including the classroom.³

She continued to perform into her eighties alongside actors like Matthew Broderick, Mia Farrow and David Hyde Pierce. She taught acting until she died in 2004 at the age of eighty-five.

The Method

Uta Hagen's method centers around her insistence on the actor's need to be open to the world around them. She touches on this in both of her books, but especially in the second, *A Challenge for the Actor*, in which she bemoans the way people have shut down their senses. It was written in 1991, so the examples are dated, but the principle is still valid,

> An interchange of ideas becomes almost impossible when so much of the conversation must be shouted above the racket of the radio or TV that seems to be turned on at all times, or above the din of most restaurants. When we are alone, we cover our ears with Walkman headphones to drown out 'noise pollution' when actually we are blocking out thoughts and suspending all imagination.⁴

She goes on to point out that our culture teaches us not to make too much noise or feel too deeply. It also wants us to alienate ourselves from both the pain and beauty of the world around us, and to boost our egos by evaluating our effect on others rather than their effect on us. When we walk past homeless people, we avert our eyes. When on a walk, we don't enjoy the beauty of the trees nearby. When we feel delight at seeing something lovely, we take silent note rather than exclaiming about it. "We must strip the cover, the hard-boiled mask, the thick skin used as a protective covering around the soul if we want to regain an artist's innocence and the intuitive responsiveness necessary for a limber, truthful, emotional instrument."⁵

Do you find this to be true of yourself? Are you constantly in a state of fixating on your phone or disappearing into your headphones? Do you really examine the world around you? Hagen has stern advice for you if you want to be an actor: "'Cease and desist' from these deadening habits. Open your senses, no matter how painful it may be. Doing so will heighten your sensitivities, which are an integral part of the actor's talent. It will also increase your understanding of the world in which you live and may even induce compassionate actions in your daily life."⁶ Her advice is to open up all five senses by engaging your eyes, ears, nose, tongue, and skin in the project of experiencing your world. Observe the feel of a handshake, the smell of your home, the sound of the air vents, the taste of cafeteria food, and what you see in the next boring classroom you enter. In other words, don't limit the moments when you think about your senses to the moments when there is something extraordinary occurring. Don't wait for the double chocolate lava cake to enjoy your sense of taste.

Hagen urges actors to also observe themselves responding to stimuli. If you take the time and attention needed to observe your reactions to your senses, you will have a treasure chest full of responses to use with your characters.

Inner Work

Hagen taught actors to find their characters in themselves. When we are children, we already naturally identify with those around us. If we see a kid being yelled at by a parent, we put ourselves in that stranger's place and imagine the pain. If we see a movie with a natural disaster, we experience it as if we were in the path of the hurricane. We naturally live in the circumstances of others. Hagen insists we should continue these empathetic fantasies as adults.

Hagen says we can find the components of any character inside ourselves. Perhaps you do not think you are shy and you are playing a shy character. In that case, remember a moment when as a teenager you attended a dance with a big pimple on your face and spilled something on your clothes. That feeling of hoping to disappear is you being shy. You can recall that and bring it to your work. You have also had murderous feelings (that you most likely did not act on), had brave moments, been a show off, been silly with a baby or animal. If you think about it, you can find every component of your new character somewhere inside yourself. Work on observing yourself.

Substitution/Transference

Sometimes as an actor you will be asked to play a role that requires you to react in a way to a circumstance that doesn't make sense to you. In this case, Hagen recommends a practice called substitution in her first book, and transference in her second. In transference, you create an altered circumstance to trigger an emotional response. She gives the example of an actor who cannot get the proper feeling of shame when her scene partner chastises her for a torn piece of clothing. Hagen suggested to the actor that she imagine this character is holding out a pair of her dirty underwear in front of her. This transference worked very well for the actor, who snatched the garment from her scene partner and hid it behind her back with obvious embarrassment.

You can also manufacture a needed experience for a role. Hagen gives the example of someone who feels they are a sloppy dresser who needs to play the part of Blanche in *A Streetcar Named Desire*. In order to drum up the appropriate care for personal appearance, an actor could find a pair of white satin dress gloves with buttons at the wrist and put them on to wear while running errands. In the course of trying to keep them pristine, the actor might gain a sense of how Blanche handles her clothing every day and then transfer that feeling and behavior to the role.

Hagen warns that we should never reveal our source material. Once others know what you are using in a moment, they will become an audience to your altered reality, and the magic of the tool will be gone. You will become self-conscious about the information you have shared, ruining the effect of the transference.

Your transference is not complete until you no longer use the source material and have transferred the needed emotions to the circumstances of the play. Once you have found a psychological tool that works, it is your job to transfer the essence of it to the scene. In the example of the dirty underwear, the job of the actor was to eventually feel the same shame when confronted with the torn shirt as with the dirty underwear.

Emotional Memory/Recall

In working with different internal acting methods, you will discover that many practitioners use variations on terms like sense memory and emotional memory. Hagen started with the term "emotional memory" but shifted to "emotional recall" to get closer to her meaning. She said, "In life, an emotion occurs when something happens to us which momentarily suspends our reasoning control and we are unable to cope with this event logically."[7] Here, the actor is in dangerous territory. When these emotions happen to us as people, we are out of control. We are controlled by the emotion rather than vice versa.

When these things happen to our characters, we can recall these moments of being overcome by emotion. The temptation is to work up our emotions so we are actually overcome on stage like in real life. This can cause actors to re-traumatize themselves on stage. Hagen teaches the actor to instead focus on the details around them in the remembered state of emotional trauma. Hagen worked to find a tiny detail about her surroundings that would trigger the essence of the feeling without re-traumatizing her. She learned from a psychologist to call these items "release objects." A Hagen actor filters through their memories, finding objects that indirectly trigger emotion without remembering the event. Armed with an arsenal of release objects, they remain present in their acting, out of past trauma, and in truthful performance.

Hagen warns against using any past pain you are not ready to talk about. If you don't have objectivity, the release object won't be useful on stage. Instead, it might trigger uncontrolled feelings. She also insists you not allow an acting teacher be your therapist. Some teachers may ask you to use your past as an acting tool, and parade that trauma in the classroom. Hagen calls this "anti-art." She recommends working privately, focusing on the item, not the actual memory. Then you can use your release object not to evoke the emotion, but as a springboard into action.

Sense Memory

Not to be confused with emotional memory, which relates to remembering emotions, sense memory relates to the recall of physical sensations directly from our senses. For example, if your job is to be hot on stage, instead of trying to think yourself into a state of heat, focus on one area of your body that will feel the heat. Hagen suggests the armpits.

Remember a sensation of stickiness, of perspiration trickling down, and *then* search for what you do to alleviate this sensation. Raise your arm slightly, see if you can pull your shirt or blouse sleeve away from the underarm to let in a little air. In that moment of adjustment, or attempt to overcome the heat you will have a sensation of heat. The rest of the body will feel hot, too.[8]

This technique requires you to figure out how you would make adjustments to alleviate the symptom of the heat, rather than trying to feel the heat itself. This same technique of recalling a localized sensation can work for innumerable sensations. It works for cold, drunkenness, headache, or heart attack.

If you are working to find a sense memory for an experience you haven't had, for example, pregnancy or being stabbed, your job is to do a little research to find out what the physical sensations are that are attached to the situation and do the same work as with a sensation you have had. For instance, the feeling of being strangled might be connected to the feeling of gasping for air after being under water too long.

Hagen warns us to realize the sensation you are replicating is not usually the point of the scene you are in. Remain in the moment of the scene and live truthfully in it while feeling the sensation as a side point. Second, if you are supposed to have a headache in a scene, and you already have a headache, don't put yourself out of control by using the sense memory technique. Stay in control at all times on stage. Hagen felt that an actor should "be the healthiest, least neurotic creature on earth."[9] She believed healthy exploration of your senses will benefit your mental health.

Work on developing your senses so you grow as an actor. If you pay attention to your senses, continually growing in sharpness of your observation, you will gain insights into human behavior and will be able to recall them more easily on stage. For instance, if you pay attention to your senses when you are talking to someone, you will notice you don't fix your focus on them when you are revealing a secret or telling a story. Instead, you check their facial expression from time to time to make sure they understood what you said. The rest of the time you are internally focused. If you try to maintain eye contact, you will lose focus.

Hagen gave instructions about specific situations that require sense memory:

- *Being in a hurry*—The scene is not about being in a hurry, but the action the actor has to perform *is* conditioned by hurry. Hagen teaches it is impossible to realistically perform "in a hurry" unless you are very precise. Think about a place you have to go to often: let's say, your acting methods class which starts at 3:45. If you are in your room, which is a ten minute walk to class, and you are doom scrolling when you realize it is 3:35, your sense of hurry will be very specific. You will feel that you can make it in time if you are just a little bit more efficient with your movements. Now, what if the clock says 3:40? Your hurry will be more uncontrolled and haphazard because of the inevitably of your tardiness. Now, what if you see it is already 3:45? Do you see how the circumstances of the hurry must be very specific?
- *Quiet*—Ask yourself: "Why must I be quiet? How far away is the person I don't want to disturb? Who are they? What would be the consequences of them hearing?" Once you have the answers to these questions, the acting will take care of itself.
- *Being drunk*—This can take many forms, and your character may experience it differently from you or your friends. It is not necessary to have been drunk in the past to play drunkenness

realistically. Obviously, study the script for clues as to how your character behaves when drunk. Then focus on the physical sensations that lead to this behavior. Dizziness is something everyone has experienced. Hagen suggests you "allow your head to feel heavy. Imagine that it's spinning and let it pull you forward until you need to support it with your hand or with your elbow on the table or the arm of a chair."[10] Other helpful sensations might be sleepiness which could manifest in your eyes with blurriness or a difficulty in staying alert. When standing, focus on straightening your wobbly legs so you can get somewhere. Don't focus on the wobble, focus on preventing it. Try to focus on only one sensation at a time and don't overcomplicate if one sensation will do the trick. It might be necessary to alternate between a few sensations to get the result you want.

Now, what if you need to feel more than one thing at a time? Perhaps you have a headache AND a backache. Or you are in a hurry AND your toe hurts. Hagen says to start with the condition you think has the least significance and add the one you will have to pay most attention to last.

Endowment

Working with props can be challenging. Your prop person may not fully understand the nuances of a particular item, and provide you with something you find unsuitable. Or perhaps the danger or expense of an accurate item are not feasible for the stage. In this case, it is your job to endow the item with meaning and sensation. For example, if you are holding a painted plastic goblet, it will not feel to you like the real goblets you would expect at the king's banquet. Even more difficult, the goblet may not have any liquid in it, and you are expected to make it look like you are drinking wine. Hagen teaches actors to endow the prop, in this case a goblet, with the proper qualities so that it reads both to the audience and the actor.

To follow her process, find yourself a heavy cup or goblet to work with. Fill it with liquid to the level you imagine your goblet would be filled with a beverage of the same temperature as the intended beverage. Now observe yourself holding the cup. How do you handle the weight of it? How do your fingers curl around the handle or stem? Do you smell the liquid before you sip it? What look crosses your face as you work with it? Now, the next time you are using your stage prop, endow it with the qualities of the practice vessel. It should handle and work for you so that you believe it is what it represents.

Now take your endowment a level deeper. Let's take a dagger as an example. Perhaps you are holding a blunt, Halloween store dagger with a retractable blade. What does a real knife feel like in your hand? Carefully play with a heavier knife or similarly shaped item. Maybe a butcher knife from your kitchen, or a replica dagger. Once you have created the endowments for weight and feel, add emotional connection. Any prop you handle on stage needs a history. The script is unlikely to give you a meaningful backstory, but your imagination can do that for you. Was this dagger a gift from your mother as a means of protection? Was it the dagger your victim used to kill your dog? Did you buy it last week? Did you spend three hours touching and handling many daggers and decide on this one? The story of your prop will make it live for your audience because it will live in your imagination. Hagen called this particularization.

It is also important to particularize your costumes. Hagen asks, will you

> put on the tights of Hamlet to find an acceptable *pose*, or will you put them on as the clothing which belongs to you and in which you live and walk and sit and run? Will you make a hoopskirt yours by finding its sensory reality and physical assets and problems, by giving it a history of when you bought it, whether it's new or old, whether it's the finest or the poorest, etc.?[11]

People who lived before us were normal human beings. While our circumstances and fashions have changed, humans have not. As an actor, you need to find a way to wear the clothing of the past as if you were born to it. Don't fuss with the hem of your garment because it is unfamiliar. Give each garment a history and you will find yourself better able to work with and believe you chose it for yourself.

Entrances

Hagen struggled as a young actor with entering the stage with the scripted cue, "She enters." That action is not motivated, and causes actor problems. Hagen suggests a three-step method of preparation for a successful stage entry that creates a reality for a character not strictly tied to the given circumstances of the play. It propels actors onto stage with an immediate past that continues onto the stage.

The three steps are to decide:

1. What did I *just* do?
2. What am I doing right *now*?
3. What's the first thing I want?[12]

Your character history is not useful here. The technique digs into only the past few seconds. Hagen uses the example of a character that is arriving home to prepare a fancy meal at home. They have just been shopping, and the delivery of the groceries should be any minute. The phone is ringing on stage. Using the three questions listed above, the actor could create a suite of answers that get them onto stage in a motivated state:

1. "You *just* saw a roach on the welcome mat.
2. You *are* using the wrong key in the door.
3. You finally *get* the door open and shiver in disgust as you *sidle* to the phone, looking for more roaches in route."[13]

Or you could use a different set of answers:

1. You *just* had to walk around a person panhandling on the doorstep.
2. You *are* prepared with your key because you want to get in quickly.
3. You get in the door and bolt it quickly before answering the phone because you are nervous that someone will try to follow you in.

These simple actions, once developed for your character can be used repeatedly for every entrance in a run, or they can be changed daily. If a fresh approach will be helpful, then add a roach to your imagined doormat, or a cat, or anything else.

Destinations

The work you are doing to motivate your movement onto stage should also be used while on stage. Keep asking yourself, *what just happened* in my mind? What *is happening now*? What does my character *expect to happen* next? The answers to these questions might be different each performance. Your character might be thinking about a missing shoe one day, and then next might be haunted by something dumb they said to a crush yesterday. All of these inner objects must be unorganized just like our thoughts are in real life.

Importantly, your job is to truly understand your character's expectations of what might happen next. Suspend your own knowledge of how the play ends. If you are playing Juliet knowing how the show will end, just like the audience members who have completed freshman English know it, you will miss the fresh and funny Juliet that is falling in love and believing her Romeo will grow old by her side. Try playing those expectations instead of the fore-knowledge you have of their untimely death and see what it does for you, your fellow actors, and the audience.

At all moments of life, our destination is important. Sometimes the destination is something we aren't thinking about, but we have one. Hagen writes that her primary objective while sitting and writing her books was to be helpful to her readers, but at the same time, she was always reaching for secondary objectives like a cup of coffee or a sweater on a cold morning. Those secondary objectives are reflexive and constant. They should be present for your character. Even if your character must pace, they are walking to or running away from something.

Hagen says that standing is also about destination. Your body intuitively knows there is a destination coming soon. Perhaps you are standing to signal you plan to leave a party, or you are waiting on a bus. Destination is on your mind while your body is in motion, checking your watch or glancing in the direction of the door. If a director asks you to stand somewhere on stage, it is your job to figure out where the destination of your character is after standing, and keep it in mind.

The same rule about destinations applies to your exit from the stage. Where are you going when you storm off? See it in your mind and continue your action into the wings.

The Fourth Side

Hagen calls the side of the stage facing the audience "the fourth side" instead of "the fourth wall." In realistic proscenium theatre, it is the only side of the character's environment that is undefined. It is up to the actor to bring it to life with their imagination. In Hagen's view, actors shouldn't project their presence out to the audience, even while they are attempting to be easily seen and heard.

Hagen tells us the best way to create a sense of reality on stage is to visualize the missing wall in great detail by visualizing high levels of detail on the fourth side. Unfortunately, it isn't possible for an actor to picture the wall or items on a wall and keep them anchored in one spot for the whole show. Hagen writes, "Whatever object you wish to see must be anchored to something which you can see is really there . . . Actors challenge me that they can't see anything out front on which to anchor something because it is too dark . . . this is untrue. We see the outlines of almost everything, from the people to balconies at the back."[14] Actors should choose an anchor point that is fixed in space. Hagen recommends putting five or six items such as ph0tos, windows, and clocks on the fourth wall and anchoring them on fixed points in the house.

Once you visualize a very specific window and anchor it to a specific door frame in the back of the house, you might worry the audience will see that you are looking at the back of the room rather than the fourth wall. Hagen says this won't be a problem if you find the spot on the back wall and bring it closer to yourself in your imagination.

Hagen warns against being the only actor in a play using this technique since it will throw the audience off. She sets up a fourth wall in every production, but doesn't spend much time on it when the rest of the cast isn't using the same technique. As an added difficulty, if you are playing a scene outdoors, it will be your job to imagine and anchor all *four* walls.

When the director or playwright call for the character to directly address the audience, Hagen has strong opinions about how this should be done. She suggests starting by replacing the fourth side with an imagined theatre with the same audience in attendance each night. For example, you might imagine Shakespeare's Globe when you are performing a Shakespeare piece. In this case, learn what that theatre looks like and endow the theatre with the appearance of the Globe, complete with an audience in the appropriate clothing and behavior of the audience of the era. When called upon to make direct address to people in the audience, she insists you create up to four imaginary audience members and place them in between the actual seats in your theatre. She finds it disconcerting to have actors make direct eye contact with her in the audience, and does not enjoy the unpredictability of forcing audience members in attendance to be her unwilling scene partners. Many directors and actors vehemently disagree with Hagen, but she was steadfast on this point.

Character Development

How do you begin the work of creating your character? Hagen recommends selecting a new journal, sharpening some pencils, and sitting down with the script. Begin by reading the whole play from beginning to end, even if you are only playing one scene. Read it as an outsider and take it in. Now reread the play several times, taking notes and asking the following questions:

- "What is the playwright trying to communicate?" Be careful to be flexible in thought so you can collaborate with the director's vision. It is your job to make your internals match the external acting your director asks for.
- "What does the play want?"
- "What is the texture of the play?" Your answer might be something like "rough like canvas" or "dark and syrupy like blackberries."
- Ask: "Who am I in this play?" Not: "Who is s/he/they?" If you ask, "Where was she born?" you get a simple answer like: Dublin 1865. "If, however, my first question is where and when was 'I' born, and the answer in the play is Dublin, 1865, the answer becomes loaded with new questions for which I must find answers and substitutions, using my imagination to make them *serviceable* facts."[15] Hagen suggests you make the details as concrete as possible. Ask yourself:

- What do I (my character) know about myself?
- What does my (character's) subconscious need from me?
- What facts can I find from the play about my parents, childhood, education, friends, hobbies, and interests?
- What do other characters say about me?
- How do other characters respond to me?
- What do these things reveal about my drives, my wants, my dislikes?
- What do I actually see and hear? What moves me?
- What do I want in my entire life? in the timespan of the play? in each scene? in each moment of each scene? What do I think I want *vs.* what I really want and am not consciously aware of?
- What is the obstacle to meeting each of my objectives?
- What did I see in my romantic partner when I first met them?
- What do I blame myself for?
- Allow other questions like this to pop into your mind. Be curious about who you are in this new role.

As you read, write all over your script with notes that will help you as you develop your character. Snippets of things that pop into your mind while you are reading might be something important later. Your subconscious is working whether you know it or not. Your journal is a place to write out historical information, substitutions, and other tools. Don't share it with anyone. This is yours alone, and the magic will be gone if others see it. Hagen says she uses her notebook to figure out her character's handwriting and to write notes to other characters. Only you will know what is useful to you in those pages.

Your character must live for you as a creature that had a beginning long before the play began, has time that passes while off stage—often not real time—and who will continue after the play concludes. Because of this, it is your job to not leave any detail unexplored. Dig into the circumstances the author gives you, drawings the set and prop designers give you, your research, and your imagination.

Dialects

If you are required to play a part with a dialect you aren't familiar with, it is Hagen's recommendation that you use that language 24/7 until it is natural. Watch movies with characters speaking in the cadences of your character. Try out your dialect on your friends and people behind the counters at restaurants and businesses. Stay in the dialect until it becomes natural to you so you can focus on the meaning of your lines rather than the sound of them.

Age

Aging your character up or down from your real age is a stumbling block for many actors, especially young ones. Hagen says that asking a twenty-eight-year-old to play a forty-year-old might feel impossible to the actor, but the trick is to simply adjust in your mind the age difference between yourself and the other characters. She claims that we always feel essentially the same age. Think of how you felt ten years ago. Was it much different? No? So the trick is in deciding you are ten years older than the thirty-year-old character opposite you. Though you are essentially the same age, the audience won't be able to tell if you believe they are younger than you by a decade.

If you must play someone elderly, rather than playing a caricature, pay attention to the ache in your back or feet. Work on the ache in only one place, physicalizing this malady that you have experience with, and truthfully play your part, recognizing that age is just a state of body. The essence of you remains the same at any age. If you must play someone much younger, also avoid the caricature. As you take on the younger character, physically adjust for insecurities rather than playing "awkward."

Uta Hagen's Legacy

Hagen is remembered as one of the most beloved acting teacher of her generation. She taught actors to revere the art of acting, take it seriously, and develop strong habits. The actor who follows her methods will be well prepared and in the moment. Hagen wrote two books on her acting technique. The first one, *Respect for Acting*, is still wildly popular. She, however, was dismayed by its popularity and the misunderstandings that came out of it. When she visited acting classes teaching her methods from that book, she was horrified at how it was being used and wrote her second book, *A Challenge for the Actor* as a revision of the first. Publishers refused her request to stop the publication of the first book because of its popularity.

Tips for taking this method further

- Read both of Uta Hagen's acting texts: *Respect for Acting* and *A Challenge for the Actor.*
- Watch Uta's acting class online.
- Complete Uta Hagen's challenge to observe yourself and all of the selves you are over the course of a day. Learn to play-act yourself in different situations as a way to enrich your toolkit for future roles.

Discussion Starters and Journal Prompts

- Write about an entrance you had to make on a stage at some point in the past where your focus was on hearing your cue rather than creating a continuous life for your character. How could the use of three entrances from Hagen's method help you as a performer? Write three possible ways to enter the stage with the three questions: "What did I just do? What am I doing right *now*? What's the first thing I want?"[16]

- Take Hagen seriously when she asks you to observe your world. Set aside one hour of time and put your electronic devices away in a place you cannot reach. Go for a walk or sit outside with only your thoughts and the world. Notice all five of your senses and how they play on you. When you have spent an hour without distractions from your senses, write what you learned. Was this experience a good one? Disconcerting? Were you able to unplug and think? Is this an experiment worth repeating and/or making part of your routine? Perhaps you want to try this when you are with other people so you can experiment with your own powers of observation. Can you focus on their effects on you? Can you learn things about yourself that will help you as an actor?

The Tools for your Toolbox

Activity—Three Entrances

- Remind your students of the three essential steps of preparation for entering stage: "What did I just do? What am I doing right *now*? What's the first thing I want?"[17]
- Say: "Step off stage and prepare for an entrance."
- "Today is the day of a dentist appointment you have been dreading. You have been mentally preparing yourself and want to look like you have it together when you arrive at the dentist office. After having gotten up from your bed, your first objective is to make yourself a cup of coffee in the kitchen."
  - "Step One: (offstage) What did I just do?—you are uncomfortable in your slippers because you put them on the wrong feet."
  - "Step Two: (preparing to enter) What am I doing right now?—You are cleaning your glasses because you want to avoid making further mistakes."
  - "Step Three: (entering) What's the first thing I want?—You open the kitchen door hoping your roommate cleaned up the Keurig so that you don't have to do it before you can make your cup of coffee."
- Now change it. "Same scenario this time, but":
  - "Step One—as you got out of bed you read a text message from your mom that makes you feel guilty for not calling her more often."
  - "Step Two—You are composing a response to her in your head which involves you using swear words that will make her upset. This makes you laugh."
  - "Step Three—You open the kitchen door to see that your roommate already brewed a pot of coffee so you don't have to."
- Say: "Work in pairs to create the three steps together and practice them."
- "Create an entrance on your own from a scene or play you have previously performed in. Imagine the set as it was, and the costumes, etc. Create a circumstance that propels you

onto the stage and find three different variations that would have worked in that play. Practice them."
- Discuss: "What did you learn about entrances by doing this activity? Do you think you will use this technique? Have entrances been a problem for you?"

Activity—Fourth Wall

- Bring your students to a place with mirrors.
- Say: " Lean in to see yourself one foot from the mirror and make the necessary body adjustments to see yourself clearly."
- "Step back six feet and repeat, adjusting the body."
- "Go as far back from the mirror as possible and do the same thing."
- "Attempt to recreate the appearance of looking into a mirror at the same three distances from a doorframe, using the same body postures."
- "Hagen says that you will be able to believe that you are seeing yourself in the mirror even though there is no mirror there. You can bring items from your fourth wall closer or further away from you simply by adjusting your body posture."
- "Run through the activity again with another item on a wall besides a mirror, perhaps a clock or window or door, paying attention to body posture. If possible, place that item in your imagination on a fixed spot in a theatre and use body posture to help yourself and the audience believe the item is there."
- Discuss: "What is the value of endowing a fourth wall? Was it believable to watch from the house?"

Activity—Two-Minute Public Solitude Phone Call

- Note: I find Uta Hagen's two-minute exercise is very difficult for students in today's techno-social culture. However she suggests an extension of the exercise that works better. This exercise requires your students to prepare alone in advance of class.
- Say: "In preparation for our next class, I want you to prepare a two-minute scene that recreates two consecutive minutes of your life. Write the following nine questions in your journal with enough space to fill the answers out later. The more detailed your responses, the better and more believable your scene will be."

    - Who am I? (describe personality traits of yourself as the character, your current state, your self-perceptions in this moment, and what you are wearing)
    - What time is it? (date, season, time)
    - Where am I? (country, city, neighborhood, specific location)
    - What surrounds me? (animate and inanimate objects—set pieces/props)
    - What are the immediate given circumstances? (what just happened, what is happening now)

- What is my relationship? (your relation with self, events, items, people you are not currently with but thinking of)
- What do I want? (what are your overarching and immediate goals)
- What's in my way? (obstacles, tactics to overcome them)
- What do I do to get what I want? (physical and verbal tactics and actions)

- Say: "A phone call must happen during your two-minute scene. It can be a phone call in progress when the scene starts, a call that you decide to make during the scene, or a call that you receive during the scene."
- "Your first job is to make and receive three phone calls today. Text a parent or friend to call them for an assignment. They can be business or social calls. During the calls, pay attention to what happens to you and where your attention is focused. You should take these calls in a place where you are alone and can move around. Phone calls while lying down or in a car don't make good scenes."
- "After you have observed yourself on the phone, choose one of the calls and answer the questions you wrote in your journal, making sure you understand who you are speaking with, what the call is about, and what is being said to you."
- "Gather props to recreate the space you are in. Bring them to class since you are not allowed to mime anything. If there is no door for you to use, you cannot come in or out of a door. If there is no window, it must be placed on the fourth wall so you can look out, but not interact with the window by opening or closing it."
- "Place some of the items you find your attention going to during phone calls on the fourth wall, to picture them in detail, and to do the work of anchoring them to actual places in the classroom you will perform in. Rehearse the two minutes at least ten times, improvising the conversation each time. You shouldn't write out dialog, the given circumstances will serve to create realistic dialog on stage."
- "Here are some tips for you":
  - "Make noise, swear, talk to yourself even when you aren't on the phone—the scene is not meant to be mute. You are alone. Do you make noise when you are alone? Then make noise in your scene. But don't talk in order to clue the audience in to your internal story. Your real self-talk rarely makes any sense to anyone else."
  - "Keep your tasks simple—don't try to impress anyone. You will be interesting if you are interested in what you are doing."
  - "REALLY rehearse the scene over and over. Don't just write it down and think about it. Time yourself on your last couple of runs and adjust what you are doing to meet your objectives if you find you are going over or under time."
- On the appointed day, they should perform with the goal of achieving public solitude—not entertaining the class. If their motivations are strong, their scenes will demand the room's attention. Time them and stop them if three minutes are done before they are done. The goal is 2–3 minutes. The scene should end in a timely manner if they rehearsed properly. If they have to be stopped, this is a moment to evaluate why.
- Discuss: "What did you learn from this exercise? Is public solitude possible? Desirable?"

Activity—Endowment

- For the first part of the lesson you will need a mug for each student, a pitcher of ice-cold water, and a kettle of hot water. For the second part either bring or ask your student to bring three items that need to be endowed for use on stage (lipstick, needle and thread, knife, liquor, sliced apples to stand in for raw onions)
- Provide the class the opportunity to make themselves a full cup of a piping hot beverage or simply have them sample hot water.
- Say: "Observe yourself as you take your first drink of the beverage. How do you hold the cup? How do you cool it down? How do you test it? How does the mug feel in your hands? How heavy is it?
- "Pour out the remainder of your drink and fill the cup with ice water."
- "Endow the cold water with the qualities you observed in the hot beverage. Can you recreate the experience and believe it is hot?"
- "Pour out the water and try the same activity with an empty cup. Can you equally experience the heat and feel of hot liquid? It is distracting for the audience if you do not properly endow your props with the qualities of the items they represent. How many of you have watched an actor on a television show wave a 'full' cup of coffee around as if it weighed nothing and was empty?"
- "I encourage you to continue your journey of self-observation. You will soon fill your toolbox with remembered responses to stimuli."
- Say: "Grab three items and come up with a scenario that would require using them on stage. You can work alone or in pairs."
- "Endow them with qualities they don't have—for example, weight or sharpness. Also give the items a history. When did you obtain each item? Do you have a fondness for it? Does it bring back painful memories?"
- "Rehearse an improvisation in which you interact with these endowed props. You must have an overarching objective in your scene that is not the endowed items."
- After you perform for each other and comment on the work, begin again, but this time endow the items differently. Perhaps the liquor bottle is no longer a reminder of a grandfather who has passed away, but instead is a gift from a boss who is seeking sexual favors.
- Discuss: "How can endowment benefit your work going forward?"

Activity—Conditioning Forces

- Create slips of paper with physical conditioning forces written on them: cold, heat, humidity, wind, headache, backache, sprained ankle, toothache, blister on toe or finger, runny nose, etc. and have your students randomly draw one of these forces from a hat. (save hurry and quiet for later) Ask them to return their slips of paper to the hat.
- Say: "Close your eyes and remember a time when you felt the conditioning force on your paper, focusing on the physical sensation that would happen and what adjustments you would make to alleviate the symptoms/situation."
- "Now open your eyes and rehearse this for a few moments in order to solidify the feeling in your body."

- "Perform your monologue or duo scene while facing this conditioning force."
- Discuss: "How was your performance changed?"
- Say: "Now draw another conditioning force from the hat to add to your previous one. If you draw the same one, try again for something new."
- "Repeat the previous steps, but keep the first condition while adding the second. You can alternate between the conditions, always keeping both present but not the main focus of the assignment."
- Discuss: "What was difficult about having two conditioning forces at once?"
- Say: "Now add the conditioning force of hurry to your list of conditions."
- "Close your eyes again and very specifically think about your hurry. Why are you in a hurry? What is the destination you must go to? What task must you finish quickly? How long will it take you to get there/get the task done? How much time do you have?"
- "Rehearse again, adding in hurry."
- "Now change the specific details of your hurry, and try again."
- Discuss: "When the specifics changed, how did it change the action of the scene?"
- Say: "Add the conditioning force of quiet. You may maintain hurry, or choose to let that one go for the time being. But don't drop the first two conditions."
- "Ask yourself why you must be quiet? How far away is the person you don't want to disturb? Who are they? What would be the consequences of them hearing?"
- Have them rehearse, then perform, and discuss their experiences.

Activity—Age adjustments

- Ask one student to come to the front of the room and wait on stage. Ask another student to come forward.
- Whisper into the second person's ear: "The person on stage is Lin-Manuel Miranda. Without speaking, go shake his hand."
- Discuss: "What age do you think the second actor was?"
- Say: "It is likely that being the lesser artist in the situation will make that actor behave as if they are younger."
- Now whisper new instructions "That is the disrespectful new boyfriend of your daughter."
- Discuss: "What age do you think the second actor was?"
- The result of this will be quite different. The actor will seem older, taller, more confident and purposeful. This ages them.
- Discuss: "Hagen tells us that we can play any age, not by changing ourselves, but how we view those around us." Is this a valid claim?

Activity—Obstacles

- Set your class in the audience and put a table with a stack of dishes on the stage.
- Say: "I need a volunteer."

- "Come to the stage and set the table for important guests."
- Discuss: "What you thinking about while setting the table? Were you thinking about impressing the audience? Did time drag?"
- Now give the actor this set of obstacles modified from Hagen's activity in *Respect for Acting*. (If you have enough tables and dishes, you can have everyone do this task simultaneously. Or in teams.)
    - Character—you are a perfectionist.
    - Past experience—you have no idea how to set the table for a fancy party because of your upbringing but you are aware there are rules of etiquette that your guests will know.
    - Time—you only have five minutes.
    - The objects—the dishes aren't quite right—maybe they are cracked, mismatched, dirty, or there aren't enough of them.
    - Circumstances—someone is sleeping in the next room and you don't want to wake them. Be specific about who the person is and the consequences of waking them (baby will cry, wife will find out about the surprise dinner party you are throwing for her birthday, mother will yell at you for doing it wrong).
    - The relationship—the guests are fussy people you need to impress in order to get a good letter of recommendation to grad school or for a job.
    - Place—the table is too small for the number of guests.
    - Weather—your apartment doesn't have air conditioning and there is a heat wave, or the furnace doesn't ever work right and it is freezing outside.
    - Get creative—add any sort of obstacles to your scene to make it compelling.
- Discuss: "What is the usefulness of obstacles in your work? Is it always necessary?"

13

Jacques Lecoq

The Person

Jacques Lecoq was born in Paris in 1921. He loved and participated in sports, even attending college to study physical education. Afterwards, he taught physical education and coached swimming. During the German Occupation in the Second World War, he joined a group of people who used movement to oppose fascism. He also taught physical education and worked as a physiotherapist, specializing in rehabilitation of people with paralysis. He said this work was important to his later work in the theatre because the anatomical knowledge and practice he used steered him towards his work in theatre and mime.

After the Second World War he worked in the field of rehabilitation for disabled people. It was in this post-war period that he began connecting his work with the physical body to theatre. Lecoq was a leader in a movement of practitioners who believed the actor's body, not the text, created meaning in performance. He traveled and taught his movement theories, spending six months helping actors relax in post-Nazi Germany in an international program designed to bring French and German young people together. He then lived and directed theatre in Italy where he moved in 1948 to teach movement skills at the University of Padua. He intended to stay three months, but stayed eight years. While he was there, he worked with Amleto Sartori to create leather commedia masks which he used extensively in his work.

In 1951, Lecoq moved to Milan and worked with other theatre makers in many genres of theatre, all focused on movement. He learned about Greek chorus movement which deeply impacted his work. In this period of time he created his two-year pedagogy for his future work. His school in Paris opened in 1956. It became popular, and he devoted the rest of his life to it. When Lecoq died in early 1999 he was still teaching classes.

The Method

Lecoq's life goal was to create theatre that embraced play. "My method aims to promote the emergence of a theatre where the actor is playful. It is a theatre of movement, but above all a theatre of the imagination."[1] He worked with his students to approach theatre as if it was yet to be invented. Using their poetic vision, their creative imaginations were set free.

Lecoq's method explores the form, matter, and movement of humans in space. His students have a somatic or embodying experience as they are trained through movement. In other words, movement provokes emotion and the body remembers. If you train your body by swimming, the body remembers those motions. If you learn to ride a bike, your body remembers how even without conscious thought. By using movement and play in training, Lecoq actors are embodied and ready to perform.

Training School

The students at Lecoq's school study for two years. The course of study includes body movement, vocal work, and acrobatics. The students start in silence, stripped of their past training so they can work from a place of innocence and discovery. They learn the rules of improvisation, movement technique, and movement analysis with a heavy focus on the study of nature with the goal of self-discovery and expression. In their two-year journey, students use various techniques to uncover their true selves. Some actors find they are funny, some find they are not. The physical, playful work helps them find their authentic creative being.

Lecoq used improvisation liberally in his training school. He wrote that it was essential to theatre training, but should not be allowed to be self-indulgent. "Unfortunately many people enjoy expressing themselves, 'letting it all hang out,' and forgetting that they must not be the only ones to get pleasure from it: spectators must receive pleasure, too."[2] The goal in creative expression is for actors to shine by creating a space where the audience is present in the work. Performance is for the audience. Lecoq was training his actors to be playful without selfishness. As an actor, your job is to forget your ego and your inner demons because performance is not about your own self-enlightenment.

Le Jeu

Lecoq's stagecraft is rooted in Le Jeu, a term that means playfulness. Play is a condition of acting that puts everything in movement. Players react to each other and boundaries shift from moment to moment, keeping the audience on the edge of their seats because they can feel the undecided nature of the performance. Lecoq likens this sort of acting to "the play of a bicycle chain" because in playful storytelling there is enough slack to allow freedom. If a bicycle chain is too tight, it becomes brittle and inflexible. There must be play in the chain.[3] Play also includes collusion with the audience. The audience and players are working in a space where there is fun, but also a darker, more mischievous understanding that rules will be broken.

Movement with a Capital M

Lecoq's method is firmly rooted in movement. Each move has dramatic potential ready to be harnessed. If all you do is move your head like the director asks, you will miss the opportunity to communicate an intention. Try it! Turn your head to the right. Now do it again while saying, "I hear a sound." The movement with intention has meaning, the movement without intention is just movement. Gestures become language when rooted in intention.

Gestures often reveal something a person or character is trying to hide from the world. Lecoq analyzed human movement to help performers find clear communication through breaking down each gesture. Movement breaks down into three categories:

1. Undulation: as humans walk, they rise and fall following an undulating line. The pelvis undulates laterally and vertically. The leverage point for undulation is the earth that we push away from and return to.
2. Inverse undulation: this movement is the opposite of undulation. The leverage point is the head. Something outside the body pulls the head up, mobilizing the body.
3. Eclosion: is balance between the other two and originates in the center of the body. It expands and contracts.

Lecoq developed seven laws of motion through his study of the body:

1. There is no action without reaction
2. Motion is continuous, it never stops
3. Motion always originates in a state of disequilibrium tending towards equilibrium
4. Equilibrium is itself in motion
5. There is no motion without a fixed point
6. Motion highlights the fixed point
7. The fixed point, too, is in motion.[4]

Lecoq begins his laws by stating that motion is always motivated, and never stops. He then indicates that all movement is vacillating between equilibrium and disequilibrium. Since movement is subject to the laws of gravity, humans are constantly compensating for it. The earth pulls us down, and we lift ourselves against gravity. When a person walks, the earth holds still and their body moves in relation to it. When you walk, you are throwing your body into disequilibrium and then finding equilibrium again, only to repeat the cycle.

This rule also applies to lifting something heavy. Try picking up a chair with one hand. You will automatically lean the opposite direction to counterbalance. This displacement happens to create equilibrium. What is done on the right, must also be done on the left. If you mime carrying a bucket or suitcase, if you compensate for the imaginary weight of the item, you create the illusion of weight.

Lecoq taught that movement is a displacement of space. Pressures and tensions are created when we move and you can highlight them in your movement. Lecoq wrote that performance in theatre intensifies these tensions to unnatural proportions. You can heighten tension by exaggerating the displacement of space that is occurring.

Stillness also has movement in it. Lecoq used the term Attitudes to describe powerful moments of stillness which stretch a moment. Again, he encourages heightening a moment of movement, but this time by isolating and extending stillness. This can be done by breaking a movement into preparation, pause, accentuation, and rhythm with a clear beginning, middle and ending.

- Preparation: A preparatory motion happens with each movement. For example, to throw a rock into a pond, the first motion is backwards, away from the trajectory of the rock. When

getting up from a chair, we lean back first. When jumping, we crouch first. This preparatory movement is powerful and defines the following action. You can try skipping the preparatory movement to create surprise. Or, you can do a false or oversized preparatory movement for comedic effect. Lecoq wrote that "An oversized preparatory movement for a tiny action will create a rupture that laughter will balance."[5]
- Pause: By separating the preparation from the action, you punctuate the movement. Each movement should have a moment of suspension in the action and a punctuation at the end.
- Accentuation: a quick acceleration of movement with a slight bump or explosion at the end. The movement itself accelerates quickly. The rhythm of the movement is important, but Lecoq taught that the movement should be weighted either towards the preparation or the completion, not in the middle.
- Pause: a moment of elongation at the end of the movement. The ending pause justifies the motion. It can't be skipped. Movement must have an ending, or it ceases to mean anything. Movement is communicated through its opposite.

Mime

For many people, the first image of mime that comes to mind is a performer with a painted white face and white gloves. This is not the mime that Lecoq used, and he hated to have it confused with his work. Another misunderstanding of mime is that it is a style of acting where the performer uses gestures to communicate instead of words. Lecoq says it goes much further than this.

> If I mime the sea, it is not about drawing waves in space with my hands to make it understood that it is the sea, but about grasping the various movements into my own body: feeling the most secret rhythms to make the sea come to life in me and, little by little, to become the sea. Next, I discover that those rhythms emotionally belong to me; sensations, sentiments, and ideas appear . . . I create another sea—the sea played with this 'extra' that belongs to me and which defines my style.[6]

In other words, Lecoq's mime is not simple gestural sign language. It is a complete embodiment of the action or object. He said his style of mime is embodiment that tries to create better understanding of movement.

Lecoq used mime extensively in training actors. One of the benefits of the form is the limitations on how mime must be performed. These constraints force the actor into a heightened style, adding pressure to the performance, creating detail and intention for the actor. These skills make an actor stronger in any genre. Play is enhanced and creativity is improved through limitation. For example, in mime, time is often expanded rather than contracted. An actor must show their action of making toast over five minutes instead of thirty seconds. This expansion of time is not slow motion, but a showing of every step of the movement required to complete the action. Another constraint that is often used in mime is space restriction. Space is contracted, showing what would take a lot of space occurring in a small box of three-dimensional space—perhaps a bar brawl in a space the size of a bathroom stall.

Another technique that Lecoq taught for enhancing the illusion of mime is creating a fixed point. For example if you establish that you have a hat in your hand and place it on your head, it might be believable, but it will be a stronger illusion if you establish the hat as a fixed point and move your body into it. The hat is the fixed point, and your head rises to meet it, finding resistance. By establishing a fixed point, the audience can see the movement better.

Masks

Lecoq felt that masks are essential training for acting because of what he calls the ricochet effect. Just as a shot-putter trains by running, so an actor trains by using masks. The sideways benefits of the work will be seen on stage.

Some masks are "Expressive" and useful for performance, however, "Neutral" masks are for training only. Neutral masks are made specifically to have no expression on them. These masks encourage actors to use movements economically and express emotion with their bodies rather than their face. The neutral mask is also designed to neutralize the face, eliminating internal tension. Simon Murray says: "The neutral mask allows the actor to recognize – in a playful way – that the experience of calmness and openness can be achieved only by accepting the perpetual motion between balance and off-balance. the neutral mask invites the actor to enjoy the pleasure of going off-balance so as to find a new balance."[7]

Lecoq liked his students to build their own neutral masks so they could figure out for themselves how masks function. For example, they had to discover through trial and error that a mask needs to not fit the face perfectly because a separation of mask from face is needed to make it come alive. Experimentation with masks forces actors to "isolate a character and situation. It focuses physical gestures and the tone of the voice. It elevates text above the mundane, clarifies, filters out the anecdotal and leaves the essential."[8] This clarified state allows an actor to perform playfully and with calm focus.

You might have noticed that the quote above includes a mention of the voice. It is true that many masks are silent, but Lecoq didn't want actors to fall into the trap of creating movement in masks to replace text. Instead, he encouraged them to work in ways that don't require words. He didn't want the audience to believe the actor wasn't speaking because the mask wouldn't allow them to.

Expressive masks come in several forms:

- Larval Masks: These are large and abstract exaggerations of underdeveloped human faces. They encourage big, uncomplicated play. When playing in a larval mask, the actor can either play with or against it by taking a mask that appears stupid, and playing into the unintelligent image. Or upending expectations by playing highly intelligent. Lecoq calls this richer expression of mask a counter-mask. In this portrayal there is a heightened internal conflict. As an actor, your job is to show the audience the face behind the larval mask through your actions. As you play in larval mask, ask yourself: What effect does the mask have on others? What is the opposite of the mask? How do you express the opposite while wearing the mask?
- Half-masks: These masks are speaking masks. When wearing one of these, the actor needs to find the voice and language of the mask. Commedia is a half-mask art. It is not a realistic acting form. The voices are exaggerated, and come from the type that the mask portrays. Commedia dell'arte masks demand exaggerated body postures creating heightened and archetypal portrayals.

- Red Nose/Clown: This smallest of masks leaves the actor exposed and vulnerable. Clown requires actors to acknowledge their human insecurities to the audience. An actor who shows the audience their knobby knees and internal insecurities invites the audience into their private moment. Each person can find their own clown through exploration of their fragility and usual public facade. Unlike a full mask, the red nose doesn't provide character for the actor. A red nose actor will discover that the more their weaknesses appear, the more they are themselves, and the funnier they will be. Training in clowning comes last because actors need experience with play, movement, and humility before they are ready for vulnerable form in which they must fully invest, and emotionally expose themselves in communion with the audience.
- Bouffon Mask: The physical bodies of a bouffon are extreme. They have huge bellies that almost touch the ground or impossibly long skinny legs that are balls on joints, or huge butts balanced by giant chests. Their extreme bodies allow the body to become a mask. Sometimes bouffons are confused with clowns. However, they are quite different.

  - The bouffon is part of a gang; clowns are alone.
  - The bouffon makes fun of us; we make fun of clowns. Mockery bordering on parody is at the heart of the bouffon. They don't believe in anything, and make fun of everything.
  - They are not from earth, but they delight in amusing themselves by recreating human lives. Clowns are earth bound.
  - They come to show us our own follies in a parade of ritual and mockery. Clowns show us their own follies.

One additional fact about bouffons is that they are hierarchical: both the bully and bullied know their place. Because of this, no revolt happens among the bouffon crowd.

Choral Movement

Using the Greek chorus was one of the most important parts of Lecoq's teaching method. Choral work is saved for the second year of training, when his students are already familiar with his method, and adept at mime. Lecoq believed that choral movement should have a strong sense of mime in order to maintain its poetic qualities.

The poetic existence of a chorus is a rhythmic and powerful state meant to balance the presence of a hero. He explains this phenomenon by writing that when a chorus enters the stage, "It fills the whole space, and then withdraws to one part of the stage. By so doing, it frees a new space and creates a kind of appeal to the hero. But who is able to fill this space? What balance can be found, today, between a chorus and a hero?"[9]

Choruses, according to Lecoq, are flowing and flexible. They have a center of gravity that can extend outward as far as the breath of the group allows. Their movement is not as a single group, but as an amorphous, organic entity that can break into smaller groupings that are linked by the leader, who is the center of gravity. Their movement is stylized and everyone in the group contributes, no one takes control, even though a leader often emerges. When a leader develops, it is because the rest of the chorus has selected them and pulled back rather than the leader stepping forward. The leader's voice is then supported by the entire chorus.

The structure of the chorus can take the form of a square, triangle, V, or arc. The shape it takes is in response to or anticipation of the actions of the hero. It's movement seeks to find balance on stage, or to create a void which calls for the hero to come forward. When they call a hero, they charge the space so the actor who is playing the hero must fill the void completely with their presence in order to answer the call of the chorus. Because of this phenomenon, the retreat of the chorus must be either extremely fast or deliberately slow, in a summoning. When the hero leaves the stage, the chorus is compelled to fill the void left by their exit, bringing balance and commenting on what has just occurred. They are reactive rather than active in charging the space and bringing balance to it.

In his work experimenting with choruses, Lecoq found that fifteen or seven are the best numbers of members. Seven allows for two groups of three and a mediator or leader. The number fifteen allows for two groups of seven and a leader. More than fifteen tends to feel militaristic rather than artistic. He found other numbers to be confusing or unbalanced. You can experiment with different numbers, and will likely find that eight tends to create a double block with no leader, and fourteen feels as if someone is missing. He also found that rectangle-shaped stages are the best to work in. This allows for diagonal, parallel, and angular movements. A rounded space only allows for curves.

Creating Characters

Lecoq also waited until the second year of training to teach character development. He was afraid that his students would fall back on personality rather than using play to create characters. By the second year, the foundation of mask work has taught actors to play using themselves rather than play themselves on stage.

The first stage of moving to character work in Lecoq's method is identifying an animal that helps distill the essence of the character. This way, when working on a character, the actor can play with a triangular relationship between the character, the animal, and the actor. The second step is to create a few characters based on people they have observed in public by giving them a three word description such as "kind, engaged, and quick-tempered." His students spend time improvising with each character and then the instructor throws them into a scenario that forces the characters to interact in a high pressure situation.

Approaching the Text

Lecoq teaches his students to approach the text through the body. His teaching method stays away from intellectual analysis. In order to do a reading of a new text, Lecoq had his students first make gestures of any sort as they speak the words of a script. The job of the gestures is to set the text free in the body, so the physical self is not an obstacle to the text. After the actor has gestured their way through speaking the text, Lecoq taught them to perform the gestures silently, emphasizing the motions. Movement comes first and remains primary in working with any text in Lecoq's method.

Jacques Lecoq's Legacy

Jacques Lecoq's work impacted Western theatre in major ways. His methods in movement, play, mask work, and mime are still taught at respected acting training schools. He taught countless performers and teachers to make the body more articulate and introduced the art of mime to mainstream theatre. His methods are an essential part of movement training in many drama schools. In fact, the training methods your theatre teachers use are probably impacted by the work of Jacques Lecoq.

Tips for taking this method further

- Study at Laboratoire d'étude du mouvement (LEM) in Paris.
- Apply to study with Embodied Poetics, an organization that teaches Lecoq, Copeau, and Bing in various international locations.

Discussion Starters and Journal Prompts

- Summarize the key points of Lecoq's method. Which ones seem most likely to be helpful to you in your work as an actor.
- Imagine, like Lecoq asked his students to do, that theatre was yet to be invented. Using your poetic vision and freeing your creative imagination, what sort of work would you do? How would this paradigm set you free?
- Lecoq's method explores the form, matter, and movement of humans in space. His students have a somatic or embodying experience as they are trained through movement. In other words, movement provokes emotion and the body remembers. Explain this concept in your own words.

The Tools for your Toolbox
Activity—Moving Off Balance

- Divide your class into groups of three.
- Say: "Stand in a line, shoulder to shoulder with a gap of eighteen inches or so between you."
- "The middle person should tilt their body until they are off balance towards one side. The person on that side's job is to gently catch them and return them to balance, then past balance to the person on the other side. Repeat, tipping to the other side."
- "Play this game for a while then rotate who is in the center, paying attention to the precise moment of going out of balance."

- "Repeat the activity, but now the center person should exhale while going off-balance. This is the opposite of a fear response. It encourages relaxation and enjoying the out of control sensation. Does your breath impact your internal state?"
- "Spread out and play alone with faltering, finding the moment of off-balance, catching yourself, and trying different angles of falling."
- "Take the game a step further. At the moment of falling out of balance, take one step into the fall to move forward. Enjoy the feeling of pushing into an off-kilter moment in order to find new balance over and over."
- "Don't look at the floor, but focus on the space around you, taking steps as a reaction to the space around you rather than fear."

Activity—Push and Pull

- Give pairs of students wooden sticks that are about 120cm or 4 foot long.
- Say: "Support the stick between the base of your open right palms which are facing each other, keeping the distance between your hands exactly four feet. The trick is to find the right amount of push and pull so that the stick does not fall to the ground."
- "Move around the room pushing and pulling each other through space playfully. Connect with each other and the space as you play."
- Note: Over time the connection will take on a more dramatic quality with one partner trapping the other against a wall or the floor. Dramatic relationships and emotional states will come out of the physical game that is being played.
- Say: "Put down the sticks, and instead imagine that there is a four foot string connecting your palms."
- "Stand in one place and play with the imaginary string, pushing and pulling."
- "Move the string to between your foreheads, then stomachs, knees and other body parts."
- "Move around the space keeping those strings taut."
- "Expand the distance to two meters or yards and allow the string to become slack sometimes, and test the maximum distance with stops and pulls back in."
- "Add one word statements to the game. One partner could say 'Come!' or 'Why?' Use whatever word you like as long as they are one word statements. Silence is still a perfectly good response."
- Discuss: "How does the push and pull of this game create emotions?"

Activity—Choral Text

- Pair your students and give each pair the following text on a piece of paper.

   I urge someone to move forward . . . he refuses
   I go in front and pull him by the hand . . . he resists I pull harder . . .
   he pulls me in the opposite direction I pull even harder . . . he gives in
   He comes with me . . . he overtakes me. He drags me after him . . . I resist
   I let him go . . . he escapes[10]

- Say: "One partner speak a choral text to the other, and then after a while the other take the paper and take over the speech. Trade back and forth randomly."
- "This time work additively so that instead of trading, the second reader joins the speech, both speaking in the same tone, rhythm, and cadence as one voice. In this activity the voice of the individual is not important, the chorus must be heard. In choral speech, you are the voice of the embodied text."
- "Stand with one partner behind the other. The one behind whispers the first line to the other, who speaks it full volume then listens for the next line, etc."
- "Regroup into groups of three with one whisperer and two speakers standing shoulder to shoulder. The whisperer says the first line and the two in front speak together in full voice."
- "Regroup into larger and larger groups, and continue until you have the entire group giving voice to one whisper behind."
- Discuss: "What does the choral voice feel like? What could be the importance of one chorus expressing one interpretation?"
- Say: "Divide into trios and create a scene with the choral text you have been working on. Think of vertical, horizontal, and diagonal lines of effort. Intensify the dramatic dimensions of push and pull both verbally and physically. Share the text in whichever way you like, thinking of your group as one artist expressing a text."
- Discuss: "What techniques of other groups were emotionally and visually powerful? What did you learn from choral work?"

Activity—Waking Up in Mask

- Give your students neutral masks and provide them with foam scraps and adhesive to customize theirs so that the masks don't rest on the face, and can be worn without fidgeting with them. Once they are satisfied with the fit, have them "fall asleep" in various playful positions. Remind them to use Le Jeu in their choice of position.
- Say: "Make yourself a blank slate, preparing the expressive potential of your body and emotions. Return to a place where you only know the world through gesture, movement, and touch. Think of the push and pull, and movement off balance, finding a place of open readiness."
- "Wake up in this state of innocence to experience the world as if for the first time and explore nature."
- "As you discover insects, plants, animals, and elements, momentarily embody the things you encounter as a child would."
- "Imagine you have just woken up on the shore of a deserted island. Absorb the scenery around you, react to it, and explore it, climbing cliffs, wandering through forests, wading in creeks, etc. Become the things you encounter."
- "The weather has changed. It is bitterly cold, windy, and wet."
- "Become the water. Explore all the forms it inhabits: streams, rivers, lakes, oceans, water droplets, condensation, puddles, monsoons, etc."
- "Now shift to become air: wind, breeze, hurricane, etc. "

- "Now shift to become fire: flame on a match, fire in a fire pit, forest fire, etc."
- "Now become earth: garden earth, rocks, hills, cliffs, etc."
- Optional: try different substances such as liquid, wood, metal, cardboard. Then continue on to embodying colors, words, rhythms, light, etc.
- Discuss: "Lecoq spoke of universal poetic awareness that renders the neutral mask invisible.[11] Did your work in this exercise rise to the level of poetic awareness? Did the mask disappear?"

Activity—The Escape

- Have your students put on their neutral masks.
- Say: "Go to sleep in a position of discomfort."
- "You have been imprisoned and are waking up in a dim cell. When you wake up, look around for a way of escape, find it, then run and sneak down long passageways trying to get out of the prison. You might be apprehended at any time, so be careful and watchful, aware that your absence in your cell will be noticed soon, so you must get out of the building and then the prison yard as soon as possible. You must be silent, so all communication must be gestural. End by scaling the wall and jumping down to freedom on the other side."
- Discuss: "How might the state of urgency you found in this game help on stage in a different situation? Are the masks helping you find embodiment?"

Activity—The Person Who . . .[12]

- Set up two small tables on the stage and a chair at each. They should have some distance.
- Hand two players a description of the scenario which Lecoq called "The person who believes that . . . but he is wrong!" And have them enact it immediately without planning. The description is: "Person A is sitting in a coffee shop. Person B is at a different table makes a gesture towards Person A. Person A isn't sure they know Person B, but you respond anyway. Person B gestures more boldly, smiling. Person A responds. Do this for a while. Finally Person B gets up and comes towards Person A. Person A gets up too, but Person B passes Person A, approaching an imaginary Person C in the wings."
- Discuss: "What did you notice about the rising dynamic scale of the gestures? How did the actors play the nuances of those moments?"
- Have students invent and play more scenarios of "The person who believes that . . . but he is wrong!" Perhaps the belief is that someone is waiting for them, that they are stronger, that they are hated, etc.

Activity—Equilibrium and Disequilibrium

- Say: "Spread out in pairs and hold imaginary hats."
- "Take turns placing the hats on your heads."

- "Remember the fixed point principle. Try again, this time placing the hat *near* your head and moving your head up into the hat using your whole body."
- "Discuss with your partner the merits of this method of mime illusion. Did it make it more believable to place the hat? or to put head in hat? Which is more realistic?"
- "Now each person pick up a chair with one hand and observe the displacement of your center of gravity."
- "Now mime picking up the chair, while exaggerating the displacement of your bodies to compensate. Using mirrors to watch is useful for some."
- "Mime carrying a suitcase that is heavy by using the principle of compensation. Start by picking up an empty suitcase, and compensate as if it is heavy. Then lift imaginary suitcases doing the same motions."
- "Add the concept of the preparatory movement before picking it up. First, open the hand wider and away from the handle, then reach down and grasp it."
- "Work in pairs trying these three approaches to an action of your choice":
  - suppressing the preparatory movement to create surprise
  - doing a false preparatory movement to create laughter
  - doing an outsized preparatory movement to create laughter.
- "Prepare mimed movements with all of the following steps: preparation, pause, quick acceleration of movement, end of movement, accentuation with slight bump or explosion, pause."
- Share performances with the group. Then discuss: "Who did you see make good use of displacement? preparatory movement? false preparatory movement? outsized?"

Activity—Justified Movement

- Have your students stand.
- Say: "Turn your heads to the side, then forward, then back."
- "Repeat the actions with the words: 'I listen, I look, I am frightened,' as justification for your movement."
- "Work in pairs to create a three movement, three justification acting moment where each of you have the same movements, but different justifications."
- "Stand on one side of the stage."
- "Imagine you are throwing a ball into the air and catching it again. As you do the motions of throwing it up, turn your eyes and heads to track the movement up to a moment of suspension in the air, then a return to your hands where your gaze should remain still for a moment to punctuate the end of the movement."
- "Work in small groups to do the same activity where you all see a ball thrown and watch it. You can be creative with where the ball begins and ends but must all see the same ball, have a moment of suspension and a punctuation at the ending."
- "After you have created your moments, add sound to your moment. The breath and sound should join the movement as one single movement."
- Discuss: "How does adding justification improve blocking? What did sound add?"

Activity—The Attitudes

- Have your students perform a simple wave by standing in neutral and raising a hand to say goodbye to someone, then putting the hand back down.
- Say: "Now breathe in as you raise your hand and exhale as you put it down. What does this mean? Lecoq suggests a reluctance to say goodbye."
- "Next, reverse this. What does this mean? Is it relief?"
- "Try breathing in and holding your breath while you raise and lower your hand. What is this emotion?"
- "Now try exhaling before and not inhaling until after. What quality is this?"

Activity—Character Development

- Ask each student to come to class prepared to play a character based on someone they observed in public. Ask them to identify an animal that distills the essence of that character and then to think of themselves as a triangle that is the actor, character, and animal all working together.
- Say: "Improvise a scenario in which your characters are waking up in their various homes, preparing for work, commuting to work, and performing their jobs. This is a solitary experience where each is using their imagination to fill out a character."
- "Now return to your homes and lie down to sleep."
- "This time, the 2m or 6 foot square area I've marked on the floor represents a train car. Each character must end up on the car, headed on an individual weekend outing. Wake up and prepare for your trip, then board the train."
- Once everyone is on the train, say: "Keep acting while I ask a few questions:
  - "Which of the characters like to be looked at? Which thinks everyone is watching them, but no one is? Which used to catch attention, but doesn't anymore?" etc.
  - "Which characters are certain of where the train is going and when to get off, what to do, exact plans? Which are uncertain or unprepared?"
  - "Which are the types that go out on the weekend to quiet bistros? loud dance clubs? stay home and cook? go to museums?"
  - "Which characters are pushed from behind to go places? Which are pulled from the front?"
- After they commute for a while, say: "The train is stopping at an unexpected place with a loud noise. You are stuck in the car together, uncertain of what is happening. Go ahead and interact as your characters."
- Repeat this exercise with another, opposite character.
- Now have them get on the train again, and say: "Play both characters alternately by switching back and forth. You can use a prop or clothing item to indicate the change (turn a cap around? remove a sweater?) or not."
- Discuss: "Did you manage to maintain playfulness? How was this mode of character development different from other methods you've tried?"

Activity—Find Your Clown

- Bring in a trunk of ridiculous disguises: wigs, beards, giant sunglasses, capes, crowns, etc.
- Say: "Come put on a disguise and play for a while!"
- Discuss: "Do you notice a lack of inhibition while you wear a disguise?"
- Now give them a red nose to replace all the other silly disguises.
- Say: "Working in front of a mirror, discover your usual walking mode. Don't adjust it because you can see yourselves!"
- "Now exaggerate your own way of walking. If you are usually hunched over, be more hunched. If you swing your arms, swing more. This is the rediscovery of your childhood bodies that moved naturally without the expectations of society encumbering you—and leaning into them."
- "Now come onto the stage using your walk one at a time while the rest of the class watches. Your job is to 'discover' the audience. This moment is not for performance, but for genuine discovery of yourselves in connection *with* the audience rather than *for* the audience."
- "Improvise something based on what you see and feel. Don't plan anything, and be brave even though you will feel very exposed."
- Discuss: "How was that activity for you? What did the nose do for you? Were you able to be yourself completely? Did you lean into your insecurities?"
- Say: "Think of a task that you can accomplish that most or all of the other students in the class cannot. Perhaps the splits? or a body contortion?"
- "Create a short clowning moment by exploiting your ability by struggling to complete it. Then when a sudden sound or action startles you, do it effortlessly."
- "Perform these bits for the audience."
- Discuss: "Did you get the laughter with the failure as well as the unexpected success? Did the constraint of the assignment make you more creative?"

Activity—Bouffon

- Start by reviewing what a bouffon is, and asking the class to draw a few examples either alone or in pairs. Discuss their sketches.
- Now provide the class with materials to create their own bouffon masks for themselves: cloth, foam, rubber, clothes, objects, ribbon, string, elastic bands, plastic sheets, etc. As well as tools: tape, staplers, scissors, etc. Ask them to create roughly shaped and expressive grotesque bodies that are not natural human shapes, either spindly and extended or bouncy and bulbous. When complete, remind them that these forms are meant to be flexible and rudimentary. They will develop over time.
- Say: "You are children in a city park playing in a sandbox. Rediscover what it is to be children. Find the playful, aggressive, possessive, comic, lonely, obsessive. Re-establish the rules of fairness and justice of childhood play spaces."
- "Play at being a grown-up, allowing yourself to strive for possession of power, and power over others. Invent rituals, but don't get angry with each other. Accept the hierarchy that develops

as you play. If someone disciplines you, accept and revel in your place in the invented world. Ask for more of it!"
- "Choose a scenario to play, for instance a union on strike and the police patrolling. Make fun of the characters you are playing, switch sides from time to time just for the fun of it!"
- Discuss: "What does it feel like to be a bouffon? How is this role like a whole-body mask? What value does the alien and mocking perspective of a bouffon gang bring to the theatre? How would you describe this form of performance to others?"

Activity—A Balanced Stage

- Start by having your students wander around a rectangular space. Use spike tape or benches to indicate the edges of the space if it is not already rectangular.
- Say: "On my signal, form groupings of seven or three."
- "Move as a group, discovering who the leader is."
- "Move apart to find the maximum distance you can be apart from the other members without the chorus breaking up. This is the threshold of stress."
- Discuss: "What did you learn about grouping sizes? Does Lecoq's rule of seven seem right to you? How did the leader emerge from the group? How far could you spread out and still be a chorus? Was it the same for every chorus group?"
- Now move your students to the outside of the rectangular space. Choose one person to begin.
- Say: "The space is balanced around a center axis. The first person must take a position in the center to create balance in the space. They will stand still. When they feel the time is right, they will move outside the center creating an imbalance. The next person must join them on stage and react to balance them. Again, both will stand still."
- "Each of you will add yourself to the space one at a time to balance an imbalance created by the chorus on the stage when they create an imbalance. The new person becomes the leader, and those on the stage must move to balance their actions."
- "Play the game silently."
- Discuss: "Did you notice anyone who added themselves when an imbalance did not exist? Did you sense a bond with the performers when you were on the outside? What did that feel like? Performers, how did the watchers help you? Did you find you had more weight in different positions on stage? Do you think the group achieved a harmonious relationship with time, space, and each other?"
- Play again, this time with a hero on stage that the chorus must balance.
- Say: "The hero must have equal weight to the entire chorus. Starting with one member, then slowly adding others and finding a balance between the chorus and hero."
- "When the hero feels it is time, they must fall to the ground, breaking up the chorus. In that moment, the chorus will choose a leader to remain and confront the hero. The leader must not step forward, choosing themself. Instead, the other members retreat, leaving the leader who accepts their responsibility to be the voice of the chorus."

14

Augusto Boal

The Person

Augusto Boal was born in Brazil in 1931. He noticed the injustice and oppression of the world from a young age. He describes a tearful Sunday night when he was nine. He wanted to be friends with the animals that lived in his yard, but knew this was impossible. "We appeared to be friends: we weren't; The truth tormented me: I lived in the big house, destined for a brilliant university future . . . They, on the other hand, lived on Death Row, destined for the cooking pot . . . True friendship cannot exist between two individuals when one is eternal and the other perishable."[1] This terrible understanding of oppressor and oppressed deepened when his pet goat, Chibico, became aggressive while they were playing one day, and was served for dinner later that week.

After he earned his chemistry degree at the age of twenty-one, his father sent him abroad to study. He considered many places, but ultimately chose Columbia University because while he worked on his graduate degree in chemistry, he could also study with a playwright he admired. While in New York he was introduced to the methods of Brecht and Stanislavski, formed connections with the Black Experimental Theater, and directed plays. The roots of his future work with the oppressed had already begun.

When he returned to Brazil, Boal didn't seek a career in chemistry. Instead, he directed for the intimate Arena Theater in São Paulo, creating an acting laboratory to prepare his company for the stage. He was always socially active, adapting classical theatre pieces to push for social change. His audiences were invited to discuss the plays after each performance, allowing them to be active participants. In 1964 a new military regime took control of the government. He continued his work, even directing a play about fascism, *The Resistible Rise of Arturo Ui* by Brecht in 1971. Soon after this, he was kidnapped off the street, arrested and tortured. Because the government was afraid of retribution from the public if Boal was killed in prison, they released him and unofficially advised him to flee Brazil. He took their advice and left his beloved homeland. He was deflated. He reflected about this sad time, "it was impossible to live in Brazil. We could not speak about what we really wanted . . . We tried to resist. It is difficult to confront tanks with stage sets, guns with music. We lost."[2]

He traveled in South America with a group of actors, inviting common people to suggest solutions to oppressions his actors performed on stage. The actors would try out these ideas in an improv style performance. His most famous form of theatre, Forum Theatre, began in 1973 when an audience member at one performance could not explain what she wanted an actor to try on stage for her. Boal invited her to try out her idea herself. She eagerly did, and a new form of Theatre of the Oppressed was born. At first it was difficult for him to let the audience have control of the narrative. He had wanted to show the audience truth. Over time, he realized that the audience often had a perspective on a problem that he could learn from. He became a teacher/artist whose job was to listen and not interfere, trusting the process. He wrote, "When I started out in the theatre I was speaking about myself, my neighborhood. I knew the truth: I doled out advice. But I discovered that you could not liberate anyone by occupying their space, taking their decisions."[3]

In 1979 Boal was convinced to train others to use the Theatre of the Oppressed in France. He later regretted not establishing a permanent school there, but it was a good start. Hundreds of people learned the form at that time and have spread it to all the corners of the world.

He returned to Brazil in 1986 after fourteen years in exile and formed the Center for the Theatre of the Oppressed in Rio de Janeiro. This group still works to fight oppression and advocates for human rights.

In 1992 he was elected to the office of City Councilor in Brazil. He used Theatre of the Oppressed to find out what his constituents needed. Thirteen laws were enacted in Rio de Janeiro as a result. Boal said the Theatre of the Oppressed was able to convert the people's desires into law. In this way, Boal used theatre to bring about actual political change. He felt all theatre is political because, "Those who try to separate theatre from politics try to lead us into error."[4] In other words, he taught that theatre makers must be political because pacifying the powers that be is also political through its omission of activism.

Boal died in 2009 at the age of seventy-eight.

The Method

Most people would classify Boal's work as a style of theatre, rather than an acting method. However, Boal's methods are worthy of examining for your acting toolbox. Boal saw theatre as a place of self-discovery. "This is the theatre I believe in: the place where we can stand and see ourselves. Not see what others tell us we are, or should be – but see our deepest selves! Theatre is the place where we can look at ourselves and say: 'I am a man, I am a woman: I am me!'"[5] As you work through Boal's unique method, you may find that you find yourself and your power as a performer.

Boal believed in the democratization of theatre. "We all are theatre, even if we don't make theatre."[6] Boal claims that all human beings are actors because all of us take action. We are all also spectators because we observe. His term for both his audience and his actors was "spect-actors" because everyone was involved in both performance and observation in his form of theatre.

Boal's Actors

On one hand, it is unnecessary for anyone to train using Boal's methods in order to participate in his theatre, since the spect-actor is brought on stage to participate with no training. On the other hand, those who prepare the space for the spect-actor must learn to facilitate this involvement. Boal understood that our occupation is one in which we must behave professionally: sign contracts, audition for work, appear sane. However, underneath, it is our job to portray the neurotic, criminal, and unstable. We don't usually have the luxury to play people in the peak of mental health.

This creates a problem for the actor. How does an actor find their mentally unstable characters? This work of awakening inner demons is dangerous. Boal argues that once you have awakened the Iago inside you, and introduced him to the spotlight, he might not ever be willing to go back to bed. Boal says that the actor goes "into her person, deep within, right inside, in the pressure-cooker, the place where the demons dwell at boiling point. And the actor, having patiently tamed her wildcats long ago, is once again obliged to go and waken them . . . Actors taunt the lion with a blade of grass."[7]

Boal's method teaches an actor to travel the same path to health that they travel to sickness. He writes that,

> a sick personality can, in theory, try to awaken healthy *personnages*, this time not with the goal of dispatching them back into oblivion but in the hope of mixing them into his personality. I am afraid, but inside me there also lives the courageous man; if I can wake him up, perhaps I could keep him awake . . . A well-founded hope: if the actor can become a sick person, the sick person can in turn become a heathy actor.[8]

By using Boal's method, you may be able to create images of your own reality in which you are liberated from your demons. He suggests creating mental health using the reverse method you use to create mental illness on stage.

The director who attempts to help an actor find this path is responsible for asking questions of the actor, to help them uncover the answer that is already inside them. Boal had great respect for actors and their capabilities. "Actors should, of all human beings, be the most capable of transformation, whether of themselves or in their ability to reveal this potentiality to others."[9] Boal found his actors had this ability to transform themselves, finding mental illness on stage, and mental health off of it. He believed that actors could use their work to find healing for themselves and their audiences.

Boal and Stanislavski

When Boal started working at the Arena Theater of São Paulo, he worked with his actors from a base of Stanislavski's System in an Acting Laboratory that they created together. In applying it to their reality they created "a Brazilian style of playing."[10] At first his actors were afraid of using real emotion on stage because it seemed unhealthy. It took some time, but they soon embraced the process of finding genuine emotion on stage. Boal felt Stanislavski's System was useful as long as it didn't lead to too much internal work. "Our first (and only!) guiding precept, at that time, was that emotion took precedence over all else and should be given a free rein to shape the final form of the actor's interpretation of a role."[11] What resulted was performance that audiences loved.

De-mechanization

Boal, being a trained scientist, found meaning in systematizing his process of acting. His time in chemistry classes was not wasted, though he never worked as a chemist. He created games and activities he hoped would help actors, and tested them. Through this Boal discovered that repetition was the best teacher. Like learning to ride a bicycle, coordination is difficult at first, but by repetition, riding becomes automatic. In the same way, Boal found that the process of acting becomes automatic once it is learned.

Unfortunately, once you have learned to ride a bike, you often shut down your senses and no longer notice the emotions and sensations you felt when you were learning. The same thing happens to an actor doing the same performance over and over. In this sense, the actor has to be trained to de-mechanize their senses and see and feel everything like it was new. Boal's actors did sensory exercises to help with this de-mechanization. For instance, they would swallow a spoonful of honey, followed by a pinch of salt, and then some sugar. After they went through this process, they had to try to remember and recreate the experience from sense memory.

Boal created many de-mechanization activities, helping participants "unlearn" habitual patterns of behavior. These games were designed to de-mechanize the body, the mind, and the political self. They were done in a spirit of fun, and no one was forced to participate. Especially in Boal's theatre, training was not allowed to become another oppression of the human spirit.

Character Development

The Boalian actor strives to create a character, and then willingly relinquish it to the audience. Boal taught that as the character becomes real, the audience will want to take it on themselves. He wanted this to happen because his theatre was created to make real-world social change. This emotional character development was designed to transfer emotions from the actor to the audience.

The exercises that Boal's actors did to create character started with finding the character's emotions in order to transmit those emotions to the audience. He used "transference" as a tool to create emotions. He explains transference by telling the story of an actor who was experienced with weapons, but needed to pretend to be afraid to use one on stage. They needed to find an equivalent experience in their life to transfer to the gun. In this case, the actor used memories of anticipating having to turn on the shower when the hot water was out, transferring the experience of getting up the nerve to pull the trigger of a prop. In this case, it worked just as well as if he had had the identical experience of the character.

Boal taught his actors to delve deeply into the relationships their characters formed on stage,

> In the theatrical experience, the actor must give himself utterly and completely over to his task. And his task is conflict – if both actors in a scene are really attentive to each other, like the two fighters in a boxing match have to be, the scene will always be dynamic and attractive; if everyone is concerned with himself, the scene will be divided in two and it will be boring.[12]

A character's desires must manifest in a conflict of wills between characters.

Just like Stanislavski, Boal taught that an actor's will must be specific and actionable. For example, if your character wants power and glory, you won't be able to play that well. If, instead, you focus on a desire to stab a rival with a large knife, you will be more successful. The more specific your goal, the better. If your character desires happiness, instead of using the generic goal "to be happy," you could desire a cookie dough ice cream cone, or something else very concrete that would make you happy. Boal wrote, "every idea, however abstract, has the potential to be theatrical when it manifests itself in a concrete form in particular circumstances."[13]

These specific motivations work in pairs. What your character wants has an opposite. Find it by asking what behavior your character is trying to avoid while meeting that goal. For example, Hamlet wants to avenge his father's death, but he doesn't want to kill his uncle. This leads to deeper, richer theatrical conflict. Inner conflict is deeply human and relatable. You both love your sibling and want them to go somewhere else. You want to win the love of your crush, and you don't want to talk to them for fear of rejection. Your character's reservations make them more human and three-dimensional. A character who only loves or only hates gets boring. The audience wants to see nuance. Boal believed actors should rehearse each will and counter-will separately in order to understand them better. Then, the actor can decide which will is the dominant one and play the others as complementary.

Embracing Ambiguity

When Boal was developing his working style, he found that many of the actors he encountered were disconcerted by his desire to present all ideas to the audience without landing on a particular "correct" way of being or understanding. When asked if the answer to the problem being presented was this or that, his answer was, "I wanted *this* and *that,* and a whole host of other *thats* and *thises*: I wanted the *more,* the *also,* the *maybe,* the *apart from that,* the *who knows?*"[14] In other words, he wanted the audience to understand that there were many ways to find meaning in the work, and the artists weren't trying to give them answers. The audience was being invited to think. The actor's job was to "sail on the sea of possible meanings."[15]

Boal's Theatre Styles

Now that we have explored Boal's approach to acting methods, it is worth learning about his more well-known work outside of traditional theatre. Boal developed a few styles of theatre that are still used today in theatre for social change. All of them are meant to help people recognize the big and small oppressions in their lives, and work towards understanding, empathy, and strategies for change. They all require the audience to interact with the prepared work of the acting troupe:

- *Image Theatre* is a type of theatre meant to expose truth about society. Static images blend into action. The spect-actor who participates in Image Theatre converts their oppressions

- into images that can be confronted with other images that Boal calls antibodies. After working in this style of theatre, spect-actors are armed with tools that will help them live life with more confidence, informed by the enactment of tactics. This form works across language barriers and cultural differences.
- *Invisible Theatre* happens in public with the participation of the crowd who are not aware it is a theatrical scene. In this form, actors stage a realistic scene in public with the goal of enticing the public to become involved, interacting with the scene. It is intended to stimulate debate among the populace. The result cannot have a planned resolution because the spect-actors create the resolution in real time.
- *Forum Theatre* presents the audience with an oppression depicted in a prepared scene. A company member, called the "Joker," then asks the spect-actors to propose solutions and participate in acting those solutions out. The Joker is an intermediary between the actors and the audience. They do not belong to either, just as jokers in a deck of cards do not belong to any one suit. This form of theatre is done so that the second half requires the audience to create versions of a new world, designing their own future through trial and error.
- *The Rainbow of Desire* is a theatre form in which a spect-actor uses several images to express their different desires, or colors. These are then embodied by the entire company of actors. The spect-actor can see how their desires are working against the antagonist. After watching the other actors create images of their desires, they are allowed to embody all of the images that they saw portrayed by the others. The subtitle for Boal's book about the Rainbow of Desire is *The Boal Method of Theatre and Therapy*. The Rainbow of Desire attempts to use theatre in a therapeutic way by enacting the desires of the participants.

All of these forms of theatre were designed to help humans act in our own defense. All of us have what Boal calls "cops in the head" that prevent us from action. "We define as 'cop' the image present in our heads, at a point of action, which obliges us to do what we don't want to do or prevent us from doing what we do want to do. Its presence means that our desire is diluted and that, instead of enacting our own desire, we enact the 'cop's.'"[16] Using Boal's Theatre of the Oppressed helps participants to quiet the cops in their heads, acting in their own best interest.

Augusto Boal's Legacy

Much of Boal's surviving theatre work can be categorized as drama therapy or a means of social activism rather than acting techniques. This work is powerful, and can create positive change in the participants. It supports revolutionary political transformation. He said,

> In times like ours, we need to reaffirm our identity: we must not let ourselves be globalised, robotised. Let us be who we are. I know that my nose is large, my ears are different sizes: but I know that that person is me! I will not surrender. Theatre is desire, bodily struggle, personal defense. Theatre, if it tells the truth, proffers a quest for oneself, oneself in others and others in oneself. It proffers the humanisation of humankind. This cannot be done without struggle.[17]

Boal's legacy is the empowerment of humanity to resist oppression through the arts.

Tips for taking this method further

- Read Boal's autobiography and one of his books about the power of theatre.
- Find an organization such as mandalaforchange, that uses Forum Theatre or one of Boal's other theatre forms, and join them.
- Try out some of Boal's activities with your friends or in your community.

Discussion Starters and Journal Prompts

- Summarize the main goals of Boal's work.
- Think about oppressions in your life or community and what it might mean to you if a group of theatre performers were willing to work through possible tactics with you in the safety of a theatre space.

The Tools for your Toolbox

Activity—Knowing the body

- Have your students pair up and face each other with a line on the floor in between them.
- Say: "This activity is an effort of silent communication. Since no one can talk, the give and take is negotiated by paying close attention to what your partner can do and how they are giving and taking energy."
- "Place your hands on your partner's shoulders."
- "Begin to push gradually increasing force without pushing your partner over the line. Achieve balance while exerting pressure and resisting your partner's energy."
- "Switch to back-to-back."
- "Gradually walk away from each other while maintaining contact until you are sitting on the floor back-to-back."
- "Without touching the floor with your hands, walk back up to a standing position."
- "Sit on the floor facing your partner."
- "Grab each other's wrists and place your feet flat on the floor with knees bent."
- "Using the weight of your partner as a counterbalance, stand up, then sink down to sitting again."
- "Now do it again using a see-saw motion so that one stands, then the other stands while the other sits."
- "Combine in groups of three or four and do the same activity, holding wrists and standing then sitting as a group."
- Discuss: "How was that? Boal suggested that this exercise is like democracy. Can you draw comparisons?"

Activity—Animal Pairs

- Prepare slips of paper with names of animals, two of each, but do not reveal this detail to the students yet. It is best if these are very distinct types of animals such as fish, reptiles, felines, birds, insects, etc. . . . You can even include a pair of humans for fun. Have each student draw a slip of paper, keeping their animal private.
- Say: "Silently perform the creature on your slip of paper however you like. Explore how they sit, stand, fly, eat, sleep, move, etc."
- After a while of exploration and interaction, say: "Find your mate by courting them in animal ways."
- "Once your pair has decided you are a pair, leave the playing space and quietly reveal your identity through an animal sound. If you are wrong, return to the floor and try again."
- At the end of the activity, you may ask each pair to perform their courtship for the rest of the room to watch, turning the activity into a performance.
- Discuss: "Did the chaos and theatricality of the event help you to overcome inhibitions and play with your partner?"

Activity—Image Theatre

- Start with a sculpting activity by asking participants to pair up. Select which one is the sculptor and which is the sculpture by some method: (tallest or person wearing the most black is sculptor, for example).
- Say: "The sculptor should not touch the sculpture, but rather communicate through sculpting movements how the other should shape their body."
- Give them a theme (perhaps: Monkey, Baby, Summer Vacation, Freedom, Peace) and give them 20–30 seconds to create their sculptures.
- Say: "Switch roles!" Give them another positive theme as above.
- Say: "Switch!" Give them something more negative to sculpt such as Pain, Jealousy, Loss.
- Switch and repeat.
- Say: "We are now going to work on Image Theatre. Pair up to create two person images. You may collaborate using words, but work quickly."
- "Create a Real Image of an oppression. Think of a time you felt powerless and afraid." Give them only a couple of minutes to do this.
- "Now create an Ideal Image of this oppression reversed." Give them only a couple of minutes to do this.
- "Animate a transition from the Real Image to the Ideal by creating a short scene." Give them a few minutes to do this.
- "Discuss different approaches to getting to Ideal. Try a different approach in a new scene. Boal was always after a good debate, rather than a correct solution."
- Have a few groups share their work with the class and discuss.

Activity—Forum Theatre

- Choose two volunteers and instruct them separately in their roles:
    - "Actor one: stand on stage offering your hand to Actor two. At the last minute, revoke the handshake and turn your back on Actor two."
    - "Actor two: happily go on stage to shake the offered hand."
- Take on the role of the Joker and ask the audience what they might do in this situation.
- Allow several actors to try solutions.
- Instruct a group of five volunteers out of the hearing of the class. Say: "Four of you should march in lockstep while the fifth dances. The four should safely 'shove' the dancer to the floor. After this, the fifth person begins to march with the rest."
- Have them perform the scene.
- Now, as Joker, say: "Does anyone have any ideas they would like to try?"
- Allow them to suggest and try as many solutions as you like.
- Discuss: "There are always multiple solutions and strategies for every oppression."
- Say: "Now that you are warmed up and understand Forum Theatre, I need volunteers to play: a doctor, a nurse, a psychiatric patient, four strong orderlies." Choose people to fill these roles.
- Say: "The psychiatric patient is being brought into a hospital between two orderlies and is very upset yelling 'No injections! No injections!' They are put in a cell in which they continue to yell and thrash around. The nurse who has seen this goes to the doctor to report what is happening. The doctor prescribes a sedative that should be delivered by needle. The nurse returns to the patient and tries to convince them to submit to the shot. The patient hides and screams 'No injections!' The nurse returns to the doctor who gets very angry because their orders have not been followed and insists. The nurse gathers four orderlies to catch and hold down the patient while they administer the shot."
- Once they have improvised the scene, ask the spect-actors, "Do you see something that you would like to change? If so, yell STOP! at the moment you want a change and we will change it."
- Run the scene again until an audience member calls a halt. At this point, your job is to replace the actor on stage with the person who wants to change something, and allow them to play out their idea.
- Continue to play the scene with alternative ideas as long as it seems fruitful.

Activity—The Greek Exercise or The Actor as Subject

- Break into groups of seven to nine.
- Say: "Please be careful and pay attention to your physical limitations."
- "Assign one person in each group as the spotter, to stand outside the group and watch for safety, intervening if needed."

- "Assign one person to be the protagonist. Perhaps you want to start with someone small."
- "When the protagonist makes a movement, the rest of the group must move to support their body. For example, if they move their foot, someone immediately places their body under the protagonist's foot to support it. "
- "The protagonist should move slowly, freely, floating and flying through space as if weightless while the rest of the group creates the needed and inventive base for their movements."
- If you have more than one group, at some point say: "Allow your protagonists to switch groups. This is not an assignment for the groups to swap protagonists, the will is all with the protagonist, your members simply allow your protagonist to go and accept a different one."
- Discuss: "What might be the lesson of this activity?"

Activity—Slow Motion

- Tell your actors to line up as in a foot race and crouch for the start.
- Say: "I will call the start of the race, and the LAST one across the finish line wins."
- "Here are the rules:

    ◦ Once the race has begun, you must never stop moving as slowly as possible.
    ◦ When one foot is moving in front of the other, it must raise above knee level.
    ◦ Every step must be as large as possible.
    ◦ Only one foot can be in contact with the ground at a time."

- During the race say: "Can you feel the capability of your body? Experience your muscles."
- Discuss: "What is the value of playing a game like this? Why do you think Boal liked it so much? Were you able to feel the options and capabilities of your body?"

Activity—The Bear

- Designate one participant as the bear. Have the bear turn their back on everyone else.
- Say: "Everyone else do forestry tasks such as woodcutting, planting, falling trees, etc. . . ."
- "The bear, without warning, lets out an enormous growl. At the sound, the foresters fall to the ground and play dead. The bear prowls about and tries to find a live person to eat. They may do anything short of touching the 'bodies' to get them to reveal they are alive. As soon as the bear gets someone to react, the round is over, and there are two bears for the second round."
- Continue in this way as long as entertained.
- Discuss: "If a person can deaden their senses, they can win. However, the instruction to 'feel nothing' often produces the opposite effect in which the 'dead' have hypersensitivity to the actions of the bear."

Activity—The Sound of the Seven Doorways

- Split your group in half into "door group" and "people group."
- Say: "Door Group, pair off with someone near your own height. Face each other and make doorways or arches spread out around the space."
- "Each door needs to devise three sounds: One seductive to entice people to go through their door, one of alarm to warn people to change what they are doing, and one sound of celebration."
- "People group, close your eyes. You are 'blind.' Attempt to go through all of the doorways."
- "Doors make your seductive sounds to help people find you, use your alarm sound to warn them if they are about to hit someone, and the celebration sound when they have made it through a doorway."
- "The game is over when all the blind folks have made it through the doors."
- Reverse roles and play again.
- Discuss: "What can you learn from this game?"

Activity—Kinetic and Silent Images

- This is an activity to be done with a cast of a show, but for the purposes of this class, use a scene that they have already prepared.
- Say: "Establish a place in the room that will represent the set for your scene."
- "Decide who will go first in your group."
- "Take turns rapidly going through only the motions of your scene as quickly as possible, creating a moving image of your scene."
- Once done, say: "Perform your scene together, again speeding it up and moving through your images quickly."
- Discuss: "How can going through just the motions in rapid succession give meaning to each image and motion of your scene?"
- Say: "Repeat the activity but now at the appropriate pace, still not using words, but communicating the story by movements only, as if performing for an audience of deaf people without interpreters. Do not add mime. All the blocking must stay exactly the same. Communicate at an undercurrent level"
- Discuss: "How successful were you? Do you think that this activity will improve your scene when you add the words back?"

Activity—Interjection of Interruptions

- As a way to explain how to break out of stale acting, have your actors prepare to act their scenes.
- Call one group up and give them opposite circumstances for their scene. For example, if the scene is deeply angry, ask them to play the scene in complete calmness.

- Say: "Each group should come up with an opposite circumstance for their scene. It could be a change of setting, mood, motivation, etc. Run through your scenes that way."
- "Run your scenes with circumstances restored, but with the addition of artificial pauses. Wait five to ten seconds between each line, breaking the hypnotic rhythm you are used to."
- "On this run, speak out loud while you are pausing, questioning your motivations and actions, 'Why am I angry at her? Should I tell her how I really feel?'"
- "On this run, think the opposite thing from what you are going to say while you pause. If you are about to express eagerness about something, think disinterest."
- "This time swap roles and improvise the lines you don't know exactly."
- "Run your scenes again without the interruptions, but with renewed freshness."
- Discuss: "What methods of rehearsal seemed useful to you? What other ideas do you have that might help you break out of ruts?"

15

Jerzy Grotowski

The Person

Jerzy Grotowski was born in Poland in 1933. He studied acting and directing at the Ludwik Solski Academy of Dramatic Arts in Kraków and Russian Academy of Theatre Arts in Moscow. In the beginning of his career he was the artistic director of a theatre in Opole, Poland. His company moved to Wroclaw in 1965 under the name The Institute for Research into Acting. This group actively researched the actor/audience relationship and tried to strip theatre down to what was distinctly theatre. He called this Poor Theatre. Rich Theatre, in his terminology, was a combination of different art forms.

He did not believe that theatre should be for entertainment, because theatre is ritual and communion with the audience. His performances in the early 1960s often involved actors moving through clumps of chairs, interacting directly with the audience. In this era of his work, some productions had several opening dates. He would open a show then withdraw and rework it before another opening date. He also sometimes worked on a show for multiple years and never opened it. Peter Brook said Grotowski's laboratory theatre only needed an audience occasionally.

In the late 1960s he took his acting company on international tours. He was always more popular abroad. Then, in 1970, at thirty-seven years old, he declared he was no longer interested in developing plays since theatre could not achieve his goals. At this point he shifted his focus to anthropological studies of performance. The remainder of his life was spent as a performance researcher and theoretician.

He was invited to move to the United States to work in 1982. He accepted the invitation because a state of martial law had been declared in Poland. He got his actors out of the country and received political asylum in the US. Three years later he became disillusioned with the American interpretation of his work, and moved to Italy where he established the Grotowski Workcenter.

Here he continued to work on theatre in secrecy for the remainder of his life. Theatre makers were so curious about his work that many of them attended a talk in 1988, hoping to learn what was happening in the Workcenter. However, he made it clear that "he was not there to persuade or convert. His researches were *his* and he had no desire to impose them on others."[1] People walked away from this seminar disheartened. It was clear Grotowski wasn't seeking disciples, and had moved out of the zone of theatre and into pure ideas. Practice had turned into philosophy that he would not share or use to impact current practice.

The Grotowski Workcenter was affectionately called Casa Grotowski by the inhabitants, and life there was simple. They all wore white, and worked collaboratively. Grotowski observed and took occasional notes. Each participant had nine physical exercises assigned to them. Often they sang and danced as part of the work. Food wasn't plentiful, and there was little in the way of modern amenities, not even a telephone. It was like a monastery. The work was ritualistic, experimental, and all-consuming. He called this portion of his work *Art as Vehicle* which had the goal of pursuing art with unconditional integrity. Grotowski died of leukemia and a heart condition in Italy in 1999 after fourteen years working at Casa Grotowski.

The Method

Grotowski developed detailed techniques of acting focused on the psychology of human nature as well as physical movement. However, he did not think of what he was doing as creating an acting method. In fact, he was convinced that Stanislavski had created the only acting method that was necessary. Instead, he created techniques for the removal of acting blocks. He wrote, "all conscious systems in the field of acting ask the question: 'How can this be done?' This is good. A method is the awareness of this 'how to do it.' I believe . . . One must then ask the question: 'How not to do it?'"[2] This work led to his creation of the "via negativa," which had the goal of removing the blocks that prevent actors from reaching their goals.

Profile of a Grotowski Actor

Grotowski trained his actors in a wide variety of skills incorporating mime, yoga, tai chi, and his own gestural movements. He carefully chose which activities were productive for the actor he was trying to refine. The physical training was extremely rigorous. The mental training was deeply psychological and spiritual. He called his work "the battle in art"[3] which only some artists want to engage. Grotowski worked only with actors who were willing to aggressively fight their way to the pure impulse of Poor Theatre. His method focused on using up all the actor's resources to strip away all that was not impulse. This was a system that produced deeply observable results in his actors, but it required them to sacrificially give up everything they had on the altar of their art. Grotowski accepted any acolyte who was dedicated to the work and their own growth to the full extent of their capability. This work required both the student and Grotowski to be vulnerable. Grotowski said,

> This is not instruction of a pupil but utter opening to another person, in which the phenomenon of 'shared or double birth' becomes possible. The actor is reborn – not only as an actor but as a man – and with him, I am reborn. It is a clumsy way of expressing it but what is achieved is a total acceptance of one huma n being by another.[4]

Via Negativa

The Grotowski method of acting is centered on "via negativa," a method of subtracting acting blocks. He believed that the ideal mindset of an actor was a passive readiness that "resigns from not doing it."⁵ Since Grotowski didn't believe in recipes, he knew each actor needed a different path. He helped each student find their obstacles then remove them. The Grotowski actor's job was to create a series of personal activities to rid their body of blocks.

If he was working with a tense actor, he thought about the psychology behind the tension—but not to remove it completely. He did not approve of the way many theatre schools teach complete relaxation, comparing full relaxation to a wet handkerchief.⁶ Instead, he taught actors to find out what is blocking their natural breathing and remove the block. He once worked with an overly tense actor by surreptitiously observing him when relaxed to learn his natural breathing. He then helped the actor identify and eliminate the obstacles to his natural state, getting rid of the artificial tenseness.

This via negativa permeated every part of Grotowski productions. In his work, he wanted to strip away everything including makeup and costumes, special lights, sets, and props. He said, "It also became evident that the actors . . . can 'illuminate' through personal technique, becoming a source of 'spiritual light.' We abandoned . . . everything that the actor puts on in the dressing room before performance. We found that it was consummately theatrical for the actor to transform . . . while the audience watched – in a poor manner, using only his own body and craft."⁷ It might seem crazy to you, particularly if you have experienced theatre only in the context of large budgets and effective tech, but Grotowski's audiences were enraptured by the experience of his theatre that was stripped of all the usual design. Imagine how much harder you would have to work on your craft if you had no tools to assist in the illusions you create!

Towards a Poor Theatre

Rich Theatre is the theatre you experience in almost every production you attend. It is an amalgamation of sculpture, literature, painting, architecture, lighting, and more. Grotowski used the term Rich Theatre as an insult. This type of theatre doesn't know what it is, and is trying to compete with movies and television by adding other arts to its raw power. He claimed this process dilutes theatre and makes it "rich in flaws." He calls this nonsense. "No matter how much theatre expands and exploits its mechanical resources, it will remain technologically inferior to film and television. Consequently, I propose poverty in theatre."⁸

Grotowski delighted in finding elements of theatre that could be removed without losing its effectiveness. He even eliminated the need for a theatre building by using found spaces.

Sacrifice to Theatre

Grotowski's methods were often brutally difficult and painful. He wanted his actors to give everything they had. He said,

> When I say 'go beyond yourself,' I am asking for an insupportable effort. One is obliged not to stop despite fatigue and to do things that we know well we cannot do. This means one is also obliged to be courageous. What does this lead to? There are certain points of fatigue which break the control of the mind, a control that blocks us. When we find the courage to do things that are impossible, we make

the discovery that our body does not block us . . . These are the limits we impose upon ourselves that block the creative process because creativity is never comfortable.[9]

This physical training often started after work hours in the evening and lasted well into the night, sometimes until 5:00 a.m. The actors were asked to give all they had, but allowances were made for the physical limitations of each person. Grotowski admitted anyone who wanted to put in the necessary work and sacrifice. After observing his rehearsals, Harold Clurman said, "The exercises of Grotowski are intended to make the actor surmount his supposed breaking point, to stretch him vocally and bodily so that he can hold nothing back; to remove his restraints, those 'blocks' imposed by his usual social comportment."[10]

Ritual and rigor are at the heart of the practice of Grotowski. One student compared his work with Grotowski to that of a pilgrim returning to their spiritual and cultural roots. The Grotowski pilgrimage is more about the process than the destination. The goal in the process of creation is encounters with fellow-pilgrims: director, actors, and spectators. It is a co-creation of intense effort, not a destination.

The Role of the Audience

The spectators at Grotowski shows were often seated in clusters in the acting space, so the actors had to work around them. He asked his actors not to shy away from them or ignore them, but instead to view them as ghosts or otherworldly creatures. He claimed that a psychic curtain falls between the actor and the spectator when they are very close to one another. Because of this, no one was allowed to touch any member of the audience.

Grotowski acknowledges that each audience member has different needs. "Our task as artist is to find spectators for whom the kind of work we create is truly necessary."[11] Grotowski's audience sizes were necessarily very small because he wanted to make sure each audience member got what they needed from the experience and the opportunity to confront their own responses to the work.

However, the audience was not the focus of the work. He wanted the actors to act near the spectators, not for them. Grotowski said of the actor, "he must . . . do an act of extreme yet disciplined sincerity and authenticity. He must give himself and not hold himself back, open up and not close in on himself in a narcissistic way."[12]

The Technique in Practice

Every session of Grotowski's actor training began with silent communal work consisting of "corporels" and "plastiques." Corporel exercises developed flexibility and trust in the actor's body. Starting from a place of outward-focused modified yoga, the actors trained to stretch their own self-trust through a series of tumbling activities. First, the trainees learned to perform each of the activities correctly, then they were encouraged to shift them to discover and expand the limits of equilibrium. Once that was accomplished, they created improvised, silent conversations with others using the corporels. The trainers in Grotowski's school also created specific corporel activities for each student designed to prepare them for work as a team.

The plastiques, while less physically demanding than corporels, required much more precision. A specific stream of motions were performed: for example, a movement with the impulse emanating from the spine out to the extremities resulting in specific wrist movements. These movements were combined in improvisations and conversation with other actors just as in the corporels. The plastiques unlocked the body-memory, where the student didn't direct the motions through the mind, but allowed the body to move using its impulse.

Vocal Training: Breath

Every day's training included vocal work, diction, and artificial pronunciation or incantation. Grotowski believed that the voice must carry to the spectator in such a profound way that the voice penetrates the spectator and the sound comes from every corner of the room. Carrying power can be created by:

1 Creating a tunnel without blocks for sound to forcefully be pushed out of the body
2 Amplifying the voice using resonators in the body.

Breath is the beginning place for Grotowski's vocal work and diction. He identified three types of breathing. The first is upper respiration that comes from the chest, the second is from the abdominal muscles, the third is total body breathing that incorporates both the upper and lower torso. Animals and children breathe in the third way, and Grotowski taught his actors to re-learn this technique of natural breathing.

Breath was one of the first things Grotowski evaluated when working with a new student. He immediately evaluated any difficulties they had and helped them rediscover their natural breath. In one interview, Grotowski talked at length about the issue of respiration,

> If we ask the question 'How should we do it?' . . . We can, in fact observe . . . there is no perfect type of respiration valid for everyone . . . Most people, when breathing freely, naturally use abdominal respiration, but the number of types of abdominal respiration is unlimited. And there are also exceptions. For example, I have met actresses who, having thoraxes that were too long, could not naturally use abdominal breathing in their work. For them it was therefore necessary to find another type of breathing controlled by the vertebral column.[13]

He customized his work to match the student he was working with.

Vocal Training: Voice and Resonators

Having found their natural breathing, Grotowski moved to awareness of body structures and functions to aid in developing the voice. For example, he taught his actors to find their larynx and how to keep it down while speaking. In order to be successful with this, the actor has to saturate the words with air. Trying to save breath is counterproductive. This process feels unnatural at the beginning, but can become second nature.

He used Eastern styles of vocalization extensively in training of the voice. These styles of vocalization were rooted in ancient cultures and included folk songs and chanting. Many of these forms of vocalization call for the actor to resonate different parts of their bodies. By using different structures in the body as amplifiers of the sound, vibrating them with your voice, you gain tremendous power and flexibility in your voice. Grotowski called these places in your body resonators:

- The upper head resonator is activated by pushing air into the front of the head. Place your hand on your upper forehead and make an "m" sound. This will vibrate your forehead. Grotowski recommends imagining your mouth is on the top of your head.
- The chest resonator is activated when you speak in a lower register. Place your hand on your chest and speak a sentence using a low pitch. You will feel your chest vibrating, and can imagine your mouth in your chest.
- The nasal resonator is activated when your nose vibrates with the "n" sound. This resonator has been maligned by many voice coaches, but it can be useful for some characters and to amplify your voice when needed.
- The laryngeal resonator is more typically used in Eastern and African performance styles. "The sound produced recalls the roaring of wild animals. It is also characteristic of some . . . jazz (e.g. Armstrong)."[14] Try producing a low "oh" sound while placing your hand on your throat.
- The occipital resonator is located on the back of the head. Try to find it by placing your hand on the back of your head and say "I'm speaking to the ceiling" while imagining that your mouth is on the back of your head and speaking up.
- The whole body resonator is simultaneous use of the head and chest resonators. So, for example, speak in a low pitch to activate your chest resonator automatically, but then concentrate on activating the front of head resonator.

Grotowski believed strongly in resonator work, saying, "the actor who investigates closely the possibilities of his own organism discovers that the number of resonators is practically unlimited . . . it is not enough that the actor learns to make use of several resonators, to open his larynx and to select a certain type of respiration. He must learn to perform all this unconsciously in the culminating phase of his acting."[15]

Vocal Training: Using the Room

Once an actor is contending with their own voice, they must learn to listen to themselves in the room. Focusing on the way your voice sounds from inside your head creates problems. Instead, learn to listen to your voice from outside yourself. Grotowski recommends you resonate your voice out towards a wall and listen to the echo. As you listen, begin to consciously shape your voice by practicing changing distance from a wall, visualizing it moving up and down the wall, and using different resonators. This individual research will unlock the full potential of your specific body and voice.

Grotowski reminds actors to be aware of the acoustic properties of each performance venue and try the voice out, learning where to direct the resonators to achieve different effects. It is your job to consciously use your voice and the space to meet your goals. Grotowski instructed, "Speak naturally and through these natural vocal actions set in motion the various possibilities of the body's resonators. Then there will come a day when your body will know how to resound without prompting. It is the turning point, like the birth of another voice, and can be achieved only by completely natural vocal actions."[16]

Misunderstandings

Grotowski's writing and philosophy are tricky to read and understand, and many have misunderstood him and then taught "the Grotowski Method" incorrectly. If you find his methods interesting, take the time to read his writings and learn from people who deeply understand the core of his process. The fakes are compelling and dangerous. One scholar warned that untrained teachers lead workshops after having spent only a few days with Grotowski, and they "of course, pass on grave errors and misunderstandings. Grotowski's research might be mistakenly construed as something wild and structureless, where people throw themselves on the floor scream a lot, and have pseudo-cathartic experiences. Grotowski's connection to tradition, and his link to Stanislavski, run the risk of being completely forgotten or not taken into account."[17] Grotowski claimed people often mistake aesthetics for techniques. In other words, the productions staged for an audience had extreme and experimental appearances, but the preparation was done behind closed doors, so it was too often misunderstood.

Grotowski continued to associate his method most closely with Stanislavski throughout his career. Early on he said that he was "possessed" by the System because it opened up creativity in actors. His results were quite different, but he was striving for the same goal as Stanislavski: to live truthfully on stage. Grotowski himself would caution you against using the activities at the end of this chapter as a recipe for achieving creativity. They prepare you, but they don't automatically make you ready to reveal yourself on stage.

Jerzy Grotowski's Legacy

What Grotowski leaves us is a story of a life devoted to the all-encompassing spirit of the theatre inspiring generations of actors to a life of self-sacrifice to art. He didn't call his techniques a method, but instead, said:

> When I came to the conclusion that the problem of building my own system was illusory and that there exists no ideal system which could be a key to creativity, then the word 'method' changed its meaning for me. There exists a challenge, to which each must give his own answer . . . The experience of life is the question, and the response is simply through true creation. It begins from the effort not to hide oneself and not to lie. Then the method—in the sense of a system—doesn't exist. It cannot exist except as a challenge or as a call.[18]

The main goal as you work on the Grotowski system is to avoid passivity. Don't allow yourself to be sedentary, instead work on yourself constantly, developing your craft.

Tips for taking this method further

- Work on your vocal resonators and breath control.
- Spend time with your own cultural myths and melodies, digging into your ancestral heritage to create original work.

Discussion Starters and Journal Prompts

- What are the obstacles blocking you from doing your work? What blocks you in your breathing, movement, and human contact? How can those blocks be eliminated? Grotowski wanted to take the bothersome blocks away from his actors, liberating them to be creative. What do you think his advice might be to you? What exercises would he create to help you get obstacles out of your way?
- How do you respond to Grotowski's insistence in total devotion to art, even to the point of complete exhaustion? What are the values and/or dangers of this approach?

The Tools for your Toolbox

Activity—The Cat

- Instruct your actors to lay face down on the floor with arms at right angles to the body, palms down.
- Say: "Think of a cat waking and stretching and do the motions as I call them out with feline ease." (Note: These motions are suggestions for you. They are a combination of several descriptions of the activity that are quite different from each other. The cat qualities are the important part, not the specific movements.)
- "Move into the cobra position by lifting the body from waist upward into an upright position with the elbows supporting the body's weight on the floor and the lower arms and hands resting on the floor palms down."
- "Move into a triangle by lifting the pelvis into the air with hands and feet on the floor."
- "Circle the torso to the right then to the left."
- "Relax the pelvis toward the floor then arch back up to the ceiling."
- "Extend your left leg as far as possible and shake it."
- "Repeat with the right leg then right arm and left arm."

- "Lift your right arm and left leg, then left arm and right leg."
- The sunbeam: Say: "Roll onto your back and stretch your legs straight down and arms straight up. Roll your shoulder blades down and lift your core and legs slightly so that the only parts of the body that are touching the floor are the head, shoulders, and back of the pelvis."
- "On hands and knees, stretch your spine, placing the center of gravity in the middle of your back. Continue the stretch, rolling the center of gravity to the shoulders and back."
- The litter box: Say: "On hands and knees, slide one leg backwards as if digging several times, then switch legs."
- "Roll over and fall onto your back, relaxed."
- The snuggle: Say: "Roll to your side and lay in a V shape, bending at the hips. Reach down with your arms to touch your toes. Reach your upper arm backwards to touch the floor, leaning upper shoulder down as well. Reverse."
- "While laying on your side, lift your upper body onto one elbow, lift your upper leg and hold it with your upper hand. Reverse."
- "Roll over into a child's pose."
- "Wake up stretch: slide your hands forward until upper legs are at a ninety degree angle from the lower legs."
- "Return to a standing position, then lower your head down to touch your knees with your legs together and straight."
- "Rise, then vigorously rotate the trunk of your body from the waist up."
- "Now bend your body backwards until your hands touch the floor, forming a bridge."
- "Get on hands and knees and do the bridge the body backwards again until the head touches the ground."
- "Return to a kneeling position."
- "Slide forward into cobra position."
- "Go back to lying on the floor face down as in the start."

Activity—Warm-ups

- Have your students spread out in the space and say: "Grotowski insists that every moment of training must be detailed and focused. As you warm-up, notice if the body puts up any resistance to the images you are trying to create. He said, 'The body should therefore appear weightless, as malleable as plasticine to the impulses, as hard as steel when acting as a support, capable even of conquering the law of gravity.'[19]"
- Discuss what the quote means, then get to work.
- Say: "Walk rhythmically while rotating the arms and hands."
- "Run on tiptoe. Remember the impulse to run comes from the shoulders. They should feel weightless as you run."
- "Walk around with hands on hips and knees bent."
- "Continue walking, but move your hands down to your ankles, keeping your back upright."

- "Slide your hands to the sides of your feet, straightening your knees so they are only slightly bent."
- "Keep your knees slightly bent, slide your fingers forward and hold your toes while walking."
- "Stand upright and make your legs stiff. Put your arms out forward and walk as if your hands are moving the legs with strings."
- "While standing on your feet, curl up into a ball with your hands beside your feet."
- "Take short jumps forward, uncurling your body to jump, but landing in the starting curled up position."

Activity—Flight, Leaps, and Somersaults

- Say to your actors: "Think of yourselves as birds, squatting on heels, curled up, and hop and sway as if you are about to take flight."
- "While hopping, raise your body up, flapping your arms as if you are trying to take off."
- "Now fly, using your arms in swimming motions, so that only one part of your body is touching the ground at a time after each leap."
- "Remember the flying sensation of dreaming and spontaneously create motions to communicate this form of flight."
- "Land like a bird."
- Perform a series of somersaults as each is individually capable:
  - forward, using hands as supports
  - forward, no hands
  - forward, finishing on one leg
  - forward, with hands behind the back
  - forward, with one shoulder on ground for support
  - backwards
  - if you are adept at teaching safe leaps, you can add somersaults that begin with leaps.
- Say: "Combine your flight and summersault exercises: take off, fly, perform a somersault, then return to your feet landing like a bird."

Activity—Plastic Motion

- Say to your actors: "Sit on the stage and be silent both internally and externally."
- "Think of this as researching your own body. Where are your resistances? What is your means of expression?"
- "Get up and walk around the space with your legs moving slowly while your arms move rapidly."
- "Stand still and rotate your head slowly while clapping a beat with your hands that doesn't match your head's rhythm."
- "Walk to a rhythm around the space with arms stretched out in T-pose. After a moment, begin to rotate arms, pushing elbows back as far as possible, rotating hands in the opposite directions to the shoulders."

- "Imagine you are a dolphin and walk around rotating your arms, gradually increasing the speed of the rotations, letting your body grow taller, walking on tiptoes."
- "Imagine there is a rope stretched in front of you that you are using to pull yourself forward in the space—being careful not to use your arms to pull yourself forward, but your trunk. Make large lunges that pull you forward so far that your back knee touches the ground. The movements should be sharp and strong like a ship in a stormy sea."
- "Make a jump forward on the tips of the toes, bending the knees on landing. Return to a standing position with an elastic and energetic movement and repeat the same jump forward, still on tiptoe, followed by the knee-bend. The impulse comes from the thighs which act as the spring regulating the bending phase and the jump which follows. The arms are stretched out to the side and while one palm caresses, the other repels. One must have a sensation of being extremely light, soft and elastic like foam rubber."[20]
- "Stand with your feet apart and with an impulse from the base of the spine, make four rotations of the following body parts in opposite directions:
    - head and trunk
    - spine and hips
    - left leg and thigh
    - right ankle and right arm
    - forearm and hand."
- "Stand with feet apart and stretch arms above your head with palms touching. Rotate the trunk and bend down with the arms towards the ground, circling back up and then leaning backwards into a bridge."
- "Walk. Your first step is normal, your second requires you to bend your knee until your heel touches your buttock while your body stays straight. Third step is like the first. Continue walking in rhythm with the bent steps taking the same time as the normal ones. Switch starting leg and continue."
- Discuss: "Tell a partner what you learned in your movement research. What resistances did you find?"

Activity—Pre-constructed Improvisation

- Ask your students to work in groups of four to six. Assign a director.
- Give them five minutes to pre-construct an improvised scene that has an outline of "telegraph poles" giving structure to the piece by writing it out on paper.
- Have them perform from the outline.
- Now ask each student to get out their own notebook and create two columns.
- In the first column, write everything they did in the improvisation.
- In the second column, write everything that they associated inwards: physical sensations, mental images, thoughts, memories of people and places. Tell them "While you are doing actions, in the same moment your mind's eye is seeing something, as if a memory flashes before you."[21]

- Give groups three minutes to discuss their structure and alter as desired, repeating the steps above. In this way, they can follow Grotowski's system of devising theatre, incorporating the inner associations and actions of the group.

Activity—Breathing

- Have actors lay on their backs on the floor.
- Say: "Place one hand on your chest and one on your abdomen."
- "As you breathe, you should feel your abdomen fill first then the chest in one continuous motion. It should be smooth and free of impediments."
- "Now breathe in a method from Hatha Yoga:
  - plug one nostril
  - breathe in for four seconds
  - hold breath for twelve seconds while switching to blocking the other nostril
  - breathe out for eight seconds"
- "Now stand and place your hands on your two lowest ribs."
- "As you breathe in, the place where your hands are should be the place the air fills first, with air continuing to fill the air column gradually upwards right up to the head."
- "Exhale, keeping the ribs expanded until the end of the breath, exhaling from top to bottom, again smoothly and seamlessly."
- "Stand with hands on hips and take in a fast and silent breath with the lips and teeth before saying a few words of a monologue."
- "Practice taking a breath quickly and exhaling normally."
- "Learn to keep the larynx down by placing a finger lightly on the side of the voice box and feel it go down as you take in a breath."
- "Count to ten as you exhale and observe what happens to the larynx."
- "Having identified the natural motion of the voice box, repeat this activity, trying to keep the larynx down by surrounding your words with air as you exhale."
- "Yawn, paying attention to the feeling of space in the back of the throat, and the feel of the placement of the larynx while yawning."
- "Do the counting exercise again."
- "Proper larynx positioning is key to transmitting sound, the goal is not getting a lot of words out in one breath—it is keeping the voice box down by pushing out a lot of air through an open voice box, saturating the words with breath."
- "Bend your upper body slightly forward, relax the lower jaw, rest it on a thumb, and place your index finger just under your lip, holding the lower jaw still."
- "Raise the upper jaw and eyebrows while wrinkling the forehead so that the temples feel stretched out. At the same time, contract the muscles at the back of the neck and head. Let out your voice. Check that the lower jaw is relaxed."
- "Now do the voice box activity again, keeping the internal feeling of the last exercise in place."
- "Are you learning to keep your voice box down? With enough practice, it can begin to be your natural way of speaking."

Activity—Resonators

- Ask your students to work in pairs as trying to activate the following resonators one at a time:
    - The upper head resonator: Place a hand on the upper forehead and make an "m" sound. Play with this resonator, having a conversation maintaining a visual image of their mouths speaking out of their foreheads.
    - The chest resonator: Place their hands on their chests and have a conversation as pirates using a low pitch, imagining their mouths in their chests. Experiment with speaking in their normal registers and high registers to see if they can do valley girl in their chest resonator as well.
    - The nasal resonator: Place fingers on the bridge of the nose and make the "n" sound. Have conversations trying to keep the nasal resonator vibrating. Talk about what sorts of characters might use this resonator while keeping the nasal passage vibrating.
    - The laryngeal resonator: Try producing a low "oh" sound while placing hands on throats. Hold a conversation as lions and then try other animal voices, keeping the larynx activated.
    - The occipital resonator: Place a hand on the back of the head and say "I'm speaking to the ceiling" while imagining your mouth is on the back of your head and speaking up. Now try letting the air flow freely and mewing like a kitten. Which method was more effective? Can you have a conversation keeping this resonator active?
    - Other resonators: Have the pairs try to vibrate other parts of their bodies and find resonators to share with the class. Suggest the ribcage, the abdomen, the back of the jaw, different areas of the spine, the shoulder blades, and encourage them to explore their limbs as well by picturing the sound coming out of those parts of the body.
    - The whole body resonator: How many resonators can they get working at once? Walk about and speak or hum activating as many resonators as possible.
- Say: "Try to use one resonator as the solo, and the other as a backup voice. This is how some performers seem to accompany themselves with two pitches at once."
- "Speak a few lines of a monologue in the usual way, then try again while focusing on resonators."
- Discuss in pairs: "What does resonator activation do for your performance?"

Activity—In the Spirit of Grotowski

- Invite your actors to meet at night at an appointed location and do some chanting and running, perhaps in a safe, open, section of woods. You could also look up and share the story about Dustin Hoffman and his Grotowski-style preparation for his role in *The Marathon Man*. This will help demonstrate the distinction between Grotowski's approach and other methods. The commitment required for this activity, and the resulting exhaustion will show them the sort of work required of a Grotowski actor.

16

Tadashi Suzuki

The Person

Tadashi Suzuki was born in Japan in 1939. His family was a traditional family in a small port town with three generations living under one roof. His father was a timber merchant. At fifteen, he transferred to a junior high school in Tokyo to have a better chance of getting into a good university. He was glad to get away from his family in which he endured painful punishments commonplace in Japan during an earlier era. Life in the city was exciting, and he spent his time partying, skipping class, and reading.

He attended Waseda University and joined the Waseda Free Stage (WFS), an organization protesting US military presence in Japan. The group put on plays as part of their activism, and Suzuki was embarrassed by their poor acting skills and lack of training. Because of this, he began directing to improve the company.

In the late 1960s, the owner of the Mon Cheri cafe helped Suzuki's group build a theatre above his shop. The actors raised funds to pay for the renovation and named their space the Waseda Little Theatre. It could seat no more than 120, but owning rehearsal space and having control over their productions was liberating for the group. Suzuki described this theatre:

> The theatre's small performance space, where the audience could easily sense the actor's breath and sweat . . . was a great discovery for me that the energy of the actor alone enabled the cultural activity called theatre to be accessible to so many people . . . Although I had no choice but to use the small theatre, the experiences I gained from it have, to a large degree, set my theatrical direction ever since.[1]

In 1972 he and his acting partner Shiraishi were invited to participate in an international theatre festival in Paris. While at this festival, he was inspired to create a spiritual home for his acting company outside of Tokyo. This was a revolutionary idea since there was no regional theatre scene in Japan. In 1976 he moved his company to a renovated farmhouse in the mountains of rural Toga where it remains today. This move didn't make sense to his patrons at the time, but his instincts paid off. He wanted to go to a place where like-minded artists could produce work together without compromising their ideals. Because of their location on the margins, they could focus on marginal perspectives more effectively.

There was another side benefit to the remote spot. This location extended the time people spent with theatre. Suzuki's established Tokyo audiences had to travel to Toga and back to see his shows.

The hours of travel time became an extension of the production, giving the audience an all-day pilgrimage of self-directed theatrical time.

It wasn't a foregone conclusion that his audiences would follow him, or that he could fund the project. But he was a savvy businessman, and sold five-year season passes to 500 audience members who paid up front for tickets to plays. This provided the funds for renovation. They turned the small town of Toga into an international theatre center with global impact, transforming every aspect of a dying town. Here, he was able to reinvent actor training and create a home base for his company that was both remote and connected to nature.

It would be ten more years before he realized his real dream of creating an International Theatre Festival in Toga. But by 1982, Suzuki's reach and prominence in the theatre had extended well beyond the borders of Toga and Tokyo. He was widely requested to teach his method in universities across the United States. This led to the formation of a month-long program of study at his compound in Toga each summer starting in 1988.

In 1992, he joined with Anne Bogart to create The Saratoga International Theater Institute (SITI), an international theatre company in which actors were trained equally in Suzuki's Method and Bogart's Viewpoints. The SITI Company disbanded in 2022 after thirty years of collaboration.

Suzuki is still working at Suzuki Company of Toga (SCOT) where you can travel to train or watch productions.

The Method

The Suzuki Method of acting trains the body in a demanding and precise process. This intense work requires discipline that creates an integrated "body-mind" for the actor. Anyone can learn the form quickly, but the endurance required to maintain the exercises requires months of endurance training and effort. It is exhausting and all-consuming from the very first exercise. Suzuki's method really can't be understood intellectually until it has been experienced, but understanding the philosophy behind the method makes the work richer.

Grounding the Feet

The first chapter of Suzuki's book *The Way of Acting* is titled *The Grammar of the Feet*. In it, Suzuki explains the importance of the foot in performance. He believes the grounding of the feet on the stage is the basis of all performance. He finds that actors are able to project truth to their audience when properly trained in how to use their bodies beginning with their feet. Without this foundation, actors appear clumsy no matter how well-proportioned they are.

In fact, an actor can believably represent anything with solid grounding. Even a small actor can create an imposing figure, appearing larger than life on stage. Suzuki describes this visceral grounded state:

> A performance begins when the actor's feet touch the ground, or a wooden floor, and he first has the sensation of putting down roots; it begins in another sense when he lifts himself lightly from that spot. The actor composes himself on the basis of his sense of contact with the ground, by the way in which his body makes contact with the floor. The performer indeed proves with his feet that he is an actor.[2]

This concept isn't new to Suzuki. He reminds his students that the motions of the feet on the stage are accentuated in Noh by well-trained actors. The foot is also very important in ballet and other classical performance genres.

Suzuki's training method punctuates this ground connection with an iconic stomping exercise. If you know anything about Suzuki Method, it is likely you are most familiar with this marching-style group work. If not, take a moment to look up a video online so you know what is being described here. James Brandon describes participating in early stomping activities in Tokyo before the move to Toga,

> the actors circle the stage, stamping in time to the music . . . Flat feet strike directly under the center of the body. There is fierce concentration. Every part of the body is held motionless except pile-driver legs and feet. The sound is deafening. We are on the second floor of this tiny building and with each rhythmic foot stamp, the whole structure bounces.[3]

In Japanese culture, stomping was a tradition meant to ward off evil spirits. Suzuki was inspired by this practice, but uses it for another reason. Suzuki's stomping is used to eradicate a sense of the usual use of the body. This breaking of the usual creates a powerful stage presence, where the actor is secure in their own power. That strength radiates upwards into the actor's body when they stomp. During stomping, the actors simultaneously radiate energy upwards as far as possible with the upper body, while "the lower body attempts to descend in a kind of counter-movement."[4]

Ritual

Before tackling the specifics of the physical training, it is good to understand the intangible benefits that Suzuki training gives its devotees. Suzuki's exercises are a sort of ritual through physical training that brings the mystical back to the modern theatre. He said, "In the Kabuki of Nanboku's time, the actors were in a very real sense *shamans* . . . In order to restore this kind of mystical shamanistic sense to the acting process, I have devised numerous physical exercises which help restore magical power to the actor."[5] He unapologetically asks his actors to experience the healing power of ritual performed for its own sake, not because of a deity. Valuing the ancient rituals of his culture, he has updated them to empower modern actors.

These ritualistic exercises assist performers in self-evaluation. Because the work is quite demanding, as actors persist in the exercises, they find measurable progress towards physical health and mental stamina. In the beginning, the work is a vulnerable and difficult time since new actors train in a room with veterans, and it is painfully obvious they aren't able to perform the demanding and precise work being done by others in the room. One student wrote about this, "You are vulnerable and exposed in what is essentially a solo practice and cannot hide. The fact that you are always doing what the group does exposes personal differences of even the subtlest kind. The emphasis on technique may be frustrating, with little encouragement of individual creativity."[6]

Another student, Jon Brokering, wrote about the state of readiness that Suzuki training provides:

> Even in my short-lived period of training . . . I could sense the strong moral imperative underlying the Suzuki Method. In that moment of hyper-awareness, in that neutral state of readiness, when the ego seemed to be assuaged and out of the way, I realized that what I had was not an empty, vacuous state of mind; I felt ready to move instantly in any direction, engage in any action, utter any words asked of me. More than that, I had a strong feeling inside me that I was compelled to do something. Even just standing there still and silent, I felt like the embodiment of Martin Luther's words when he declared: "Here I stand. I can do no other."[7]

The spiritual-physical-mental experience of Suzuki training brings actors to a place of awareness, readiness, and openness to critical feedback and collaborative art-making.

Repetition

Ellen Lauren, one of Suzuki's most trusted students, said

> This idea that the training is mind-numbing, or that the repetition of it is militaristic or limiting to the imagination, is, frankly, narrow-minded and a complete misunderstanding of the scope of this work. It is hard to keep your imagination and your inner world going while you're doing something over and over again, but that's the very foundation upon which rehearsal and the creative process is built. Virtuosity is accomplished by a series of logical steps that build a runway from which to get airborne. The purpose of the training is flight. But at least 80% of the time the runway is built from repetition and will, from sheer perseverance.[8]

The repetition is the point. Your work creates a strength and energy for your performance as you concentrate on continual improvement and body awareness while repeating the same action over and over.

In Suzuki's method, the goal during the repetitive work is not relaxation. It is finding the correct tension and resistance to do the work of the stage. Tension is always present in the basic stance of Suzuki work. Unlike other methods, the goal is to leverage tension, not eliminate it.

The basic stance creates a still and ready state in the upper body. In this posture, the legs are moving the body forward, but the upper body is holding back. The center or core is always engaged. The focus on the perfect form creates resistance. Resistance-energy can be compared to a puppet. The actor is a puppet with four strings attached and pulling at their body. First, one string attached to the top of the back of the head is pulling up. Second, a string pulls the actor down from the pelvis. Third, a string from the belly button pulls forward. Finally, a string pulls the actor back from the small of the back. With practice, an actor falls into this tension as soon as they engage the basic stance.

The repetition of the forms make it seem like an actor could eventually perfect them. However, a highly respected student said,

All of the exercises . . . are basically impossible. What Suzuki is asking you to do are movements that are not seen in daily life . . . that take the body out of a habitual way of moving. Then he asks you to maintain an equilibrium and steadiness as if you held a glass of water inside the body which you don't want to spill . . . So you willfully create a collision in the body and try to control it keeping a very strong specific outward focus at the same time . . . Suzuki thinks the actor should be doing something extraordinary on the stage, something that not just anybody can do.[9]

In many ways the impossibility is the point. Because actors are engaged in focusing on perfecting the imperfectible, their effort and focus create energy on stage that are irresistible for the audience.

The Disease of Agreement

Within the repetition of the exercises, Suzuki is not pushing for uniformity. Humans naturally gravitate towards being the same as those around them. Suzuki pushes his actors to find their individuality within the forms. Anne Bogart has had a front row seat to Suzuki's work for many years. She describes observing his work for the first time this way,

in this inimitable, hierarchical way, Suzuki would clap, and everybody would have to stop where they were on stage, no matter where they were and hold that position while he went up to an actor and harangued them for twenty minutes . . . and everybody just had to stand there. At one point I asked one of the Japanese actors, "Isn't that a pain, to have to stand there?" They said, "Oh, no, no, no. It's really good. Because usually he'll stop you in a moment when you're making a mistake. While he's haranguing somebody else, you have to deal with the mistake you've made . . . He likes American actors because Japanese actors really try to be the same, and American actors have the courage to be different." So what he's yelling at people about is being too much the same with other actors. The haranguing is about trying to get them to be more individual.[10]

Suzuki tries to help each actor find the body position that is right for them. His training prepares the actor for the control and strength they need to be in control of their unique body.

Suzuki's Style of Leadership

Suzuki is respected as a tough drill sergeant. He is a sort of *sensei*, a spiritual guide as well as a technical instructor. Suzuki is firm and even belligerent in the training space, and much more relaxed on campus with them in non-class or rehearsal spaces. But humility and submission to the work are required at all times. It is intense, and reflects a Japanese sense of family in relation to the patriarch. There is social and artistic freedom, but within strict parameters defined by Suzuki. It should be noted that the actors who work with Suzuki accept this style of leadership. If you attend a Suzuki workshop led by one of his students, you will very likely experience the stern, unrelenting facilitator imitating their mentor. This discipline is facilitated with an expectation of silent acceptance and obedience much like in a martial arts studio. Participants are not invited to speak unless reciting lines on command.

On the other hand, the expectation of every member of the company is very communal. While not in training, every member of the company is involved in the artistic work as well as the mundane. Everyone at Toga assists with office work and custodial support. The end result is a cohesive company of artists who are humble enough to do the least glamorous work.

Stage Awareness and Emotion

Suzuki doesn't buy the Stanislavski System's insistence on an actor feeling every emotion while performing on stage using the *Magic If*. The actor's job is not realism in acting, but rather full concentration on the fiction they are portraying. By living in the fiction of the play, the actor expresses emotion. The work a Suzuki actor does is not in historical research or personal emotions, but in living in the present on the stage under their feet. This is "stage awareness."

Suzuki's stage awareness extends to the physical space. There is a spiritual comfort that is achieved when working in a room for a long time. Your acting techniques have to be different in a large auditorium than in a small black box. This adjustment takes time and should not be ignored because your body is sensitive to the site it is in. But it is more than that. Suzuki teaches this adjustment is not just making your voice and gestures bigger. Instead, the actor must possess each unique performance environment.

An actor naturally feels uneasy in a new theatre when touring a show. This lack of ease translates into the performance. Suzuki teaches that adjusting in each space requires acquainting yourself with the space and spiritually claiming it as your own. Suzuki writes, "The actor's body and the space reveal a mutual connection. I call a space which is thus connected to the actor's body a *sacred space*."[11] The stage is the body's real home, and must be respected with keen awareness. Without connection to space, the actor's attempts will be sub-par.

Timelessness

Suzuki points out the plasticity of childhood. Children are adept at reacting physically and emotionally to a myriad of stimuli. Adults lose this flexibility without even realizing it. Young actors can rely on physical prowess to create art, but as they age, they need continuity in technique to sustain creative power over the decades of a lifetime. The aging actor must take control of the physical changes that occur naturally, developing their skills into their old age.

In fact, Suzuki teaches that the physical control required of the actor can *only* be fully realized *because of* the discipline required of an aging body maintaining control. He writes,

> as an actor grows older, his personal experience, gained in the context of a set of restrictions, comes into play. The actor undergoes various experiences so that eventually he achieves a kind of communal self-consciousness (another term, if you like, for artistic freedom). The kind of freedom to which he aspired when he was young can only truly be achieved as the body ages. Thus, all the restrictions he faces serve as a kind of lengthy initiation ceremony.[12]

By taking a long view of your craft, focusing on physical longevity, and collecting communal experiences, you will finally be able to achieve artistic freedom in your later years.

Voice

Of course, work on the body and spirit are not complete without working on the voice. Suzuki's method is designed to create efficient energy production, breath calibration, and center of gravity control in the human body. Your energy, breath, and body are interdependent. Suzuki trains the voice by focusing on a single organ, the diaphragm, which does all the work. "With time and practice, the voice shifts into the lower belly, giving great strength and allowing flexibility. Whispered recitation can be audible in a large auditorium without the vocal strain which this normally suggests. Clear articulation is also fostered by encouraging muscularity of vocal delivery."[13] Just as the body requires focus on muscle control, the voice requires muscular training. As you build energy and muscles, your vocal power will increase.

In Performance

Suzuki's actors do not use their training exercises on stage any more than a martial artist would use rehearsed forms in a sparring match. However, the physical conditioning impacts their performances profoundly by tuning their bodies and minds.

Suzuki's method does not lead to realism. However, it does create reality. Suzuki wants the people in the audience to believe what the actors are saying has reality for the characters in their circumstances. For example, in his productions, the actors do not look at each other often, instead speaking out towards the audience so they can be seen and heard well by the audience. This is not realism. Suzuki reasons, "the act of looking at someone else onstage itself is a moment of drama demanding tremendous concentration. So, what I require is that they look squarely at each other only at the most important moments—and the rest of the time they do not."[14]

Suzuki training puts actors in a position to have a heightened focus as they perform. He writes about his goals for actors who work with him during performance, "The point is not to try to use the energy of the training to create an everyday imitation, but to mimic everyday activities using the same energy, body and voice as you do in the training."[15]

Tadashi Suzuki's Legacy

Tadashi Suzuki's Method resonates strongly with actors all over the world. His methods are highly physical and often portrayed as repetitious and grueling. On the other hand, his work is renowned for its simplicity, beauty, intensity, control, and sense of community between the actors. He has worked his entire career to create a sense of the communal rooted both in the traditions of Japanese forms and fresh techniques created in his school.

Having lived a long life in the arts, Suzuki has learned both from the arts and the surrounding world. In his book *Culture is the Body*, Suzuki wrote about the paradoxes of living a life with art and hope, despite inevitable failure:

We must never forget that, in the end, we are only mortal human beings. However powerful we may feel we have become, in the end we are never able to change very much. The theatre, too, has a limited impact on the world we live in, however revolutionary and influential our work may seem. We must have courage then to continue pushing forward without doubt, despite the fact that we will never achieve what we set out to do. This is the essential, existential paradox that lies at the heart of the artist's life. We must pursue our ideals until our dying day . . . If I had to choose one thing I am most thankful for since having come to Toga, it would be the opportunity to encounter certain courageous individuals who understand that, despite whatever desperate conditions they may face, they must continue the quixotic pursuit of their impossible dreams. Armed with this knowledge, these spiritually enlightened artists have achieved a self-awareness that allows them to lead fulfilling lives.[16]

Tips for taking this method further

- Read *The Way of Acting* and *Culture is the Body* by Tadashi Suzuki.
- Look up Suzuki training online and watch groups of actors performing the various exercises he uses in his studio.
- Consider studying with Suzuki's company in Toga.
- Find a Suzuki workshop that is taught by someone who trained directly with Suzuki. Since he is still alive and working, you have a rare opportunity to work with only one degree of separation fairly easily. There are many programs out there that advertise Suzuki Method, but do not have the endorsement of Suzuki. While many of them may be quite good, try to find one that is authorized.

Discussion Starters and Journal Prompts

- After reading this chapter and watching some videos, but before doing the Suzuki activities with your class, what do you think you will feel about practicing Suzuki's methods? What do you like about what you read? What did you observe in the videos you watched? How did that change after experience?
- What connection do you feel with your acting spaces? Do you understand Suzuki's claim that the stage is the body's real home? Elaborate.

The Tools for your Toolbox

Activity—Stamping

This activity is difficult to describe if you have never experienced it. If at all possible, bring in a guest instructor for a workshop to work with your students on Suzuki's methods. There is a lineage of

Suzuki instructors who are deemed prepared to teach Suzuki's method. Simply watching a video and imitating it could be dangerous.

In preparation for the workshop, you will need to locate a space with sprung floors to avoid knee injuries. You should also instruct your students to wear socks unless you have *tabi* for them to wear.

- The instructor will play music and lead the stamping activity. Some of the rules they will teach are:
    - They should loosen their pelvic area slightly, then move themselves by striking the floor vehemently with their feet.
    - The stamping must be accomplished by striking the floor with the maximum amount of energy possible for the actor.
    - Some instructors use a bamboo pole to touch the place on the body that needs attention.
    - The stamp should be slightly ahead of the beat, never behind it.
    - The knees must return quickly to waist height, with the thigh parallel to the floor and the foot parallel with the floor, and then stamp again.
    - The stamping must be even and unremitting.
    - Breathing must be even and controlled
    - The back and shoulders must be straight
    - The arms must be rigid and straight down at the sides—Imagine holding poles in one's hands and keep those poles parallel to the ground.
    - The head must be raised as if a puppet string is pulling up the back of the top of the head
    - The upper body moves upwards as far as possible; the lower body does the opposite in counter-movement.
    - Their bodies must move forward with power from their core.
    - As the music comes to an end, the instructor will ask them to collapse to the floor and stay motionless in a state of quiet for at least 20 seconds. "Something just happened. Stay in the stillness."
- The instructor will likely have the students repeat this activity a few times and then switch to the next movement activity.

Activity—Sitting Statues

- If you cannot get a Suzuki Instructor, you can lead a few activities like the ones below. In advance of this class, have your actors to memorize the following monologue of Menelaus from *The Trojan Women*:

    > O splendor of sunburst breaking forth this day
    > Whereon I lay my hands once more on Helen my wife;
    > And yet it is not so much for the woman's sake I came to Troy,
    > But against that guest proved treacherous who like a robber carried the woman from my house

- Say, "Remember that in the Suzuki Method, the instructor IS the obstacle for the student. They will create impossible goals that you cannot attain. But you must try to meet them anyway. The activities you will be doing will require focus. Stay in character as devotees of the Suzuki method. You are not to speak or laugh during the lesson. Your job is to learn through listening, working on the body and inner monologue, not through questions. We will not discuss this activity along the way, and I will remain in role as a stern instructor."
- "Sit on the floor and pull your legs into your chest, curling your head down onto knees. Place your hands on your legs, but don't use them to support your legs so your core strength is holding you rather than your arms."
- "When I call out 'One!'—tilt your bodies slightly back to balance on your coccyx, with feet lifted off the floor and flexed so the audience can see the soles of the feet, eyes looking straight out and arms curved loosely around your legs without touching them."
- "When I call out 'Two!'—shoot the legs forward together while the body leans backwards to create a new center of balance, arms relaxed at the side with fists on hips, eyes still focused forward over your feet which are just barely off the ground."
- "When I call out 'Three!'—repeat position two, except shoot the legs out wide open at a 45 degree angle."
- "I will call out the different positions at random intervals, always giving a signal to return to your initial relaxed fetal position between poses." Note: I use a bamboo pole striking a cardboard box as the signal to return to neutral. It is important that this signal be loud and sharp. A clap is not loud enough.
- "If I call out 'Speak!' begin reciting the Menelaus monologue until I stop you with the sound that signals going back to fetal position. As you recite, only breathe at the ends of lines."
- "Think of the recitation as a release of energy."
- After you have worked with them for a while, take a pause and discuss: "This exercise shows you how to use your voice and body from your center. Can your character be possessed and driven by the text? Can the text come from your center?"
- Try again with the same activity. Say: "Choose your own position when I signal, but keep your body balanced on your coccyx and your appendages off the ground. Allow the text to come from your center."

Activity—Throwing The Feet

- Say: "Stand in lines with your heels together and feet turned out in box position. Keep your spine straight for the entire exercise. Remember the string pulling your head up."
- "When I call out 'One!'—lift your right leg outward and stamp it down to the right. The end result of this motion is that your center of gravity is over your right leg and your left leg is straight. The stamping should be firm and loud, but the control of the center of gravity should prevent your upper body from moving."
- "When I call out 'Two!'—pull your left leg in to put you back into box position."

- "When I call out 'Three!'—lower your center of gravity, flexing your knees, until your buttocks rest on your raised heels. This should be a movement that has great painful restraint and discipline." (Do this to a countdown from you—anywhere from three to ten seconds. They must pace themselves so they reach their heels when you say one.)
- "When I call out 'Four!'—slowly raise back to box position, again using restraint. Your upper body should be free of tension while your legs are exercising control and your core is straight and engaged."
- Repeat these steps, but this time begin with the left foot.

Activity—Crossing the Stage

- Say: "Stand in a line, shoulder to shoulder at the far upstage. Each of you take a pose in which your arms reach out in some way towards the audience. Hold this pose perfectly still while you maintain eye contact and begin to walk slowly downstage."
- "Every step is careful, and as slow as possible, with each step landing in front of the other foot, as slowly and deliberately as possible, rolling from heel to toe."
- "Create forward motion with your core."
- "When you reach the front of the stage, maintain eye contact, but slowly return your arms to neutral position."
- Stand in stillness until the last person has arrived and experienced the stillness.
- Command firmly, "Speak!" at which time, the students recite the monologue they have prepared to the audience, projecting the exertion and energy out.
- Discuss: "Suzuki training is a structured system which aims to build speed, strength of energy, stamina, stability and concentration in a modular manner. It moves from the simple to the complex, and from the mechanical to the creative.[17] Did you feel this? What do you imagine years of training would accomplish in you with many repetitions and modifications?"

17

Harold Guskin

The Person

Dubbed "The Great Guskin," Harold Guskin was an American actor, director, and acting coach. He was born in 1941 in New York City. Initially entering the arts world as a trombonist, Guskin was fascinated by theatre and acting, so one day he joined an acting class and volunteered to go first in an improvisation activity so he wouldn't lose his nerve. He tells this story in his book *How to Stop Acting*. The assignment given him by his instructor was to enter through a door at the upstage of the classroom theatre and communicate what the weather was outside just by the way he entered. In that moment, he created a vivid scene in his mind of the cold Irish countryside. He was lost and stumbled into a pub.

> I came in through the door. I shook the rain from my hat and coat. After a moment, I realized something was wrong. There was silence. I looked around the pub. Unfriendly men were looking at me. I smiled, walked to a table, sat down, and waited for someone to take my order. No one came. I didn't look up. I was chilled and afraid. I felt unwelcome, utterly alone. I waited. The silence seemed dangerous. Suddenly I slammed my fist on the table and yelled, "What the hell are you looking at!"
>
> The class roared with laughter. I hadn't realized it was funny. But what surprised me most was that, while I had been aware that I was on stage the entire time, that awareness was not in the least distracting. My concentration was on this strange thing happening to me in the pub of my mind.[1]

This experience hooked him into acting right away. After studying theatre at Rutgers University and later at Indiana University, he taught at the collegiate level for a while. Finally, unhappy with academias, he moved on to work at the Public Theater where he taught acting.

Later in his career, Guskin began to coach actors. He worked with Kevin Kline at the beginning of his acting work, and helped other actors, like Christopher Reeves, later in their careers when things began to fizzle. He also worked with Glenn Close, Michelle Pfieffer, and many others, such as James Gandlofini, who he assisted during the second and third seasons of *The Sopranos*. Although he felt he was a very strong director and actor, he chose to pursue actor coaching, believing he had a greater impact on the field this way. He was a persistent coach who pushed his clients to greatness, caring more about their connections to their work than the work itself. He never advertised his business, instead picking and choosing his clients from the pool of people who found him.

Guskin died of a pulmonary embolism in 2018, just short of his seventy-seventh birthday. Sadly, his health had been declining due to a rare dementia-causing disease called primary progressive aphasia which made it impossible for him to continue his work in his final decade of life.

The Method

New York magazine ran a story by David Blum in 1989. He wrote about Guskin's approach to directing, "you must let people be themselves and do whatever they want; then, when the time comes to take the stage, the character will be a part of the actor. Don't play the character, Guskin likes to say—let the character play you."[2] His entire method is to help actors stop acting, simplify their work, and react genuinely each time they hit the stage or screen.

According to Guskin, the most common ailment actors face is their own fear of how they might appear to others, resulting in over-analyzation or over-intellectualization of their characters. At the beginning of his actor training the usual methods were very helpful. He studied many of the acting methods detailed in this book, but was particularly interested in digging into the methods of Stanislavski. He wrote character biographies in detail, determining their super-objectives, objectives, motives, and actions. He became obsessed with character work. However, after a while, it became painfully obvious to him that he wasn't performing freely enough on stage.

Guskin recalled the moment when he improvised coming in from the cold, and realized that he needed to begin improvising every moment on stage while staying completely true to the words of the text. So he created his method requiring actors to let go of the creation of characters in order to live in the moment, always reacting naturally to what is being said and done in real time. This can cause fear in an actor, because the desire to control what is happening is an actor's way of handling the fear of looking foolish on stage. Guskin taught his actors to trust that when the time came, they would know which words came next, if they lived fully as themselves on stage.

In a 1995 *New Yorker* profile, John Lahr puts it this way,

> Guskin is peddling not a system but a process. He believes that actors are athletes of the spirit, who have to be trained to show us those places in the heart where we (and they) hide feeling away. This is a courageous job and a hard one. It takes a certain kind of vigilance and tact to pry out the emotional stuff and shape it into character.[3]

Taking it off the Page

Guskin's method requires actors to work on their acting every day by saying their lines out loud. If all an actor does is think about character, they won't be connected to the text, which is the actor's work. The first step of Guskin's process is called "taking it off the page." The job of an actor, even an inexperienced one, is to connect themself to the text, this way connecting themself to the character. As they do, they become less afraid of not finding the character.

Guskin would coach you to stay in the moment, being present to the text and yourself at the same time, "floating with the line."[4] He taught that your instincts and text will lead you. This floating quality is important to Guskin's method. It requires you to avoid intellectual choices at the beginning of the process. Instead, you take the time to breathe and explore.

Here is how this part of the process looks: The actor takes a monologue and looks at the first phrase while breathing in and out. Reading the text internally, the actor does not speak, but thinks only about these words in their head. Then, looking up from the page, the actor speaks the line. It is important for the actor to avoid thinking of what the appropriate reaction is to that line. Instead, the actor should say exactly what the words mean to them in that moment. Guskin teaches actors to say the words as soon as they have exhaled so they don't have time to censor the thought of feeling. This exhalation has the added benefit of ensuring "that it is your own voice that you are using, not a phony, artificially projected actor's voice."[5]

Sometimes the most genuine response to a line is nothing. In that case, the actor should deliver the line with nothing behind it. This is often the best way to deliver a line that feels corny or overly dramatic. If the actor feels nothing, then the actor should speak it flat and move on to the next phrase. Perhaps something unsolicited and surprising will happen with the next phrase. This very gentle way of approaching the text allows an actor to live moment to moment in rehearsal and on the stage.

If you are struggling with being in the moment, try to purposefully react in ways that are varied and inappropriate for the text. Follow your instincts. Sometimes, Guskin says, if you don't allow the inappropriate impulse to happen, you will not be able to get past them. Try it in a rehearsal or on your own, so that when performing for an audience, you won't be pulled towards that idea anymore. Lahr writes, "Guskin is unrepentant. 'Reject justification,' he tells his students. 'It has to be, simply, 'I did it because I did it. I wanted to do it.'"[6] If you have an irrational or tyrannical idea while taking it off the page, he feels it is best to try it out. If it doesn't work, it will leave you alone. If it does work, it is often the best idea you will have in your entire process of taking it off the page. It is likely this idea will stick long term.

All of this requires the actor to stop caring about how their acting comes out. Letting go of the fear of the unknown and uncontrolled creates the possibility for varied and real moments on stage.

Another piece of taking it off the page is physicalization. Sometimes choosing to move to a new position between each phrase is helpful in releasing physically locked acting techniques. An actor can physicalize the image of the words, putting their body in a pose or acting out the words before they speak them. Try it! Find a position, look at the text while breathing in and out, physicalize the phrase, breathe in and out again, speak that phrase as it comes to you, move to a new position, and repeat.

Guskin suggests you practice this process with monologues first, before you add a scene partner. When you are ready to add a partner, start by remembering to be in the moment. While you do not have to look at your partner while they speak, you should not look at the page. Listen to them and then look at your line, breathing in and out, and then say the line as it comes to you, allowing your partner's emotions to color the way you read your lines. Don't impose your way of working on your scene partner. Let them do their own work while you do yours.

Guskin warns actors to never memorize their lines. Instead, keep taking it off the page, and the lines will come to you on their own. Soon you will discover that you don't have to look down to know what comes next.

Exploring the Role

Guskin felt strongly that actors need to get out of their analysis mode at the beginning of the process. He saw many actors had been trained to start outside the character by analyzing the interior of their character in a distant way. While this works to some extent for all actors, it did not work long term for him. He encouraged his long list of actors to get out of the habit of doing research first because the research diminished their instincts. Knowing too much about a character before working on the script gets in the way of inspiration. Guskin reminds us even Stanislavski wanted his actors to avoid interfering with their own subconscious at work.

Often when Guskin worked with an actor, they came to him feeling insecure. They felt they could not meet the challenge before them because they were inadequate, rather than understanding that it was the method or technique they had been working with which was failing them. He taught them to trust the text in the moment, and this was very helpful to many as they built characters. So Guskin pushed his actors to let go of the goal of consistency. Method actors are trained to find the same emotion in every instance of a scene. Guskin countered that consistency is not necessary or desirable because it often causes the actor to lose spontaneity. The trade-off is not worth it.

If we are to believe that a better way to more effective acting is by resisting analysis, rejecting consistency, and by taking the character moment by moment, then how do we build a character that the audience will understand and believe? Guskin shows this is another instance where the actor has to rely on the text. If the actor stays in the moment and allows the text to mean what it means each time, the words "*come together as the character only for the audience,* as the lines, action, and story unfold before them in performance. *That is not the actor. The moments are the actor. The character is the text.*"[7] The playwright put all the pieces of the story and character together in the words. Knowing this frees the actor from worrying about a consistent character, and allows them to live moment to moment in the text. Guskin gives one caution, as actors are working using in-the-moment impulses: as you follow your impulses in rehearsal, it is important to never act on aggressive or threatening impulses that might harm another actor without the guidance of a director or choreographer. Actors should indulge their impulses in the moment, but refrain when injury could occur.

Guskin encourages actors to take the words off the page, and by working through them over and over, the character will become real. They will discover that the character begins to talk to them, even challenging the actor by asking questions such as, "Why are you yelling those words?" The actor can listen to the character, who is really their instincts, telling them to try something different or to slow down.

This process takes time. When the actor takes the time to slow down and allow the process to happen naturally, they will find their choices will not be predictable or boring. This is also true of small parts. Often an actor given a small or ensemble role will overdo their moment of glory in order to make that character count. Instead, prepare yourself as if you are the star of the show. This doesn't mean he wants actors to try to do a lot. Instead, remember that each line or thought is just another moment in the life of the character. "So don't make it a big deal . . . Let the lines, no matter how few, take you to your imagination."[8] Flesh the character out by learning as much as you can from the text, and then allow the character to talk to you.

Work from the Negative

Another way Guskin recommends finding a character is by discovering what a character is not. He compares this process to a sculptor working in marble. By chipping away the pieces that are not part of the artwork, the artist finds the masterpiece. In the same way, an actor can "work from the negative." This process looks like trying out options and discarding what doesn't work. Before you begin, however, resist the temptation to mimic the usual approach to a character. For example, if an actor playing Stanley in *A Streetcar Named Desire* begins with an assumption that his job is to imitate Marlon Brando, he might never discover the Stanley he was meant to play. If instead he begins by discarding everything Brando did and tries everything else, he might find gold. What will be left after discarding the conventional and rejected options, will be the character. That character will be the actor. The actor no longer has to act—they have found the character and can work with freedom.

Take the Script at its Word

Guskin helped actors avoid over-analysis by avoiding working on subtext too quickly. Actors often enjoy delving into the meaning below the words, but in most cases, the character says what they mean. Try first taking the script at its word. When an actor tries to play the subtext too much, it is often out of fear the audience won't see what the actor is playing. Actors can learn to trust the audience to understand what is happening. The audience loves to see past the words to the story, and the actor shouldn't make it too obvious. It is more fun for the audience to figure it out.

Playing with Tempo and Pitch

Even in consideration of his method's effectiveness in creating truthful characters, Guskin points out that actors often approach a character with their own rhythms or the rhythms of previous characters they have played. It often takes persistence and patience to shift into a new character. Guskin states that most of the problem comes from a feeling that a prior rhythm was working for them and its difficult to let go of the comfort of a functioning character for the uncertainty of something new. One way to combat this is by slowing way down or drastically speeding up line delivery. By practicing with a completely different pace, the correct rhythm will emerge and free the actor to be a new character. The actor has to resist the desire to be interesting, and work instead on the lines as they come off the page.

Another technique is working in vocal variety, oftentimes choosing the opposite of what is comfortable. For example, going up in pitch at the end of a line instead of down. Guskin pushed his actors to keep trying new things until the new character is uncovered.

Research can be an important part of the work of uncovering characters, but Guskin felt research needs to come after the words had been taken off the page. Using the text to guide research is more helpful than doing a ton of research before knowing the character's words. Actors will find the specific qualities of their characters from the text, but research can help inform how that character interacts in their world. The actor must find the character and work in the character's reality.

Auditioning Tips

Guskin often prepared his clients for auditions. He found they naturally did what we all do: feeling nervous about impressing the casting director, they often did their worst work for roles they wanted the most. He told them to stick with what they already know, and to take the text off the page in auditions just as they would at home or in a rehearsal. His advice was to let the casting team see them exploring in front of them, not worried about getting it right. They will see the way you work, that you are open to trying different things, and why they need you in the role.

While preparing for auditions, work on taking the text off the page as usual, but also take the other character's lines off the page. Verbalize their lines and then paraphrase them. Then, speak your thoughts about their lines. Ask them questions. Guskin suggests you spend more time on the other character's lines than your own. This will help you to empathize with your scene partner, and to listen better because you will be in a responsive state.

To follow Guskin's suggestions, on the day of an audition, dress to feel the part you are auditioning for. Do not dress to look like the character; this would make you look amateurish and desperate. However, if your character is moody and aloof, find clothes in your closet that make you feel that way. If your character uses sex appeal as a weapon, instead of wearing a provocative dress with high slits or a low neckline, wear something that makes you feel attractive and powerful. If you walk into an audition with a calm attitude, ready to work on the character with a few ideas that interest you, and trust the text to help you in the moment, you will assist the director in seeing your instincts and how you as the actor connect with the character. Remember you cannot give a performance in an audition. What you can give is a view of yourself in collaborative exploration with the director and the playwright's words.

Lastly, stop looking for the right choice, whatever that means to you. There isn't a right choice, only options that may or may not work. Try what you believe in the moment, and the next time, try something else. This will give the casting team an opportunity to see your capabilities, and that you are able to work on a variety of options rather than getting locked into one idea. You cannot guess what the director wants—you can only try interesting ideas. If the director gives you direction, try what they ask you to do. If it doesn't work for you, the next time try something else, but not what you were doing before.

Sometimes in auditions you are asked to read with a reader who will give the line to you in a flat or unhelpful way. Perhaps you will be paired with an actor who is inexperienced or counterproductive. It is not their responsibility to give you a reading that will help you. It is your responsibility to listen to the line and respond to it.

Guskin repeatedly addresses the fear actors live in. He recommends attacking fear in the audition room by taking your time and standing in silence for a long moment. "Let the silence make the reader and anyone else in the room look up and stop what they're doing. Then take a breath and begin."[9] He recommends that as soon as you realize you are afraid of something, do it until you feel the fear intensify and then dissipate. This will give you the freedom to move past your fears and do the work you know how to do. By attacking your fear, you will take control of the audition room and make the casting director pay attention. Even if you don't get the role, they will remember and respect you as an actor who has confidence, flexibility and freedom.

In Rehearsal and On Stage

Guskin teaches that the actor's job in the rehearsal room is to explode the moments. The director's role is to move things along. This tension can add to conflict, but if you, the actor, are ready to do your work, the director will be more pleased in the end with the work you do than if you had presented yourself as a puppet, ready to do whatever you are asked. Guskin breaks the process down into eight steps.

1. *Table work*. In this stage of the process, the actors and director sit around the table, read through the text and discuss it. As an actor, your job is to keep exploring your part and taking your lines off the page. Do not read your scene partners lines while they are speaking, but listen to them.
2. *Physical exploration*. At some point, the need to physicalize the lines will become apparent. Ideally, at this time, the director will allow the actors to get up from the table and try things out. The director and stage manager will establish what the set and props will be, and the actors will explore the physical space as they say their lines, continuing to take them off the page.
3. *Direction*. At this point, the director may need to offer some guidance for the blocking of the show. If the work the actors have done organically does not meet the needs of the show, or could be enhanced, a skilled director will offer their suggestions and allow the actors to explore them.
4. *Off book*. The actors will gradually come off book naturally because of the process of taking the text off the page. This freedom from the script will allow the actors to explore the text more and more deeply together. Unfortunately, many directors are not patient enough during this portion of the work. They might be looking for performance-ready work too soon. If this is the case, you cannot expect the director and your fellow cast mates to follow your process. Instead, you will need to do work at home, taking your lines off the page as slowly as you need to so you are more ready to work at the pace your director asks for in rehearsal. Guskin reminds actors to give up their egos by keeping your own method private. At the same time, you can take suggestions from others as long as you have the freedom to work the way you want to. He writes that he always does whatever he wants in the process, but, "I always . . . let everyone else feel that I need their *help* to do my best work. And I do! . . . Theatre is a joint effort."[10] While you are working, remember to give your fellow artists the benefit of the doubt. Assume the best of everyone, including directors. When you work this way, if you allow your ego to affect your work, you will not be successful. You must make sure when you talk to your director that they understand you are *having* a problem—you are not *being* a problem. If what the director asks you to do isn't working for you, admit it is your problem and try to find another approach that works for both of you.
5. *Homework*. Now begin doing research. Look to the text to tell you what you need to learn. If you are required to knit on stage, find someone to learn from. Watch them work, and try to imitate their movements. Work on knitting during rehearsal on the sidelines even when you aren't required on stage. If you are playing a war veteran, find veterans to interview and observe. Watch documentaries. Let your research seep into your work on stage. The text remains the base, but your homework will bring nuance to your work and influence the other actors around you as well.

6 *Exploring and repeating.* As you work, you will eventually find a slate of choices that work well. Sometimes you will lock in a great choice very early in the process, and if you try to change it, you may find you need to go back to your first impulse. Don't fight this, but keep trying new ideas as they occur to you until you are sure they don't work. You will know you have landed on a repeatable choice when you feel free every time you make that same choice.

7 *Repeating and exploring.* On the other hand, it can be dangerous to stop thinking about the moment and trusting in choices you have always made. Guskin puts it this way, "He will get ahead of himself on stage, because he will be thinking about what's coming, not where he is at the moment. His instinct will shut down. He may think he is safe, but his acting will have lost its edge."[11] Working with your scene partner, try something different even after the show opens if things feel stale for you. If you were exploring in rehearsal, you won't throw your scene partner off when you explore in performance. Always allow yourself to make the same choice again in the moment, but also allow yourself to make a new choice. This exploration is not to subvert the will of the director, but to respect the work by keeping it alive. "If all we know is what we will say, but not how we will say it, instinct will be free to take us there in a new creative way."[12] (A caution from the author: Be aware of the constraints of exploring during a run. If you don't hit your marks, you might be in the dark since the lighting design can't change on your impulses. You can, however, make choices that enliven the acting and stay within the limitations of a completed design and the safety of other actors. Don't change your blocking without permission.)

8 *Surprise.* During a long run, sometimes it is necessary for actors to try new things and surprise themselves. Instead of allowing yourself to slide into the safe laughs you always get, try something new and see if you get a different response. If it doesn't work, you can choose to go back to a tried and true option—but don't decide what you will do until you are in the moment. Let your work surprise you.

Harold Guskin's Legacy

Harold Guskin's book *How to Stop Acting* gives a practical approach to acting and auditioning that has been useful to many actors. The legacy of his work is in the performances captured on film by the actors he coached, and in the work of actors like yourself who take his tips and tricks into auditions and rehearsals. By simplifying your approach to the work, and improvising the meaning of the words during every performance, you will prove his methods can keep a performance alive even during a long run.

Tips for taking this method further

- Read Harold Guskin's book *How to Stop Acting*.
- Watch the video by Jesper Trier, *Guskin's "The Breathing Thing"* and try this technique.

Discussion Starters and Journal Prompts

- Summarize Guskin's acting method in two sentences for an actor who has never heard of him.
- Do you like Guskin's idea that you should avoid research before you begin working on a role? Does his claim that early research is counterproductive and inhibits your instincts compel you?
- How do you feel at auditions? What piece of advice from Guskin would you like to take with you to your next audition? How will that help you to succeed?

The Tools for your Toolbox

Activity—Take it off the Page

- Hand the students a monologue to work on. Guskin suggests Chekhov's *The Three Sisters*. For men, Tuzenbach in Act I, beginning with, "The longing for work..." For women, Irina in Act I, "Tell me, why am I so happy?"
- Say: "Spread out in the space and quiet yourself."
- "Look at the first phrase while breathing in and out and then speak the line immediately after the exhale."
- "Use your own voice, not an acting voice. Stay in touch with yourself as you explore the text."
- "Practice taking it off the page for a few moments."
- "Find a new position in the room as you prepare to work on physicalization."
- "Read the first phrase again in your mind while breathing in and out. As soon as you finish reading it over a few times, physicalize the words however you imagine them without judging your motions."
- "Say the words after an exhale."
- "Continue to find a new position, read silently, physicalize, then speak after an exhale. Then move to a new place and repeat."
- "This time, try a very different vocal cadence from your usual impulse."
- "Listen to the pitch at the end of each line and reverse what you were doing last time."
- "Slow your pace way down, then try speeding it way up."
- "Can you find the character's rhythm somewhere in the mix?"
- "Try changing the physicalized rhythm of the character from what you've done before."
- "Try this method on your monologues between this class and the next session. Strive to do it as long as you can maintain interest, then stop and come back to it several times a day. Don't try to memorize the words, but continue to work on taking it off the page. Abandon the physicalizations when they are no longer necessary for freeing the words. After the second or third day of working on the monologue, begin to read the play, taking breaks from time to time to take the monologue off the page."
- Discuss: "How does it feel to breathe the text in and out internally before speaking with connection to the room instead of the page?"

Activity—Explore a Character

- Give each pair of students a scene that features two characters.
- Say: "Find another pair to watch you work, and take turns demonstrating. First, try doing a cold read of this scene as you usually would, reading the lines while looking at the page. Then, try doing the cold read by taking it off the page, making a connection with your scene partner. Neither of you should look at the page while either of you speak."
- Discuss: "What are the benefits and drawbacks of using this technique in an audition? How does it feel to watch and to perform?"
- Say: "Now work alone for ten minutes, taking your lines off the page using the Guskin techniques of physicalization and changing cadence and pacing."
- "For the next five minutes, think about the change your character goes through from beginning to end and condense your lines into a monologue that spans the change. Speak it as you physicalize."
- "For the next three minutes, take your partner's lines off the page, exploring what their character is saying."
- "Find your partner and go back to the full script and your own part, taking it off the page with them for the next ten minutes. Don't look at the script when your scene partner is speaking a line, and exhale before you speak each time. Keep trying new choices even if you find options that are working. There might be a better choice down the road."
- Try Guskin's five different ways: "do it for laughs, then for interior values, then for anger, then for tenderness, and then for petty (bratty) values. Finally, after exploring . . . each of these ways, do it however it comes out."[13]
- Discuss: "How does 'the five ways' impact your performance? What came out when you allowed whatever happened to happen? Is this method worth using in scene work in the future?"

Activity—Work from the Negative

- Give your actors a page from a screenplay of a movie all of them will be familiar with—perhaps a famous scene from *Star Wars*, *The Lion King*, or *the Wizard of Oz*. Break them into groups so that everyone has a role to play.
- Say: "Talk together about the iconic performances of the original actors. What sort of personality did each actor take on in the role? What made those performances so iconic?
- "Work on the scenes together, taking the text off the page, and rejecting all of the choices of the original performers. Find different vocal rhythm and pacing, different emotional choices, different meaning, and different essence for each character. Reimagine to make the acting completely different."
- Have the actors perform their scenes for the class and discuss: "What moments did you see where taking the negative space from an iconic performance led to gold?"

18

Anne Bogart

The Person

Anne Bogart was born 1951. As the only girl in a Navy family, her aspirations were not taken very seriously. She wasn't sent to a good school like her brothers, or expected to accomplish much beyond marriage to an officer, and this neglect frustrated her. She fell in love with theatre as a teenager when she attended a production of *Macbeth,* drawn to the energy and focus of the actors even though she didn't fully understand the play. "In the theater, I found a site of grace. The theater demanded creativity and helped me to survive and construct fruitful bridges to other people and their experiences."[1] She poured her energy into high school productions, then studied theatre at Bard College. Afterwards, she moved to New York and immersed herself in experimental theatre while she earned her masters in theatre at New York University. She began teaching at the university's newly formed Experimental Theatre Wing (ETW) after she graduated.

Bogart made a very important contact in 1979 when she met Mary Overlie. They were both on the faculty of ETW where they worked together on projects. Overlie, a choreographer, had developed a system called View Points to explore what performance is. Bogart worked with Overlie on a few projects and watched her use them in dance, and she felt the View Points addressed many problems she was having in theatre. Then Overlie went to Europe for a decade and the two lost touch. Bogart and Overlie separately developed the method in different directions. Bogart worked with a co-director, Tina Landau, who also found the View Points to be useful. Over time, their version of the system came to be called Viewpoints.

The women who developed Viewpoints worked with it from their unique perspectives. Bogart says of Overlie, "Mary is an innovator and inventor and explorer. She goes into herself and comes out with something truly original. I'm a scavenger. I look around and go, 'I like that. And I like that and that, and I think I'll put them all together.'"[2] And she did. Her version of Viewpoints is distinct from the original. When Overlie heard from a friend that Bogart and Landau were publishing a book on her method, she was happy View Points was being used. But it hasn't always been easy to let go of the system and let it change and grow. Bogart says it has been an uncomfortable, but open issue for them. The discomfort comes because Overlie feels very strongly about the six View Points she developed (Space, Shape, Time, Emotion, Movement, and Story), and the Bogart/Landau iteration of the system doesn't include some of Overlie's elements. Instead, they developed nine Viewpoints, more than half of which are their own invention.

All three practitioners believe it is a flexible system. Overlie says,

> Anne is a good example of this because she never really studied Viewpoints with me. She just came in contact with me. I have for years and years and years observed that if you get one little scale of them and you get that down, they will recreate themselves. If you spend time, all the rest of it is there. That's why you ended up with this funny little machine—because it recreated itself for you in a system that wasn't mine.[3]

Bogart is collaborative and works in the mode of collage, taking pieces of styles and melding them together. Another example of this trait is the SITI Company. In 1992, Bogart co-founded the SITI Company with Tadashi Suzuki. This troupe of actors trained equally in Viewpoints and Suzuki as two separate disciplines, but they connected with each other at complementary areas of overlap. Bogart stayed active with the SITI Company until it had its final season in 2022.

She currently runs the graduate directing program at Columbia University and continues to write.

The Method

Bogart and Landau define Viewpoints as "a philosophy translated into a technique for (1) training performers; (2) building ensemble; and (3) creating movement for the stage."[4] Bogart was initially interested in Overlie's View Points because they addressed acting problems she was struggling with. Three of these problems are:

- Problem 1: The Stanislavski System as it was Americanized by Strasberg was useful for camera acting, but it locked actors into overly realistic acting. Viewpoints, focused on movement, brings emotion out of actors as they work together. Rather than delving into psychology, fresh choices come from awareness of space and time.
- Problem 2: Actors don't practice ongoing training. Viewpoints provides actors a practical way of collaboratively training in their craft.
- Problem 3: Actor's focus on the word *want* in performance and rehearsal. Bogart believes language is important, and artists should be careful selecting a vocabulary. She feels the word "want" implies there is a right and wrong choice a director desires. Her approach is to collaboratively seek what the *play* wants, discovering what the piece is. Viewpoints sets the tone for actors to create together, taking responsibility as co-creators of the work.

Beyond solving acting problems, Viewpoints has many advantages. It:

- is non-hierarchical and collaborative.
- requires only your presence and attention.
- allows actors to carry their past into the present moment.
- preserves individuality through unison movement.
- works against human nature that encourages uniformity.

- provokes open awareness of your body in space and in relationship with others, as well as in relation to the room.
- means the script doesn't outrank the performance space. All elements are equal.

Viewpoints works within the limits of what you have, which is energy. Bogart writes, "We inhabit a vibrational universe. Everything moves. Nothing is at rest and everything is energy at different levels of vibration. Even objects that appear to be stationary are in fact vibrating, oscillating, and resonating, at diverse frequencies."[5]

The Viewpoints

Viewpoints is a game-like, facilitated movement activity created by the participants. Each of the participants has a part in creating the shape of the work, and an equal responsibility to be present and alert to the room. The Viewpoints are categorized under the titles TIME (Tempo, Duration, Kinesthetic Response, Repetition), SPACE (Shape, Gesture, Architecture, Spatial Relationship, Topography) and VOCAL. Those features describe a practice that is "attempting to construct moments of shared resonance between the stage and the auditorium, between actors and audience, among bodies, objects, ideas, and moments of being."[6]

Participants listen to a facilitator call out instructions to explore various Viewpoints, and respond collaboratively with others. For example, the facilitator might say, "Begin walking in the space as if the floor were a grid, following the lines. You can make turns on impulse, exploring individually, but your turns should be angular or sharp. This is **Grid Topography**." After this instruction, the participants begin moving silently in the room, walking on an invisible grid. These exercises usually continue for at least ten minutes, but sometimes for hours at a time. The following is a definition of each of the Viewpoints.

Viewpoints of Time

- **Tempo**—This Viewpoint relates to the rate at which a movement occurs. Try creating any motion, making sure it is well defined and repeatable. Do the motion at slow, medium, and fast tempos. There are six tempos in Viewpoints: the slowest you can go and still call it movement, very slow, slow, medium, fast, very fast, and hyper-speed.
- **Duration**—This Viewpoint is the amount of time a movement or sequence of movements takes to complete, or how long it is continued. As a default, most people work in average durations. This Viewpoint encourages stretching or shortening rather than the safety of medium.
- **Kinesthetic Response**—This Viewpoint takes the control of movement from the individual. Each person surrenders the pressure to be interesting, and lets everything around them provide the impulse to change.
- **Repetition**—This Viewpoint involves either repeating based on your impulse or repeating something outside yourself.

Viewpoints of Space

- **Shape**—Shape breaks down all movements into shapes that are curved, straight, or a combination of both. Some movements are rounded, others are angular. They can be stationary or moving, and can be formed with the body alone, in relationship with the architecture of the space, or with other bodies.
- **Gesture**—Gesture describes a movement with a defined beginning, middle, and end. A gesture can be made with a single body part or in combination with other parts. Behavioral gestures are those that represent concrete, external everyday motions like a wave or swinging a bat. Expressive gestures are internal and express internal emotions, desires or values.
- **Architecture**—Architecture is the Viewpoint that engages the space around us. The aspects of the space engaged in architecture are:
    - solid mass: the structure of the space and the furniture within it.
    - texture: the type of material.
    - light: both light and shadow.
    - color: noticing and reacting to the mood and contrasts of colors surrounding us.
    - sound: we create sound with our bodies in movement.
- **Spatial Relationship**—Spatial Relationship draws attention to the space between bodies in the space, and between bodies and the architecture. In this Viewpoint, actors explore the many ways bodies can be grouped and tell stories with proximity.
- **Topography**—Topography refers to the pattern or design created in space by bodies in motion.

The Vocal Viewpoints

The Vocal Viewpoints dissect sound the same way the physical Viewpoints dissect movement. In Vocal Viewpoints, participants become aware of sound as something separate from its meaning. There are twelve Vocal Viewpoints:

- **Pitch**—we all have a range of pitches that we can produce from low to high. These ranges are limited, but can be stretched with work.
- **Dynamic**—we can produce sound at different volumes. This can change quickly or slowly. Our voices can alternate between nearly inaudible to yelling.
- **Tempo**—we can vocalize at different paces.
- **Duration**—we can choose how long we hold one sound.
- **Acceleration/Deceleration**—we can speed up or slow down sounds.
- **Timbre**—the timbre (pronounced tam-ber) of the voice refers to where it is produced in the body. You can use resonators in your chest, nose, throat, etc. to create different sounds.
- **Shape**—we can work to create round, soft, fluid, sharp, spiky, and percussive sounds. It is a more subjective Viewpoint. What makes a sound round? or sharp?

- **Gesture**—vocal gestures are broken down into expressive and behavioral just like movement gestures. Behavioral gestures are sounds that people make in their everyday lives: coughing, clearing throat, sniffling, etc. Expressive gestures are more abstract. These are the sounds of grief, justice, home, freedom. They require the actor to play with their voice.
- **Architecture**—we can play with the sonic qualities of the room by experimenting with bouncing sounds off of walls, corners, and furniture, or by sending our voices to different textures of surfaces and objects.
- **Repetition**—we can repeat each other and ourselves.
- **Kinesthetic Response**—we can give control of our voices to outside stimuli, being responsive to others.
- **Silence**—we can stop our voice, holding in potential energy.

This long list of Viewpoints is easier to understand by experiencing. Gather a group of interested people and try some of the activities at the end of this chapter to really grasp it. People do not need to be trained artists to perform Viewpoints exercises, but many companies of experienced actors start each rehearsal with them.

The Four Energies

There are four main energies to work in when using the Viewpoints.

1. Horizontal energy: This is the easiest to access and most beginners are immediately dominant in horizontal energy as they move around the space. It connects the actor with the other actors and with the surrounding world.
2. Vertical energy: This is the energy connecting the actor to the universe and the ground. The actor is the line connecting heaven with earth.
3. Heavy energy: This is a young and unrefined energy that bounces off the environment. It doesn't tire and is easier for the beginner to access.
4. Light energy: This energy takes maturity to cultivate. It is more nuanced. The energy is less visible, but much more is happening internally.

These energies can be intentionally harnessed by actors in a scene. Think about using vertical energy if your partner is stuck in the horizontal; find characters with heavy and light energy to play off each other. The key is to work intentionally with your energy.

The Benefits of Viewpoints for the Actor

Bogart lists some benefits of Viewpoints:

- **Surrender**—In trusting your collaborators and the space, you don't have to make something happen. Instead, you can trust it will occur.
- **Possibility**—By removing hierarchy and the need to meet the desires of the director, actors are freed to explore a multiplicity of possibilities, and then to make a choice.

- Choice and Freedom—"Viewpoints leads to greater *awareness*, which leads to greater *choice*, which leads to greater *freedom*."[7] As time goes on, you find more and more freedom in your work.
- Growth—By working with Viewpoints, your awareness of your limitations, patterns, and habits increases, giving you the gift of an option to grow.
- Wholeness—We are awakened to how stuck we are in our heads most of the time. "Through Viewpoints we learn to listen with our entire bodies and see with a sixth sense. We receive information from levels we were not even aware existed, and begin to communicate back with equal depth."[8]
- Stress Relief—We can use our frustrations and other emotions, harnessing them as energy. Using them in Viewpoints work can inspire you and your collaborators. "The frustration generates a storehouse of energy useful in locating the necessary stubbornness and courage, patience, and energy for creative expression. The transformation is a kind of spiritual alchemy."[9]
- Articulation—We can harness voice and movement in communication. It takes bravery to let the speaking of words carry you, making meaning as you go. Words, like all of theatre, are ephemeral. You can use movement to point to the meaning when words aren't articulate enough in the moment.

Compositions in Rehearsal

In Bogart's rehearsals, the actors start with Viewpoints and then Bogart often uses a technique called composition in her rehearsals. In this method of devising theatre, actors borrow from other art forms to create new forms of theatre. Bogart gives her actors an assignment with an intention and a structure as well as a list of components to include such as: stillness, "symmetry versus asymmetry, use of scale and perspective, juxtaposition . . . objects, textures, colors, sounds, actions."[10] The actors then work in a limited amount of time to create a performance based on the structure given. Oftentimes this list of components are related to the play being rehearsed, and the work they do in compositions informs the direction of the piece.

She teaches her students to pay attention to the material so they know what form it needs to take. What does the work want from you? Your job in rehearsal room is not to please others, it is to be the voice of the art. Bogart writes that composition work "is the act of writing as a group, in time and space, using the language of the theatre."[11] She recommends the director closely monitor the group to make sure they are working on their feet and feeling "Exquisite Pressure"[12] to get the work done, while having the right balance of limitations and inspirations to stay focused rather than becoming overwhelmed.

Viewpoints in Performance

Of course, Viewpoints are not literally performed on stage. Neither are the Compositions. However the exercises help actors develop a more wide-open ability to perceive while learning how to give and take focus. As they train together, participants learn to support the moment as it unfolds on stage. "We are telling stories all of the time. Our body tells a story. Our posture, our smile, our liveliness or fatigue, our stomach, our blank stare, our fitness, all speak, all tell a story. How we walk into a room tells a story. Our actions relate multiple stories. We invest our own energy into stories. Deprived of energy, stories die."[13] Viewpoints work in rehearsals prepares actors to enliven stage articulation of stories.

Acting is Attention and Attitude

Actors have control of a very few things. Bogart suggests attention and attitude are the two most important elements you have control over. You can gain skills in paying attention while you are on stage for long periods of time. You can cultivate an attitude that features the *will* to get yourself on stage (feedforward) and the *grace* to receive feedback. Feedforward and feedback must balance between effort and surrender.

Think of the right attitude as the tightness of a guitar string. It can't be too tight, or too loose. This is not a black and white attitude, it is an attitude of balance between too much and too little. It is the middle way. If you pay attention with readiness, and allow doubt to keep you on your toes, seeking the middle, you will find the right attitude. Bogart reminds us not to be confused by the term "right" here. The right attitude requires us to make good mistakes. Bogart writes, "In the face of an exceedingly complicated world, there are too many people who are invested in 'being right.' These people are dangerous. Their authority is based upon their sense of certainty . . . Innovation results from trial and error. The task is to make good mistakes, good errors, in the right direction."[14] Allow mistakes to happen in the interest of making progress as an artist.

This isn't easy because it's natural to feel humiliated by mistakes that lead to imbalance. Both artists and their characters want to correct imbalances, however, the joy of art comes from the restoration of balance after error. "Becoming conscious of error is how we learn and how we change. Our mistakes can teach us who we are . . . In the midst of the realization that we are wrong, we transform our understanding of ourselves as well as our ideas about the world. But we live in a culture that simply does not value error enough."[15] Bogart has learned in her work to embrace her errors, reject a need to feel right, and recognize that each of her past errors led her to change. If you let them, Viewpoints can teach you these skills too.

Anne Bogart's Legacy

Anne Bogart teaches us to make art with openness and focus. She wants us to jump in and make Viewpoints our own. Bogart and Landau write, "Almost always, the exercises were born out of moments of terror . . . We are torn between the desire to provide a map for you and the desire to tell you to rip up this book and enter the terror for yourself . . . We hope maybe to have indicated a path but not cleared it, leaving you to work through the most thorny areas."[16] It's time to try it out for yourself and see how it speaks to you.

Tips for taking this method further

- Read any of Anne Bogart's books. I recommend you start with *And Then, You Act: Making Art in an Unpredictable World*.
- Find opportunities to participate in Viewpoints workshops.

Discussion Starters and Journal Prompts

- After reading about the imperatives of Viewpoints, decide which of them will be the hardest for you to accomplish and write about the struggle.
- Bogart says that acting is attention and attitude. What does this mean to her? How are you engaging your own attention and attitude in your work?

The Tools for your Toolbox

Note on preparing your space and participants for Viewpoints

- If possible find a sprung wood floor, not carpeted or concrete.
- Sweep the floor to clear anything sharp or dangerous in the room.
- Remove all excess furniture and designate another space for storing the participant's things.
- Ask participants to come into the space in non-restrictive clothing and with bare feet, hair pulled back, and no jewelry.
- Note: Bogart and Landau's book has a treasure trove of activities for you. If you want to do more than an initial trial of the work, *The Viewpoints Book* is a required purchase for your program. I have selected a few activities for you representing Viewpoints, skipping many essential steps in an effort to help you sample the process.

Activity—Introducing Viewpoints

- Every new bullet point below is a separate instruction. When your participants have worked long enough with one bullet point, clap and read the next prompt.
- Say: "Every time I clap, I will give you a new instruction. Continue working when I clap, allowing the new prompt to inspire changes to your way of working."
- Clap then say: "Begin walking in the space as if the floor were a grid, following the lines. You can make turns on impulse, exploring individually, but your turns should be angular or sharp. This is **Grid Topography**."

- "Allow all of the visual information in the room to come to you at the same time using soft focus."
- "I will now clap and call out various **Tempos**. You are currently moving at a medium tempo. Continue moving on the grid in the tempo I indicate. Stay safe. Soft focus will help avoid injuries."
- Clap then call one of the tempos. (The slowest you can go and still call it movement, very slow, slow, medium, fast, very fast, and hyper-speed.) Practice all the tempos.
- Say: "You may now switch tempos at will. Surprise yourself by changing tempo."
- "While continuing to work with tempo, now think about the **Duration** of your tempo. Play with varying the length of time you stay at each tempo, sometimes for a short time, others for a very long time."
- "You may add the elements of moving backwards and sideways, still on the grid."
- "Think about levels. Make yourself higher on the grid, or low to the ground. Bring your attention to the vertical space while you work on tempo and duration."
- "Until I clap again, focus on stillness and top speed."
- "When you are in top speed, keep an inner slowness or calmness. When still, focus on inner momentum."
- "Keep working with tempo and duration, the how of movement, but now focus on the when. Allow yourself to be triggered to change by the Viewpoint of **Kinesthetic Response**. Use the movements of others around you. If someone stops, let that trigger something in you. Don't try to be interesting. Take in all the information around you and let it transform you. This portion of Viewpoints is receiving and reacting."
- "Change the trigger for new movements to the Viewpoint of **Repetition.** Everything you do should be a repetition of what someone else is doing. Copy one person's tempo and another's floor pattern, but every move should be surrendered to the effort of repeating others. Maintain *soft focus* for safety as you work, paying attention to everything around you."
- "Relax from holding onto any one Viewpoint. Use all of the ones that have been introduced, moving naturally using your instinct."
- "Notice the Viewpoint **Spatial Relationship** by noticing the spacing between bodies. You are fairly evenly spaced, since people tend to work in medium values."
- "With my next clap, focus your movements only on distance between bodies. Work in extremes with very close proximity or far distance as a goal. Be spontaneous. Create different groupings and patterns."
- "Stop. Notice how the spatial relationships in the group have changed: are they more interesting or powerful? Something occurs when we pay attention to space."
- "Begin to work in a topography of circles instead of grids."
- "Switch to a topography of zigzags and diagonals."
- "Everyone move to the outside of the space."
- "Imagine the topography of the space dissolving. Begin to create your own topography using your feet. Imagine they are covered with red paint. Move around the space painting your own topography on the floor."

- "Switch back to working on a grid, but this time change the size of your canvas. If you have been spreading your paint all over the space, begin to work in a small, defined area. If you have been defining a small canvas, work on a bigger one."
- "Begin to define the frame shape you are painting using the Viewpoint **Shape**. Your frame can be oblong, square, triangular, etc. Work within your shape, painting in contrasting and complementary shapes."
- "Stand still in space and become aware that your body is making a shape in space as a silhouette. Make angular shapes with your body."
- "Begin making curved shapes."
- "Create both curved and angular shapes with your silhouette at the same time."
- "Think about your shapes being fluid, moving from one to another smoothly."
- "Think about your shapes as traveling through space, and begin to move around the space creating shapes"
- "Begin combining with ensemble members to create shapes collaboratively. These shapes should be defined, legible, and in motion, merging and breaking away to make other shapes with other partners."
- "Create **Expressive Gestures** by thinking about your shapes as having distinct beginning, middle, and end."
- "Create expressive gestures that communicate the feeling of joy."
- Choose one or two more from: Anger, Fear, Freedom, Justice. The cosmos.
- Say: "Try your own expressive gestures with other emotions and ideas. Let the gestures move through space, refine, repeat, and evolve."
- "Notice parts of your body you are ignoring, and bring them into your gestures."
- "Freeze for a moment as we transition to **Behavioral Gesture**. Behavioral gestures are everyday actions you would see an ordinary person do outside the theatre. The pose you are currently in is more abstract. Think about the abstract expressive gesture you are in and what a related behavioral gesture might be. Smoothly shift from your current pose to the new one you thought of."
- "Move around the space making behavioral gestures related to body and health."
- Choose from this list or invent your own: "Try out behavioral gestures of cavemen, Renaissance era people, Western movies, Romcom, Superhero."
- Say: "Stop. Shift your focus to the **Architecture** of the room. Become aware of the floor, walls, furniture, and other solid objects in the space."
- "Dance and move with the architecture."
- "Shift your attention to the textures around you, letting the texture of things affect your movement."
- "Work off of architecture features far from you in the room. Allow the far wall or the ceiling to inspire movement."
- "So far we have been moving with the architecture alone, now change that. Join other people around you by moving with what they are inspired by. Don't stick to your own activity. Explore the activities of others."
- "Begin walking on a grid again, using soft focus and a medium tempo."

- "Free yourself from the grid and walk around finding doorways to walk through between two other people. As people walk, the doorways will move, but keep looking for as many doors as possible to walk through."
- "Change your tempo using kinesthetic response, responding to the tempo changes of others and their passage through doors."
- "Add stops to your tempo changes. Remember that stops are full of energy."
- "Follow someone. It is fine if lines form."
- "You may turn away from people rather than following them if you want to."
- "Only move in diagonals. All of the rules are still in play."
- "Sit quietly and close your eyes. Focus on your senses of smell, hearing, and touch. Feel the energy around you without the benefit of sight. Relax."
- Discuss: "What did you notice? What benefit could Viewpoints have for you in your acting? In your lives?"

Activity—The River and Tag Shape

- Ask everyone to stand in a circle. Establish rules around physical contact before starting this game. It is fine to play this game with no touch.
- Select a volunteer.
- Say to the volunteer: "Run into the center of the circle and create a shape."
- "Someone else run in and add to the shape."
- "Continue adding people until the entire group is part of the shape."
- Comment in a neutral way when you see examples of repetition and opposition in the shapes.
- Release everyone besides three who have created strong and dynamic shapes. Comment on what makes their shapes interesting and useful. Release them.
- Repeat the activity without comment.
- Say: "Return to your circle. We are going to play again, but this time when a third person joins the shape, the first needs to exit so that there are never less or more than two shapes in the center of the circle."

Activity—Life Story

- Say: "Stand spaced evenly around the four sides of the acting space."
- "Simultaneously Tell your life story using movement, criss-crossing and curving around the space. Maintain soft focus. Work to tell your story using the Viewpoints. Think about the size and shapes of different periods of your life. Is there repetition in your life? What tempos do each of your life stages have?"
- "As you finish your story up until now, return to an edge and wait, watching and reflecting."
- "Repeat the life story activity, this time telling the story of your character."
- "Share your work with a partner and verbally dissect what you discovered."

Activity—Flocking

- Say: "Spread out on stage facing downstage in the shape of a diamond so the person most downstage cannot see any of the others. This person is the leader."
- "Leader, begin moving in smooth motions. Everyone else copy the movements of the leader, trying to create the illusion that you are all moving together without a leader. Not everyone can see the leader, rely on following others who can."
- "At some point, the leader will turn their body so they can see the others. At that point, the person at a different point who can no longer see anyone else becomes the new leader. Continue moving for a while, allowing former leaders to recede into the group so other people can have a turn as the leader at one of the points."

Activity—Vocal Viewpoints

- Have everyone spread out, standing in the space.
- Say: "Play with your voices and find a three syllable gibberish word to work with."
- "Play with the Vocal Viewpoint **Pitch** by speaking your gibberish word as low as possible, then bring up the pitch each time you repeat the word until you get to the highest speaking pitch you can safely produce."
- "Try saying the first syllable in a low pitch, the second in a high, and the last in a medium pitch."
- "Play with pitch."
- "Play with the Vocal Viewpoint **Dynamic** by producing your word at a barely audible level and then the loudest possible."
- "Play with your voice alternating between nearly inaudible to yelling on each syllable and finding the levels in between."
- "Play with the Vocal Viewpoint **Tempo** by creating different rhythms with your word."
- "Play with the Vocal Viewpoint **Duration** by speaking your word very slowly and very quickly."
- "Play with the Vocal Viewpoint **Acceleration/Deceleration** by working on slowly increasing and decreasing the speed of your word.
- "Play with the Vocal Viewpoint **Timbre**. Bogart really admired and studied Grotowski's method of acting. One of the most useful aspects of Grotowski's work for the actor is the use of the body as a resonator. We are going to explore Grotowski's resonator activity using your gibberish word." (Find the exercise in the Grotowski chapter if you need help with this.) Lead them in vibrating their upper head, chest, nasal, laryngeal, occipital, and whole body resonators.
- "Play with the Vocal Viewpoint **Shape** by creating round, soft, fluid, sharp, spiky, and percussive sounds with your gibberish. Think about what makes a sound round? or sharp?"
- "Play with the Vocal Viewpoint **Gesture** starting with Behavioral gestures by making sounds that people make in their everyday lives: coughing, clearing throat, clucking, shushing, sniffling, etc."

- "Make behavioral vocal gestures that communicate the weather."
- "Now communicate personality (bossy tsk tsk, nervous teeth grinding, etc.)."
- "Make expressive gestures of the voice by creating sounds of grief, justice, home, freedom. These are subjective and require you to play with your voice."
- "Play with the Vocal Viewpoint **Architecture** by exploring the sonic qualities of the room. Move around and experiment with bouncing sounds off of walls, corners, and furniture. Send your voice to different textures and objects."
- "Pair up and sit on the floor facing your partner."
- "Play with the Vocal Viewpoint **Repetition**. One of you say your gibberish word, coloring it with Vocal Viewpoints. Your partner should try to repeat you exactly. Switch back and forth, taking turns being the leader of the game."
- "Keep playing, but now reverse the dynamics the person you are repeating used."
- "Come sit in a circle and close your eyes."
- "Play with the Vocal Viewpoint **Kinesthetic Response**. In kinesthetic response each person gives over the control of their voices to outside stimuli. Start with the word *Viewpoints*. Work to be responsive to others, playing with the timing of your words, creating a sonic version of the movement Viewpoints."
- "Add the Vocal Viewpoint **Silence**. Remember that silence holds potential energy. Treat silence proactively rather than passively."

Activity—Composition of Loss/Reunion

- Note: I have simplified an activity from Bogart and Landau's *The Viewpoints Book* for the purposes of beginning actors. I recommend going straight to the source and using "Composition Assignment 3: Loss/Reunion"[17] if you have a more advanced group or more time.
- Say: "Divide into groups of four or five and assign a director."
- "You will be working outside the theatre, and each group will design their own set by finding a site-specific performance space."
- Give them the following list of instructions on slips of paper, or have a scribe from each group write your instructions:

  - There are no blackouts allowed.
  - Time limit for performance: 5 minutes at most.
  - Rehearsal time: 20 minutes (this forces them to get to work on their feet).
  - The structure follows the structure of: The Meeting, Something Happens, Loss, The Reunion.
  - Include all of the following ingredients in no particular order:
    - Revelation of an object
    - Revelation of the space
    - A moment of at least 5 seconds where everyone is looking up

- [Fill in the blank] item or element overused
- A visual reference to a famous movie
- A surprising entrance
- An awkward moment of stillness
- Fifteen consecutive seconds of [fill in the blanks]
- A moment of unison movements
- A few lines of text chosen by the instructor, from any source, the same text given to every group.

- Check in with each group repeatedly, making sure they are on their feet and working out their piece. Give them more time if they are all still engaged in the thick of devising. If one group is done while others are still working, give them more surprise challenging ingredients to add to their piece such as: Sound from three different sources, singing, etc.
- Once they are mostly ready, have the class rotate to watch each of the compositions.
- Discuss: "How did the ingredients impact the audience's experience? How did the collaboration go—breakdowns, easy flow? What moments made your pulse race? What moments created empathy? What moments of use of the text were particularly creative? What did you notice about repetition? What did you notice about use of sound? How could an activity like this enrich the rehearsal for a scripted show?"

19

Declan Donnellan

The Person

Declan Donnellan was born in England to Irish parents in 1953. When he was a college student, Donnellan studied English and Law at Cambridge. He was not educated in acting or directing formally, but while he was directing a play in 1980 at the age of twenty-seven, he realized this was something he could do. He has been doing it ever since. He is best known as a stage director and as the co-founder of the Cheek by Jowl theatre company, which he founded with Nick Ormerod, his regular stage designer and domestic partner in 1981. They find the independence of working on their own projects to be rewarding, as they can choose the play, the actors, and the venue, then just put on the play.

He has directed for plenty of impressive theatres such as the Royal Shakespeare Company, the Royal National Theatre in London, the Old Vic, the Maly Drama Theatre of Saint Petersburg, and the Bolshoi Ballet. He also directed the 1992 short film *The Big Fish* and the 2012 film *Bel Ami*, which starred Robert Pattinson, Uma Thurman, Kristin Scott Thomas, Christina Ricci and Colm Meaney. He has worked all over the world, including forming an acting company in Moscow in 2000.

These theatrical credits are impressive, and not nearly a complete list, but what is most impressive and important about Declan Donnellan for our purposes is his acting method. His techniques will remind you of other methods already outlined in this book, but his approach for helping actors get out of their heads and into the moment makes him a truly useful teacher for directors who have struggling actors, and for actors who need to get out of the trap of their own character development.

Donnellan published his book *The Actor and the Target* in 1999 in Russian. It has since been translated into at least fifteen languages and has become a cult favorite of actors and directors worldwide for its ability to break actors out of their heads. I have found it to be extremely practical and useful for my students. I hope it is useful to you as well.

The Method

Donnellan personally translated his own acting text into English, explaining the methods he has found useful for actors in his long career as a director. He begins by explaining we are born with the preparation for acting within us. Donnellan says that acting isn't second nature to us because it is in our "'first nature' and so cannot be taught like chemistry or scuba diving."[1] Our characters are as natural as we are because we interact with targets the same way our characters do. It may take a bit for you to grasp the concept of targets, but it is an effort many actors have found worthwhile.

The Actor Wobbles

Donnellan's book is an attempt to help actors who are blocked become un-blocked so they can discover and reveal to the audience who the character is. In his experience of working with actors from many different cultures and languages, he has found the words they use when they are stuck sound about the same. He has categorized these actor complaints into eight statements he correlates with the legs of a spider. If an actor cannot answer one of these questions about the character, it creates a wobble point for the actor, making the entire character unsteady. The eight statements that reveal a wobble are:

- I don't know what I'm doing.
- I don't know what I want.
- I don't know who I am.
- I don't know where I am.
- I don't know how I should move.
- I don't know what I should feel.
- I don't know what I'm saying.
- I don't know what I'm playing.

Have you ever heard yourself say one of these things? Have you spoken to a director or complained to a fellow cast-mate about one of these things? Donnellan explains these problems are inextricably linked to each other. You can't solve one problem neatly and then move on to the next. They are too interconnected.

One thing you might have noticed is that every one of these statements are very strongly "I" statements. "I" exists twice in each one. All of these statements also assume there is an answer the actor is entitled to. Donnellan calls these two things the "know" and the "I." Every one of these statements has two "I"s and a "know." These words are seeking what is missing: The Target. It is difficult to tie down a definition of Donnellan's target.

The Target

Donnellan defines the target first by what it is not: "The target is neither an objective, nor a want, nor a plan, nor a reason, nor an intention, nor a goal, nor a focus, nor a motive. Motives arise from the target."[2] Further, the "why?" of acting can block an actor, a target cannot. Here is where Donnellan diverges from Stanislavski and so many other acting teachers. He says that the problem is often not in an actor's lack of understanding of what they want or need as a character.

So, if the target is not one of those things, then what is the target? Simply put, the target is what the character sees. Freedom for the actor comes from seeing the target. Donnellan points out that "the very word *theatre* comes from the Greek *theatron,* which means 'a place for seeing.'"[3] He pushes the actor to stop analyzing the character's inner life and focus on what the character sees outside themself. The core of Donnellan's method is learning to use the eyes to solve self-consciousness and blocked acting. Sight is everything, and the crux of dynamic acting.

Donnellan's method is impactful for the blocked actor because it helps them open up, seeing what the character sees. Instead of trying to figure out what the character feels, the actor can make use of the sight of the character. For instance, when playing the problematic Petruchio, an actor might get stuck thinking about what Petruchio wants and create a hateful, misogynistic man on the hunt for a rich wife at whatever cost. Instead, if the actor opens outwardly to see what Petruchio sees when he beholds the shrewish Kate, he might instead create a character that sees a woman who has never truly been seen. In that simple shift, Petruchio becomes a man who recognizes the beauty of a misunderstood woman and treasures her. If the actor can see through the character to what the character sees, essentially using the character as a mask, then they can bring that character to life. If, on the other hand, the actor tries to monitor or control how the audience sees the character, the actor has devolved into showing. It is more powerful and much easier to see what the character sees instead of showing how the character feels.

It is a simple principle, but there are many complexities. Donnellan categorizes these complexities into six rules.

The rules are:

1 There is always a target.
2 The target always exists outside and at a measurable distance.
3 The target exists before you need it.
4 The target is always specific.
5 The target is always transforming.
6 The target is always active.

I will deal with these rules one at a time, though they are difficult to tease apart. They are so interconnected that you will find a lot of overlap between them.

There is always a target

Donnellan is quite clear about this rule. A target is always there for the actor, and "The actor can do nothing without the target."[4] For example, an actor can't play "I laugh." That action has no target. A properly targeted action like laughter could be stated, "I fight to contain laughter" or, "I fight for breath" or, "I see joy that I can't contain." In any of these scenarios, the actor is seeing something from the perspective of the character.

Another example is the hard to play, "I die." Try replacing the statement with "I welcome death"—your character sees death coming and welcomes it. By creating a targeted action and using that in place of the dead action of "I die," you have created a word picture of a goal that can actually be acted upon.

While we are on the topic, Donnellan also says that it is impossible to act a "be" verb. You cannot, for instance, act, "I am angry." You *can* act, "I kill her with my eyes." Notice that the second statement gives the actor something to see. There is comfort in this concept. Because there is always a target, the actor cannot be alone on stage even if they are performing a monologue. It is the actor's job to see the target from the character's perspective and react to it.

The target always exists outside and at a measurable distance

Donnellan is equally firm about this rule. He explains that your eyes have to move and search for the target, just as when you are asked a question, your eyes search for the answer. The eyes always have to see something, whether that thing is real or imaginary. Even a headache, which is obviously inside the head, is outside the consciousness. It has to be separate from the self. You cannot fuse with the target, and you cannot find it inside of yourself. The good news is this creates a built-in obstacle for the actor to overcome. As the actor is performing a character's death, and using the target statement "I struggle for life," the actor must see life as a thing outside of themselves, and reach for it with their eyes.

Landing on and committing to the target is the second half of the process. Ineffective actors never find their target, but if an actor can discover the outside targets that influence their character's thoughts and decisions, they have found a powerful space to exist in, and the audience will see and experience it too. Audiences love to be in on the secret inner life of the character, and you can share it with them by searching for it with your eyes and reacting when you find and return to it.

The target exists before you need it

Donnellan says our eyes search for the thing that will exist in the future even before it exists in the present. Ask someone to tell you what life will be like for them in five years, and their eyes will begin to move around in an attempt to see that future reality. As actors, we often blind ourselves to the future. We block ourselves by not allowing our eyes to roam in search of the target outside ourselves. While as people we are aware of both the internal and the external, the internal is not useful to the actor because it doesn't read well for the audience. Donnellan says that it helps the actor to "transfer all inner functioning, all drives, feelings, thoughts and motives, etc. from inside and relocate these impulses in the target."[5] Actors can only act in relation to the external target. That target already exists and cannot be manufactured. It must be found. The actor is served by being curious about the target and literally looking for it. This requires you to be present to your character at all times on stage, and to trust that your target is findable.

The target is always specific

Donnellan explains the specificity of the target by talking about how the target is always split. In other words, there are always **two possible simultaneous outcomes** of a situation in the present. There is a better possible outcome and a worse. The character sees both possibilities as current reality. The stakes in a situation are huge because the character sees both the worst and the best futures at once. Donnellan uses the example of Juliet to explain this split-target idea. The actor playing Juliet has sent her Nurse to make arrangements to meet with Romeo later. While her Nurse is gone, Juliet soliloquizes onstage on whether or not her Nurse will help her with her romance. Will she tell her parents and prevent the union? Or will she keep Juliet's secret and help her marry Romeo? Her internal answer during this performance, if following the split-target model is "My Nurse will protect me **and** my Nurse will betray me." Until the moment she knows which answer is true (and she might never figure it out), both answers exist for Juliet, and this creates unbelievable tension and appropriately high stakes. Actors cause roadblocks for themselves when they only see one of these possibilities at a time. Both possibilities need to be symmetrical, pulling the actor in two equal directions. They are equally powerful images for the character.

This concept of developing two equally possible outcomes is something we can all feel familiar with. We are always trying to **create the positive outcome and prevent the negative**. Donnellan calls this "thinking in doubles" and he illustrates this again using an actor playing Juliet who targets her work with the actor playing Romeo by thinking, "*I try to seduce Romeo, and I try not to repel him.*"[6] The two thoughts are playing for her at the same time are highly specific and exact opposites.

Also, we will do better to **ask ourselves more specific questions**. For example, asking, "Who am I?" is not as helpful as asking, "Who would I rather be?" at the same time as "Who am I afraid I am?"[7] Questions that are full of contradictions are much more useful to the actor. They are also much more specific. For example, if you are playing the part of Angelo in *Measure for Measure*, as you interact with your world you might equally consider the identities that he wants and fears at the same time. He can reasonably feel, "I am afraid I exploit my subjects," and "I believe I am a good ruler." You can find this in other characters as well. Batman is always equally sure he is a villain at the same time that he believes he is a hero. Kate in *Taming* is equally sure that she is the only reasonable human in her world, and that she is a crazy person.

The target is always transforming

The actor needs to watch as targets transform before them. This does not mean the actor has to maintain constant eye contact with their scene partner. On the contrary, they may avoid eye contact and concentrate on some stage business. Both targets (the scene partner and the stage business) exist at the same time. This leaves the actor with what Donnellan calls an uncomfortable choice: to see or to show. Sometimes actors want to make sure the audience understands what is happening, so they choose to show that action. When they choose to do this, they are pretending instead of acting and they risk losing the audience. Instead, the actor must see the target and interact with it.

It is helpful to recognize that thoughts are also targets. They cannot be contained in one position. They are always transforming. The audience wants to see our thoughts happen before we speak them, and watch as we see our thoughts change and morph. Donnellan says, "Before the old thought has time to expire, the new thought is clambering over its body."[8] In other words, an actor can be more free when they realize thoughts are constantly interrupting each other. New thoughts are always interrupting each other and the new is much more exciting to the character than the old. The target moves and transforms just as thoughts move and transform. The actor cannot control this and must allow it to happen. Actors must learn to recognize the freshness of each moment and live in that reality.

The way this process can feel in rehearsal and in performance is freedom for the actor to explore the world and future of the character. The actor must first choose a path for their target—a journey, if you will.

In any given scene, an actor must have a path from one target to the next. They might play with several different versions in rehearsal and then experiment with different ones in performance. As long as trust has been established between scene partners, and the rules are clear about what can and what cannot change, this can give life to a scene. Donnellan gives the example of Juliet in the balcony scene. "Perhaps Juliet starts by seeing a potential rapist and ends up seeing a son who must be mothered. Perhaps she begins by seeing a Romeo who is bright, strong, and deep, and ends the scene less sure, or vice versa."[9] Either way, the scene has somewhere to go, and the actor begins a journey of changing vision.

Fun tip: You can use the **Double Take** in which you delay your reaction to a target. In this moment, when the target transforms in front of you, your audience can observe your delayed processing. Donnellan gives a fun example. Imagine your character is pruning chrysanthemums when a vicar (priest or pastor) comes on stage.

Step one: 'Good morning, vicar!'—you look at him.

Step two: You then look back at the chrysanthemums.

Step three: While still looking at the chrysanthemums, you realise that the vicar is not wearing any trousers.

Step four: You look back at him aghast.[10]

The way your focus shifts from the vicar to the flowers and back again is an example of your target shifting for comic effect. In step one, your character sees what they believe to be reality. They "see" a respectable public figure, return focus to their work, then allow their actual sight to replace the expected visual input.

The target is always active

Just as the target is always changing, it is also always active. Whatever that target is doing must be viewed as something the character wants to change. Our words are a tool we use to change our hearers. It is also true that the target gives us little choice in our actions. When a character makes a choice, even though there are many possible options, the target compels them to only one. The character chooses by reducing their options to one.

Even though it might seem counterintuitive, the acting space is also an active target in Donnellan's method. He reminds us that the balcony scene in Romeo and Juliet is iconic because the balcony is an active obstacle for the lovers. The space actively separates their passion.

Also, the character is always actively hiding an alternative vision of themselves. Remember the split targets? If you build for yourself a list of personality traits your character exhibits, you might find it useful to think about the alternative version of your character repressing the opposite personality traits. For instance, Kate the Shrew is strong, loud, confident, self-sufficient, and proud. It might be useful for the actor playing Kate to recognize that under all of that bravado, Kate is suppressing the weak, quiet, worthless, dependent, and humiliated self. Donnellan would call this the un-Kate. The actor who plays Kate with the understanding that Kate exerts a tremendous amount of energy to guard against the un-Kate peeking out, will find a nuanced performance comes more naturally. She will see the hidden un-Kate lurking in every corner, waiting to be seen by the audience and the other characters on stage. "We all have an identity, and for each identity there is an equal and opposite un-identity. Neither is the truth, but both, as long as they are considered jointly, can dynamise the actor."[11]

Other thoughts beyond the rules

Another concept Donnellan uses to help actors who are stuck, is reminding them that their scene partner is not responsible to give them anything. It is the job of the actor to see their acting partners, and believe they are giving them everything needed to play the scene well. "It is the actor's challenge to believe, more than his partner's problem to convince him."[12] For example, consider an actor who is playing royalty. If the actor simply sits on the throne to claim her queendom, she is not fully employing her ability to control the room. She must instead believe the other characters in the room would be truly shocked if she were to sit on the floor to talk to the court jester. She will only feel free in playing the queen when she believes the other actors in the space see her as the queen. This is not their responsibility. It is hers.

The actor cannot truly act an emotion. They can, however, show that emotion is impeding them from reaching a goal. In this way, an actor who wants to cry on stage is missing the point. Instead, your character can show the audience that tears are preventing you from appearing pulled together in a moment when they desperately want to impress others. Think about all the ways your character's emotions can get in the way of a goal the character has. This annoyance can help you make your character more human.

Another blocking agent that Donnellan warns about is the tendency to label a character good or evil. Judgmentalism is beneath the dignity of an actor. We may judge an action, but not an identity.

Masks as a tool for the blocked actor

Donnellan finds masks useful in training actors because they are a way to obliterate the face of the actor without concealing the eyes. A mask could be helpful for an actor who needs help discovering the target. An actor can physically see that they are required to look through their character (the mask) to see the target. A mask can also remove the self-consciousness of the actor and give them permission to do forbidden things. The mask takes the blame. Since actors tend to be afraid of being seen, the masks can help actors feel less self-conscious.

The Blocked Body

Donnellan writes that we stop our bodies from their full movement when we fear what our muscles might do. Our muscles want to participate in every action we do, but we usually limit our efforts to those muscles required to do the action. For example, when lifting a glass of water, we only involve our hand and arm muscles. Why don't we allow our feet and back to assist? Donnellan says that "The first step in liberating the blocked body is to acknowledge the degree to which we keep it caged."[13] Once we have realized that our every muscle wants to assist in our movement, we can make our movement easier by allowing them to work. This attention paid to our bodies can free us to recognize the tremendous effort our characters are expending in order to suppress and limit our muscles. If we let that suppression go, our energy can shift to the moving targets all around us.

The Rhythm of Three

Donnellan sums up the human condition in this way, "Everything we do fails. Every reaction an actor might play fails."[14] Spelled out, this means all actions and text come from the repeated rhythm of three actions:

- to try to alter something or someone
- to see it hasn't worked
- to try another tactic to alter them.

This series of actions is grounded in the realization that humans can never achieve pure contentment. Because of this, even in a moment of loss or victory, a new desire is discovered. We are always existing in the striving. In this sense, we don't ever truly feel pure despair or pure joy. Hope is present in despair and vice versa. Imagine a new phone gleaming in your hands. This is joy and delight, but there is the nagging thought that you might scratch the screen too. Both are present in that moment of pleasure.

As you begin your efforts to try out Donnellan's methods for potential addition to your acting toolbox, remember that the core of it is your vision. Seeing is everything. What can you do as an actor when you spend your energy not on internal analysis or holding back your impulses, but instead, spend it on seeing what your character sees? Can you help yourself, your scene partner, and your audience by empathetically exploring the world of your character with your eyes?

Declan Donnellan's Legacy

Donnellan's legacy will likely be the way he articulates the orientation of the actor's vision towards an external target. By teaching actors to think outside themselves, and providing directorial insight into how to unblock actors, Donnellan has unlocked many struggling actors. I am grateful that he has published his book so his way of framing acting has spread far beyond his physical sphere of influence.

Tips for taking this method further

- Read Declan Donnellan's book *The Actor and the Target.*
- Score your current scene or monologue with a target map, detailing the shifting focus of the character, then attempt to follow the eye line of your character, focusing on what you have written.

- Look up Cheek by Jowl's production of Pericles and watch it. Do you see evidence these actors are using Donnellan's methods?

Discussion Starters and Journal Prompts

- Summarize Donnellan's acting method in two sentences for an actor who has never heard of him.
- What impression do you have of Declan Donnellan's method after reading this chapter? Are you compelled by it? Do you want to try his ideas to see what happens? Why or why not?
- Which of the legs of the spider most often cause you difficulty? What does Declan recommend for solving that problem?
- Do you experience the "you" and "un-you" phenomenon in your real life? Do you think that all characters have this problem? Are there some characters that are not hiding a secret version of themselves?

The Tools for your Toolbox

Activity—Rule One: There is always a Target

- Have the class walk about the room.
- Say, "Now die with the action 'I die.'"
- Give the students slips of paper that have these six target statements written on them. You can add others.

    - I welcome death
    - I fight death
    - I mock death
    - I struggle for life
    - I choose death
    - I succumb to death.

- Say: "Walk about again and absorb your target statement."
- "Perform your new death scene using your target statement."
- Discuss: "What was the difference between your first and second death. How is the addition of a target helpful in acting this scene? What does it do for the actor? What does it do for the audience?"
- Now try a new action: I laugh. Have the class come up with new target statements and try them out. Alternatively, have each student act out their chosen target statement and then have the class guess which one they used.

Activity—Rule Two: The Target always exists outside and at a measurable distance

- Say: "Pair up and sit facing each other."
- "Decide who is first speaker in each pair."
- "If you are a listener, both listen and observe the speaker carefully. Notice movement and focus."
- "Speakers. Answer the question 'What did you do yesterday?' Take time and be specific about an order of events from waking until time is up."
- After one minute, say: "Switch roles!"
- Discuss: "What did you observe in the mannerisms of the speakers. What happened in the movement of the eyes? What are they searching for? Is that the target? Do our characters make similar efforts to find what they are looking for? Could our characters benefit from having a Target?"

Activity—Rule Three: The Target exists before you need it

- Say: "Pair up sit facing each other. Ask your partner what they are planning to do during Spring Break or another upcoming school vacation."
- "Pay attention to what your partner's eyes do when they are looking for the answer in the future."
- "Spend a few minutes studying your monologue to find moments when the character is looking to or thinking about the future."
- "Practice saying a short portion of the monologue to your partner, imitating the eye movements you observed when your partner talked about the future."
- "Now try to actually see the future while saying that portion of the monologue without trying to imitate the eye movements."
- Discuss: "Talk to your partner. Did you notice a difference between the two attempts at seeing the future? How was if for actor and audience?"

Activity—Rule Four: The Target is always specific

- Say: "Choose one character you are working on and brainstorm a list of things the character is afraid they are."
- "Now brainstorm a list of things they hope they are."
- "Select a specific moment in the text and write some double statements that are exact opposites of each other from the brainstorming lists you just created."
- "Work in pairs, trying out your specific split targets."
- Discuss: "What discoveries did you make?"

Activity—Rule Five: The Target is always transforming

- Say "Get in your scene groups and get out your scripts."
- "Spend a few moments arranging your environment." (chairs, props, etc.—either real or imagined).
- "Rehearse, trying to see through the eyes of the character and notice things in the room and about your scene partner. Allow your character's minds to wander in the same way our minds wander in real life. Remember what Donnellan wrote: 'Before the old thought has time to expire, the new thought is clambering over its body.'[15]"
- "Play the scene a couple of times, trying out different trains of thought, exploring the idea of a transforming target before the eyes of your character."
- If time allows, have scene partners perform for the class or for each other using this new transforming target activity.
- Discuss: "What are the ramifications of acting onstage in this way?"

Activity—Rule Six: The Target is always active

- Give your actors a copy of a scene to work with. I suggest *The Taming of the Shrew* II. i. Give them a quick synopsis of the play to this point, remembering that some of your students won't know enough about it to be able to accomplish the activity.
- Have your class suggest the characteristics of Kate and Petruchio. Write them on a white board.
- Remind your students that the character is always hiding an alternative version of themself. Ask for the characteristics of the un-Kate and the un-Petruchio and write them down. Say: "What is the alternate version of Kate that she is trying to repress?" For instance, Kate the Shrew is strong, loud, confident, self-sufficient, and proud. Kate may be suppressing the un-Kate who is a weak, quiet, worthless, dependent, and humiliated person.
- Pair your students up. Gender isn't important. Say: "Run this scene while playing both the self and the repressed un-self. Repeat the activity several times, each time focusing on hiding the un-self from the other. Switch roles between readings."
- Discuss: "How could this type of character work dynamize another character you are working on?" If time allows, have them work on a list of the self and un-self in another character they are preparing.

Activity—The Blocked Body: A glass of water

- Place glasses of water on a table for your actors.
- Say: "Reach out and pick them up then set them down again."
- "Try again while thinking about which muscles are employed in the task of picking up the glass."
- "Could the task be easier if you allow other muscles to help with the task? Can you use your ankle or toe to make this job easier? Try it."

- "Donnellan's philosophy is that all of our muscles want to participate in every action because they were made to move. If we don't hold them back for fear of what they might do, they will joyfully participate in every action."
- Try another activity in which students can add muscles to the task that might otherwise be left out.
- Discuss: "How might careful shutting down of muscles be expending more energy than if we allowed our whole bodies to participate in the work of acting? Do you think focusing the effort of all of our muscles onto the task might reduce nervous actor tics?"

Activity—Ground energy

- Say: "Lie on the floor and feel the energy coming from the ground and through you."
- "Experience the relaxing of your muscles and the power of the ground energy working on your bodies."
- "Speak lines from a scene or monologue while gathering energy from the floor."
- "Sit on the ground cross-legged and try the same thing. Can you channel the energy from the ground into your voice?"
- "Stand up and repeat the same power of the ground, feeling the energy coming up from the feet and through your body."
- "Try moving while speaking. Can you retain the ground energy?"
- Discuss: "How does grounding work for you? Are you able to access ground energy while standing?"

Activity—Character development

- Say: "Form groups of three."
- "Each person should take on an archetype: an older grounded person, a younger flighty person, or an animal."
- "Using these characters, create a fable. A fable is a short story, usually involving animal characters, that communicates a moral. You have five minutes."
- Perform these fables for the class.
- Then, have the students ask themselves the following questions: "What does my character see when I look at the other characters? What does my character need from the other characters? What does my character think the other characters need from me?"
- Then say: "Rehearse again while focused on the targets of your characters."
- Re-perform one or two of the pieces and comment on how targeting changes the dynamic for the audience.

20

Patsy Rodenburg

The Person

Patsy Rodenburg was born in 1953 in London. As a child, speaking did not come to her naturally. She had a speech impediment and was sent to elocution classes. She did so badly that her teachers never called on her. Even so, she loved words, and discovered Shakespeare at the age of nine. When she writes about this wordless period of her life, she says, "this passion stayed locked inside me and couldn't find expression in my voice. Until the age of 13 I would never speak to strangers, although my friends say I have made up for it since."[1] She eventually found her voice, and wanted to help others succeed like she did. When she enrolled at the Central School of Speech and Drama to study acting, she realized right away she wanted to specialize in voice training to help people find their voices.

As a voice coach, Rodenburg started by working with anyone who wanted to improve their speaking. She experimented with the voices of actors, teachers, prisoners, and singers. This work, and her skill in returning individuals to their natural voice and presence earned her the job of director of the Guildhall School of Music and Drama in London at only twenty-eight years old. She has been working there ever since. The program was a bit of a mess when she took over. One teacher was regularly rolling around in a dark classroom with his students, all of them naked—a method that seems horrific to modern sensibilities, but all too common in the 1980s. Other teachers, though not as shocking, were not effective either. She did the difficult job of firing them and replaced them with teachers who helped create an effective and prestigious program.

She has also taught in New York and worked with the Royal Shakespeare Company and the Royal Shakespeare Theatre. She has worked globally with the Moscow Art Theatre, Complicité, Cheek by Jowl, and Comédie-Française. Her list of students is a who's who of actors that includes Daniel Craig, Orlando Bloom, Ewan McGregor, Dame Judi Dench, Sir Ian McKellen, Daniel Day-Lewis, Nicole Kidman, Hugh Jackman, and Natalie Portman. She has published several books on the subject of voice coaching. All of them give her readers encouragement and practical tools to find their voices for stage and life.

Rodenburg is also a humanitarian who has worked in UK prisons, with the poor in India, Northern Ireland, Gaza and the West Bank, sex workers in Amsterdam, tribes in Africa and Aboriginal communities in Australia. Her work with all these communities is an effort to break down communication barriers. Some of her most inspiring work has been in helping women in patriarchal society find their voices and power, balancing female empowerment with a need for safety in their home cultures.

The Method

Rodenburg has written extensively on the fears and traumas that lock our voices up. She points out that when we are born, we have a natural, free voice; but through trauma or societal conditioning, we get locked into bad vocal habits. She writes,

> What I believe is that every human voice has thrilling potential waiting to be discovered and unleashed. And I do mean every human voice. As soon as any of us surrenders to a defeating habit and says, "I have a bad voice", what happens? . . . We begin to second-guess every statement we utter and each sound we make. A negative myth about a bad voice compromises our right to speak.[2]

As you work on your voice and breath, believe that you have the right to speak, the right to exist, and the right to claim your power. Some people shrivel and their voices are locked up and quiet, others bluff and push their voices out in a general and overbearing way. When you believe you have the right to speak, you will claim your open, powerful, interactive voice. Rodenburg's methods can help you do that, starting with understanding the structure of your body.

The Anatomy of the Voice

Human beings breathe and speak without thinking about how. Rodenburg starts work with her students by teaching them how human sound is created:

1. We breathe in through our mouth or nose.
2. Our breath goes into our lungs, providing oxygen to our body and expanding our ribcage.
3. Our diaphragm moves down, creating a column of air to support the voice.
4. Breathing out, our muscles move, regulating the voice.
5. Air passes over the vocal folds forming shapes creating different pitches of sound that can be resonated in various body parts.

As you breathe, you can become aware of this column of air, the placement of your shoulders, the expansion of your ribcage, the downward motion of your diaphragm, the air passing over your vocal folds. Your voice is an effort of your whole body. Paying attention to your body, you will likely discover you are habitually holding your body in a way that fetters your voice. The sooner you identify and break these habits, the better. Rodenburg tells her students "You aren't training to reinforce what you already do but to move into new and dramatic areas of change."[3] Don't worry if this change feels uncomfortable, even wrong, as you begin the process of reclaiming natural breath. We are naturally uncomfortable with the unfamiliar.

Your Centered Body

Rodenburg writes that our daily lives don't require the physical alertness our ancestors needed. Horseback riding, walking long distances on uneven turf, wielding swords, hunting and gathering: all of these required a tremendous amount of core strength. If our ancestors weren't strong enough, they died. Our lifespans are much longer now because the dangers and strains on our bodies are much less, but our bodies and voices are also weaker. This makes performance challenging because we don't hold our bodies in a ready and centered way most of the time.

In finding your physical center, posture is important. When Rodenburg asks her students to find a good posture, she asks for a relaxed body in its centered, natural balance. Your body needs to find it over and over, as you move out of center intentionally for a role or unintentionally because of habits.

As you work, try to find an alert state where your body is in its natural, centered posture. Of course, sometimes you will play a character who is physically weak and/or mumbly. This must be a choice. Rodenburg claims you can play weak and mumbly as long as you have engaged energy held in your body supporting your character.

The centered body is not self-conscious. Be body positive! Allow your core to expand and make room for your breath. Have the costumer measure you at your fullest size. Don't hold your stomach in. Instead, take a full breath and expand your ribcage. This way you will be able to breathe properly while in costume. The centered body is always attractive.

The Second Circle

Rodenburg developed a principle called the Second Circle to help her students find the proper focus in performance. She describes three embedded circles of attention, like a target with First Circle in the center and Third Circle on the outside. These three states of presence exist both on and off stage. On stage, it is necessary to identify and stay in the Second Circle most of the time. Off stage, you may find that leveraging the first or third circle can be a powerful tool. Which circle do you live in most of the time?

In the First Circle the person:

- is in the state Rodenburg calls *denial*.
- has energy that is connected to itself, inwardly focused.
- is lonely because they withhold expressive energy.
- is absent or hidden from others in social circles.
- says their lines to themselves; the audience is irrelevant.
- speaks after an impulse rather than acting on the lines.
- is trapped, shy, uncertain, sometimes speaking with eyes closed or glazed over.
- is perhaps listening, but not sharing.
- can intentionally place focus inward, hiding their power, avoiding the notice of others in order to find safety or escape a situation.
- can intentionally give focus to another actor or event by withholding their presence from the stage.

In the Third Circle the person:

- is in a state that Rodenburg calls *bluff.*
- has energy connected to self in an outward push.
- is lonely because they have no receptive energy.
- tramples over others in social circles.
- is performing outwardly for the whole world in general.
- uses general eye contact, and listening is absent.
- often yells, overacts, and cuts other actors off.
- often tries to fill the space without fully connecting to the language.
- is afraid of failure and cannot take in feedback.
- is seeking, but does not have power.
- can take control or gain immediate compliance.
- projects a force field to protect themselves.

In the Second Circle the person:

- is in a place that Rodenburg identifies as *centered.*
- is connected to self and others simultaneously.
- has energy that is intimate, compassionate, powerful, and contagious, transforming their ability to communicate effectively.
- is both receptive and expressive with others.
- is attractive (no matter their physical appearance) and compelling in social circles.
- is speaking specifically to another human rather than at the crowd.
- has focus that can shift rapidly from person to person, but only attaches to one person at a time.
- is centered and in a ready place in the body and mind.
- is connected specifically to scene partners.
- is open, ready, and strong.
- is listening as well as speaking.
- is connecting on equal terms, even if there is a hierarchy.
- speaks text to connect.
- is open, vulnerable and in a real place of power.

Picture a First Circle person sitting curled up in a corner, listening but trying to avoid being noticed. Imagine a Third Circle person standing up with arms outstretched, not making eye contact with anyone but saying "Look at me!!!" The Second Circle person is also standing, but they are making eye contact with someone, giving and receiving energy. This Second Circle existence can transform your life on and off stage. If you have ever been told you don't have "It," you can find "It" by being present in the Second Circle. "It" isn't a miracle or a special gift given to only some of us. Rodenburg believes everyone can turn on the It Factor.

In your life, you can probably think of moments of Second Circle existence. These are connected to others in specific, intimate moments of give and take. If you are blessed, your childhood was full of these moments where you unselfconsciously interacted with your parents and family, secure in unconditional love. If not in your family, maybe you have found a friend or partner you are able to connect with on equal footing. Good conversations happen in the Second Circle. We are clicked in and listening, responding and giving focus to the person we are in conversation with. These moments on stage are riveting to watch. They are in real life too.

In her work with women in oppressive societies, Rodenburg teaches them to leverage the First Circle for safety, escaping the notice of the authorities. She also teaches them to leverage their Third Circle selves to repel predators. The Second Circle, for these women, is reserved for safe situations where they can express their right to speak.

So, how does Rodenburg suggest you move into the Second Circle? She writes:

1 Be available for transformation. Being in the Second Circle requires willingness to embrace change because the Second Circle is in the present which is always transforming.
2 Recognize power is not force and stop being afraid of it.

    ◦ In the Third Circle you might feel safe from ridicule and failure because of the force field you have placed around yourself to exert control over others. This is force, not power. Your status will grow as you let go of force.
    ◦ In the First Circle, you might withhold expression to protect yourself from notice.
    ◦ If you move into Second Circle, Rodenburg says your "life will have more texture, color, and fun. You will be able to gauge other people's feelings better and understand your own."[4] The joy of Second Circle is in understanding that power comes from equality.

3 Center your body. Being centered connects you to your natural body. The Second Circle body accepts itself freely, rejecting a distorted, self-conscious body that is trying to appear more appealing. "A centered body deemed 'ugly' by the cosmetic world is distinctly sexier than a distorted 'beautiful' body."[5]
4 Breathe to the whole room. Experiment with breathing to the whole space when going into an interview or presentation. You will be more connected and confident; therefore, impressive and approachable.
5 Place your voice in the present. The First Circle voice is in the past, apologetic for breaking the silence. The Third Circle tramples the present and lands in the future.
6 Listen in the Second Circle. When we listen in First Circle, we hear but are not open and trusting enough to respond with truth. When we listen in Third Circle, we hear words and interpret them based on our own perspective. In Second Circle we are on equal footing with our audience and scene partner. We are able to react in real time.
7 Practice being in Second Circle as much as possible on and off the stage. Your struggles with acting will greatly diminish if you can learn to stay there.

Voice Meets Text

After a year of working on their presence, breath support, and voice, Rodenburg introduces her students to text work. The first step is taking ownership of the text. This requires actors to fully understand every word and allusion. Rodenburg points out that when an actor doesn't have the text handled well, the audience worries about them. If an audience is worried, their focus shifts from the story to you as a person.

Once you understand the text, you need to speak it completely. "Every syllable, vowel and consonant should be in your mouth, not half there or forgotten."[6] The voice that speaks clearly comes from a centered voice and body. In that Second Circle place, you think, feel, and speak the text simultaneously. It is easy to do all the blocking, generally be in character, and say your words correctly; it is hard to think, feel, and speak the text every performance.

Voice Tips

As a vocal coach, Rodenburg has practical tips for circumstances you encounter on stage.

When dying:

- Make every word count. Your character might be weak or fighting, but they want to be understood, so they conserve their strength for clarity.
- Troubled breathing is a part of playing death. Ask yourself "Where does the pain or lack of breath emanate from the body?"
- As you die, breathe out a dramatic sigh or groan to cleanse your breath and place your intake of air low in your body.
- Once you are dead, focus on calm breathing to minimize chest movement.

When playing illness:

- Research the effects of the illness on a person's breath and voice.
- Research treatments in the time of the play and how they impacted humans.
- When off stage, hydrate well and breathe through your nose.
- While on stage focus your energy on your deliberate movement and speech.
- When coughing on stage, stay very well hydrated.
- Cough thinking of a yawn. If you need a phlegmy cough, bite your tongue to increase saliva and swallow just before you cough.

When playing drunk:

- Be careful not to overact.
- Think of the vocal liberation of someone who is drunk. They speak more confidently, loudly, and with the belief they are interesting to everyone.
- Alcohol should make your character a bigger version of themselves, with diminished motor skills.
- Drunk people don't listen well.

When you rehearse in one space and then transfer to the stage:

- Take time in advance of the transfer to breathe in the performance space and find the vocal requirements of the room.
- Use this knowledge as you work in the rehearsal room.

Can You Handle Shakespeare?

As her actors gain comfortability with the text, Rodenburg introduces them to heightened text, like Shakespeare. She instructs them to *learn the text accurately* and to *practice regularly*. The goal with heightened text is to really feel the language, making it a comfortable friend rather than an awkward stranger.

Your voice needs to be free to communicate the heightened emotions in classical texts like Shakespeare. "When actors perform in musicals, it is understood that they can sing. When you perform a Shakespeare play, it should be understood that you can speak and be thrilling to listen to."[7] If you feel you aren't up to the task of this language, or think you aren't suited for the work, it is probably because you are not yet trained. Once you learn a state of readiness and use of body and voice, you will have the power to perform Shakespeare with ease. Everyone who puts in the work can handle any text.

Rodenburg writes repeatedly that Shakespeare is your ally, and learning to embody his text will help you become a powerful performer. Shakespearean acting "needs a profound understanding of language and how it works. Actors have to engage fully with language before it can engage an audience . . . if you trust him, he is easier to speak than a screenplay. As you learn to decipher the text, you quickly learn that he is on your side."[8] With Shakespeare the word comes first, not last as in many modern scripts. Start with the words. You CAN handle Shakespeare.

The Rules of Shakespeare

Once you understand the rules of Shakespeare, you can break them intentionally. Shakespeare breaks his own rules all the time, and these moments are acting tips for an astute actor who is paying attention. Rodenburg calls these broken rules "acting notes."[9] One Shakespeare rule is that his characters function best in Second Circle. He wrote his plays for the highly interactive Elizabethan stage where groundlings were rowdy and easily distractible. They needed to be drawn in with personal attention. Romeo's lines in II.ii of *Romeo and Juliet* before he approaches Juliet on the balcony work on a wholly different level when spoken to someone on the front row than when spoken in Third Circle, to everyone in general. Try it! Speak the following shortened monologue in Third Circle as if to the universe, ignoring the stage directions I have added:

> *(crouching in the aisle tap an audience member on the shoulder and say:)*
> But, soft! what light through yonder window breaks?
> It is the east, and Juliet is the sun.
>
> *(now jump on the stage, look out at the horizon, and say the following lines, but check in with your audience scene partner to see if they are listening and agreeing with you:)*
> Arise, fair sun, and kill the envious moon,
> Who is already sick and pale with grief,
> That thou her maid art far more fair than she.
>
> *(come to the front of the stage and talk directly to a new person:)*
> It is my lady, O, it is my love!
> O, that she knew she were!

> *(crawling closer to Juliet's perch speak to a new person:)*
> She speaks yet she says nothing: what of that?
> Her eye discourses; I will answer it.
>
> *(start to speak and then think better of it, explain yourself to someone.)*
> I am too bold, 'tis not to me she speaks:
>
> *(Get close to your first audience member again and lean your head in your hands, saying to them)*
> See, how she leans her cheek upon her hand!
> O, that I were a glove upon that hand,
> That I might touch that cheek!

Now try it again, this time imagining you are making contact with different audience members as directed in the added stage directions. Do you see how the words were written to connect Romeo to the audience? Do you also see how much that young man enjoys his words?

This brings us to another important Shakespeare rule: Shakespeare's characters live in a world that is about the words. They love speaking! Their words and thoughts have structure, and they care about being understood. They delight in strutting their superior grasp of language. They speak while thinking deeply, without taking a breath to ponder. No pregnant pauses allowed! They fearlessly verbally process and their emotions change as they speak. Rodenburg reminds us Shakespeare's text doesn't deal in subtext the way many modern scripts do. Shakespeare's characters mean what they say they mean. They lie sometimes, but the audience always knows what is going on.

The Givens—the Structure of Shakespeare's Text

Rodenburg's next Shakespeare rule is every word is essential to the flow of a thought, and must be fully enunciated. Think about the sounds of the words as you say them. Don't shy away from the way they are put together. Shakespeare bunches similar vowels and consonants near each other on purpose in the form of assonance and alliteration. Enjoy the feel of the repeated sounds on your tongue. Try speaking and enjoying the comedy of Bottom's speech as Pyramus in *A Midsummer Night's Dream* V.i:

> Sweet Moon, I thank thee for thy sunny beams;
> I thank thee, Moon, for shining now so bright;
> For, by thy gracious, golden, glittering gleams,
> I trust to take of truest Thisby sight.
> But stay, O spite!
> But mark, poor knight,
> What dreadful dole is here!
> Eyes, do you see?
> How can it be?
> O dainty duck! O dear!
> Thy mantle good,
> What, stain'd with blood!
> Approach, ye Furies fell!

> O Fates, come, come,
> Cut thread and thrum;
> Quail, crush, conclude, and quell!

"Speaking the text makes you laugh. The sounds, the rhymes, the abundance of the alliteration, the pettiness of the onomatopoeia are silly. You don't need to be an expert to realise the silliness because it feels silly as you speak it."[10] The text teaches you to speak it properly if you trust it.

The next building block is the iambic heartbeat of Shakespeare's text. When you learn to understand the predictable iambic pentameter as it is written, you will notice the moments when the heartbeat is off—a beat is skipped or an accent is flipped. These moments should attract our attention to what is happening. Shakespeare is giving you acting notes!

Rodenburg introduces the de dúm of iambic rhythm using a line from *Sonnet 12*: "When I do count the clock that tells the time." As you say the line, you feel the accented and unaccented syllables. It follows the rules of ten syllables with regular *de dúm* rhythm. The second line breaks the rules: "And see the brave day sunk in hideous night." It has an extra syllable and the accents aren't regular. The predictability is broken. As an actor, you can feel the emotion of "hideous night" in the way the words are spoken. We can ride the waves of the text, allowing the rule-breaking to teach us and reinforce meaning.

In dialog, lines are often shared between characters. Sometimes syllables are missing indicating pauses. Sometimes the text is relentless and no pauses are allowed. Look at this scene between Kate and Petruchio in *The Taming of the Shrew* II.i:

> Petruchio
>   Alas, good Kate, I will not burden thee,
>   For knowing thee to be but young and light —
> Katherina
>   Too light for such a swain as you to catch,
>   And yet as heavy as my weight should be.

Notice these lines are in regular iambic rhythm. Both of them are in control of their breath as they size each other up. They are well matched. The scene continues with a shared line:

> Petruchio
>   'Should be'? Should buzz!
> Katherina
>   Well ta'en, and like a buzzard.

Now we have eleven syllables. They are speaking quickly and slightly off kilter. A little later they continue the full lines with some irregularities:

> Katherina
>   If I be waspish, best beware my sting.
> Petruchio
>   My remedy is then to pluck it out.
> Katherina
>   Ay, if the fool could find it where it lies.

> Petruchio
>> Who knows not where a wasp does wear his sting —
>> In his tail.
> Katherina
>>   In his tongue.
> Petruchio
>>   Whose tongue?

The shared line above is split into three lines with only eight syllables. This leaves room for a two syllable pause. Where that pause is placed makes a difference in the balance of power. If it is before "In his tail," then the playfulness of Petruchio is highlighted. If it is before "In his tongue," then Kate is shocked or stumbling to catch up. If it is before "Whose tongue?" then Petruchio is left fumbling or amazed by Kate. It is easy to see how understanding and leveraging the language of Shakespeare's text can be an asset.

Another Shakespeare rule is that each line has its own rhythm as a unit, but complete thoughts must also be respected. An experienced Shakespearean actor finds the full thought and speaks evenly across line ends if the thought is not complete. They help the audience feel the completeness of the lines while also expressing in complete thoughts. For example, take a look at Hermoine's monologue in *The Winter's Tale* III.ii and find where the first thought ends:

> The crown and comfort of my life, your favour,
> I do give lost; for I do feel it gone,
> But know not how it went. My second joy
> And first-fruits of my body, from his presence
> I am barr'd, like one infectious. My third comfort
> Starr'd most unluckily, is from my breast,
> The innocent milk in its most innocent mouth,
> Haled out to murder: myself on every post
> Proclaimed a strumpet: with immodest hatred
> The child-bed privilege denied, which 'longs
> To women of all fashion; lastly, hurried
> Here to this place, i' the open air, before
> I have got strength of limit.

Do you see that these thirteen lines are ONE thought? As an actor, you must deliver it with that understanding. Can you keep the energy moving to the end of the thought? Knowing this, it is helpful to learn the text in complete thoughts, rather than one line at a time. In some cases, you will need to memorize thirteen lines at a go in order to get in a complete thought. Other times a thought is only one syllable.

Another aspect of Shakespeare's structure is liberal use of opposites or antithesis. Antithesis explores the pendulum of our thoughts and feelings bouncing from one extreme to the other. You can avoid a two-dimensional portrayal by believing both opposites fully. For example, look at antithesis in Romeo's dialog:

>   What fray was here?
> Yet tell me not, for I have heard it all.
> Here's much to do with hate, but more with love.

> Why then, O brawling love! O loving hate!
> O anything, of nothing first create!

As you deliver these lines, respecting the opposites, you must fully embrace the hate before you jump to love; you envision brawling then love, love then hate, anything then nothing. It requires you to be in the Second Circle to do it well enough for your audience to also see the contrast.

Notice the last two lines of this rhyme. Shakespeare's lines don't rhyme all of the time, but when they do, it's tricky. The rhyme is there on purpose, so you can't ignore it. Figure out why it is there. Is it because the character is trying to soothe you into not noticing the evil behind the lines? Is it because the character is showing off? or being childish? And when the text moves from rhyme to blank verse or prose, what does that signal? Is there a shift in the thoughts and tactics of a character? Are two characters finding connection by rhyming with each other? Are the lines a challenge to the other like in a rap battle? Is the rhyme internal? mid-thought? or is it sing-songy, with thoughts completing the line hypnotically?

If your character is like Trinculo from *The Tempest* and speaks only prose, what does that mean? Likely, it is because they don't have the ability to think with agility. If your character switches between styles like Hamlet does, it is because he is extremely skilled with communication. Why does he switch when he does?

It is important to pay attention to the language games the characters play. Are they using irony? puns? repeating words? These are not accidental and shouldn't be ignored. For example, repeated words give the character the opportunity to mean something different each time they say the word.

One more Shakespeare rule for the actor involves monologues, or soliloquies. Rodenburg says, "Soliloquy has the dramatic effect of making the audience complicit with the character, for good or ill."[11] Soliloquy gives the audience a job to do: they must keep secrets and explore the morality of the thoughts of the characters. The audience knows that Hamlet is suicidal, but his mother doesn't know. The audience knows that Iago is out for revenge; Othello is fully unaware.

Do you see how much richer your understanding of the text can be if you understand the structure and design of each line?

Patsy Rodenburg's Legacy

In her books, Rodenburg tells stories of people from many walks of life who were withdrawn and needed to unlock their power and voice. She also tells stories of the opposite sorts of people who use bravado to protect themselves from critique and vulnerability. The answer was always found in reclaiming a Second Circle presence that is open, at ease, and centered in a natural body and voice. As these people reclaimed their natural state, their lives were transformed. Much more than a legacy of voice and acting technique, Rodenburg's legacy is in helping people find their voice, and use their presence intentionally. She writes,

> I have spent my life working on voice, language and effective delivery. It is my passion and I only started this journey because of my own fears and struggles to communicate. I understand the pain and distress concerned with any inability you experience when your communication fails and I honour the struggle you face as you attempt to improve your voice and your verbal impact on the world.[12]

Tips for taking this method further

- Start by reading *The Second Circle* to gain an understanding of the open and intimate place that acting and existing can come from.
- Now move on to *The Actor Speaks* then *Speaking Shakespeare*. The first is a step-by-step description of Rodenburg's training program with activities you can do on your own to find your vocal power. The second applies these principles specifically to Shakespeare.

Discussion Starters and Journal Prompts

- Articulate your fears and joys surrounding performing Shakespeare. How has reading about Rodenburg's method changed your desire to tackle the bard's classics?
- Think about the Second Circle. Do you experience the Second Circle in any of your personal relationships? Does fear hold you back from Second Circle with any of your relationships? What activities put you in the Second Circle, and which push you into First or Third? Have you used the Second Circle on stage? Have you ever had a scene partner meet you there? The audience?

The Tools for your Toolbox
Activity—Natural Body Position

- Have your actors remove footwear, spread out, stand comfortably with feet apart, and say: "We are going to find your natural, centered body."
- "Stretch your arms up and shake out your body."
- "Relax your arms at your sides and lift and drop your shoulders."
- "Rotate your shoulders."
- "Circle each arm clockwise, one at a time, letting the whole body participate, and let the arms find their place when dropped."
- "Hold your hands behind your back and lift as high as possible, then release."
- "Bring your feet together and slowly undulate your spine like a snake."
- "Place your feet under your hips and let your spine slump, then lift gently from the center of the stomach."
- "Sit cross-legged on the floor. Can you find a position of ease and balance in your spine?"
- "Get on your hands and knees and drop and raise your core through the spine."
- "Stand with feet comfortably apart. Hug your body with crossed arms reaching for your shoulder blades. Keep the touch gentle and shoulders released."
- "Keeping the hug, bend your knees slowly and fold at the waist."
- "Breathe deeply several times, feeling the back open."

- "Drop your arms, then slowly come up through the spine, not letting the chest do the work. Let your shoulders find their natural position."
- "Open your arms out in welcome and allow energy to flow through your arms, dropping the shoulders."
- "Allow your arms to return to their position at your side."
- "Let your head drop to your chest, keeping your jaw free."
- "Massage the back of your neck with your hands, keeping shoulders relaxed."
- "Swing your head from shoulder to shoulder gently."
- "Lift your head and balance it on top of your spine."
- "Let your head fall back gently, with jaw relaxed, then lift it again."
- "Let your head rotate from shoulder to shoulder in the back."
- "Rotate your head in a full circle while circling your shoulders."
- "Make circular chewing motions, remembering to treat your jaw gently."
- "Bunch your face up."
- "Relax, letting your face find its position. Repeat several times."
- "Massage your jaw hinges."
- "Smile and open your jaw big enough to put two fingers between your lips."
- "Chew around for ten seconds."
- "Open your jaw and stretch your tongue flat onto your chin then slide it back in. Repeat several times."
- "With the balls of your feet on the floor, rotate each ankle, one at a time."
- "Plant your feet firmly and lean forward, feeling slightly more weight on the balls of your feet and big toe than on the heels and sides of your feet."
- "Place your feet wide apart and parallel."
- "Keep your spine straight while bending your knees"
- "Place a hand on your lower stomach and breathe deeply enough to move the hand at least five times."
- "While standing, keep your stomach and thighs from tightening up."
- "Imagine that the ground is unsteady beneath you like you are riding a subway or bus while standing. Adjust your stance so you are relaxed and unlocked in your body."
- "Open yourself to both the internal and external world."
- "Swing your arms up to the sky in a gesture that starts from your feet and continues up to the gods. You should look up, but remain grounded. Imagine you are getting ready to dive into a pool."
- "Now breathe and let your arms spread out wide, radiating energy from your fingertips out to the sides."
- "Allow your head to find its place at the top of your spine."
- "You are embracing the world. This Da Vinci pose is designed to help you find your balanced, open, human energy that is grounded, with energy flowing from the ground out your hands and head."
- "If you feel vulnerable in this state, that is because you have abandoned tension and need to learn to replace it with a state of readiness."

Activity—State of Readiness

- Say: "We are going to do a few activities that will teach you the state of readiness. Once you find it, you can find it again easily."
- "Walk around the room as if you have an urgent errand. While you walk, remember to feel centered on the ground without looking down. Your speed can be any pace as long as it is done with intent. Try a couple of different speeds from slow to fast."
- "Now stop and stand still but continue feeling the urgency filling you. Do you feel more alert and three-dimensional?"
- "Find a spot on the wall and push against it. There is someone you love on the other side of that wall and you need to push it down to free them. Do you notice that there is no tension or stiffness in the way you are pushing? Do you feel the power of your breath? This is a state of readiness. You aren't locked when you are ready."
- "Now stop pushing and stand with the memory of the power of breath and body."
- "Alternate between walking urgently and pushing the wall for a couple of moments, noticing your state of readiness, and finding your freedom and power."
- "Pick up a chair and hold it over your head. Breathe and feel your breath go down. Notice that you can't hold any tension in your body while you do this task."
- "Speak some lines of Shakespeare while walking, pushing, and holding up the chair."
- "Try speaking in a deadened state."
- "Try speaking from a state of readiness while holding bad posture, by centering your body and breath beneath the posture."
- Discuss: "What does the state of readiness feel like? Can you hold that memory, building up the practice of finding it and using it no matter what posture your body is in?"

Activity—Breath

- Say: "Stand comfortably and breathe in gently then release your breath slowly and gently on an *s* sound. The goal is to expand your capacity through daily practice so you can do this exercise for ten, then twenty, even thirty-five seconds."
- "Now do the exercise on *v*"
- "Release your air on a *z*, recovering your breath before any squeezing occurs. You should feel the muscles around your abdomen and ribcage working rather than collapsing your chest."
- "Over a count of ten release the breath on *ha*, crescendoing and then decrescendoing over the next 10 seconds."
- "Release on *z* and recover, then begin again several times in a row. Rodenburg says you have gained the capacity for Shakespearean text when you can do this seven times in a row with ease. The goal here is to learn when a recovery breath is needed, and how to take it with ease."
- "Take a yawn breath in order to feel the openness of the throat."
- "Count while yawning."

- "This time, think of yawning while counting. Do you feel the open throat?"
- "Follow me through a line from *Twelfth Night* II.ii practicing breath support."
    - "Breathe in 'I'"
    - "Breathe in 'I left'"
    - "Breathe in 'I left no'"
    - "Breathe in 'I left no ring'"
    - "Breathe in 'I left no ring with'"
    - "Breath in 'I left no ring with her.'"
- Discuss: "What does breath control do for supported voice, comprehension of words for the actor and audience, and sound of the voice?"

Activity—Resonators

- Say: "Spread out. We are going to warm-up our resonators by sending a humming sound to our head, nose, face and throat while touching the place we are sending sound to."
- "Repeat: 'O for a Muse of fire, that would ascend The brightest heaven of invention!'" (*Henry V* prologue)
- "Say it again, sending it to your head resonator. Speak the line softly until you vibrate the top of your head with the sound. Then speak in full voice."
- "Now your nose resonator. Speak softly until you vibrate your nose."
- "Now face."
- "Now throat."
- "Use your chest resonator while visually focusing on a point in the audience above your eyeline. Remember not to push your voice down into your throat or chest."
- "Remember to release tension, stay focused outside not sinking down into yourself, and keep your head and body still."
- "Speak the text in an exaggerated range from high to low."
- "Return to a normal delivery with your resonators activated. Do you find your voice to have more range, variety, and body?"
- "Repeat the line with the goal of elegance, beauty, control, etc."
- Discuss: "What are the felt benefits of this warm-up?"

Activity—Clear Speech

- Say: "Try making a series of consonant sounds: b, d, g, r, l"
- "Make chewing motions with the face."
- "Without voice, say the following two lines, experiencing every syllable of every word, giving it a beginning, middle, and end."
    - "What studied torments, tyrant, hast for me?" (*The Winter's Tale*, III.iii)
    - "Weary with toil, I haste me to my bed." (*Sonnet 27*)

- "Speak the lines with full voice. Do you find the text is easier to speak and get your mouth around?"
- "Focus on the vowels. Place them as far forward as you can, and speak only the vowels of a line."
  - "Woe the while! / O, cut my lace, lest my heart, cracking it, / Break too!" (*The Winter's Tale*, III.ii)
  - "No longer mourn for me when I am dead / Then you shall hear the surly sullen bell / Give warning to the world that I am fled / From this vile world, with vilest worms to dwell." (*Sonnet 71*)
- "Now pronounce the words with all the sounds."
- Discuss: "What emotions lie in the sounds? Do you find the story or subtext in the vowels? Has your clarity increased by isolating the vowels or consonants?"

Activity—Walk the Text

- Say: "Pull out your monologues and analyze the breaks in thought, marking where each thought ends."
- "Walk the text, making a turn on each new thought."
- "Add more turns on the next walk, turning when a shift happens mid-thought."
- "Speak the speech while rooted to the ground, but expressing the shift of thought as you move towards a resolution."
- Discuss: "Did you find that shifts of thought can be expressed if you feel the movement, even if you don't physically move?"

Activity—Iambic Pentameter

- Print out Sonnet 12:

    When I do count the clock that tells the time,
    And see the brave day sunk in hideous night;
    When I behold the violet past prime,
    And sable curls all silver'd o'er with white;
    When lofty trees I see barren of leaves
    Which erst from heat did canopy the herd,
    And summer's green all girded up in sheaves
    Borne on the bier with white and bristly beard,
    Then of thy beauty do I question make,
    That thou among the wastes of time must go,
    Since sweets and beauties do themselves forsake
    And die as fast as they see others grow;
       And nothing 'gainst Time's scythe can make defence
       Save breed, to brave him when he takes thee hence.

- Say: "Hum the first two lines, noting the regular iambic of the first line and the irregular rhythm of the second. Respect the rhythm built in. Don't try to force it to follow the rules, but learn from the irregularities."
- "Work in groups of two or three to find the heartbeat of Sonnet 12, noting regular and irregular lines. Articulate what the irregularities can teach you."
- "Now recite it to each other, first emphasizing the beat, then focusing on the meaning. Do they match up? Does emphasis help clarify the text?"
- "Pull out your Shakespeare monologue and walk the iambic in it."
- "Perform for a partner and discuss how each of the monologues has a different character rhythm built in."
- "Release the iambic and perform without emphasizing it, but letting it exist in the words."
- Now give them IV.i of *The Merchant of Venice*

    Portia.   A pound of that same merchant's flesh is thine:
       The court awards it, and the law doth give it.
    Shylock.   Most rightful judge!
    Portia.   And you must cut this flesh from off his breast:
       The law allows it, and the court awards it.
    Shylock.   Most learned judge! A sentence! Come, prepare!
    Portia.   Tarry a little; there is something else.
       This bond doth give thee here no jot of blood;
       The words expressly are 'a pound of flesh:'
       Take then thy bond, take thou thy pound of flesh;
       But, in the cutting it, if thou dost shed
       One drop of Christian blood, thy lands and goods
       Are, by the laws of Venice, confiscate
       Unto the state of Venice.
    Gratiano.   O upright judge! Mark, Jew: O learned judge!
    Shylock.   Is that the law?
    Portia.   Thyself shalt see the act:
       For, as thou urgest justice, be assured
       Thou shalt have justice, more than thou desirest.
    Gratiano.   O learned judge! Mark, Jew: a learned judge!
    Shylock.   I take this offer, then; pay the bond thrice 2265
       And let the Christian go.
    Bassanio.   Here is the money.
    Portia.   Soft!
       The Jew shall have all justice; soft! no haste:
       He shall have nothing but the penalty.

- Discuss: "In pairs or trios, count out the syllables and find irregularities. Which lines are shared? Which lines are fewer than ten syllables? Where should a pause be added?"

Activity—The Second Circle

- Have your students sit cross-legged on the floor.
- Say: "Experience your own breath and body. This is the First Circle. Stay focused on receptive energy, but do not send any out."
- "Stand up and imagine your energy shifting out, pressing forward. Become aware of your presence filling the space and moving outwards. This is the Third Circle. You should feel expansive and general. Try to encompass everything in the room at once."
- "Did you sense the Second Circle on the way to the Third? Drop into a state that is present and open."
- "You can appear to be in the physical state of the First or Third circle, while interacting in the Second. Try it."
- "Deliver the beginning thought of your Shakespeare monologue in the First Circle."
- "Try it in Third Circle."
- "Pair up and engage with a partner in the Second Circle while performing."
- "Try slipping between circles as you deliver the speeches again. Listener, try listening in all three circles."
- Discuss with your partner: "What did you learn? Is it annoying to listen in the Second Circle while your partner is delivering in the First or Third? Is the reverse true?"
- "Spread out and stand comfortably."
- "Examine your stance. If your feet are spread wider than your hips, you are in Third Circle, if narrower, you are in First. If your feet aren't fully on the ground, you are in First, if too solidly placed to move into the next movement, you are in Third. Adjust your stance to shoulder width with feet fully touching ground, put weight on balls of feet, ready to spring into action. This is feet in Second Circle."
- "Check that the knees are soft and not locked."
- "Check that your pelvis is not thrust forward, holding you back in Third."
- "Slump your spine to feel First Circle, then to pull the spine up rigidly to feel Third. Now find the place of ease between these that is the Second Circle spine."
- "Let your shoulders find their natural place, not rounded or lifted."
- "Is your head balanced like a ping pong ball on the top of a spout of water, floating and flexible, not rigid or slumped?"
- "Re-check each part of your body to make sure you are fully in the Second Circle. It will take vigilance to learn to stay in Second Circle. If practiced outside as well as inside the theatre, it will become your natural state of being."
- "Put a hand in front of yourself and breathe to it. Feel the moment the breath connects with your hand."
- "Breathe short of it—the First Circle."
- "Breathe past it—the Third."
- "Breathe to a point farther out in the room. It is still Second Circle if your breath is sent to it specifically, not trampling over it, but reaching toward it."
- Discuss: "Rodenburg claims that you can control a room with Second Circle breathing. What do you think of that claim?"

21
Chelsea Pace

The Person

Chelsea Pace is an intimacy coordinator, choreographer, and educator for stage and film. She is also a movement specialist. She has been researching intimacy work for more than a decade. In that time, she founded Open Intimacy Creatives in 2024 and co-founded the company Theatrical Intimacy Education (TIE) in 2017, where she serves as Head Faculty. In this capacity, she shares her work internationally with performers and artistic teams.

She has developed ethical and simple systems for staging intimacy that can be used by anyone, creating safety and a language for communicating boundaries in a non-threatening, desexualized way. Her focus is on the artistry and storytelling of the moments, figuring out how to make intimacy choreography better each time, and getting everyone to say exactly what they mean as they work together. She encourages companies to, for instance, let an actor know that full rear nudity is desired for a role before they accept it. This gives the actor a chance to consider and consent or decline with full information. The actor is also encouraged to be honest about what works for them. The result of this honesty and specificity is a less awkward, more efficient process in which the intimacy director keeps things moving, consistent, and aesthetically appropriate for the mood of the piece. The guesswork is removed and the actors feel safe and heard.

Pace was the intimacy director of the Broadway production of *A Strange Loop*. Regionally, she has worked at La Jolla Playhouse, Signature Theatre, Studio Theatre, Folger, Woolly Mammoth, and Philadelphia Theatre Company.

Pace was awarded The Kennedy Center Gold Medallion in 2021 for the clarity of her staging intimacy system which centers the vulnerable. Her book, *Staging Sex: Best Practices, Tools, and Techniques for Theatrical Intimacy*, was released in 2020.

She also serves as intimacy coordinator for TV and film. Her credits include *A League of Their Own* and *Wu-Tang: An American Saga*. She specializes in "staging queer intimacy, complex stories of consent and/or non-consent, kink, and supporting productions with inclusive, thoughtful, professional, trauma-informed, and culturally competent choreography."[1]

The Method

This chapter is a slightly different one. In it, I am highlighting what I consider to be the best and easiest method for staging any sort of touch on stage. The culture we work in is much different than the culture theatre was born into. For the first time in human history, we collectively hold consent as a primary value. It seems as the world moves on from the social isolation and distancing of the Covid-19 pandemic, we are even more acutely aware of touch as something that should always be consensual and safe. The book *Staging Sex* was written before the onset of the pandemic, but was released in the early days of lockdown.

I hesitated to include it here, not because I don't wholeheartedly recommend it to everyone in theatre, but because I fear you will read this chapter and then not buy her book. I promise you that you need it. This chapter is intended to begin to shift your processes as an actor or teacher and alert you to the fact that we can't do things the way we always have anymore. Buy *Staging Sex*. Then buy it for everyone you know who has a theatre career. It is a required purchase for all of my directing and performance students and has a place of honor on my bookshelf.

Chelsea Pace has developed a system of staging touch simple enough for a conscientious teenager to use when staging a scene with peers. At the same time, it has the power to revolutionize the culture of established theatres worldwide. It is time to make this change. Actors are not separate from their characters. When a character touches another, it is the actor who experiences the intimacy. Henry Bial wrote,

> When a character disrobes, it is the actor's body that is exposed. When two characters kiss, it is the actors' lips meeting. And when characters simulate sexual activity, it is the actors who may find themselves a little too close to their co-worker's 'naughty bits' with disturbing regularity. The oft-repeated disclaimer 'it's just a play' flies in the face of a wealth of experience that convinces us otherwise.[2]

Old Approaches

The rehearsal room is powerful, and has a hierarchy. It is difficult even for well-meaning people to manage intimacy competently and safely. In the absence of good techniques, theatre professionals have taken several approaches:

- The director says "Just kiss each other." This is easy for the director because it takes them out of the position of dictating something uncomfortable. However, it isn't okay because it is awkward and vulnerable for the actors to guess what will look good.
- The director says "You guys talk this out and decide what to do." This approach is taken because the actors understand the characters and will theoretically only suggest things they are comfortable performing. This isn't true because actors often suggest things they are uncomfortable with to please the director.
- The director says "You guys talk it out and decide what to do in another room." We do this to take the power dynamic out of the picture. Unfortunately, the actors often still create scenes that one or both of them are uncomfortable with.

In all three of the preceding scenarios, the director is in a tough spot if they want to change what the actors have created. It's tricky to tell them that something so vulnerably created is boring or awkward. So professionals try some other techniques that might work because the actors aren't put on the spot:

- The director models the intimacy they want to see with an assistant. This is the fastest way to teach choreography of any kind. In intimacy scenes however, this crosses all kinds of boundaries including asking actors to visualize their director in compromising positions.
- We ask the choreographer to stage the intimacy because choreographers know how to plan and teach people to move. But they lack the training in intimacy work, and the skills are not the same.
- We sit in a circle and talk about the intimacy and the scene to understand each person's relationship to intimacy. In this case, we are trying to consider everyone's boundaries and traumas to help them work through the scene. This makes the work unsafe for everyone involved setting you up to hear about past traumas when the rehearsal room isn't the place for therapy, and likely no one in the room knows how to handle those intimate revelations.

There are more methods, but all of them lead to the same set of awkwardnesses and traumas. Pace says that the problems created by most intimacy rehearsals are:

1. The dynamics of the rehearsal room make consent tricky and leaves the door open to abuses of power.
2. Even in the absence of abuse or wrongdoing, the nature of theatrical intimacy makes actors psychologically, physically, and emotionally vulnerable, and good intentions on the part of their directors and scene partners are not sufficient to protect them . . .
3. Intimate moments onstage are part of the story and deserve the same attention to detail and careful crafting as any other moment of theatrical storytelling.[3]

Directors often don't feel that they have a special power in the rehearsal room that would intimidate an actor, but by virtue of their position, they do. Actors are trained to always say yes. They want to make the director and other actors happy so they will be cast/hired again. They want to please. It is hard to break this habit, and not everyone can do it. Therefore, a new culture of consent needs to be built. This new culture must normalize actors saying no, desexualize intimacy and touching, and be choreographed using standardized language.

Will intimacy still be weird? Yes. But it can be safe.

Boundaries

Boundaries are very complicated. They are hard to make, hard to enforce, hard to respect. Pace writes, "most people spend a fair amount of mental energy negotiating boundaries, their own and everyone else's, on matters ranging from parking spaces to pronouns . . . Given the overlapping, intersecting, idiosyncratic and evolving boundaries in any theatrical endeavor, it is no wonder that staging intimacy is specially charged for both actors and directors."[4] Because boundaries are so complicated, it is important to help everyone in the room feel comfortable and safe. Boundaries are the tools that allow us to continue in relationship with others.

The Ingredients For Choreography

Anyone can learn to be an intimacy choreographer by learning the ingredients for creating safety and clarity in the rehearsal room. There are situations that call for hiring a specialist in intimacy work, but many situations will best be handled by members of the artistic team who are already in the room.

The desexualized language that Pace uses teaches directors how to create clear directions for movement and touch. As you work with your director or scene partner, you can create a storytelling moment using the following elements of vocabulary:

1 Opening and closing distance—To talk about touch, decide who closes the distance between the bodies, and who opens the space after the touch ends. This language is desexualized because it is applicable to anything. You can ask an actor to close the distance between themself and a prop as easily as between themself and another actor. Actors can also close or open the distance mutually. Bodies have many parts, and it must be clear how the distance is closed for each point of contact. Perhaps the distance between mouths is closed, but the distance between pelvises remains open. Or, maybe after a kiss, the distance is opened first from the lips and later the chests.

2 Levels of Touch—You can talk about the levels of touch in different ways. Pace suggests using the language of three levels to indicate how firm the touch will be. One way is to label these levels as Skin/Muscle/Bone. A skin level touch is very light; a bone level touch is deep. Muscle level touch is in between. Some artists might prefer Pace's other suggested terms: Powder/Paint/Clay or Touching/Moving/Pulling. You can use whichever terminology works best for you. Use this terminology when you talk about an actor touching a piece of furniture the same way you would another person or themselves. By using this terminology all the time, it becomes desexualized and understood.

3 Tempo and Counts—Directors and actors can create consistent and safe choreography by learning to create tempos and counts for a moment of intimacy. Actors will notice that what feels like three counts to them, might feel like five to another. A common understanding of what is meant by a specific count is important.

4 Shapes—Most moments of intimacy can be described as arcs, angles, or figure eights. Discussing and planning the shapes of movements is very helpful in desexualizing the motions.

5 Destination—Movement happens not only in shapes, but with destinations. You can provide a map of where the touch will occur and where it moves to.

6 Eye contact—Discussion of moments when eye contact is sought, avoided, and found is very helpful in storytelling and takes the pressure off the actors to decide what is appropriate and when.

7 Visible power shifts—Who is in control of a moment is an important component of intimacy. The important distinction here is the power structure must be visible rather than psychological. Be careful to not use the names people use when describing sexual positions in this conversation. Instead say "Person A closes the distance between his body and the chair in a one count while Person B's hand is on his left shoulder. Person B closes the distance between

her pelvis and Person A's upper thighs . . . ." Always keep the descriptions of the power shifts equally desexualized: "Person A increases the level of touch to bone level and shifts his weight onto his right arm, closing the distance between his pelvis and Person B's pelvis."
8 Breath and sound—"Making intimate sounds can be embarrassing. Actors are often nervous or self-conscious about making sound or even bold choices about breath."[5] Using the words short, long, shallow, deep, high, low, or sharp can help actors move past ambiguity and remove some of the embarrassment. Instead of asking for a gasp of pleasure, a director can ask for "a short, sharp intake of breath." Instead of asking for a moan, a director can ask for "a low oh sound for a count of two."
9 Gravity and weight—An actor can be asked to use less or more gravity when leaning against another body. The use of the terminology of imagining less gravity in the moment can help alleviate awkwardness. You can also think about shifting weight. Practicing these prompts using a chair instead of another person can help to desexualize the work.

A note about kissing: Kissing is the most often used element of stage intimacy. Pace insists there is almost never a reason for lips to be open. If a director is asking for something that requires you to open your lips or your partner to open theirs, it is best to ask for a way to communicate the story in a different way. Perhaps an added hand movement or shift of weight or shape can create the mood or story that open lips might in real life.

All of the nine tools of language and choreography above should be established, and they should be rehearsed with hands as placeholders before the kiss is practiced. Once the kiss is practiced, the director and actors should suggest tweaks using desexualized language and questioning "How would you feel about shifting from skin to muscle level touch after three counts?" Then, after choreographed and agreed upon, the stage manager should document every detail of the instructions and keep them written in a place where they can be referred to if it feels like a change is happening. Kisses often get shorter over a run, and an actor can ask to review the choreography with the stage manager instead of saying "Kiss me longer!" to their fellow actor.

What Can One Actor Do?

As an actor, you can't control the culture of the room, but you can contribute to its safety in a few ways:

1 Remind yourself and others that their boundaries are good exactly as they are.
2 Allow your own boundaries and the boundaries of others to change by checking in with yourself and others to see if things are the same or different today. Ask your scene partner before each rehearsal if their boundaries are the same or if they want to go over them with you.
3 Remember to ask to touch others. Theatre people have the reputation of being touchy-feely, but this isn't necessarily true of most artists. Our culture of saying yes has created a room full of people who allow others to hug them when they do not actually want to be touched.

4 Replace the question "Can I touch your shoulder?" With "How would you feel about me touching your shoulder?" The first question requires a yes or no answer, and your partner has been conditioned to say yes. The second question requires thinking about and articulating a response that is more likely to be truthful. "Open questions create opportunities for everyone to consider what is being asked of them and to make suggestions that work for their boundaries."[6]
5 When someone reveals something traumatic or becomes emotional, learn to say "Let's get you some support" rather than trying to become their therapist. And follow through. Sometimes the effort required to get help is more than someone can manage on their own.
6 Suggest that your director read *Staging Sex* and incorporate language in rehearsals that work well. If your director isn't on the same page with you, you can work outside the rehearsal room with your partner in order to create safety by going through boundary practice and check-ins with Pace's terminology or your own. Pace suggests the following three terms:

   a. Button—instead of requiring an activated person to say "stop" or "no," giving them a term that implies a pause to consider is often more accessible. This pause gives the actor a chance to think and find a yes in the moment. It might be an alternative touch, or a shift. It might be that after thought, they agree the suggested action is the best one. It also does not require an explanation. No one has to divulge their trauma in order to be respected as they process.
   b. Fences—actors take turns first showing, then telling what parts of their body have boundaries around them by miming fences around parts of their body. A "fences session" gets the actors who will be in contact with each other face to face and exploring boundaries in a clear way without giving reasons for their boundaries. Reasons are unnecessary since actors respect what they are shown without question.
   c. Gates—sometimes actors need to open a fence and allow contact they wouldn't usually allow. For example, an actor would need to open a gate on a rehearsal when a kiss is choreographed, or an assault is blocked. In these cases, actors receive a warning in advance that the gates will need to be opened for a particular rehearsal. You should also have consented to the activity when you auditioned for the role, being informed in advance that your character would be kissing another.

7 Use placeholders before you run the actual intimacy to check that you are on the same page. For example, when asked to do a stage kiss, you might perform the kiss with your hands first to make sure you understand what is being asked for in the same way as your partner and the director do.
8 Ask the stage manager to document the choreography of the intimacy so it can be checked during the run of the show to make sure "the artistic vision of the director is being honored."
9 Encourage and model desexualized language surrounding the intimacy. It is common for actors to deal with discomfort by joking about stage intimacy, but everyone should be speaking professionally about the intimacy choreography with desexualized language always. You can model this for others.
10 Learn to de-role with your partner. Breaking the illusion after each performance is sometimes the best way to protect your mental health and that of your partner. This is especially

important if your characters engage in stage violence of any type. Here are a few possible ways to de-role:

a. Create a moment where you communicate with words or actions that you see and respect the actor even if your character does not. You might routinely meet just off stage after a scene with a forced sexual encounter and say "My character shoves and treats you in abusive ways while trying to have power over your character using demeaning names and physical violence. But as an actor, I am doing choreography. I'm speaking the text and performing the opening and closing of distance. I would never do these things or say those words to you."

b. If your partner does not want to participate, you can do these things on your own with the help of a mirror or quiet statements to yourself. You might say to yourself, "As the character Juliet, I am in love with the character Romeo. In that role I feel very close to Romeo and express that with physical movements, words, and eye contact. As an actor, I am using intimacy choreography, speaking Shakespeare's words, and using my imagination. I do not have those feelings for the actor who is playing Romeo. I respect them as a scene partner and fellow actor."

c. Choose a moment on stage, agreed upon by your scene partner, where you touch or make eye contact as actors rather than characters to non-verbally communicate your mutual care/respect for each other as actors even though your characters do not.

11 Own up to your mistakes when they happen. Tell the other person that you recognize you touched them without permission or violated a fence. Whether accidental or not, the apology should be sincere. Then thank them for helping you grow as a person.

Ground Rules

There are some basic rules that Pace asks everyone to follow when working with staging intimacy:

- The timing of intimacy choreography should be published and decided on with lots of notice—at least 24 hours—so nothing is sprung on the actor.
- The people in the room for the choreography should be decided on in conjunction with the actors. Anything from the full company to just the actors, director, and stage manager are okay, though no one should be required to watch if it will be activating for them.
- Stage chemistry should not be a goal that is in anyone's mind. Actors can be taught to be vulnerable and open with their partner.
- Nudity and stage intimacy should be part of the casting call, and only actors who have agreed to them should be considered for the role.
- Intimacy calls should be run by the stage manager before every performance.
- Provide warnings to the audience if there will be any physical contact between an actor and an audience member. Non-consensual touch is never okay in performance. The audience members in potential contact zones should know what they have agreed to, and that there are rules for them when in contact with actors as well.

Tips for taking this method further

- Buy and read *Staging Sex* by Chelsea Pace. Then give a copy to your collaborators so you can be on the same page when you work together.

Discussion Starters and Journal Prompts

- Think about your history with stage intimacy and reflect on the insecurities and struggles you have had in the past. Do you like what you read in this chapter? Does it address your concerns? Are there more questions you have?

The Tools for your Toolbox

Activity—Boundaries Practice

- A full detail of this activity is in chapter one of Chelsea Pace's *Staging Sex*. I recommend you lead the activity with her book rather than this one. It is laid out clearly there.
- You can also use the Boundaries practice as your characters. Remember, your character may be in a place or culture where the rules around touching are quite different from yours.

Activity—Practicing Desexualized Language

- Have your students pair up and tell them to decide who is A and who is B.
- Say: "You will be practicing using desexualized language for moments of intimacy starting with opening and closing distance."
- "Sit facing each other and put out your right hands towards each other, but leaving six inches of space between palms."
- "Person A, close the distance between palms. Now Person A, open the distance between palms."
- Do a few variations on this activity until you are sure they are all on the same page.
- Now add story to the activity. Say: "I am going to suggest a few scenarios and you should talk to each other about how to tell those stories with just your palms and opening and closing the distance. Remember to keep the language desexualized and practice the terminology of opening and closing distance:"
    - A seduction
    - A reunion of friends after a long separation
    - Unequal interest between two people

- ○ The end of a first date—a decision made between a kiss or handshake
- ○ A goodbye
- ○ The balcony scene from Romeo and Juliet.
* Now have your actors get a chair to work with. Tell them you are moving on to levels of touch.
* Have your students direct each other to make contact with the furniture piece using the terminology of the three levels of touch, trying each of the three suggested levels in the three forms: Powder/Paint/Clay or Skin/Muscle/Bone or Touching/Moving/Pulling
* Say: "discuss each of the suggestions and decide which of them will be your chosen vocabulary for the exercise as a pair."
* "Create a choreography for the other with several steps to it using the language of closing and opening distance and levels of touch with the chair."
* Once they have played with this for a moment, say: "Go back to your choreography with your hands and deepen the work you did with opening and closing the distance by adding levels of touch. Practice your choreography."
* Now tell your actors you are adding tempos to the work.
* Say: "Tap your feet to find a common rhythm for a ten count."
* Discuss why people might have different tempos in different situations and why they might differ from a scene partner.
* Say: "Now each pair should create a choreography for interacting with a chair for the other with several steps to it, using the language of closing and opening distance, levels of touch, and tempos."
* Once they have played with this for a moment, say: "Now add tempo to the hand choreography you completed in the previous activity."
* "It is time to add shape and destination to your choreography. Begin by touching the chair in arcs, angles, and figure eights."
* Tell them to try a choreography you will call out to them: "Close the distance between your hand and the seat of the chair over a five count. When your hand reaches the chair, trace an arc shape using powder level touch moving from the front edge of the chair to the back for a count of three. Finally, open the distance with a two count."
* Have them discuss with their partner how they each did something slightly different with the same instructions.
* Now say: "Add shape and destination to the movements you have been working on using your hands."
* Now, it is time to stretch the movement work to a choreography using more than hands. Give your actors the scene when Romeo and Juliet first meet at the ball as a structure. Gender doesn't make any difference for this activity. It is perfectly useful to gender swap or work with a same sex partner in this activity. Say: "I am going to choreograph a touch between you (not a lip kiss) which adds the aspect of eye contact. It is the first time you are touching each other. Create a map of the event and then perform it. I will guide the activity."
* First, have them use the terminology of "How would you feel about my hand touching your forearm like this?" (demonstrating on their own body) Remind them that their partner

is free to suggest an alternative touch if the suggested one doesn't feel right for that moment to them. I suggest having two trusted students model a suggestion followed by an alternative suggestion.
- Say: "Now work on creating a choreography for Romeo and Juliet's first touch by talking about opening and closing distance, level of touch, shape, destination, and eye contact."
- Practice the motions first with hands as a placeholder, then when both people understand the motions, transition to touching other body parts as agreed upon.
- Now have them use the same language to discuss the balcony kiss and try the same conversation about the dynamics and movements and practice with hands. Add the concept of visible power shifts and have them add one to their palm kiss. (Do not move on to having their mouths touch each other for this activity.)
- Say: "As a final step, write down the choreography you have created as practice for documenting a choreography using desexualized language."
- Discuss: "We covered a lot of material in one activity. What are the most important takeaways you learned? How would you feel if you were cast in the role of Romeo or Juliet, and a director used this system to stage your kiss? What kind of bravery would be required of you? Would Pace's terminology make it easier for you to be brave?"

Part II

Partial Chapters

22 Lee Strasberg
23 Frank Silvera
24 Barbara Ann Teer
25 Susan Batson
26 David Mamet

Appendix of Additional Methods

I struggled to title this section of my manuscript because it seems to defy categorization and because the practitioners included here do not lend themselves well to classroom activities. You might ask why I include them at all, if I couldn't justify placing them in the body of the book. Good question.

As for Strasberg, his imprint on acting in America is impossible to ignore. I believe actors should know the roots of the work they do. I have my students learn about him in conjunction with Stella Adler. It always leads to fruitful discussions of boundaries, mental health, and power dynamics in the rehearsal room.

Mamet is too interesting to ignore although he's problematic. I contend he is worth knowing about. For some students, his theories are the trick to get them out of their heads and back into a better, unlocked state.

The answer is easy with Silvera, Teer, and Batson. I wanted to include as many influential practitioners from the Global Majority as possible. As I researched these three compelling theatre leaders, I learned enough to extend their influence by compiling what I could find in dissertations and magazine articles for you here. Maybe in a subsequent edition I will be able to unearth enough material to move them where they deserve to live, next to their well-documented peers.

22

Lee Strasberg

The Person

Lee Strasberg was born in Austrian Poland, now part of the Ukraine, in 1901. He immigrated to New York in 1909. When he was young he had a few actor credits, partly because he spoke Yiddish. He wrote about these younger acting days with some puzzlement since he really didn't remember much about them or think of them as important in his development. He wasn't planning a theatre career at the time. He does remember loving the sound of his voice reverberating in the theatre.

In the early 1920s, he was working as a wigmaker when he joined the dramatics club at Chrystie Street Settlement House "because I was looking for female companionship."[1] He was still not envisioning a life on the stage, but he began to attend many plays and witness problems actors had with finding consistency from performance to performance. He became curious and began to read about theatre, learning as much as he could. One book he read was Gordon Craig's book *On the Art of Acting*. Craig posited that actors are not artists because they cannot control emotions and repeat them night after night. Strasberg spent his life trying to prove Craig wrong.

When the Moscow Art Theatre toured America in 1923 and 1924, Strasberg attended many of their performances and commented that while the technical capabilities of the company were not strong (bad makeup, poorly lit, ragged costumes), the actors themselves were a true ensemble, with appropriate humor, lack of sentimentality, and a distinct creation of performances without stars at the helm. The actors disappeared into their characters. It was these performances that inspired him to get serious about acting and become a professional actor. He studied first at a conventional theatre school and then moved on to the American Laboratory Theatre where he learned the System from Stanislavski's students, Richard Boleslavsky and Maria Ouspenskaya who had immigrated to the US.

At the time, the Lab was taught in a two-year sequence. Year one was mostly with Ouspenskaya with curriculum covering given circumstances, characterization, and affective memory. The second year was with Boleslavsky which was more invested in text work. Strasberg did not stay for the second year.

The next step of Strasberg's career was potentially the most important one. Along with Cheryl Crawford and Harold Clurman, he founded the Group Theater and was the primary acting teacher. It was in this capacity that he created an acting method that was a rival to Stanislavski's System. In fact, his method was not referred to as the Strasberg Method, but simply, "The Method" and produced what today we call "Method Acting." The Method had many facets, but focused on using past memories and emotions to create consistent emotion on stage. Everyone in the Group learned it, but it was not popular with all of the members. Notably, Stella Adler was unhappy and felt that Method Acting had spoiled acting for her. She sought out Stanislavski in Paris in 1934 and found out his System was not as much like Method Acting as Strasberg claimed.

After weeks of private lessons with Stanislavski, Adler returned to the US and delivered a lecture to the Group Theater attempting to clear up the confusion. In this lecture she questioned Strasberg's methods and proposed newer, less personally invasive methods of creating emotion on stage. Strasberg was not happy. The next night Strasberg gave a counter-lecture in which he stated, "I teach the Strasberg Method, not the Stanislavski System."[2] This public acknowledgment that his Method was significantly different from the System was a watershed moment for him. It opened up a huge rift in the Group Theater, leading to his departure in 1936.

When he wrote about this break from the System, he said, "in view of the many discussions and misunderstandings as to what 'the system' is and what it is not, plus the confusion about the earlier and later periods of Stanislavsky's work, I was unwilling to make Stanislavsky responsible for any of our faults." He considered his Method to be based on the System, clarified by Vakhtangov, and added to by his own interpretation and procedures. He continued: "Through our understanding, analysis, applications, and additions, we have made a sizable contribution to the completion of Stanislavsky's work."[3] When he writes "we" in the above quotes, he is referring mostly to himself, considering his additions to Stanislavsky's System to be superior to the developments Stanislavski had made to his System during the same time period.

He continued to teach his method and became the Artistic Director of the Actor's Studio in 1951. In that role, he continued to coach actors and to direct on and off Broadway. He called his Method a "peculiarly American version of Stanislavsky."[4] This American acting training gave actors a place to hone their skills, a community of fellow artists, and a unique sort of psychotherapy without trained therapists present.

In 1970, he opened the Lee Strasberg Theatre & Film Institute with branches in New York City and in Hollywood with his third wife, Anna. Both here and at the Actor's Studio, Strasberg's Method was used to train an impressive list of film actors. It drew some criticism as it was perceived as "cultish" by some, but Strasberg got obvious results in his work with his actors.

Near the end of his life, Strasberg played a role in *The Godfather, Part II*, probably his most famous acting work. He died of a heart attack in 1982 at the age of eighty, the day after he was notified he had been elected to the American Theater Hall of Fame.

The Method

Strasberg's method of acting had many elements of Stanislavski's System as it existed in the 1920s, but it was deeply fixated on affective memory, which was one small portion of The System. His training with Maria Ouspenskaya and Richard Boleslavsky started Strasberg out in a Russian way, but his unique spin on it changed the way American actors were trained and viewed by the world.

"In popular culture ... the Method is associated with an authentic and uniquely American acting style ... references to it usually call to mind portrayals of tough, moody, sexually potent male characters. Method acting has become associated with a handful of male stars, whose ... performances stand out from the ensemble."[5] As these associations are almost 100 years old, you might not know about James Dean and Montgomery Clift, but their sexually unfulfilled brutality and barely held together social manners were synonymous with the Method in the twentieth century.

Incidentally, though Marlon Brando is widely reputed to be a Method actor, he was a student of Stella Adler who did not teach the Method. In fact, Brando despised the exploitative tactics of Strasberg's Method. Strasberg, however, liked to claim Brando as one of his students so much so that he was listed in Strasberg's obituary.

The Problem of Replicability

Strasberg was concerned with creating a replicable way for actors to convey emotion on the stage. He writes that a piano player has an instrument that can exactly replicate the art from performance to performance. But when an actor tries to "play" themselves, they often get a result they weren't trying for. In fact, they might play the same notes each time and get different results. Actors want to produce truthful, predictable, moving performances every time, but they can't because emotions are tricky. They can't simply correct errors to perfect their performance. If an actor finds a way to express an emotion one night, the next night they might feel stale using the same formula. Strasberg wanted to keep actor impulses fresh.

He knew this was not an easy task since, "The actor must guard against a search for perfect solutions. Neither on the stage nor in life do we find perfect solutions."[6] Even so, Strasberg created the Method to find good solutions. His solution was not intellectual. Strasberg fought against intellectualizing acting, believing the playwright has already created the necessary material the actor needs to accomplish their goals. If the play is funny, the actor doesn't need to try to be funny. Instead, "All that remains for the actor is to create as fully as possible the reality of that situation. He does not need to be funny—but the results will be."[7]

Relaxation

Every activity of the actor, according to Strasberg, must begin with complete relaxation. This portion of Method is very like Stanislavski's System. Strasberg taught his students to search for tension in their muscles and release it. Actors need to work on this constantly, as it is hard to maintain a tension-free body. Physical relaxation is relatively easy to do, but mental relaxation is much harder.

As students started with relaxation, they were also routinely reminded to go back to relaxation exercises if they became fearful when working on emotions. He wrote "There's no real fear in merely being emotional, but I don't want to encourage the sense of fear which may work against the effort you're making. Trust yourself and have faith and commitment in what you're doing."[8]

Concentration

In Strasberg's Method, relaxation itself is not the goal. In fact, Strasberg claimed the only purpose of relaxation is to find concentration. "Everything the actor does is a two-sided action. Relaxation is connected with concentration."[9] Concentration skills allow the actor to focus on the imaginary reality that truthful performance requires.

An actor can begin the process of concentration by focusing on an object, for instance, a table. By simply staring at the table, nothing will happen, but if the actor starts thinking about the table and asking questions about its height, weight, etc. they will find they are concentrating on the table. However, in a play, the actor often has to do a more difficult task: concentrate on an imaginary object.

The training leading to this ability to concentrate starts with familiar objects. The Method actor is asked to explore the object that holds their morning beverage. This vessel is explored for all of its sensory values. How heavy? What texture? What temperature? What color? What scent? After doing this preparatory work, the actor can then recreate the sensation of a hot mug without the physical object. In this exercise, the sensations of the cup and liquid are re-experienced, but the actor remains relaxed and recalls the sensations without moving.

Once this is done, the actor can move on to re-experiencing a morning ritual like shaving or applying makeup while looking in a mirror. The exercise begins at home where the actor looks at themselves for ten minutes, trying to establish all their features. Next they perform the task, paying careful attention to all the sensations of their five senses. Once in class, they try to recreate this morning ritual without seeming rehearsed. Strasberg claimed this is hard because humans are not equipped to imitate life. They have to believe what they are doing is real.

The Private Moment

After successfully completing the concentration exercises, the actor in Strasberg's class could move on to private moment work, often a recreation of showering, usually without actual nudity. The students were asked to take on the feeling of nakedness and make it real to themselves. These actors were instructed to "pick something that you would never do in front of anyone. If someone interrupted you and asked what you were doing you would say, 'Oh, nothing at all.'"[10] You can see how this activity could easily become inappropriate or appear to be out of control.

Strasberg, however, thought this activity was important in reaching the goal of forgetting the audience and creating ease in acting. These exercises got a bad reputation because, while they were usually mundane sorts of moments, it was not unheard of for an actor to perform naked or choose an activity that was shocking. Nothing was off limits, though most people chose activities that would not be considered lewd. Students were required to pass this test before being allowed to move on to emotional memory activities.

Emotional Memory

Strasberg writes that when he began exploring acting methods "I discovered that there was a central debate in terms of acting: Does the actor actually experience the emotion he is portraying, or should he demonstrate the emotion without experiencing it?"[11] Strasberg's answer is definitive: actors must genuinely experience the emotion each time on stage. A difficult task, made more difficult for professional actors who expect emotion to reliably return for eight performances a week.

Strasberg's solution to this problem was an activity called emotional memory. This exercise awakens emotions for use on stage. Strasberg claimed "If you have enough faith to permit the lines to come out organically as a result of the exercise, they will come out convincingly."[12]

Before an emotional memory exercise began, the actor put themselves in a complete state of relaxation, often in a chair in the center of a classroom with the teacher and classmates. At this point the actor would identify a memory attached to a needed emotion. Strasberg taught the moments that are best for use in emotional memory work are the most heightened past experiences. These experiences needed to be at least seven years old, because if a memory has lasted that long, it is permanently useful for the actor.

Strasberg didn't pressure his actors to use memories they were uneasy about dredging up in the classroom. He said, "We never push it. We take the thing that they're less afraid of. I prefer to deal with something less strong … An exercise may act as therapy rather than a theatrical device. I don't get involved in therapy. I never push the student who says 'I'm a little uneasy about going into that area.'"[13]

Once the appropriate memory was selected, it was time to find emotional memory objects. To do this, the actor was asked to recall the environment around them a few minutes before the height of the emotion occurred. Without trying to create the emotion, the actor worked with a coach to talk through everything that occurred prior to, during, and after the emotional event. The actor answered questions about the sensory details of the experience. The coach asked about the colors and textures of surrounding objects, prompting the actor to think in detail. They then talked through the words spoken in as much detail as possible, the clothing worn by everyone involved, what the people in the room were doing, sensory details, etc. Everything was important.

The coach reminded the actor not to tell the details of the story for the others in the room since they are only interested in the surrounding environment. At some point, emotions would come unbidden as the actor recalled a detail. It could be a half-empty wine glass, a tie, or the feel of a shirt on the body. The actor kept working until they found several objects in the memory that brought up a strong emotion when remembered. These details become the actor's golden keys to unlock emotions. Sometimes one remembered object would stop working, if an actor had identified backup golden keys, they could substitute them to find the needed emotion.

The observers in the room were important not just for support, but also so the actor would be used to being observed while experiencing the emotion and be able to use their golden keys on stage. Strasberg said actors who did the work alone at home found they could not use the keys when observed from stage. However, once the session was done, the actor was encouraged to repeat the activity on their own, recalling only the golden keys to find the emotion. With practice, it would take less and less time to recreate the feeling needed on stage.

Strasberg felt the results were more than worth the emotional pain and fear required to break down the barriers that actors hold in suppressing emotion. His actors had some issues with this emotional memory technique, but he defended it to the end. For instance, the actors would claim their golden keys no longer worked. He insisted this was because they were doing it wrong. When he worked with them again, he could coach them to find the details they had been leaving out, and the key would work again.

Strasberg enjoyed the closeness that resulted from his students unblocking memories with each other. He was unashamed of the work, citing Freud as proof.

> Often when you re-live an emotional memory and use it in your work, it's one that has been sublimated, in the Freudian sense. When the emotion is released, the feelings remain, but the block is eliminated. It's freed. You feel as if you've been absolved. The therapeutic value in art is the living out of emotions that made you feel guilty, for example, or have been otherwise stifled . . . All art is revelation.[14]

Others complained the time it took to recall the emotion on stage took them away from connection with their scene partner. This phenomenon is problematic on stage, but it doesn't matter in film. Perhaps this is why so many Method actors found success in film. They are able to recreate an emotion in a believable way take after take. Since the camera doesn't often encompass more than one actor at a time, the connection with a scene partner is not as important.

Adjustments

Strasberg sometimes used what he called adjustments to help his actors in tricky stage moments. These adjustments were not directly related to memory, but came from personal understanding of circumstances. For instance, once, when an actor could not get angry enough on stage using emotional memory activities, Strasberg asked the actor what made him angry. He answered that seeing someone else being wronged always got him angry. Strasberg instructed the actor to imagine someone close to him being wronged. That adjustment worked to achieve the results needed.

Adjustments and affective memory were not required in stage moments where the actor was successful at creating truthful emotions. In fact, Strasberg reserved those techniques only for problem moments. "When you're in trouble and things aren't working, then use what you've learned to create the proper reality. Either way you take risks, have courage, and let your truth come out."[15]

Improvisation

Once an actor had worked through emotional memory activities, they were ready for scene work. One activity Strasberg liked to do with casts was to improvise scenes that did not appear in the play. For instance, if he was working on *The Cherry Orchard*, he might have the actors have a picnic in the orchard five years before the beginning of the play, imagining the setting and creating a history together.

He also led improvisations of scenes actually in the play not using the author's words so the actors could respond honestly to the actions of the play. The author's words would be substituted later. Strasberg also liked to assign improvisations where the actors were asked to act out a theme of the play rather than the plot.

He thought improvisation stimulated genuine responses in the actors. He wrote,

Many actors believe that they truly think on the stage. They do not accept the premise that their thought is tied only to the memorized lines of dialogue. In the process of training or of rehearsal, I will often deliberately change objects, partners, or other details and demonstrate to them that they go right on doing and saying what they have prepared to do. Often an actor enters a scene and, because he already knows the outcome, is playing toward that end. By improvising, the actor finds a way to play the scene more logically and convincingly.[16]

Director's Role

The Method teaches that directors should be in control of what happens on stage. Method actors are conditioned to respond easily and quickly to a director's wishes. Unlike the System, where it is the actor's job to analyze the text, in Strasberg's Method, the director has that responsibility. The Method frees the actor from script analysis, and sends them instead to work on whatever personal experience will enable them to create the needed effect on stage. Strasberg said, "In the theatre, the director with complete authority is an absolute necessity."[17]

However, the actor is responsible for doing the work of improvising in their own rehearsals, making decisions, and coming up with ideas for their character. They should not, however, try to articulate their theories to the director. Instead, the actor must use their theories in rehearsal while following the director's instructions so the director can see the actor's ideas of the role. This avoids misunderstanding. If the director asks for an adjustment, the actor should be able to accomplish the changes without discussion or dissent.

The Controversy About The Method

Contemporary teachers rightly feel there is need to be cautious with plenty of Strasberg's techniques. He is not purely to blame for all of the bad in Method Acting techniques, but he was the most visible, driving force of it. His intentions were good, but the results have been harmful to many. In the words of Cynthia Baron, who studied the impact of the Method extensively,

> Between the summer of 1931 and the summer of 1934, Strasberg's insistence that actors relive traumatic personal experience had come to be seen as 'a destructive burden,' because 'almost everyone had a painful tale to tell.' Younger players . . . were reduced 'to a pulp'; even established performer Morris Carnovsky 'wandered around like a white ghost after some emotional memory sessions'; and he also determined that a reliance on emotional memory 'dissipated its effectiveness.' [Some Group members] saw that Strasberg's approach led to 'a number of physical and emotional breakdowns among the members' and they objected to Strasberg's Method because it involved 'digging into [one's] subconscious life and not with trained psychiatrist.' By summer 1934, 'the inner turmoil created by [Strasberg's] confusing and painful obsession with emotional memory was undermining the confidence of the company in themselves and in their director.'[18]

It got so bad that one actor, Ruth Nelson, having witnessed Strasberg's emotional abuse, got up on stage and stated she was going to kill him. He ran out of the theatre, and someone else took over that particular show for the remainder of its rehearsal period. No one came to his defense.

Stella Adler's own assessment was "Many of the actors from the beginning suffered strain, despite the importance of relaxation in actor's work. to a large extent, this was because the actor was asked through the use of this 'Affective Memory' or emotional substitution to deal consciously with that part of himself which was intended to remain unconscious."[19]

In a more recent interview, Britney Spears revealed why she no longer acts.

> My problem was . . . with what acting did to my mind . . . I started Method acting—only I didn't know how to break out of my character. I really became this other person . . . I ended up walking differently, carrying myself differently, talking differently. I was someone else for months while I filmed *Crossroads*. Still to this day, I bet the girls I shot that movie with think, *She's a little . . . quirky*. If they thought that, they were right.
>
> That was pretty much the beginning and end of my acting career, and I was relieved . . . I hope I never get close to that occupational hazard again. Living that way, being half yourself and half a fictional character, is messed up. After a while you don't know what's real anymore.[20]

There are techniques to de-role. If you ever try Method Acting, please learn and use these techniques.

I hope you read this chapter with the curiosity of a scholar and the interest of an actor who wants to learn everything that will help you grow in performance. Please also be sure to keep yourself safe both mentally and physically as you work. I, and your acting teachers, want you to find the art in yourself without bringing your trauma into the theatre. I strongly encourage each of you to find a good therapist and maintain a lifelong habit of working on yourself, be mentally as healthy and stable as possible, AND act with honesty and conviction on stage. If you are ever in an acting class or rehearsal situation that asks you to violate your memories in a way that feels damaging, get out. It isn't worth it. Your body doesn't know the difference between simulated trauma and real trauma. You don't need to sit naked in a circle or discuss your experience with sexual assault in an acting class. Nor do you need to weep in class about a painful divorce or betrayal in order to find your character's pain. Please don't. Find a teacher who will help you work safely.

Just as you would walk out of an acting situation where real firearms with real bullets were being used on stage, walk out of an acting situation that puts your mental health in jeopardy.

Lee Strasberg's Legacy

Lee Strasberg spent his career trying to elevate and raise the standards of the field of acting. Lola Cohen, who worked closely with Strasberg in the last five years of his career and later wrote a book with transcripts of his acting classes, said that he was driven to push students to accomplish more than they thought possible.

> His expectation of seriousness, discipline and passion in the student was manifest in his energetic urgings, praise, and exhortations in which he used humor, wit, and sometimes biting commentary. Some students took his comments personally, although that was not his intent. Throughout his teaching process . . . logical, truthful, and believable dramatic behavior was made possible on stage, and it further enabled actors to achieve those values and results in performance after performance.[21]

Although his Method has earned a poor reputation in contemporary society, his work in the latter half of the twentieth century forever impacted the art of acting.

Discussion Starters and Journal Prompts

- Summarize the impact of Method Acting on the latter half of the twentieth century. Do you see any of its effects remaining in today's acting culture? What do you think made Strasberg's Method so popular in its time? Did you find anything in The Method compelling for you as a performer?

The Tools for your Toolbox

Activity—Relaxation

- Say: "Find a comfortable position where you might be able to fall asleep."
- "Curl your toes and uncurl them, relaxing all tension in the toes."
- "Rotate your ankles and relax them, releasing all tension."
- Continue through the body, relaxing each part in turn.
- Strasberg paid particular attention to three places:
    - "Imagine the tension melting away from your temples, the place we put tension when we are trying to think too much."
    - "Relax the bridge of your nose where we put tension because our eyes are moving around so much."
    - "Relax the muscles from the sides of the nose that connect to the mouth and chin, the muscles that work our face in our tics, like chewing our lips or sucking our cheek in."
- When they are completely relaxed, go to a student and lift and drop their arm. If it doesn't drop, then it isn't relaxed. Try this with several students.
- If they aren't relaxed, have them tense the muscles of the arm as tightly as possible for a moment, and then have them relax it. "Sometimes the way to find relaxation is the opposite." After they tense and relax, try lifting and dropping the arm again to see if it worked for them.
- While your students are in this relaxed state, say: "listen to the sounds in the room. Listen deeply to everything that can be heard."
- "Imagine you are in orbit around the earth in a vessel with sound controls."
- "Turn up the knob to listen to all of the laughter on earth. Is there a lot of laughter? How varied are the voices and cadences of laughter?"
- "Turn down the laughter and turn up the crying."
- "Relax the bridge of your nose, your facial muscles including your temples."
- "Turn down the crying and turn up the sounds of lovers whispering to each other."

- "Switch to the sounds of gunshots and war."
- "Notice that some of the noises we listened to were real, and some were imagined."
- Discuss: "What did you learn about your powers of relaxation?"

Activity Note

Much of Strasberg's work is now considered dangerous. Affective memory work is not recommended even as an experiment.

23

Frank Silvera

The Person

Frank Silvera was born in Kingston, Jamaica on July 24, 1914. His father was a Spanish Sephardic Jew and his mother was native Jamaican. This made him feel out of place in every setting because he was neither Black nor White. However, his appearance was such that he was often not believed when he claimed his Black heritage. He could pass as white, but didn't want to. He considered himself to be Black and wanted to help Black actors find humanity and recognition.

He emigrated to the United States in childhood. His racially ambiguous appearance allowed him to play non-Black roles. Luckett writes: "He was dismayed and rightfully disappointed with the racism that Blacks endured in the entertainment industry. The fact that Black actors were almost always hired to portray demeaning roles and had very few options to receive formal acting training compelled Silvera to begin coaching many Black actors and to provide a space for them and others to train."[1]

He tried to do research, but he couldn't find any Black actor-specific books in the Boston Public Library. So, he decided to study how to be an actor without considering race. He looked to other Black actors who had succeeded as well as all the acting techniques he could find. Through much hard work he became a successful actor. His Broadway debut was in 1945 in the play *Anna Lucasta*. He became a respected Broadway actor and had more than forty roles in film and 150 on television.

In 1952, Silvera gave a speech at the Television Authority Convention clearly laying out the plight of Black members of society because of their exclusion or stereotypical portrayal on screen. White people who had no contact with Black people believed these stereotypes, which negatively impacted the Black experience in life. This speech could have ruined Silvera's career. It didn't.

He attended University of California at Santa Barbara, teaching a course for high school and college theatre teachers there.

He developed his Theatre of Being while playing King Lear in 1963, the role that earned him a nomination for best Broadway actor of the year. That same year he founded the American Theatre of Being in Los Angeles where he trained actors in his method. This school was a low-cost program, and more than half of his students attended on full or partial need-based scholarships. Silvera helped found several other acting groups in Los Angeles, New York, and Boston during the last few years of his life. He died in 1970.

The Method

The goal of the Theatre of Being is for the actor to experience their character rather than portray them. Silvera wanted to help the Black artist remove stereotypes and create real characters that represent people who have not been acknowledged in society.

Shakespeare

In 1963, Silvera was acting in a Shakespeare play while also being involved in the Civil Rights movement and the March on Washington. He noticed that Shakespeare's writing reveals the chaos of human nature. The characters in *King Lear* encounter people who have differences from them. Silvera realized that "Lear was forced to acknowledge he needed other people,"[2] and he believed white people could also acknowledge their existence was dependent on the lives of Black people. As Silvera studied Lear, he saw Shakespeare's characters had the same tendency as modern humans to build compassion and empathy towards others as they understood them better. As he processed this ability of people to grow in understanding with exposure to people who were different, he changed his personal tendency to sit and accept the current reality. Instead, he concentrated his efforts on improving the lives of Black people both in the theatre and in society by changing the way they are depicted on stage and film.

Silvera's movement started with attempting to improve the training of Black actors so they could meet the expectations of the American theatre. In 1960s America, there were very few training programs for actors of color. His Theatre of Being trained an integrated group of actors that were majority Black. His school was recognized by Actor's Equity, affording this group professional status. His training was integrated, but not specific to Black actors. He wanted to help society accept the human bond we all share, so the training his artists received was not specific to Black artists, instead focusing on the training all human artists would benefit from.

He felt that accurate images of people of color were the most effective way to increase empathy in society. He understood that changing laws would only treat the symptoms of racism. He wanted to make lasting change, so he focused on the root cause of racism instead. Because African Americans were not portrayed in the media, their very Being was denied. This absence led to a lack of understanding, leading society to ban people of color from their establishments and mistreat them. In a brochure about his acting school, he addressed the question of why his school was necessary. "WHY? Because responsible theatre can enlighten, ennoble, and liberate our humanity ... Because cultural genocide can only be prevented by the communication of accurate images—the strengths and foibles, passions and compassions—of the varieties of ethnic and racial existence ... And, because of LOVE."[3]

Being

One of Silvera's tenets of acting is that actors must not seem to be, but actually BE. He taught his students to create a complete existence for their characters that he called *Being*. That state of Being, in his experience creates empathy and compassion for the character in the actor. Silvera defined a "being" actor as an actor who can identify with the character and their point of view. This identification leads to the ability to portray the character truthfully. By so closely identifying with the character, the actor and character merge, creating a complete Being.

In the United States, the omission of Black bodies in portrayals of normal life pushed the Black culture into a state of invisibility. One scholar paraphrased Silvera's position, "this segment of the nation's populace has been thwarted in achieving its full Being and forced to endure real circumstances in unreal existences."[4] When a person's existence is denied, they are forced to live a partial, or *skinless* existence. An actor's job is to bring a character into being, avoiding the skinless portrayal.

As an actor preparing for the role, Silvera coached his actors to emphasize nuance and fully embodying the character while empathizing with them. The actor was taught to believe the character is a human with a message for the actor to give their voice and body to until the actor's perception merges with the character's. Silvera believed the depiction of accurate humans on stage could purge the audience and society through catharsis into accurate understandings of others, including people of other races. Through realistic portrayal, audiences are able to understand the humanity of others they previously dismissed or ignored.

The character development that Silvera sought was deeper than simply making a character real. That portrayal had the intention of teaching the world what it was like to live in someone else's skin, creating empathy. "Silvera trained his actors to stop portraying and showing symbols, and to strip away the 'seeming to be' so his audience would know what they heard and saw was a real happening and was a truth. It was honest. It was felt. It was experienced."[5] In that experience, understanding of the humanity of each person would be realized.

In a pamphlet about his method, Silvera wrote:

> The art of the actor in
> A Theatre OF BEING
> Consists in so involving an audience in the
> NOW HAPPENING EXPERIENCE
> That the conventional references are shed
> And they are moved to participate
> And thereby become
> Enlightened and
> Enriched
> By the experiences they join[6]

This enriching experience of enlightenment could only happen if the character existed as a real figure on the stage.

> 'Being,' theatrically to Silvera, was for 'King Lear' or 'Othello' to appear on stage themselves without anyone questioning their reality. That is to say, the portrayal was not a portrayal in the traditional sense but an experience of the character, through being, so realistic that the audience could not or would not consider it as a performance but be so involved or consumed as to enter with the performers into the staged reality.[7]

Beyond Stanislavski

Silvera focused on concentration and motivation as Stanislavski did. He wanted truth in performance. Neither teacher wanted actors to use stereotypical gestures or portrayals on stage. Neither of them thought that a hand behind the ear to hear better was truthful. Stanislavski wrote that an actor should imagine themselves in the place of the character, Silvera wanted his actors to BE the character.

There are some significant differences between their techniques. For example, Silvera asked his actors to delve deeply into the character, the playwright, and the culture and politics of the character's world, just like Stanislavski, but he did not allow them to look into their own past. He felt it was self-defeating to bring an actor's past trauma into the theatre. Silvera pointed out that people have a hard enough time talking through their problems with a therapist, so how would using these experiences make them better communicators on stage? Actors should instead seek what could be true on stage rather than what was true in their past. Stanislavski did not fixate on using past experiences in actor preparation, but it was one of the tools he taught.

Perhaps a more important difference between Silvera and Stanislavski was the end goal of their life's work. Stanislavski was seeking Truth in Art. He was not trying to change society through his methods, bringing acceptance of underrepresented people through his work. Silvera was.

Silvera in Rehearsal

Silvera felt it is important to take time with the process. Nothing was just a short exercise. He began each rehearsal with breathing or meditation exercises that usually lasted more than two hours. Then, as he worked with his actors, Silvera would push them to find the truth through their experience of the author's words. He would say to his actors, "go to the challenge . . . what does it take for you to open up your mind and deal with the word to find the experience?"[8] Lines were not important in rehearsal, because Silvera believed they would become the true words of the character. By the end of the process, no ad-libs were allowed. If an actor could not find their line, he would sometimes release the other actors and work one-on-one with the actor with the problem, helping them find the reason they were blocked in that moment and helping them mentally bridge from the moment before to the missed line.

One of his actors, Louis Gossett, characterized the work Silvera did with him as career changing. He said, "Frank Silvera is the man singularly most responsible for opening up my instrument, so that I could be able to see the endless possibilities of achieving incredible momentum as an Actor."[9] This momentum was an important part of Silvera's work. The actor needed to be in the moment and feeling the forward motion and truth of the scene. Another actor, Esther Rolle, felt that working with Silvera permanently impacted his actors. She also described the momentum of Silvera's work that Gossett mentioned, "He insists that you go back, beyond the confusion of current meanings, to the original and Be. If you have the courage to do this you are forever changed, and your acting and your very being are better for it. It's like getting out from under a great load."[10]

Like some other acting teachers, Silvera had some unusual methods that required the actors to simply go with his ideas. Once, he had his cast move in together, share chores, and spend time talking about their feelings about the other characters during their rehearsals.

Frank Silvera's Legacy

Frank Silvera's concepts in acting intentionally went beyond the work of his actors. He wanted to both make a place for Black artists in culture, and change culture at the same time. Silvera's Theatre of Being had the goal of enhancing the status of the Black American in media with the goal of changing cultural understanding of African Americans in every American household. Tommie Stewart, the premier scholar of Silvera's work claimed that Silvera "questioned, experimented, and tampered with the universality of man through theatre."[11] He believed that if Americans were exposed to the truth, not academically, but in their souls, racism would be removed from society.

Frank Silvera was part of a movement that led first to including Black people in media at all, then to helping bring those depictions closer to reality rather than caricature.

Tips for taking this method further

- Apply to study the Theatre of Being at the College of Visual and Performing Arts at Alabama State University, a HBCU.

Discussion Starters and Journal Prompts

- Explore the depictions of Black people in the media when you were a child. Perhaps explore other depictions of underrepresented people. Were the depictions you consumed accurate? Did they help you grow in empathy? If you could change something about how a category of people are depicted in the media, what would that change be?
- Summarize Silvera's Theatre of Being. What steps could you take to approach Silvera's ideal in your own work?

24

Barbara Ann Teer

The Person

Barbara Ann Teer was born in St. Louis, Illinois in 1937. Her parents were teachers and activists. She was a dancer first, taking dance classes with her sister at their aunt's private dance school. Teer was a talented dancer, and she planned to earn her way onto the stage and into a big city with her gift. She earned her bachelor's degree in dance education at the University of Illinois at Urbana-Champaign at the age of nineteen. After that, she studied modern dance in Europe, took pantomime classes from Étienne Decroux in Paris, worked as a dance captain for Agnes DeMille on Broadway, and performed as a dancer in Brazil before a knee injury ended her dance career. She turned to acting, training with Sanford Meisner. She had several notable acting jobs and a few minor film roles.

She found herself in the unenviable position of being a talented Black actor in a white theatre. She chose to style her hair in an Afro and refused to change it to a more white hairstyle in order to get roles. This left her mostly unemployed as an actor. At one point when she did have a role in a play with an all-Black cast, she noticed and commented on the fact that the crew and production team were all white. She was dismissed for being militant.

During this time, she was dismayed by what she saw and experienced. One article described how she felt, "The Western dance aesthetic had no room for jazz . . . and as for the plays she did, she felt they 'never dealt with me as an individual. And since white people were writing all the plays, you would get one-dimensional characters—the Black people anyway.'"[1]

Not only did Teer suffer discrimination because of her race, she was also fighting an uphill battle because she was a woman. Men of all races dismissed and denied her efforts because of her gender. The men in charge didn't know what to do with her brilliant power and light. She did not diminish herself to meet their expectations and make them comfortable. This didn't always work in her favor.

She began to teach in 1964, working with youth at the Group Theater Workshop which later became the Negro Ensemble Company. She felt the acting techniques she had been taught were not helping the Black youth she was working with. Her technique did not know how to channel the power and emotion of Blackness. One biographer wrote,

> By the late 1960s, Teer had grown disenchanted with the direction Black theatre was taking and the limited roles that she was being offered. She felt that Black theatre needed to be grounded in the

realities of Black people and in 'non-Western' performance traditions. She sought a theatre that would nourish the spirits of Black people rather than feed the commercial theatre with its emphasis on reaching the Broadway stage.[2]

She felt that the roles available to Black women were demeaning, presenting them as "jezebels" or slaves. She wanted them to create their own theatre where they could represent themselves as they really were.

Knowing that Western theatre was built on the denial of African roots in theatre, focusing on Greek influences instead, she published a Manifesto in 1968 entitled *The Great White Way Is Not Our Way–Not Yet*. In it she cut ties with establishment theatre and argued for the establishment of a Black theatre in Harlem that would nurture the Black creative soul. And then she acted, founding what would become the National Black Theatre (NBT) of Harlem that same year. Rather than trying to fit in with, and meet the expectations of American theatre, her company could follow their own roots and find legitimacy in their own community's approval. The training in this theatre utilized African American cultural traditions instead of Eurocentric ones. This work was difficult, and required them to work without performances for the first two years as they established a Black theatrical standard that is based on the Black lifestyle.

They created six goals:[3]

1. the creation and perpetuation of a Black art standard
2. eliminating the competitive aspect of commercial theatre
3. re-educating audiences
4. restoring spirituality and a cultural tradition that had been stripped from Blacks in America
5. creating an alternate system of values to the Western concept
6. creating a Black theory of acting and liberation

She encouraged her students to work on changing themselves from the inside out rather than trying to change the world around them to feel happier. She said, "Learn to stop taking your relational cues from the outside world. Begin taking all your cues from the 'heart.' Ask yourself the questions: What do I care about? What are my concerns? What is my commitment?"[4]

The NBT was located in Harlem, a predominantly Black neighborhood, and was intentionally established there to nourish Black people. Her students were predominantly Black, but also Hispanic and other races as a small minority. She was their "warrior mother" who practiced "ruthless compassion."[5] and her goal was the communion of all races, creeds, and colors—with an emphasis on African ways of being. The work her students did was unapologetically rooted in the culture and history of Black people: ritualistic, spiritualistic, and improvisational in nature.

In 1972, Teer received a Ford Foundation Fellowship which allowed her to travel to Africa where she spent most of her trip in Nigeria being initiated as a Yoruba priestess. This training rooted her acting methods in Afrocentric mission and curriculum. After this trip, she made frequent visits to Nigeria, other African countries, and the Caribbean.

In 1986, President Ronald Reagan declared the NBT a national treasure when he awarded a NEA Challenge Grant to the organization. When she died in 2008, Teer was seventy-one. Her homegoing celebration was a joyful, colorful procession of people from all walks of life that traversed from the NBT to the Hudson River. Teer's Theatre is still New York's oldest company devoted to Black theatre.

The Method

Teer's method is called the Teer Technology of the Soul. Teer claimed that soul, "is the awesome gift, a cultural phenomenon that swells up inside where the spirit resides. It can be present when a person is in touch with the divine energy of God."[6]

The Technology of the Soul focuses on six goals:

1. Self-affirmation—She had her students look into mirrors every day and admire their bodies, as well as asking them to do anatomical research so they could become more and more informed about each part of their bodies.
2. Cooperation—She pushed her students to be engaged with each other, their culture, and their community. Church attendance as a group was required, as was attendance at the Apollo comedy club, and at social functions at local bars. Community service in Harlem was also required.
3. Education—She educated her students on the histories and cultures of Black people from many countries.
4. Spirituality—She had her students study spiritual release and meditation which encouraged them to take time for themselves to get in touch with their feelings, finding harmony between body, mind, and spirit. This training included visits to Black Pentecostal churches and knowledge about the occult.
5. Values—She worked collaboratively to create Black values for theatre that were not based on the white establishment theatre.
6. Liberation—She taught her students to claim their power, and resist the notion that they are oppressed. Rather than living as victims, they were taught to seek better pay instead of bemoaning their poverty, and to control their energy for fearless performance.

The goal of Teer's method for Black actors was to get them to a place where they cared more about their own internal sense of worth than the approval of others. This did not mean that she was satisfied with selfish students, focused only on themselves. An important part of their work was community service.

Terminology

Part of what Teer did as she founded the NBT was create a new way of talking about the art. She wasn't interested in making Black people fit the container that White people had created and gatekept. "Much of Teer's approach has involved changing the terminology and definitions used to describe the NBT. She invoked associations in labeling the NBT a 'Temple of Liberation, designed to preserve, maintain, and perpetuate the richness of the Black life-style.' Teer called the NBT's plays 'revivals' or 'rituals.'"[7] She sometimes called her performers liberators.

Performance Goals

Teer's NBT set five goals for performance. These goals all had the intention of liberation for the performers as well as the audience. Because of this, every production of the NBT had to meet all five goals:[8]

1. RAISE THE LEVEL OF CONSCIOUSNESS by liberating spirits and strengthening minds of all involved.
2. BE POLITICAL by dealing with existing oppression in a positive way.
3. EDUCATE by bringing knowledge already within the person to the surface and giving new knowledge and truth.
4. CLARIFY ISSUES by enlightening the participants about why many negative conditions and images exist in their community, thus eliminating negative conditions while strengthening positive conditions.
5. ENTERTAIN.

In order to meet these goals the actors had to discover the secret of soul. Teer taught the secret of soul is found in going down into self and the earth to create movement, praise, singing, and a release of the spirit. The soul is grounded and derives its power from the earth.

Teer wanted the audience to be involved in the performance in such a way that that they would be liberated and reclaim their spiritual freedom. She believed active involvement would bring freedom to both actors and spectators. The spiritual community of these performances often included planned and spontaneous audience interaction.

Stanislavski

Teer asserted Stanislavski's use of the *Magic If* was counterproductive to Black Americans because imagining they were living in a character who had not experienced racism or who could get a prestigious job would make them angry rather than allow them to live the truth of a different character. This tool of The System created an additional layer of negativity a Black actor had to deal with before they could do the work of acting. Instead, she encouraged them to study their roots, or soul. She believed researching the history and cultures of Black people in America, Africa, South America, the West Indies, Guyana, Haiti, and Trinidad helped her community in self-discovery and the establishment of a Black art standard.

Barbara Ann Teer's Legacy

One scholar wrote that "Teer's intellectual and artistic endeavors redefined the revolutionary theater of the Black Arts Movement by incorporating a holistic approach to performance that privileged the spiritual, artistic, and psychological liberation of both participants and performers."[9] Her work improved the lives of many actors and created a place for re-defining art on the terms of the artist. Her theatre still stands as a testament to her legacy.

That theatre, the National Black Theatre, claims its rich heritage and history,

> More than five decades after its founding, NBT's core mission remains the same: to be the premier producer of transformative theatre — theatre that enhances African American cultural identity by telling authentic, autonomous, multifaceted stories of the Black experience. NBT is now envisioned as a means to educate, enrich, entertain, empower and inform national consciousness around social justice issues that impact our communities.[10]

They are doing this with great success, even transferring their work to Broadway. Teer's vision of creating art that would nourish Black artists, and educate the wider world is a reality.

Tips for taking this method further

- Study the history and culture of Black people from all over the world.
- Find ways to affirm yourself and your wild spiritual, emotional, artistic soul through repeated affirmations and radical acceptance of you.

Discussion Starters and Journal Prompts

- How do you feel about Teer's approach to reforming establishment theatre by creating a separate theatre movement? What are the arguments for abandoning the negative to start fresh *vs.* the arguments for transforming the theatre from within? Did she have other good options?
- What is the value of Teer's warrior mother approach of ruthless compassion? Can you find a way to apply this to your own practice?
- Both Teer and Silvera taught that some of Stanislavski's methods were counterproductive to Black actors. Do you agree with this?

The Tools for your Toolbox

Activity—Teer Acting Class Sampler

- Say: "Before you take your place in class, first hug yourself, then hug every other person in the room, then hug yourself again."

- "Take out your phone and turn it to selfie mode. Repeat two of Teer's mantras to your image:
    - "Hello, beautiful, you are Somebody."[11]
    - "I am not ugly. I am a human being made in the image of God. God is beauty; therefore, I am beauty . . . I am not ignorant. I am a learned individual. Much of my education has involved misrepresentation of the truth but I am embracing true knowledge; ignorant people do not embrace true knowledge; therefore, I am not ignorant."[12]
- "Now, sit quietly, breathing in positive energy and breathing out negative."
- Say: "Teer's methods encourage actors to get in touch with their power. You can transform your life, increasing your ability to attract, hold prosperity, life, happiness, and joy."
- Play African drum pieces of various West Indian, African, and South American artists.
- Say: "Move to the music."
- "Show (love, pride, joy, ecstasy) in your body movements."
- Perhaps read or recite poetry while they move, guiding them in various ways.
- Discuss: "What did that feel like? Why did you move the ways you moved? Teer said, 'The Evolutionary Movement was designed for the student to experience his body as a 'cosmic miracle,' so that his self-consciousness would dissolve. Through this experience the student would begin to know more about his body and thereby be more exuberantly alive.'[13] Did you experience this?"

25

Susan Batson

The Person

Susan Batson was born in 1943 in Massachusetts to noted Civil Rights activist Ruth M. Batson and her husband John. She was part of the theatre world from the age of eight when she began working at Adele Thane's Boston Children's Theater. She attended Emerson College and earned a degree in theatre arts. Afterwards she earned a fellowship to train with Uta Hagen and Herbert Berghof in New York. She was an original cast member of the Broadway musical *Hair*.

Batson is a member of the Actor's Studio and has studied with an impressive list of twentieth-century acting teachers including Harold Clurman and Lee Strasberg. Her method is rooted in the Americanized version of Stanislavski as taught by Lee Strasberg.

Racism played a large role in holding her back from roles she could have earned. She worked hard, and was impressive as an actress. Despite hardship, she persisted in seeking roles and played roles in at least eleven movies and was featured on television in more than a dozen episodes, including an appearance in a 2017 episode of *America's Next Top Model* and a 1991 episode of *Law & Order*.

She founded the Susan Batson Studio with her son Carl Ford in 1996 where she still offers workshops. She has coached Nicole Kidman, Oprah Winfrey, Tyler Perry, Tom Cruise, Zac Efron, Chris Rock, Jamie Foxx, Liv Tyler, Jennifer Connelly, Kirsten Dunst, Common, Janet Jackson, Rihanna, and many other well-known performers.

Batson has received a New York Drama Critics Award, an LA Drama Critics Award, and an Obie Award. She continues to work as an actress and teacher.

The Method

Batson is a woman with a knack for helping actors find their characters. She writes,

> Acting is a craft—a disciplined art form that uses everything that makes an individual artist unique—from the DNA up. When you can find the joy of using the good, the bad, the ugly, the evil, and the sublime in yourself to create a scripted character, you're on your way to expertly practicing this craft. The more you're willing to share the events and sensations that have made you who you are, the better an artist you will be.[1]

Batson teaches that every person creates a public persona to help them survive despite childhood trauma and conditioning. That public persona masks unfulfilled needs in the person's experience. Characters are the same. "Unfulfilled *Need* is the universal truth at the heart of all characters. There's an unfulfilled *Need* 'to be somebody' inside arrogant cruelty . . . There's an unfulfilled *Need* 'to be accepted' at the core of a loner's rebellious anarchy."[2] As an actor, you will find some characters are more aware of their unfulfilled need than others, but all of them have a need that is opposite of their public persona.

Your Instrument

Batson teaches that we are an instrument which requires us to take responsibility for ourselves in our work. Our instrument is made up of six elements:

1 Physicality—This is a flexibility and timeless physicality of body capable of creating a beautiful and effortless movement quality.
2 Intelligence—You use your brain to "make smart, specific, and truthful choices that embrace your character, the circumstances, and the story."[3]
3 Imagination—You have to leverage your imagination to put yourself in the circumstances of your character.
4 Emotion—The actor's job is not emoting, but releasing the truth of a sensation.
5 Sensory Faculties—the actor must store the physical reality of the sensory world of the character and use it on stage.
6 Empathy—Your ability to be generous and non-judgmental with your character are essential "It's a privilege to share your skin with a character."[4]

Acting is not therapy

While some acting teachers tell actors to leave their personal baggage at home or in the office of a therapist, Batson encourages her actors to use their baggage. She writes,

> Acting is not therapy. It's personally enlightening, but it's not therapy. In fact, a lot of what I encourage actors to do, a therapist would forbid. A therapist asks you to change, control or modify your behavior. I tell you to USE IT! Acting demands that you celebrate the wild, the sinful, or the painful places within you. Use your imagination to expose and lift what's already inside you into art.[5]

Character Development: The Journey of the Need

Every character has three dimensions: public persona, need, and tragic flaw. The need pushes a character to action. As the show progresses, the need also has fewer and fewer options to express itself as the script limits the circumstances. The public persona of the character covers up the need as best as it can, but the tragic flaw of the character makes that difficult. "In those climactic moments, the *Tragic Flaw* carries the greatest danger for the character. The *Tragic Flaw* also holds the greatest potential for redemption if the pressure of that jam-up can be relieved."[6] It is in the flaw of the character that we see what they are made of. Do they crumple because of it, or grow through it?

Batson insists that every person has these three dimensions, and the only way to overcome your own tragic flaw is to allow your need to live in the open, not allowing your public persona to rob you of open expression. This takes courage because self-analysis can be scary. But, Batson teaches that doing this work will unlock creative tools for you in character development. "Through this process of discovery you may even find new ways of building your own character and of identifying and maintaining your own moral center."[7]

The journey of the need is a seven-step process that each actor can use to analyze each character they play:

1. Define the root need of the character, finding a way to identify with this need by recalling how the same need was unfulfilled in your past.
2. Spend time recalling sensations of that unfulfilled need in relation to a person who could have met the need but didn't.
3. Figure out what that person could have done to meet the need but didn't. What are the obstacles and conflicts that prevented them?
4. Discover your own tragic flaw by asking yourself what happens when you can't solve your need?
5. Imagine your own inner child, and promise to protect that child's dreams. This will make accessing memories from the past safer for you as the actor.
6. Spend time recalling the sensations of a person who helped to meet your need at some point in the past.
7. Engage your imagination to visualize a world where the need has been fulfilled.

This process must remain private. It is not a communal experience. Batson insists this privacy will enable the actor to do better work with the character they are working on.

Incidentally, Batson insists this process must also be applied to props you use on stage. Ask yourself: What unfulfilled need does the prop represent? Why does it exist in your world? Does your need compel you to glance at it often? To handle it carefully? To keep it between you and others?

Sense Memory

Batson teaches that an actor's job is to find honest sensation in acting. Batson is particularly interested in leveraging the inner child to reach this goal. She teaches that children abandon themselves to made-up realities, and adult actors must do the same. Our inner child is "alive, energetic, and creative . . . every act of creation and imagination begins with our inner child."[8]
Batson entered the argument of the American giants Strasberg and Adler about using past trauma on stage by saying,

> from today's distance, their argument is moot. The truth of your actor's own life—the sights, sounds, feelings, sensations, thoughts, and dreams you carry inside of you—are what stock your memory *and* fuel your imagination. It's a waste of actors' personal resources not to utilize the energy and authenticity of their own lives . . . Sense Memory is a complement to the imagination, not an alternative to it. Imagination has to have fact and experience on which to feed.[9]

Batson studied with Strasberg, and has boiled down his techniques to a series of questions that an actor can self-guide themselves through to enliven a sense memory. First, the actor relaxes and locates the memory they want to use, then they ask themselves eleven questions:[10]

1. How long ago was it?
2. Time of year?
3. Time of day?
4. What clothing did I have on?
5. What did I need?
6. What were the conditions of the place I was in?
7. What will I always remember about the place?
8. If there was a person there: What was their strongest physical feature? Human quality? Rememberable actions and words of that person in the moment? What did I want to say to them that I didn't?
9. Did I repeat a behavior?
10. What words or actions did I hold back even though I wanted to do or say them?
11. Why didn't I do or say those things?

The goal of these questions is to stir up sensations, not just the idea of an emotion or an emotion itself. Batson insists that honest sensations must come first in communicating emotions. "If the sensation is strong and Honest, an actor will naturally communicate that emotion."[11]

Into-Me-See

The intimacy an actor has with their character and the audience is what Batson calls "into-me-see." It requires you to be open, exposing the truth of real sensations. There must be a feeling of safety for you, and a sense that there are no observers. In order to reveal yourself, you need to be able to let down your defenses.

Batson uses a technique for focusing the actor's attention on the fourth wall without thinking of the audience. She selects someone or something that brings strong feelings and carries a need. The reality of that person, place, or thing placed on the fourth wall has the ability to focus the actor's concentration towards the fourth wall without having to think about the audience. This placement on the fourth wall doesn't require visualizing the thing or person there, but simply allowing yourself to experience "a flow of sensation" in the body "a sensation of wanting to be with whatever it was"[12] just as you sometimes feel someone is with you in spirit, you can feel your imagined person or thing is there. There is an activity at the end of this chapter describing this process for you to try out.

Script Analysis

Batson uses and expounds on Stanislavski and Strasberg's script analysis methods. She teaches there are different sorts of beats (bits) and each beat has a purpose. Once an actor figures out which type each is, they can then follow the rules of that type of beat.

- Exposition: The actor understands that this beat is factual and necessary. This is the exposition where the conflict is set up. In this type of beat, the actor must simply tell the truth by stating the facts.
- Character Statement: This is like an adjective. The actor describes this beat with an action: "to charm," or "to joke," etc.
- Statement of Need: This type of beat is about the internal life of the character. The actions in this type of beat are more about need. A need "to reveal a weakness" or "to confess a feeling."
- Statement of Conflict: These beats require an aggressive action like "to force" or "to crush."
- Operative: These beats move the story forward. They are things like entrances or exits, stage directions. The actor's job is "to do as told in the script."

When she worked on a scene, Batson created a chart that had four columns. The first was to identify the beginning and end of each beat. The second was to describe which sort of beat it was (see above), the third was the action, the fourth was personalized material or notes to herself.

Monologue Preparation

Batson recommends actors have at least three monologues prepared for auditions. One needs to be comic, one dramatic, and the third should be classical. Whatever you select for those three should show you off. By show off, she doesn't mean you should be an over-actor. She means each monologue should have a beginning, middle, and end, giving you a chance to show your ability to tell a story. And as you prepare them, remember that "Each should be considered a multi-colored mini-drama created to give the actor a full plate, and the audience an elevated experience of traveling through 'the wilderness of human nature.'"[13] The full experience of your monologue isn't contained only in the words you speak. You must also build a backstory for your character in order to stimulate your imagination through the previous circumstances of your character, adding to the multi-colored mini-drama.

An important step for a Batson actor in monologue work is to do emotional flexibility preparation through emotional/sense memory activities intended to bring you closer to your truth.

Personalization is another step that can help with monologues. First, she tells her actors to think of a person from their lives that represents the unfulfilled need of their character. Once identified, the actor should think of:

1. the strongest physical feature of that person
2. their strongest human quality
3. what type of energy they project (warmth, anxiety, etc.)
4. something they said that stuck
5. identify what the actor needs from them, exploring until they can actively use that need on stage
6. imagine things the actor always wanted to say or do to the person, but didn't

7 imagine that person in front of the actor who then says to the image, "I see you as . . ." and fill in the blanks
8 next, the actor tells the image what they specifically need: "I need . . ."
9 finally, the actor tells the image who they are: "I am . . ."

Batson claims that as you work creating sensory conditions for your monologue, your truth will be found:

> Only great actors can make the proper Choices. The mediocre ones slide and glide about on the playwright's words. As an actor who begins using **Emotional/sense Memory, Personalization,** and **Sensory Condition**, you will have countless opportunities—not to float on seas of generalities and words, but to make specific choices of your own Truth that will bring your own unique sparks of realization into the playwright's written words.[14]

Susan Batson's Legacy

Susan Batson is a teacher and coach that has impacted the performances of many actors. Her legacy is in the expansion and teaching of Strasberg's Method from her own perspective.

Tips for taking this method further

- Enroll in courses at the Susan Batson Studio. Most of these are held online, so they are accessible to anyone.

Discussion Starters and Journal Prompts

- As you examine Batson's method, how do you see it as the same or different from Strasberg's Method? Are there key differences that make it safer?
- Do you see connections and direct contradictions between her work and the work of Frank Silvera and Barbara Ann Teer? How did she combat racism in a different way than these other practitioners?

The Tools for your Toolbox

Activity—The Wall

- Say: "Think of a person that has a strong unfulfilled need associated with them for your character. Perhaps the person is a parent who did not adequately meet your character's need for attention."

- "Now think of an object connecting that person and the unfulfilled need. The thing could be a cell phone that might distract the parent or a frisbee that the two of you could play with together, meeting the need of attention."
- "Now think of a place such as a childhood living room or backyard to set this need in."
- "Face the fourth wall and name the three elements of person, object, and place one by one. You don't need to speak loudly enough for others to hear you. This is a solitary exercise."
- Now ask a series of questions that they should answer silently to themselves:
    - "Embody your character and answer the following questions for yourself. What is the need this person represents for you?"
    - "What are your feelings about this person?"
    - "Describe the appearance, clothing, smell, feel of this person."
- Say: "Now associate the sensations of that person on the fourth wall."
- Now ask questions about the object:
    - "How does it feel to handle the object?"
    - "Think about textures, weight, color, temperature, etc."
    - "What is the need that is associated with the object?"
- Say: "Associate the sensations of that object on the fourth wall."
- Now repeat the activity with the place:
    - "What are the sensory elements of the place?"
    - "How is the place connected to the person?"
    - "What is the need associated with the place?"
- Say: "Associate the sensations of the place on the fourth wall."
- "Don't visualize these things but think of their essence and the need they represent as floating between yourself and the audience."
- "Now, sit on the stage and imagine your character is psyching themself up to make a phone call to the person on the fourth wall. When you're ready, pantomime picking up the phone and dialing."
- "Have an improvised conversation with that person, dropping into the intimacy of an honest phone call."
- "Don't drop your head or hide, but stay open to the essence of the person you're talking to between yourself and the audience. Have this quiet conversation where their character gets to say the thing they have always wanted to without being overheard."
- Discuss: "How did placing the essence of the unfulfilled need on the fourth wall feel for you? Batson encourages her actors to do this activity first for themselves, then for their characters. What do you like about this? Do you worry about it for your health and safety as an actor?"

Activity—Emotional Flexibility

- Gather your students and talk to them about the fact that Batson teaches her students to use Strasberg's sense memory activities. As you do this activity, remind them to stay aware of mental health and safety. They should stay away from memories that are recent or traumatic.
- Say: "Think of a time you felt betrayed and remember the sensory elements of the space around you at that time. Think about smell, taste, touch, sight, and sound. Focus on the senses, not the event."
- "Think about the person that you felt betrayed you. Focus on the sensory elements of the person, not the person themself."
- "Now focus on a sensation of disgust or revulsion."
- "Once you are in this state of feeling betrayed and a sense of disgust, imagine that you are Hamlet, returning home from college to attend your father's funeral. When you get home, you discover that your mother and uncle are in a relationship. They have encouraged you to cheer up and go back to school. You can hardly wait for them to leave. As soon as they leave, you say:

    Oh that this too, too solid flesh would
    Melt and thaw itself into a dew.
    Oh that the everlasting had not
    Fixed its cannons against self-slaughter
    Oh God—God!"

- "Perform these lines with the feelings and sensations from the emotional flexibility exercise."
- Discuss the use of past memories and personal experiences in performance. "Does it help? Is it healthy? Does moving to the sensations rather than the specifics make it better? Can a positive sense memory exercise help bring you out of this place of disgust and revulsion afterwards? Do you have other de-roling activities that help when pulling out of sense memory?"

26

David Mamet

The Person

David Mamet is a playwright, filmmaker, and author who was born in a suburb of Chicago in 1947. His mother was a teacher, and his father a labor attorney who was a child of poor Jewish-Russan immigrants, but achieved the American dream, finding success and financial freedom.

Mamet was always dramatic, and started performing early. He acted in plays and on television, and even had his own radio show for Jewish children. As a teen and young adult, Mamet had jobs as a cab driver, a magazine editor, and a busboy for The Second City (an improv theatre that is the training ground for many *Saturday Night Live* comedians). He studied at Goddard College, but credits his education to the Chicago Public Library where he read. He wanted to be a professional actor and even studied with Meisner for a year, but when he wasn't invited back for a second year, he realized he wasn't really an actor; so, he learned to write and direct in order to stay involved in theatre.

At twenty-four, he began to teach acting at Goddard College as an artist-in-residence. One person described his course,

> Mamet comes into the classroom and says, "Here are the rules: If you're not on time, get out. If you don't prepare the scene exquisitely, get out. If you ask student questions, I'll *throw* you out. One person can teach you how to act on this campus and it's me. If you want to learn how to act I'll be your teacher. If you have any other motives, get out."[1]

Despite his youth and arrogance, Mamet's teaching, playwriting, and directing began to get attention, and he was invited to teach at Yale Drama School and New York University. He and his students founded the Atlantic Theater Company that is a producing house and an acting school attached to NYU's BFA program.

Mamet has written at least forty plays, the first one in 1970. Not much later he captured the attention of the theatre world with a trio of off-Broadway productions: *The Duck Variations*, *Sexual Perversity in Chicago*, and *American Buffalo*. Later, he won the Pulitzer Prize for *Glengarry Glen Ross* and received an Academy Award nomination for *The Verdict*.

Never one to be quiet about his opinions, Mamet is pro-Israel and quick to point out anti-Semitism when he sees it. His outspokenness has made him a controversial figure for many reasons. From a young age he made himself the enemy of formal education, claiming that university training is a waste of time, upsetting academia. After being a liberal in his younger years, his political views shifted far right in the early 2000s, surprising and further frustrating left-leaning Americans. He argued against gun control laws, harshly criticized the NFL anthem protests, endorsed Donald Trump as a great president, and spoke in favor of legislation limiting the teaching of sexual orientation and gender identity in schools in Florida.

Despite the fact that his career is riddled with controversy, his philosophies on the theatre are worth examining and reacting to. He was, after all, reacting against the methods of his teachers, and breaking new ground for his actors—something most important figures do.

The Method

Mamet loves theatre, and he has a million critiques of it. He writes that the art form we love is full of difficulties and problems. Chief among these problems is the over-complication of the art of acting. He writes, "As actors, we spend most of our time nauseated, confused, guilty. We are lost and ashamed of it; confused because we don't know what to do and we have too much information, none of which can be acted upon; and guilty because we feel we are not doing our job."[2] In Mamet's mind, the answer to this nauseated state of being is to get on the stage and serve the text.

What is the Actor's Job?

Mamet writes that actors need speech training, the ability to move freely, find relaxation, and act on simple actions the text asks for. This simple formula, in Mamet's opinion, means an actor should not waste themselves in acting school, or try to dissect acting into methods requiring emotional turmoil, or bother with script analysis, or frustrate themselves trying to become a character. He believed these tasks are ultimately impossible and only produce guilt in the actor.

Mamet also teaches it is impossible to force anyone to feel anything. No one likes to be told how to feel, and no one can actually create an emotion in their real life, even if they want to. Do you know anyone who has learned to be happy simply because they wanted to? Mamet says there would be no need for therapists if humans were capable of creating desired emotions on command.

Mamet writes that when an actor forces an emotion in themselves on stage, the effort takes them out of the moment and puts them into their head. It isn't productive and leads either to guilt because they can't accomplish the emotions their teachers have requested, or to an inflated ego based on perceived success. Both of these remove the actor from being in the moment.

According to Mamet, the beginning and end of an actor's job is to "show up, and use the lines and his or her will and common sense, to attempt to achieve a goal similar to that of the protagonist."[3] He asks his actors to tell the story without making any personal comment on it. The actor's job is to speak for the character, not moralize.

Mamet on Stanislavski and Strasberg Techniques

In a chapter titled *Ancestor Worship*, Mamet claims the mental health and success of actors depends on their rejections of both Stanislavski and Strasberg's Methods of acting. "The Stanislavski

'Method,' and the technique of the schools derived from it, is nonsense. It is not a technique out of the practice of which one develops a skill—it is a cult."[4] He claims actors who found success through these manipulative methods of acting were successful because of natural talent, not training. After all, schools teaching these methods selected naturally talented students who could already act. He goes further, claiming these actors succeeded *despite* their training rather than *because of* it.

Mamet came out against many other tenets of System and Method. For instance, they taught concentration as a cornerstone of their methods. Mamet writes that concentration is self-absorption and boring for the audience. Besides, he says, you can't force yourself to concentrate. He also writes that trying to improve truthfulness on stage is counterproductive because it just complicates their acting.

Importantly, Mamet has a lot to say about emotions on stage. The audience goes to theatre to experience emotions, Mamet believes the actor should not. In fact, he claims it is impossible to live emotionally in given circumstances since emotions are unpredictable. We all idolize ourselves and think we will handle a cancer diagnosis with heroism. But the truth is not usually what we imagine.

Mamet asks us to not waste time delving into our sense memories or given circumstances. Our characters, by very nature of being in a play, are in the given circumstance of a crisis. Since we don't know what we would really feel in a crisis, we can't predict our character's emotions either. After all, Mamet reminds us, the work of a crisis moment in life is to *suppress* our emotions and deal with what is happening. For example, when a car accident happens we tell ourselves, "Stop freaking out and get out of the car. Act as calmly as possible while you talk to the other driver, exchange information, call the police, take pictures, call your parents and significant other and whoever is expecting you at this moment." Did emotion happen in this crisis? Certainly, but the events of the day are much more pressing than your desire to curl up into a ball and cry about the damage or the other driver's lack of car insurance. So, on stage, feeling the emotions in the midst of crisis can bring actors further from truth in performance.

Mamet tells us that our performance is not strengthened by intellectually analyzing the character arcs or trying to create emotional control in a moment. It takes bravery to step on stage with uncertainty, feeling underprepared, but since we cannot control the outcome of any moment, Mamet teaches his actors to just go for it with bravery. As you approach moments on stage, you will be forced to deal with what actually happens. You will see and feel things you did not expect. If you are trying to have control, what you achieve is only the illusion of control.

Actors cannot control what they believe on stage. If an actor is going onto the stage to play a scene where they find out their brother was killed in an accident, they *cannot* actually believe their brother has died. What they *can* do is imagine what that moment would be like. But actors don't understand this. Mamet says actors often feel they must stay in a "magical state of psychosis," forgetting that they are actors in a play "and somehow 'become' the characters. As if acting were not an art and a skill but only the ability to self-induce a delusional state."[5] Mamet compares our desire to forget we are acting to a musician or dancer trying to not know they are playing a violin or dancing. That is absurd. Performing art requires the artist to know what they are doing. We are performing choreography when we do our blocking. We are reciting lines when we speak them on stage. We should know what we are doing. It is uninteresting to the audience to watch a self-deluded person who thinks the stage is actually a colosseum.

Since you can't control so many things, Mamet encourages you to stop feeling guilty for not being able to control them, and stop believing that other actors are able to control them using technique. They can't. Start working on controlling the controllable. Find the actions that are like what the playwright suggested your character might do. Make these actions doable, and do them. That is your most important job. He wrote, "'Technique' is the occupation of a second-rate mind. Act as you would in your fantasy. Give yourself a simple goal onstage, and go on to accomplish it bravely."[6] Everything else is out of your control.

Auditions

Mamet believes the reason auditions are difficult is because theatre is meant to be in the presence of a supportive audience. Mamet claims the people gathered to cast the show are not there to create the communion of an audience. He thinks they are usually there looking at you as a potential waste of their time. It is easy to internalize the judgment we feel as we audition, and internalizing negative thoughts about your work is destructive to your success in the audition. Your job as an actor is to communicate the play to the audience, not to please casting directors, who can feel like the barrier between you and your goal of performance. In most cases, you cannot ignore the casting directors. You can, however, keep them in perspective. You are not working for their respect, but for your own. If you are asking yourself how to please them, you will fail.

Mamet's best advice to you about auditions is twofold: (1) Go make your own work which allows you to skip past the gatekeepers. (2) If you have to audition, enjoy yourself despite the casting team as if they were "an inevitable and preexisting condition, like ants at a picnic."[7] You are a unique human being with something to say. Say it, and don't internalize the criticism of the gatekeepers.

Rehearsals

Mamet cautions that rehearsal is not a place for intellectual work. Mamet believes rehearsals should be efficient and not waste time on script work or interpretation; the author already did that work for you. Mamet encourages simplifying rehearsal by focusing on two things: blocking and intentions. This work on intentions might seem contradictory, since he wrote so often about not intellectualizing, but he does want the actor to think about motivation. He says any action more difficult than "open that window" is too complex; but he also claims actors need to find what their characters want. The actor should reduce the character's desire to something actionable. For example, if you decide that Hamlet's objective is to learn what is rotten in the state of Denmark and restore order there, that actor might use the tools: "to interrogate, to confront, to negotiate, to review ... All of the above are simple physical *actable* objectives. They do not require preparation, they require *commitment*."[8]

Mamet teaches that an actor should go to rehearsal with mind and spirit ready to find and perform the actions of a character truthfully and simply, this practice in rehearsal means the actor will also perform them in front of an audience. Once you find your character's task in each scene, you may discover the task does not relate to the overarching purpose in the play. That is fine. Focus on one scene at a time, since the playwright took the time to create the overall structure. If you trust the work of the author, you don't have to spend time on looking at character arc.

You can find a simple action for each scene and do it. In fact, he states the words are much less important than your intention. Your job is to find a simple action for each scene, go onto the stage and do that action. Then, "simply open your mouth and let the words come out however they will—as if they were gibberish."[9] Mamet teaches that the actions, not the words, carry the meaning. Your actions conflict with the actions of your antagonist, creating drama. As you say the words that are set, it doesn't matter how you pronounce the words, Mamet believes the audience will understand what you mean, and that is all you need to focus on.

Habits of Good Character

In theatre, we use the word "character" to mean only one thing: the person you are portraying on stage. Mamet says that this is a false construction, since when you are on stage, you are yourself. Character is not a costume that can be taken off and put back on again when needed. Character instead is building your own self-respect for who you are. Mamet writes: "Act first to desire your own good opinion of yourself."[10] You can work to delight the audience and feel good about your character by moving your focus from being good at school, to being good on stage.

Anyone can develop good habits by repeating a desired behavior. Mamet says that actors should cultivate a few good habits:

- Cultivate the habit of compartmentalization. Leave the theatre at the theatre, and the street on the street.
- Cultivate the habit of generosity. Everyone is doing their best. It is pettiness to try to change someone else instead of yourself.
- Cultivate the habit of knowing what is controllable. Don't waste time being mad at yourself for something you can't change.
- Cultivate the desire to give yourself the gift of manageable self-improvement.
- Cultivate the habit of being proud of your accomplishments.
- Cultivate a love of theatrical skills. Practice theatre adjacent skills like juggling, tango, voice, etc.
- Cultivate a spirit of humility. As you work on things that are hard, you will find peace in knowing you have done as well as you could at a tough skill.
- Cultivate a habit of mutuality. As you work with your peers to create, you will be creating real theatre. This rising *with* your fellow artists instead of rising *above* your fellow artists will avoid the tendencies of loneliness and divisiveness in the theatre.

Audience

Mamet's advice about approaching an audience is simple. Don't underestimate or patronize them. "Now I've been working with audiences thirty years or more, in different venues. And I've never met an audience that wasn't collectively smarter than I am and didn't beat me to the punch every time. These people have been paying my rent, all my life. and I don't consider myself superior to them and have no desire to change them."[11] He adds, "the purpose of art is not to change but to delight. I don't think its purpose is to enlighten us. I don't think it's to change us. I don't think it's to teach us."[12] Your job as an actor is not to teach the masses. Serve the play.

Mamet doesn't think that studying theatre helps actors serve the play. He writes that your audience will teach you how to act and direct. If you go to grad school for theatre instead of going to the theatre to do theatre, you might even damage yourself as an artist. All you need to learn, he believes, you can learn by observation, tutoring, and personal practice. By performing in front of an audience, you learn about what works and what doesn't. If you pay attention, they teach you what you need to change and what to keep.

David Mamet's Legacy

Mamet's legacy is yet to be fully realized. He is a person who has encouraged actors to simplify their practice, and know what their role is. Maybe most importantly, he teaches that you shouldn't let anyone tell you not to be an artist. And he has lived his motto that "The theatre belongs not to the great but to the brash."[13]

Tips for taking this method further

- Read David Mamet's book *True and False*. It is an easy read, and will give you a much more full understanding of Mamet's acting philosophy.
- Try focusing your efforts on finding your own approval, cultivating good habits and serving the script/audience rather than seeking the approval of your teacher. Can you learn through being on stage and from your classes with the goal of artistry rather than validation?

Discussion Starters and Journal Prompts

- Summarize how Mamet is reacting against Stanislavski's System and the American's Method. In what ways are you compelled by his theories? In which ways do you disagree with him?
- Can you think of any ways in which Mamet actually agrees with other acting methods, though he says he does not?
- How do you feel about learning from someone you disagree with on some level? Do you think it is valuable to study a philosophy taught by a person who is canceled in popular culture?
- Mamet tells actors to cultivate eight habits. Which of them do you think are the most important? Why?

The Tools for your Toolbox

Activity—Just Act

- Read the following quote to your students:

    The actor is onstage to communicate the play to the audience. That is the beginning and end of his and her job . . . The actor does not need to 'become' the character. The phrase, in fact, has no meaning. There *is* no character. There are only lines upon a page. They are lines of dialogue meant to be said by the actor. When he or she says them simply, in an attempt to achieve an object more or less like that suggested by the author, the audience sees an *illusion* of a character upon the stage. To create this illusion the actor has to undergo nothing whatever. He or she is as free of the necessity of 'feeling' as the magician is free of the necessity of actually summoning supernormal powers. The magician creates an illusion in the minds of the audience. So does the actor.[14]

- Give them scenes to act with only a few minutes to look over the dialog.
- Discuss: "Did freeing yourself from the guilt of being underprepared or untalented help you on stage?"

Conclusion: Missing Chapters

I have worked to find new and diverse voices from the Global Majority to highlight in this book. I am keenly aware this book features too few women and too few people of color. The scope of this project didn't allow me to do primary research, so there are many gaps I hope to fill in future iterations. I am aware of a couple of coming projects that will help you in your quest for more methods from the Global Majority. I heard a rumor that Freddie Hendricks is working on publishing his method. A couple of his students have published some details about him in *Black Acting Methods*. One of these students, Dr. Sharrell Luckett is also currently working to publish her own acting method designed to highlight Afrocentric acting approaches.

Some of you may be aware of someone who has a useful method of acting that I did not cover. Please reach out to me to suggest their inclusion in future volumes or editions. I'm not hard to find on social media, through my place of employment, or through my publisher. I'm taking suggestions!

Or, perhaps you know someone personally who is doing exciting work right now. Document their work! Write about the exciting things that are happening under your nose so that the rest of us can benefit. I mourn the loss of the work of the undocumented. A word of affirmation to you: many teachers of acting don't think that they are creating a method that is valid beyond their classroom. They are often wrong.

Maria Ouspenskaya, a powerfully effective acting teacher with acting techniques of her own is not included in this book because she chose not to publish any of her own writing saying, "I do not believe that it is possible to learn acting from books . . . An actor masters his art in only two ways—first, by living, secondly, by practice."[1] This sentiment limited her work and influence to only those fortunate few who took a class from her during her lifetime. If you know someone like this, don't let their work go undocumented! If you are that person, please leave a legacy for future generations of actors. Don't let imposter syndrome take away your legacy.

Notes

Preface

1. Moore, xvi.
2. Spolin, *Theater Games for Rehearsal: A Director's Handbook*, 3.
3. Carnicke, *Stanislavsky in Focus*, 3.
4. Meerzon, 23.

Chapter One: Beginnings

1. Butler, xiv–xv.
2. Quintilianus, viii.
3. ibid., 345.
4. ibid., 364.
5. Bogart, *The Viewpoints Book*, 148–9.
6. Hill, 219.
7. Francis, *The Athenæum*, 219.
8. Allen, *The National Review*, 103.
9. Archer, *Masks or Faces*, 196–8.
10. Butler, xv.

Chapter Two: Konstantin Stanislavski

1. Cole, 484.
2. Stanislavski, *My Life in Art*, 458.
3. ibid.
4. Moore, 6.
5. Merlin, 18.
6. Stanislavski, *An Actor Prepares*, 78.
7. Moore, 30–31.
8. Stanislavski, *Building a Character*, 85.
9. Knébel, *La Palabra en la Creación Actoral*, 24.
10. Stanislavski, *An Actor Prepares*, 37.

11. Carnicke, *Dynamic Acting through Active Analysis*, xiv.
12. ibid., xx.
13. Stanislavski, *An Actor Prepares*, 13.
14. Moore, 35.
15. Carnicke, *Dynamic Acting through Active Analysis*, 153.
16. Thomas, 45.
17. ibid.
18. ibid., 113.
19. Moore, 18.
20. Stanislavski, *My Life in Art*, 569.
21. Barton, 131.
22. Stanislavski, *An Actor Prepares*, 33.

Chapter Three: Vsevolod Meyerhold

1. Pitches, 42.
2. ibid., 3.
3. Law, 97.
4. ibid., 231.
5. ibid., 124.
6. ibid., 99.
7. ibid., 125.
8. ibid., 103.
9. Pitches, 55.
10. ibid.
11. ibid., 61.
12. ibid.
13. ibid., 53.
14. ibid., 56–7.

Chapter Four: Jacques Copeau

1. Cole, 219.
2. Evans, 62.
3. Cole, 219.
4. Hodge, 53.
5. Cole, 222.
6. ibid.
7. Evans, 99.
8. Brestoff, *The Great Acting Teachers and Their Methods*. Vol. 2, 47.
9. Frank, 588–9.
10. ibid.

Chapter Five: Rudolf von Laban

1. Adrian, *Actor Training the Laban Way*, 161.
2. ibid., 162.
3. ibid., 23.
4. Ewan, *Laban's Efforts in Action*, 175.
5. ibid., 187.
6. ibid., 194.
7. Bloom, *The Laban Workbook for Actors*, 154.
8. Ewan, 126.
9. Bloom, 90.

Chapter Six: Michael Chekhov

1. Chekhov, *On the Technique of Acting*, 16.
2. ibid., 4.
3. ibid., 45.
4. ibid.
5. ibid., 46.
6. ibid.
7. Rushe, 103–4.
8. Chekhov, *Technique*, 36.
9. ibid., 89.
10. ibid., 56.
11. Hodge, 72.
12. Rushe, 54.
13. Chekhov, *Technique*, 137.
14. ibid., 26.
15. ibid., 95.
16. Petit, 33.
17. Petit, 39–41.
18. Chekhov, *Technique*, 33.
19. Rushe, 114.
20. Petit, 35.
21. Ashperger, 299.

Chapter Seven: Maria Knebel

1. Knebel, *Active Analysis*, 88.
2. Hodge, 103.
3. Hodge, 101.

4. Knébel, *Poética de la Pedagogía Teatral*, 12.
5. ibid., 34.
6. Knébel, *La Palabra en la Creacioón Actoral*, 17.
7. Knébel, *Poética*, 101.
8. ibid., 27.
9. Knébel, *Palabra*, 86.
10. Knebel, *Active Analysis*, 127.
11. ibid., 68.
12. ibid., 121.
13. ibid., 27.
14. Carnicke, *Dynamic Acting through Active Analysis*, 118.
15. ibid., 106.
16. Hodge, 111.
17. Hodge, 104.

Chapter Eight: Bertolt Brecht

1. Brecht, *Brecht on Theatre*, 9.
2. ibid., 14.
3. ibid., 187.
4. ibid., 45.
5. ibid., 94.
6. Lewis, 59.
7. Brecht, 95.
8. ibid., 173.
9. Hodge, 121.
10. Brecht, 201.
11. Brecht, 126.
12. "Epic Theatre . . ."
13. Brecht, 186.
14. ibid., 235.
15. Crawford, 263.
16. Harrop, 310.

Chapter Nine: Stella Adler

1. Clurman, *The Fervent Years*, 53.
2. Adler, *The Technique of Acting*, 6.
3. Rotté, *Acting With Adler*, 17.
4. Adler, *Technique*, 9.
5. ibid., 11.
6. Rotté, 42.

7. ibid., 56.
8. ibid., 62–3.
9. Adler, *Technique*, 26.
10. Rotté, 61.
11. Adler, *The Art of Acting*, 44.
12. Adler, *Technique*, 41.
13. ibid., 47.
14. Rotté, 134.
15. ibid.
16. Adler, *Stella Adler on America's Master Playwrights*, 239.
17. Balcerzak, *Beyond Method*, 108.
18. Rotté, 78.
19. Adler, *Playwrights*, 3.
20. Adler, *Technique*, 7.
21. Adler, *Playwrights*, 204.
22. ibid., 205.
23. ibid., 208.
24. ibid., 210.
25. ibid., 225.
26. Baron, *Modern Acting*, 247.
27. Adler, *Technique*, 1.
28. Adler, *Ellen*, "Letter to the Editor."
29. Adler, *Technique*, 9.

Chapter Ten: Sanford Meisner

1. Meisner, *Sanford Meisner on Acting*, 5.
2. ibid., 12.
3. ibid., 13.
4. Esper, *The Actor's Art and Craft*, 8.
5. Silverberg, *The Sanford Meisner Approach*, 9.
6. Meisner, 11.
7. Meisner, 33.
8. Silverberg, *Larry Silverberg's Meisner Complete*, 20.
9. Meisner, 36.
10. ibid., 34.
11. Esper, 250.
12. ibid., 86.
13. ibid., 167.
14. ibid., 20.
15. Meisner, 79.
16. ibid., 115.
17. ibid., 87.

18. Esper, 9.
19. Silverberg, *Complete*, 23.

Chapter Eleven: Viola Spolin

1. Sills.
2. ibid.
3. Spolin, *Improvisation for the Theater*, 19.
4. Spolin, *Theater Games for Rehearsal*, 1.
5. Spolin, *Theater Games for the Lone Actor*, 16.
6. Spolin, *Improvisation*, 6–7.
7. Spolin, *Lone Actor*, 117.
8. ibid., 120.
9. Spolin, *Improvisation*, 219.
10. Spolin, *Lone Actor*, 7.
11. Cole, 645.
12. Spolin, *Lone Actor*, 12.
13. ibid., 18–19.
14. Spolin, *Improvisation*, 53.
15. ibid., 114.
16. ibid.
17. ibid., 224.

Chapter Twelve: Uta Hagen

1. Hagen, *A Challenge for the Actor*, xxi.
2. ibid., 21.
3. O'Driscoll.
4. Hagen, *Challenge*, 74.
5. ibid., 84.
6. ibid., 75.
7. Hagen, *Respect for Acting*, 47.
8. ibid., 55.
9. ibid., 59.
10. Hagen, *Challenge*, 179.
11. Hagen, *Respect*, 135.
12. ibid., 97.
13. ibid., 99.
14. ibid., 107–8.
15. ibid., 153.
16. ibid., 97.
17. ibid.

Chapter Thirteen: Jacques Lecoq

1. Lecoq, *The Moving Body*, 104.
2. ibid., 16.
3. Murray, *Jacques Lecoq*, 68.
4. Lecoq, 94.
5. ibid., 86.
6. ibid., 69.
7. Murray, 133.
8. Lecoq, 102.
9. ibid., 137.
10. ibid., 86.
11. ibid., 45.
12. ibid., 34.

Chapter Fourteen: Augusto Boal

1. Boal, *Hamlet and the Baker's Son*, 31.
2. ibid., 281.
3. ibid., 338.
4. Boal, *Games for Actors and Non-Actors*, 17.
5. Boal, *Theatre of the Oppressed*, foreword.
6. Boal, *Hamlet*, preface.
7. Boal, *The Rainbow of Desire*, 37.
8. ibid., 38–9.
9. Hodge, 310.
10. Boal, *Hamlet*, 146.
11. Boal, *Games*, 29.
12. ibid., 40.
13. ibid., 42.
14. Boal, *Hamlet*, 150.
15. ibid., 150.
16. Boal, *Rainbow*, 149.
17. Boal, *Hamlet*, 314.

Chapter Fifteen: Jerzy Grotowski

1. Wolford, *The Grotowski Sourcebook*, 382.
2. Grotowski, *Towards a Poor Theatre*, 207.
3. Richards, *At Work with Grotowski on Physical Actions*, preface.
4. Grotowski, *Towards*, 25.

5. ibid., 17.
6. Cole, 532.
7. Wolford, 31–2.
8. Grotowski, 19.
9. Wolford, 40.
10. ibid., 161.
11. ibid., 110.
12. Worthen, *The Idea of the Actor*, 162.
13. Nair, *Restoration of Breath*, 140.
14. Grotowski, 154.
15. ibid., 36.
16. ibid., 228.
17. Richards, 4.
18. Hodge, 202.
19. Grotowski, 135.
20. Grotowski, 140.
21. Richards, 12.

Chapter Sixteen: Tadashi Suzuki

1. Carruthers, *The Theatre of Suzuki Tadashi*, 15.
2. Suzuki, *Culture is the Body*, 68.
3. Carruthers, 21.
4. Suzuki, *The Way of Acting*, 10.
5. Beeman, *Tadashi Suzuki : The Word Is an Act of the Body*, 89.
6. Allain, *The Art of Stillness*, 99.
7. Nobbs, *Insights We Got from Tadashi Suzuki*, 3.
8. Allain, 49–50.
9. Carruthers, 97.
10. Bogart, *Conversations with Anne*, 479–80.
11. Suzuki, *Way*, 91.
12. ibid., 51.
13. Allain, 127.
14. Suzuki, *Culture*, 175.
15. ibid., 176.
16. ibid., 102.
17. Carruthers, 95.

Chapter Seventeen: Harold Guskin

1. Guskin, *How to Stop Acting*, xiv.
2. Blum, *Hollywood Shakespeare*, 34.

3. Lahr, *The Great Guskin*, 46.
4. Guskin, 5.
5. ibid., 7.
6. Lahr, 49.
7. Guskin, 4.
8. ibid., 139.
9. ibid., 87.
10. ibid., 104.
11. ibid., 112.
12. ibid., 115.
13. ibid., 30.

Chapter Eighteen: Anne Bogart

1. Bogart, *And Then, You Act*, 19.
2. Bogart, *Conversations*, 471.
3. ibid., 483.
4. Bogart, *The Viewpoints Book*, 7.
5. Bogart, *Art of Resonance*, 7.
6. ibid., 8.
7. Bogart, *Viewpoints*. 19.
8. ibid., 20.
9. Bogart, *And Then*, 20.
10. Bogart, *Viewpoints*, 13.
11. ibid., 137.
12. ibid., 139.
13. Bogart, *What's the Story*, 1.
14. ibid., 37.
15. ibid., 42.
16. Bogart, *Viewpoints*, xi.
17. ibid., 150.

Chapter Nineteen: Declan Donnellan

1. Donnellan, *The Actor and the Target*, 2.
2. ibid., 27.
3. ibid., 22.
4. ibid., 18.
5. ibid., 22.
6. ibid., 72.
7. ibid., 99.
8. ibid., 185.

9. ibid., 214.
10. ibid., 19.
11. ibid., 104.
12. ibid., 37.
13. ibid., 151.
14. ibid., 200.
15. ibid., 85.

Chapter Twenty: Patsy Rodenburg

1. Rodenburg, *The Right to Speak*, 3.
2. ibid., 19.
3. Rodenburg, *The Actor Speaks*, 11.
4. Rodenburg, *The Second Circle*, 29.
5. ibid., 38.
6. Rodenburg, *Speaking Shakespeare*, 6–7.
7. ibid., 53.
8. ibid., 4.
9. ibid., 5.
10. ibid., 81.
11. ibid., 188.
12. Rodenburg, *Power Presentation*, x.

Chapter Twenty-One: Chelsea Pace

1. "Chelsea Pace".
2. Pace, *Staging Sex*, xii.
3. ibid., 6.
4. ibid., 1.
5. ibid., 57.
6. ibid., 16.

Chapter Twenty-Two: Lee Strasberg

1. Strasberg, *A Dream of Passion*, 11.
2. Baron, *Modern Acting*, xvi.
3. Strasberg, *Dream*, 84.
4. Cole, 622.
5. Baron, 61.
6. Cole, 627.

7. Strasberg, *Dream*, 165.
8. Cohen, *Acting One*, 6.
9. Strasberg, *Dream*, 130.
10. Strasberg, *The Lee Strasberg Notes*, 25.
11. Strasberg, *Dream*, 30.
12. Strasberg, *Notes*, 27.
13. ibid., 30.
14. ibid., 28.
15. ibid., 14.
16. Strasberg, *Dream*, 108.
17. Baron, 123.
18. Baron, 124.
19. Cole, 605.
20. Leonard.
21. Cohen, xxvii.

Chapter Twenty-Three: Frank Silvera

1. Perkins, *The Routledge Companion to African American Theatre and Performance*, 192.
2. Stewart, *The Acting Theories and Techniques of Frank Silvera*, 47.
3. ibid., 188.
4. ibid., 13.
5. ibid., 75.
6. ibid., 142.
7. ibid., 26.
8. ibid., 80.
9. ibid., 82.
10. ibid., 83.
11. ibid., 93.

Chapter Twenty-Four: Barbara Ann Teer

1. Clapp, *Barbara Ann Teer Was Unapologetically Black*.
2. Perkins, *The Routledge Companion to African American Theatre*, 130.
3. Thomas, *Barbara Ann Teer and the National Black Theatre*, 79.
4. Thomas, 173.
5. Forsgren, *Set Your Blackness Free*, 143.
6. Thomas, 89.
7. Thomas, 133.
8. Teer, 87.
9. Forsgren, 137.
10. "Our Story . . ."
11. Thomas, 107.

12. Thomas, 108.
13. Thomas, 103.

Chapter Twenty-Five: Susan Batson

1. Batson, *Truth: Personas, Needs, and Flaws*, 7.
2. ibid., 19.
3. ibid., 35.
4. ibid., 41.
5. ibid., 7.
6. ibid., 24.
7. ibid., 28.
8. ibid., 48.
9. ibid., 82.
10. ibid., 84–5.
11. ibid., 84.
12. ibid., 105.
13. Batson, *Attention Will Be Paid*, 4.
14. ibid., 7.

Chapter Twenty-Six: David Mamet

1. Brestoff, *The Great Acting Teachers and Their Methods*. Vol. 2, 200.
2. Mamet, *True and False*, 5.
3. ibid., 12.
4. ibid., 6.
5. ibid., 67.
6. ibid., 120.
7. ibid., 51.
8. ibid., 74.
9. ibid., 62.
10. ibid., 41–2.
11. Mamet, *Three Uses of the Knife*, 25.
12. ibid., 26.
13. Mamet, *True*, 107.
14. ibid., 9.

Conclusion: Missing Chapters

1. Carnicke, *Stanislavsky in Focus*, 61.

Bibliography

Adler, Ellen. "Letter to the Editor." *New York Times*, May 30, 1997.

Adler, Stella. *Stella Adler on America's Master Playwrights: Eugene O'Neill, Thornton Wilder, Clifford Odets, William Saroyan, Tennessee Williams, William Inge, Arthur Miller, Edward Albee*. Edited by Barry Paris. New York, NY: Vintage Books, 2012.

Adler, Stella. *The Art of Acting*. Edited by Howard Kissel. Lanham, Maryland: Applause Theatre Books, 2000.

Adler, Stella. *The Technique of Acting*. New York, NY: Bantam Books, 1988.

Adrian, Barbara. *Actor Training the Laban Way : An Integrated Approach to Voice, Speech, and Movement*. New York, NY: Allworth Press, 2008.

Allain, Paul. *The Art of Stillness : The Theatre Practice of Tadashi Suzuki*. New York, NY: Palgrave Macmillan, 2003.

Allen, W. H. *The National Review, Vol. 3*. London, UK: W. H. Allen & Co., 1884.

Archer, William. *Masks Or Faces? : A Study in the Psychology of Acting*. Longmans, Green and Co. New York, NY: 1888.

Aristotle. *Rhetoric*. Edited by Richard McKeon. Translated by W. Rhys Roberts. Vol. Book III. Random House, 1941.

Ashperger, Cynthia. *The Rhythm of Space and the Sound of Time: Michael Chekhov's Acting Technique in the 21st Century*. ProQuest Ebook Central. Brill, 2008. https://ebookcentral.proquest.com/lib/carroll/detail.action?docID=556850.

Babbage, Frances. *Augusto Boal*. New York, NY: Routledge, Taylor & Francis Group, 2018.

Balcerzak, Scott. *Beyond Method : Stella Adler and the Male Actor*. Detroit, MI: Wayne State University Press, 2018.

Baron, Cynthia. *Modern Acting : The Lost Chapter of American Film and Theatre*. Bowling Green, OH: Palgrave Macmillan, 2016.

Barton, Robert. *Acting: Onstage and Off*. Orlando, FL: Holt, Reinhart and Winston, Inc., 1989.

Batson, Susan. *Attention Will Be Paid*. Thornton, CO: self published, 2014.

Batson, Susan. *Truth: Personas, Needs, and Flaws in the Art of Building Actors and Creating Characters*. Middleton, DE: self published, 2020.

Beeman, William O. "Tadashi Suzuki : The Word Is an Act of the Body." *Performing Arts Journal* 5, no. 2 (1981): 89.

Bloom, Katya, Barbara Adrian, Tom Casciero, Jennifer Mizenko, and Claire Porter. *The Laban Workbook for Actors : A Practical Training Guide with Video*. Edited by David Carey and Clark Carey. New York, NY: Methuen, 2022.

Blum, David. "*Hollywood Shakespeare : Joe Papp Sprinkles Stardust on 'Twelfth Night.'*" New York Magazine, June 19, 1989, 28–35.

Boal, Augusto. *Games for Actors and Non-Actors*. Translated by Adrian Jackson. New York, NY: Routledge, Taylor & Francis Group, 2022.

Boal, Augusto. *Hamlet and the Baker's Son: My Life in Theatre and Politics*. New York, NY: Routledge, 2001.

Boal, Augusto. *The Rainbow of Desire: The Boal Method of Theatre and Therapy*. Translated by Adrian Jackson. New York, NY: Routledge, 1995.

Boal, Augusto. *Theatre of the Oppressed*. New York, NY: Theatre Communications Group, 2018.

Bogart, Anne, and Tina Landau. *The Viewpoints Book: A Practical Guide to Viewpoints and Composition*. 1st edn. Theatre Communications Group, 2005.

Bogart, Anne. *And Then, You Act: Making Art in an Unpredictable World*. Routledge, 2008.

Bogart, Anne. *Art of Resonance*. New York, NY: Methuen Drama Bloomsbury Publishing Plc, 2021.

Bogart, Anne. *Conversations with Anne: Twenty-four Interviews*. New York, NY: Theatre Communications Group, 2012.

Bogart, Anne. *What's the Story: Essays about Art, Theater and Storytelling*. New York, NY: Routledge, 2014.

Boleslavsky, Richard, and *Rhonda Blair. Acting: The First Six Lessons: Documents from the American Laboratory Theatre*. London: Routledge, 2010.

Brando, Marlon, and Robert Lindsey. *Brando: Songs My Mother Taught Me*. Toronto: Random House of Canada, 1994.

Brecht, Bertolt, and John Willett. *Brecht on Theatre: The Development of an Aesthetic*. New York, NY: Hill and Wang, 1992.

Brestoff, Richard. *The Great Acting Teachers and Their Methods*. 1st edn. Smith and Kraus, 1995.

Brestoff, Richard. *The Great Acting Teachers and Their Methods*. Vol. 2. Smith and Kraus Publishers, 2010.

Butler, Isaac. *The Method: How the Twentieth Century Learned to Act*. Bloomsbury Publishing, 2022.

Carnicke, Sharon Marie. Dynamic *Acting through Active Analysis: Konstantin Stanislavsky, Maria Knebel, and their Legacy*. New York, NY: Methuen Drama, Bloomsbury Publishing Plc, 2023.

Carnicke, Sharon Marie. *Stanislavsky in Focus: an Acting Master for the Twenty-First Century*. New York, NY: Routledge, 2009.

Carruthers, Ian, and Yasunari Takahashi. *The Theatre of Suzuki Tadashi*. Cambridge, United Kingdom: Cambridge University Press, 2004.

Chekhov, Michael Aleksandrovic, and Bella Merlin. *The Path of the Actor*. London and New York: Routledge, 2005.

Chekhov, Michael, and Mel Gordon. *On the Technique of Acting*. Harper Perennial, 1991.

Chekhov, Michael. *Lessons for the Professional Actor*. Edited by Dierdre Hurst Du Prey. New York, NY: Performing Arts Journal Publications, 1985.

Chelsea Pace. Accessed November 9, 2023. http://www.chelseapace.com/new-page-1.

Clapp, Deb. "Barbara Ann Teer Was Unapologetically Black." *American Theatre*, April 10, 2020. https://doi.org/https://www.americantheatre.org/2020/04/10/barbara-ann-teer-was-unapologetically-black/.

Clurman, Harold. *The Fervent Years: The Group Theatre & the 30's*. New York, NY: Da Capo Press, 1983.

Cohen, Robert. *Acting One*. 5th edn. McGraw Hill, 2008.

Cole, Toby, and Helena Krich Chinoy, eds. *Actors on Acting*. New York, NY: Crown Trade, 1970.

Coveney, Michael. "As He Likes It." *Guardian*. Accessed March 30, 2023. https://www.theguardian.com/stage/2006/feb/04/theatre.

Cowart, Tia Shaffer. "Former Students' Perceptions of How Theatre Impacted Life Skills and Psychological Needs." Liberty University Scholar's Crossing, 2013. https://digitalcommons.liberty.edu/doctoral/709/.

Crawford, Jerry L., Catherine Hurst, and Michael Lugering. *Acting in Person and Style*. Fifth ed. Dubuque, IA: Brown & Benchmark Publishers, 1995.

Cynkutis, Zbigniew, Khalid Tyabji, and Paul Allain. *Acting with Grotowski: Theatre as a Field for Experiencing Life*. London: Routledge Taylor & Francis Group, 2015.

Donnellan, Declan. "Declan Donnellan Discusses Acting. Cheek by Jowl." Accessed January 11, 2023. https://youtu.be/YdWDXyC-MV8.

Donnellan, Declan. *The Actor and the Target*. Theatre Communications Group, 2011.

"Epic Theatre and Brecht Spass and Gestus." BBC Bitesize. Accessed November 8, 2023. https://www.bbc.co.uk/bitesize/guides/zwmvd2p/revision/7.

Esper, William, and Damon DiMarco. *The Actor's Art and Craft: William Esper Teaches the Meisner Technique*. New York, NY: Anchor Books, 2008.

Esslin, Martin. "Jacques Lecoq obituary," January 22, 1999. https://doi.org/https://www.theguardian.com/news/1999/jan/23/guardianobituaries.

Evans, Mark. *Jacques Copeau*. New York, NY: Routledge, 2006.

Ewan, Vanessa, and Kate Sagovsky. *Laban's Efforts in Action: A Movement Handbook for Actors*. New York, NY: Methuen Drama, 2019.

Fergusson, Francis, and Francis Fergusson. "The Notion of 'Action.'" Essay. In *Sallies of the Mind*, 247–9. Routledge, 2018.

Forsgren, La Donna. "'Set Your Blackness Free': Barbara Ann Teer's Art and Activism during the Black Arts Movement." *Frontiers: A Journal of Women Studies* 36, no. 1 (2015): 136–59. https://doi.org/https://doi.org/10.5250/fronjwomestud.36.1.0136.

Francis, J. *The Athenæum: A Journal of Literature, Science, the Fine Arts, Music, and the Drama*. London, UK: John C. Francis, 1883.

Frank, Waldo. "Copeau Begins Again." Essay. In *Theatre Arts Monthly* 9, edited by Edith Juliet and Rich Isaacs, September 1925, 9:585–92. 1924. Theatre Arts, Incorporated, n.d. Accessed November 16, 2023.

Ghosh, Manomohan. *The Natyasastra: A Treatise on Hindu Dramaturgy and Histrionics*. Calcutta: Royal Asiatic Society, 2002.

Grotowski, Jerzy. *Towards a Poor Theatre*. New York, NY: Simon and Schuster, 1968.

Guskin, Harold. *How to Stop Acting*. 1st edn. Farrar, Straus and Giroux, 2003.

Hagen, Uta, and Haskel Frankel. *Respect for Acting*. Hoboken, NY: John Wiley & Sons, Inc., 2009.

Hagen, Uta. *A Challenge for the Actor*. New York, NY: Scribner's, 1991.

Harrop, John, and Sabin R. Epstein. *Acting with Style*. Boston, MA: Allyn & Bacon, 2000.

Hartnoll, Phyllis, and Enoch Brater. *The Theatre: A Concise History*. London: Thames & Hudson, 2012.

Heilman, Pamela Sue. "The American Career of Maria Ouspenskaya (1887-1949): Actress and Teacher." Dissertation, *LSU Historical Dissertations and Theses*. 6890., 1999. https://digitalcommons.lsu.edu/gradschool_disstheses/6890.

Henshaw, Wandalie. The "Open Scene" as a Directing Exercise. *Educational Theatre Journal*, Vol. 21, No. 3 (Oct., 1969), pp. 275—84. https://doi.org/10.2307/3205468

Hensley, Brandon. "Memories of a Rockhaven Nurse." *CV Weekly*, November 14, 2013.

Hill, Aaron, and Urania Hill. Johnson. *The works of the late Aaron Hill, esq; . . . Consisting of letters on various subjects, and of original poems, moral and facetious. With an essay on the art of acting. Printed for the benefit of the family*. 1753.

Hodge, Alison. *Actor Training*. New York: Routledge, 2010.

Hutchinson, Anjalee Deshpande. *Michael Chekhov and Sanford Meisner: Collisions and Convergence in Actor Training.* New York, NY: Routledge, 2021.

Knebel, Maria. *Active Analysis.* Edited by Anatoli Vassiliev. Translated by Irina Brown. New York, NY: Routledge, Taylor & Francis Group, 2021.

Knébel, María Ósipovna. *La Palabra en la Creación Actoral.* Madrid, Spain: Fundamentos, 2018.

Knébel, María Ósipovna. *Poética de la Pedagogía Teatral.* México, D.F.: Siglo XXI, 1991.

Lahr, John. "The Great Guskin." *The New Yorker,* 71, no. 4 (March 12, 1995): 44.

Law, Alma H., and Mel Gordon. *Meyerhold, Eisenstein and Biomechanics: Actor Training in Revolutionary Russia.* Jefferson, NC: McFarland & Company, 2012.

Leach, Robert. *Stanislavsky and Meyerhold.* Peter Lang AG European Academic Publishers, 2003.

Leonard, Elizabeth. "Britney Spears Opens Up: 'Finally Free' to Share Her Story in a Bombshell Memoir & New Interview–'No More Lies.'" *People Magazine,* 23 Oct. 2023.

Lecoq, Jacques, Jean-Gabriel Carasso, and Jean-Claude Lallias. *The Moving Body (Le Corps Poétique): Teaching Creative Theatre.* Translated by David Bradby. 3rd edn. New York, NY: Methuen Drama, Bloomsbury Publishing Plc, 2020.

Leigh, Barbara Kusler. "Jacques Copeau's School of Actors: Commemorating the Centennial of the Birth of Jacques Copeau." *Mime Journal,* 9 and 10 (1979): 4–75. https://doi.org/10.5642/mimejournal.

Lewis, Robert. *The Tulane Review,* Volume 6. New Orleans, LA: AMS Press, 1961.

Luckett, Sharrell D., and Tia M. Shaffer. *Black Acting Methods: Critical Approaches.* New York, NY: Routledge, 2017.

Mamet, David. *True and False: Heresy and Common Sense for the Actor.* Vintage Books, 1997.

Mamet, David. *Three Uses of the Knife.* Vintage Books. 1998.

Meerzon, Yana. *The Path of a Character: Michael Chekhov's Inspired Acting and Theatre Semiotics.* Frankfurt am Main, Germany: Peter Lang, 2005.

Meisner, Sanford, and Dennis Longwell. *Sanford Meisner on Acting.* New York, NY: Vintage, 1987.

Merlin, Bella. *The Complete Stanislavsky Toolkit.* London: Nick Hern Books, 2016.

Meyerhold, V. E. *Meyerhold on Theatre.* Edited by Edward Braun. London: Bloomsbury Methuen Drama, 2016.

Monday, Mark. *Directing with the Michael Chekhov Technique: A workbook with video for directors, teachers and actors.* New York, NY: Bloomsbury Methuen Drama, an imprint of Bloomsbury Publishing Plc, 2017.

Moore, Sonia. *The Stanislavski System: the Professional Training of an Actor, etc.* 2nd edn. Penguin Books, 1984.

Morrison, Patt. "Lee Strasberg, Mentor of Method Actors Dies." *Los Angeles Times,* February 17, 1982.

Murray, Simon David. *Jacques Lecoq.* New York, NY: Routledge, 2018.

Nearman, Mark J. "Zeami's Kyui. A Pedagogical Guide for Teachers of Acting." *Monumenta Nipponica,* 33, no. 3 (Autumn 1978): 299–332. https://doi.org/10.2307/2383994.

Nair, Sreenath. *Restoration of Breath: Consciousness and Performance.* New York, NY: Rodopi, 2007.

Nobbs, John, and Jon Brokering. *Insights We Got from Tadashi Suzuki, the Shogun of Toga: Actually he didn't tell us anything, but he gave us the keys and we filled in the gaps.* East Brisbane, Queensland: Frank Theatre Press, 2016.

"Our Story." National Black Theatre. Accessed November 8, 2023. https://www.nationalblacktheatre.org/our-story.

O'Driscoll, Pauline. "Introduction to Uta Hagen – Who Was Uta Hagen." Web log. Pauline O'Driscoll (blog), January 2023. https://www.paulineodriscoll.com/news/introduction-to-uta-hagen-who-was-uta-hagen/.
Pace, Chelsea, Laura Rikard, and Shealyn Jae. *Staging Sex: Best Practices, Tools, and Techniques for Theatrical Intimacy*. New York, NY: Routledge, 2020.
Perkins, Kathy A., Sandra L. Richards, Renée Alexander Craft, and Thomas F. DeFrantz, eds. *The Routledge Companion to African American Theatre and Performance*. New York, NY: Routledge, 2020.
Petit, Lenard. *The Michael Chekhov Handbook: For the Actor*. New York, NY: Routledge, 2020.
Pitches, Jonathan. *Vsevolod Meyerhold*. London: Routledge, 2003.
Quintilianus, Marcus Fabius, and John Selby Watson. *Quintilian's Institutes of Oratory: or, Education of an Orator in Twelve Books*. Bohn, 1909.
Richards, Thomas, and Jerzy Grotowski. *At Work with Grotowski on Physical Actions*. New York, NY: Routledge, 1995.
Rodenburg, Patsy. "About Patsy." Official website of Patsy Rodenburg, Master Voice Teacher. Accessed May 30, 2023. https://patsyrodenburg.co.uk/about/.
Rodenburg, Patsy. *Power Presentation: Formal Speech in an Informal World*. New York, NY: Penguin, 2009.
Rodenburg, Patsy. *Speaking Shakespeare*. New York, NY: St. Martin's Press, 2002.
Rodenburg, Patsy. *The Actor Speaks: Voice and the Performer*. New York, NY: Palgrave Macmillan, 2002.
Rodenburg, Patsy. *The Right to Speak: Working with the Voice*. New York, NY: Bloomsbury, 2019.
Rodenburg, Patsy. *The Second Circle: How to Use Positive Energy for Success in Every Situation*. New York, NY: W.W. Norton & Company, 2008.
Rodenburg, Patsy. *The Woman's Voice*. New York, NY: Methuen Drama, 2023.
Rotté, Joanna. *Acting With Adler*. Pompton Plains, NJ: Limelight Editions, 2000.
Rushe, Sinéad. *Michael Chekhov's Acting Technique: A Practitioner's Guide*. New York, NY: Methuen Drama, 2019.
Saint-Denis, Michel. *Theatre: The Rediscovery of Style*. Theatre Arts Books, 1960.
Sills, Aretha, and Carol Sills. "Viola Spolin Biography." Viola Spolin. Accessed August 31, 2023. https://www.violaspolin.org/bio.
Silverberg, Larry. *Larry Silverberg's Meisner Complete*. Hanover, NH: Smith and Kraus, 2019.
Silverberg, Larry. *The Sanford Meisner Approach*. Vol. 1. Smith & Kraus, 1994.
"Spass and Gestus—Epic Theatre and Brecht—GCSE Drama Revision—OCR—BBC Bitesize." BBC News. Accessed August 25, 2023. https://www.bbc.co.uk/bitesize/guides/zwmvd2p/revision/7.
Spolin, Viola. *Improvisation for the Theater: A Handbook of Teaching and Directing Techniques*. Third ed. Evanston, IL: Northwestern University Press, 1999.
Spolin, Viola. *Theater Games for the Lone Actor*. Edited by Paul Sills and Carol Sills. Evanston, IL: Northwestern University Press, 2001.
Spolin, Viola. *Theater Games for Rehearsal: A Director's Handbook*. Evanston, IL: Northwestern University Press, 2010.
Stanislavski, Constantin. *Building a Character*. Translated by Elizabeth Reynolds Happgood. New York, NY: Routledge/Theatre Arts Books, 1987.
Stanislavski, Constantin. *Creating a Role*. Translated by Elizabeth Reynolds Hapgood. New York, NY: Routledge, 2003.

Stanislavski, Konstantin. *An Actor Prepares*. Translated by Elizabeth Reynolds Hapgood. Routledge/Theatre Arts Books, 1988.

Stanislavski, Konstantin. *My Life in Art*. Translated by J. J. Robbins. Read Books Ltd., 2018.

Stebbins, Genevieve. *Delsarte System of Expression*. With the address of François Delsarte before the Philotechnic Society of Paris. E.S. Werner, 1892.

Stewart, Tommie Harris. *The Acting Theories and Techniques of Frank Silvera in his "Theatre of Being."* Ann Arbor, MI: UMI Dissertation Services, 1994.

Strasberg, Lee. *A Dream of Passion: The Development of the Method*. Edited by Evangeline Morphos. New York, NY: Penguin Books, 1987.

Strasberg, Lee. *The Lee Strasberg Notes*. Edited by Lola Cohen. New York, NY: Routledge, 2010.

Suzuki, Tadashi, and J. Thomas. Rimer. *The Way of Acting: the Theatre Writings of Tadashi Suzuki*. Theatre Communications Group, 2014.

Suzuki, Tadashi. *Culture is the Body: The Theatre Writings of Tadashi Suzuki*. Translated by Kameron H. Steele. New York, NY: Theatre Communications Group, 2015.

Teer, Barbara Ann. "Dr. Barbara Ann Teer's Letter to the Future." The Public Theatre. Accessed October 26, 2023. https://publictheater.org/contentassets/a5af18066c8540c5b7ac2d4b5b2285a7/pdf-resources/letter-to-the-future-by-dr.-teer.pdf.

Thomas, James, and María Ósipovna Knébel. *A Director's Guide to Stanislavsky's Active Analysis: Including the Formative Essay on Active Analysis by Maria Knebel*. London: New York, 2016.

Thomas, Lundeana Marie. *Barbara Ann Teer and the National Black Theatre: Transformational Forces in Harlem*. New York, NY: Routledge, 2016.

Vakhtangov, Yevgeny. *The Vakhtangov Sourcebook*. Translated by Andrei Malaev-Babel. New York, NY: Routledge, 2011.

Wolford, Lisa, and Richard Schechner. *The Grotowski Sourcebook*. London: Routledge, 1997.

Worthen, William B. *The Idea of the Actor*. Princeton, NJ: Princeton University Press, 1984.

Index

actions 15, 19, 20-1, 23, 24, 28, 30, 76-7, 79, 83, 86, 91, 93, 95, 98, 111-18, 120-1, 140-1, 147, 150, 157-8, 164, 166, 194, 220, 250-1, 290, 310, 315, 317-8
Active Analysis 23-25, 30, 88, 93-5
actor blocks/obstacles 138-40, 196-8, 220-2, 244, 246, 249-50, 289-90
Adler, Stella xii, xiii, 23, 73, 109-121, 122, 284, 286, 287, 292, 308
alienation effect 100-2
animal work 39-40, 45-6, 50, 52-53, 54-5, 141-2, 174, 177-8, 180, 190, 200, 207, 254
Aristotle 4
athletics 33, 46, 58, 220
atmospheres 73, 76, 77-8, 82, 90
audience 3, 5-6, 9, 17, 21, 22-3, 31-2, 36-7, 43, 77-79, 90, 99-104, 119, 129, 142, 158-9, 169, 173, 183-4, 186-8, 195, 197-8, 208-9, 214, 222-3, 245-7, 265, 279, 288, 297, 301, 303, 309, 316, 317, 318-19
auditioning 224-6, 310, 317

Batson, Susan 23, 284, 306-13
BESS 58-61
Berghof, Herbert 151, 306
Bing, Suzanne 44-6, 175
bits/beats 20, 24, 28, 309-10
Biomechanics 31-6
Boal, Augusto 183-94
Bogart, Anne 7, 209, 212, 229-42
Boleslavsky, Richard xii, 109, 285-6
bouffon 173, 181-2
Boyd, Neva 135
Brando, Marlon 116, 118, 223, 287
breath 6, 26, 46, 59, 63, 66-7, 68-9, 180, 197, 199, 206, 214, 221, 227, 256-7, 259-60, 268-9, 272, 277
Brecht, Bertolt 99-108, 116, 183
Brook, Peter 102, 195

center 33-4, 58-9, 73-5, 84, 170, 173, 203, 211, 217-18, 257-60, 266-7
character development 47-8, 60-1, 64, 73-4, 104-5, 106, 113-16, 119-20, 128-9, 141-2, 159-61, 174, 180, 186-7, 220-2, 228, 245-9, 254, 280, 297, 307-8
Chekhov, Anton xii, 12, 14-15, 21, 41, 72, 90, 227
Chekhov, Michael 9, 12, 72-87, 88-9
circles of attention 17, 257-9
Clurman, Harold xii, xiii, 109, 122, 151, 198, 285, 306
clowning 32, 173, 181
commedia 32, 44, 54-5, 168, 172
communion 22-5, 95, 124, 173, 195, 301, 317
concentration 16-17, 26-7, 89-90, 210, 213-14, 288, 298, 309, 316
Copeau, Jacques 43-55, 175
counter-actions (*see also* tactics) 21, 23, 28, 93
Craig, Gordon 285
Crawford, Cheryl xii, 122, 285

dactyl 35, 38-9
Decroux, Étienne 48, 300
dialects 160
Diderot, Denis 9-10
directing 19, 24, 36, 47, 76, 89, 91, 93-5, 112-3, 142-3, 158-9, 185, 224-6, 233-4, 274-7, 291
A Doll's House 36, 40, 129
Donnellan, Declan 243-54

emotion memory/affective memory/ emotion recall xiii, 23, 89-90 , 122, 154, 288-90, 298, 308-10, 316
emotions 3, 6, 8-12, 15-16, 19, 22, 32, 36, 46-7, 49-50, 57, 72, 76, 80, 99-102, 106, 112-13, 120, 124, 127-9, 131, 141, 153-4, 169, 172, 176, 185-6, 213, 221, 230, 234, 249, 285-7, 290-2, 307, 309, 313, 315-16
endowment 115, 156-7, 165

energy 7, 13, 33, 58, 60, 78, 81, 83, 91, 111, 189, 208, 210–12, 214, 218, 231, 233–5, 250, 254, 257–8, 264, 267, 272, 302
ensemble 14, 43–4, 48, 50, 122, 141, 212–3, 230, 233, 285
etudes 24, 30, 35–6, 93–5
exits and entrances 108, 112, 146, 157, 158, 161–3, 174, 242, 310

first time, the 23, 91–2, 101, 123–4, 177
Forum Theatre 183, 188, 191
fourth wall 23, 31, 142, 158–9, 163–4, 169, 309, 312

gestures 3, 5–9, 46–7, 62, 76–7, 81, 83, 97–8, 101, 102–3, 106, 170, 174, 221, 232–3, 238, 298
gestus 102–3, 104, 107
getting out of your head 124, 128, 243, 284
given circumstances 15, 18–19, 93, 111–15, 122, 128, 154, 157, 163–4, 307, 316
Greek chorus 4, 44, 54, 168, 173–4, 176–7, 182
grotesque, the 36–7, 181
Grotowski, Jerzy 195–207, 240
grounding 8, 17, 47, 49, 58, 60, 204–5, 209–10, 254, 267
Group Theater, the xii, xiii, 73, 109, 118, 122, 124, 135, 151, 285–6
Guskin, Harold 219–28

Hagen, Uta xiii, 151–67, 306
Hauptmann, Elisabeth 99
Hill, Aaron 8–9, 12–13

images 30, 73–5, 76–7, 92, 141, 185, 187–8, 190, 193, 203, 207, 221, 296, 303, 311
imagination 17, 19, 21, 26–7, 43, 45, 64, 72–8, 81–2, 91–2, 111–12, 118, 128, 156, 159, 168, 211, 307–8, 310
improvisation 45, 71, 94, 126–7, 135, 137–8, 169, 205–6, 220, 290, 301
impulse 47, 54, 60, 74, 84, 124–9, 138, 196, 199, 203, 205, 221–2, 226, 231, 246, 250, 257, 287
internal acting *vs.* external acting techniques 3, 8–10, 15, 57, 62, 80, 100–1, 153, 185, 250, 316

Jingjù 100
jo-ha-kyu (*see also Otkaz, Posil, Tochka*) 6–7, 13

kinesphere 58, 59, 63, 66
Knebel, Maria xii, 19, 45, 88–98

Knipper, Olga xii, 90
Kyogen 101

Laban, Rudolf von 56–71
Landau, Tina 229–30, 235, 236, 241
Lecoq, Jacques 48, 168–82
Le Jeu 169
living truthfully under imaginary circumstances 22, 25, 123–4
Luckett, Sharrell 295, 321

Magic If, the 19, 28, 128, 213, 303
Mamet, David 284, 314–20
masks 4, 10, 36, 44, 46–7, 50–55, 100, 172–4, 177–8, 181–2, 245, 249
Meisner, Sanford xiii, 122–34, 300, 314
memorization 94–5, 115, 127, 134, 221, 227, 264
Method Acting xii, xiii, 222, 286–7, 291–2
Meyerhold, Vsevolod xii, 31–42, 89, 95
mime 45, 52, 133, 164, 170–5, 179, 196
mirrors 6, 8, 11–12, 33, 50, 106, 163, 179, 181, 279, 302
Modern Acting xiii, 110, 118, 123
monologues 23, 90, 92, 96–7, 119–21, 217, 220–1, 227, 246, 250, 252, 254, 261–2, 264, 270–2, 310–11
Moscow Art Theatre (MAT) xii, 14, 20, 32, 72–3, 88–9, 285
Motokiyo, Zeami 6–7, 13
movement
    as character development technique 5–6
    body posture 110–11, 266–7
        see Biomechanics
    corporels and plastiques 198–9, 204–5
        see Laban (LMA)
    movement qualities (Chekhov) 74–5, 84–5
    with intention 169–70

negative, via or working from 196–7, 223, 228, 247
Nemirovich-Danchenko, Vladimir xii, 14, 31, 89
Noh 6, 7, 32, 101, 210

objectives 20–1, 24, 76–7, 91, 158, 160, 220, 244, 317
observation 52–3, 89–90, 95, 97–8, 102, 110, 132, 140, 152–3, 155, 162, 165
obstacles 21, 126, 160, 164, 166–7, 246, 248, 308
Otkaz, Posil, Tochka (*see also jo-ha-kyu*) 35, 41–2

Ouspenskaya, Maria xii, 109, 285-6, 321
Overlie, Mary 229-30

Pace, Chelsea 273-82
pantomime 32, 47, 49, 51-53, 94, 312
Piscator, Erwin 99
physicalization 112-13, 137, 221, 227, 228
the pinch and the ouch 126, 132
play (*see also* spass and Le Jeu) 34, 40, 43, 136, 142, 168-9, 171, 174, 181
playwright 18, 21, 72, 91, 99, 112, 116-7, 222, 287, 317-18
Plutarch 3
Poor Theatre 195-7
preparation, pause, accentuation, pause (*see also* jo-ha-kyu) 170-1
private moment 288
professionalism 25, 318

Quintilian 5-6, 8, 11-12

radiating 59, 63, 74-5, 77-9, 81, 83-7, 91, 210, 267
readiness 16, 33, 177, 196, 211, 235, 261, 268
realism 3, 31-2, 36, 40, 82, 99, 100-1, 105, 213-14, 230
rehearsal (*see also* Active Analysis) 3, 24, 34, 47-8, 76, 95, 102, 127-8, 140-1, 143, 198, 221-2, 225-6, 233-5, 247-8, 260, 274-8, 291, 298, 317-18
relaxation 16, 26-7, 78, 197, 211, 287-9, 293-4, 315
repetition 124-6, 130-4, 186, 211-12, 226, 231, 233, 237, 239, 241
resonators 199-201, 207, 232, 240, 269
Rich Theatre 195, 197
Rodenburg, Patsy 255-72

Sanskrit drama 5
Second City, The 136, 143, 314
sense memory 154-5, 186
script analysis 18, 46, 63, 91, 114-17, 140-1, 159-60, 174, 220, 222-3, 225-6, 259-60, 309-10, 315

Shakespeare, William 7-8, 44, 99, 159, 261-5, 268, 270-2, 296
Sills, Paul 135, 136
Silvera, Frank 284, 295-9
SITI Company 209, 230
space awareness 138, 143-5, 200-1, 213, 231-2, 260
spass (*see also* play) 103-4
Spolin, Viola 135-50
spy back 79-80
Stanislavski vii, xii, xiii, 3, 7-8, 9, 10, 14-30, 31, 57, 72-3, 109, 185, 196, 201, 285-7, 298, 303, 315
  Stanislavski's System (historical info) xii, xiii, 15, 88, 109, 123, 286
  criticism of 47, 93, 126, 136, 213, 230, 244, 315-16
Strasberg, Lee xii, xiii, 109, 118, 122, 284, 285-94, 306, 315-16
substitution/transference/adjustments 153-4, 186-7, 290
subtext 14, 21, 27-8, 90, 93, 223, 262, 270
super-objective 20-1, 30, 76, 91, 98, 220
Suzuki, Tadashi 208-18, 230

table work 19-21, 23-4, 30, 93, 225
tactics (*see also* counter-actions) 21, 71, 164, 188, 250, 265
taking the first thing 126-7
Technology of the Soul 302
Teer, Barbara Ann 284, 300-5
tempo-rhythm 22, 28, 33, 97, 223
Theatre of Being 295-6
Theatre of the Oppressed 184
Thespis 4
throughline of actions 20, 93, 113

Vahktangov, Yevgeny xii, 286
Viewpoints 229-42
voice techniques 6, 17-18, 59, 63, 103, 110, 140, 149, 199-201, 214, 232-3, 240-1, 256, 260, 269-70

Williams, Tennessee 116-17